Tools of Culture

Japan's Cultural, Intellectual, Medical,
and Technological Contacts in
East Asia, 1000-1500s

Tools of Culture

Japan's Cultural, Intellectual, Medical, and Technological Contacts in East Asia, 1000-1500s

Edited by
Andrew Edmund Goble,
Kenneth R. Robinson,
and Haruko Wakabayashi

Published by the Association for Asian Studies, Inc.

Asia Past & Present: New Research from AAS, Number 2

Asia Past & Present: New Research from AAS
A series edited by Martha Ann Selby

"Asia Past & Present: New Research from AAS," published by the Association for Asian Studies, Inc. (AAS), features scholarly work from all areas of Asian studies. In addition to scholarly monographs, translations, essay collections, and other forms of scholarly research will be considered for publication. AAS particularly hopes to support work in emerging or under-represented fields. For further information, please visit www.asian-studies.org.

Formed in 1941, the Association for Asian Studies (AAS)—the largest society of its kind, with more than 7,000 members worldwide—is a scholarly, non-political, non-profit professional association open to all persons interested in Asia.

Published by:
Association for Asian Studies, Inc.
825 Victors Way, Suite 310
Ann Arbor, Michigan 48108 USA
www.asian-studies.org

Library of Congress Cataloging-in-Publication Data

Tools of culture : Japan's cultural, intellectual, medical and technological contacts in East Asia, 1000–1500s / edited by Andrew Edmund Goble, Kenneth R. Robinson, and Haruko Wakabayashi.
    p. cm. — (Asia past & present: new research from AAS ; no. 2)
  Includes bibliographical references and index.
    ISBN 978-0-924304-53-8 (pbk.) 1. Japan—Civilization—East Asian influences. 2. Japan—Relations—East Asia. 3. East Asia—Relations—Japan. I. Goble, Andrew Edmund, 1952– II. Robinson, Kenneth R., 1962– III. Wakabayashi, Haruko Nishioka, 1967– IV. Association for Asian Studies

  DS821.5.E18T66 2009
  303.48'252050902--dc22

                              2008055026

Cover Image: Sculpture of Lanxi Daolong (foreground) with Man'anpō medical text (background).

Contents

Abbreviations

The following abbreviations are used in the notes and in the bibliography. Each work also has an entry in the bibliography of primary sources.

CWS	*Chosŏn wangjo sillok*
DNBZ	*Dai Nihon Bukkyō zensho*
DNKR	*Dai Nihon kokiroku*
GBSS	*Gozan bungaku shinshū*
GBZS	*Gozan bungaku zenshū*
GR	*Gunsho ruijū*
HC	*Haedong chegukki*
KI	*Kamakura ibun komonjo hen*
KT	*Kyŏngguk taejŏn*
NBI-Ky	*Nanbokuchō ibun Kyūshū hen*
NET	*Nihon emaki taisei*
NKBT	*Nihon koten bungaku taikei*
NST	*Nihon shisō taikei*
SNKBT	*Shin Nihon koten bungaku taikei*
SS	*Shiryō sanshū kokiroku hen*
STYS	*Sinjŭng Tongguk yŏji sŭngnam*
SZKT	*Shintei zōho kokushi taikei*
T	*Taishō shinshū Daizōkyō*
ZGR	*Zoku gunsho ruijū*
ZHST	*Zōho shiryō taisei*

Contributors

Robert Borgen is Professor of Japanese Literature and History at the University of California, Davis. His research focuses on Heian court culture and relations with China. In addition to his book *Sugawara no Michizane and the Early Heian Court*, he has published articles on the Tenjin cult and the monk Jōjin. His most recent publications are "A History of Dōmyōji to 1572 (or maybe 1575): An Attempted Reconstruction," *Monumenta Nipponica* 62 (Spring 2007); and "Jōjin's Travels from Center to Center (with Some Periphery in Between)," in Mikael Adolphson et al., eds., *Heian Japan: Centers and Peripheries* (Honolulu: University of Hawai`i Press, 2007).

Martin Collcutt is Professor of East Asian Studies and History at Princeton University. His publications include *Five Mountains: The Rinzai Zen Monastic Institution in Medieval Japan* (Cambridge: Council on East Asian Studies, Harvard University, 1981); "Muso Soseki," in Jeffrey P. Mass, ed., *The Origins of Japan's Medieval World* (Stanford: Stanford University Press, 1997); "Nun Shogun: Politics and Religion in the Life of Hōjō Masako (1157–1225)," in Barbara Ruche, ed., *Engendering Faith: Women and Buddhism in Premodern Japan* (Ann Arbor: Center for Japanese Studies, University of Michigan, 2002).

Andrew Edmund Goble is Associate Professor of History and of Religious Studies at the University of Oregon. His research has covered aspects of medieval Japanese social, intellectual, and political history and most recently issues of medicine and society. Previous publications include *Kenmu: Go-Daigo's Revolution* (Cambridge: Council on East Asian Studies, Harvard University, 1997); "Medieval Japan," in William Tsutsui, ed., *A Companion to Japanese History* (Oxford: Blackwell, 2007); "Medicine and New Knowledge in Medieval Japan: Kajiwara Shōzen (1266–1337) and the *Man'anpō*," *Nihon Ishigaku Zasshi* 47.1 and 47.2 (2001); and "War and Injury: The Origins of Medieval Japanese Wound Medicine," *Monumenta Nipponica* 60.3 (2005). He is currently completing *Confluences of Medicine: Illness, Buddhism, and Society in Medieval Japan*.

Kosoto Hiroshi is Professor and Head of the Department of Medical History at the Oriental Medical Research Center of the Kitasato Research Institute. His research has covered the transmission of Chinese medical knowledge to Japan; traditional Chinese medicine; medieval Japanese medical writing; Japanese printed editions of Chinese medical works; and extensive bibliographical study of early Chinese medical writing, particularly of the Song through Ming eras. Among his extensive publications (see also the bibliography in this volume) are the multivolume *Wakoku Kanseki isho shūsei* (Entapuraizu, 1988–92); *Chūgoku igaku koten to*

Nihon (Hanawa Shobō, 1996); *Nihon Kanpō tenseki jiten* (Taishūkan Shoten, 1999); and *Mawangdui shutsudo bunken yakuchū sōsho Wushier bingfang* (Tōhō Shoten, 2007).

Murai Shōsuke is Professor of Japanese History at the University of Tokyo. His research covers a wide range, and he is particularly interested in issues of movement and change in medieval Japan. His research on interactions among China, Japan, and Korea during Japan's medieval era has fundamentally transformed the field of early Japanese history. Among his major publications are *Ajia no naka no Nihon chūsei* (Azekura shobō, 1988); the six-volume *Ajia no naka no Nihon shi* (coeditor) (Tokyo Daigaku Shuppankai, 1992); *Chūsei Wajinden* (Iwanami Shoten, 1993); *Nanbokuchō no dōran* (Yoshikawa Kōbunkan, 2003); volume 10 of the Chūō Kōron History of Medieval Japan, *Bunretsu suru ōken to shakai* (Chūō Kōronsha, 2003); and *Chūsei kokka to zaichi shakai* (Azekura Shobō, 2005).

Kenneth R. Robinson is Senior Associate Professor of History at International Christian University, Tokyo. His publications on Chosŏn-period foreign relations include "Centering the King of Chosŏn: Aspects of Korean Maritime Diplomacy, 1392-1592," *The Journal of Asian Studies* 59.1 (2000); on Tsushima include "An Island's Place in History: Tsushima in Japan and in Chosŏn, 1392-1592," *Korean Studies* 30 (2006); and, among other topics, on Korean cartography include "Chosŏn Korea in the Ryûkoku Kangnido: Dating the Oldest Extant Korean Map of the World (15th Century)," *Imago Mundi* 59.2 (2007).

Saeki Kōji is Professor of Japanese History at Kyushu University. His research interests include the urban and commercial development of Hakata as a medieval city, premodern trade networks in maritime Northeast Asia, maritime and land archaeology, the role of overseas Chinese merchants in premodern trade, and trade pottery in East Asia. Among his publications are *Yomigaeru chūsei 1, Higashi Ajia no kokusai toshi Hakata* (coedited, Heibonsha, 1992); "Hakata," in *Iwanami kōza Nihon tsūshi*, vol. 10 (Iwanami Shoten, 1993); volume 9 of the Chūō Kōron History of Medieval Japan, *Mongoru shūrai no totsugeki* (Chūō Kōronsha, 2003); and *Kaidō Nihonshi, 49, Iki, Tsushima, Matsura hantō* (editor Yoshikawa Kōbunkan, 2006).

Peter Shapinsky is Assistant Professor of East Asian History at the University of Illinois at Springfield. His work focuses on the social history of seafarers labeled pirates in the maritime networks linking Japan and East Asia in the fifteenth and sixteenth centuries. His doctoral dissertation (University of Michigan, 2005) was "Lords of the Sea: Pirates, Violence, and Exchange in Medieval Japan." His most recent publication is "With the Sea as Their Domain: Pirates and Maritime Lordship in Medieval Japan," *Seascapes: Maritime Histories, Littoral Cultures,* *and Trans-oceanic Exchanges*, ed. Jerry Bentley, Kären Wigen, and Renate Bridenthal (Honolulu: University of Hawai`i Press, 2007).

Ivo Smits is Professor of Japanese Arts and Cultures at Leiden University. His publications include a chapter on Heian literature for the forthcoming *The Cambridge History of Japanese Literature* (Cambridge University Press); "The Way of the Literati: Chinese Learning and Literary Practice in Mid-Heian Japan" in *Centers and Peripheries in Heian Japan*, ed. Mikael Adolphson, Edward Kamens, and Stacie Matsumoto, Honolulu:University of Hawai'i Press, 2007); "Teika and the Others: Poetics, Poetry, and Politics in Medieval Japan," *Monumenta Nipponica* 59 (2004); with Michel Hockx, *Reading East Asian Writing: The Limits of Literary Theory* (London, New York: RoutledgeCurzon, 2003); "Song as Cultural History: Reading *Wakan rōeishū*," *Monumenta Nipponica* 55 (2000); with Leonard Blussé and Willem Remmelink, *Bridging the Divide: 400 Years of the Netherlands-Japan* (Leiden: Teleac/NOT and Hotei Publishing, 2000).

Haruko Wakabayashi is Japan Memory Project Research Fellow at the Historiographical Institute, University of Tokyo. Her publications include "The Dharma for Sovereigns and Warriors: Onjōji's Claim for Legitimacy in *Tengu zōshi*," *Japanese Journal of Religious Studies* (Spring 2002); "Tenpen chii no kaishakugaku: *Gyokuyō* ni miru chūsei no saigai ishiki," in Masuo Shin'ichirō et al., eds., *Kankyō to shinsei no bunkashi*, vol. 1 (Bensei Shuppan, 2003); "Hell Illustrated: A Visual Image of *Ikai* That Came from *Ikoku*"; "Sangoku shisō and Japan's Identity in the Buddhist Cosmology as Depicted in the *Konjaku mongatarishū*" in *Practicing the Afterlife: Perspectives from Japan*, ed. Susanne Formanele and William R. LaFleur [Vienna: Verlag Der Osterreichischen Akademie Der Wissenschaften, 2004]; and "Emakimono no naka no Ippen: *Ippen hijiri-e* ni miru Ippen no yugyō," in Imai Masaharu, ed., *Nihon no meisō 11: Yugyō no sutehijiri Ippen* (Yoshikawa Kōbunkan, 2004).

Preface

The present volume is an outgrowth of an international, bilingual conference held at the University of Oregon in 1997. That conference, "Tools of Culture: Japan's Technological, Medical, and Intellectual Contacts in East Asia, 1100–1600," was made possible by a generous grant from the Japan Foundation. Supplementary funding, and the provision of facilities and services, came from a number of sources at the University of Oregon. Particular thanks is owed to the Office of the President, Dave Frohnmayer; the Office of the Vice-Provost for Academic Affairs; the Graduate School; College of Arts and Sciences and Dean Joe Stone; the Department of History's Speakers and Events Committee; the Department of East Asian Languages and Literatures; the Oregon Humanities Center; and the Office of International Affairs. Cynthia Brokaw and Robert Felsing provided positive counsel. The Center for Asian and Pacific Studies (Stephan Durrant, Sandi Leavitt, Steve Crowe, and John Labrousse) handled the logistics and financial arrangements. The conference benefited from the varied contributions of graduate students Alex Bay, Morgan Day, Brett Walker, Loyd Willaford, and Michael Woods. Dick Easley and Lin Hueping hosted a wonderful reception at their White Lotus Gallery. The University of Oregon catering services provided excellent fare throughout. Yoko McClain hosted participants for dinner one evening. Above all, special thanks to Michiyo Horiguchi Goble for her support and organization throughout, and her assistance in hosting participants.

The conference was held over a five-day period, on three of which there were seven presentations. The remaining two days were devoted to discussion and assessment. Papers were distributed and commentators assigned in advance. Most papers and presentations were in English or Japanese, the two working languages of the conference, but in a few cases Chinese was also used. Participants were selected after consultation among Andrew Goble, Kosoto Hiroshi, and Murai Shōsuke. Papers were presented by Robert Borgen, Cynthia Brokaw, Lucille Chia, Chen Jie, Martin Collcutt, Wayne Farris, Andrew Goble, Guo Xiumei, Ann Jannetta (unavoidably, in absentia), William Johnston, Kosoto Hiroshi, Mayanagi Makoto, Murai Shōsuke, Kenneth R. Robinson, Saeki Kōji, Ivo Smits, Takahashi Kimiaki, Haruko Wakabayashi, Brett Walker, Wang Tiece, and Yonetani Hitoshi. James Mohr and Jeffrey Hanes served as "outside" discussants for the Johnston and Walker papers, respectively. The conference was stimulating, the quality of papers high, and visits to Crater Lake and a vineyard memorable.

The shape of the present volume has been influenced by a number of different elements, including individual research schedules. Several of the conference papers were parts of ongoing research that later appeared as monographs; a number of them have appeared as articles in various languages and in a range of scholarly journals or collections. The essays in the present volume reflect extensive postconference reflection, and most of them are on topics that are new since the conference. Thus, while this volume had its genesis in the conference, the contents represent new research and engagement of scholarship since that time.

We would also like to express our thanks to the following for their invaluable assistance as the volume took shape. Kosoto Hiroshi and the Department of the History of Medicine at the Kitasato Research Institute have provided research and other facilities to Goble for a decade and a half, which has greatly assisted the editorial process. Guo Xiumei has been especially helpful in sharing her knowledge of Chinese medical literature. Peter Shapinsky provided the translation and adaptation of Saeki Kōji's paper. Bruce Batten generously produced the maps that appear on the following pages. The suggestions of the three anonymous readers of the manuscript have been very helpful.

Finally, but not least of all, we would like to express our gratitude to Jon Wilson and Gudrun Patton at the Association for Asian Studies. Their meticulousness and patience in the editing and production of this book have been invaluable.

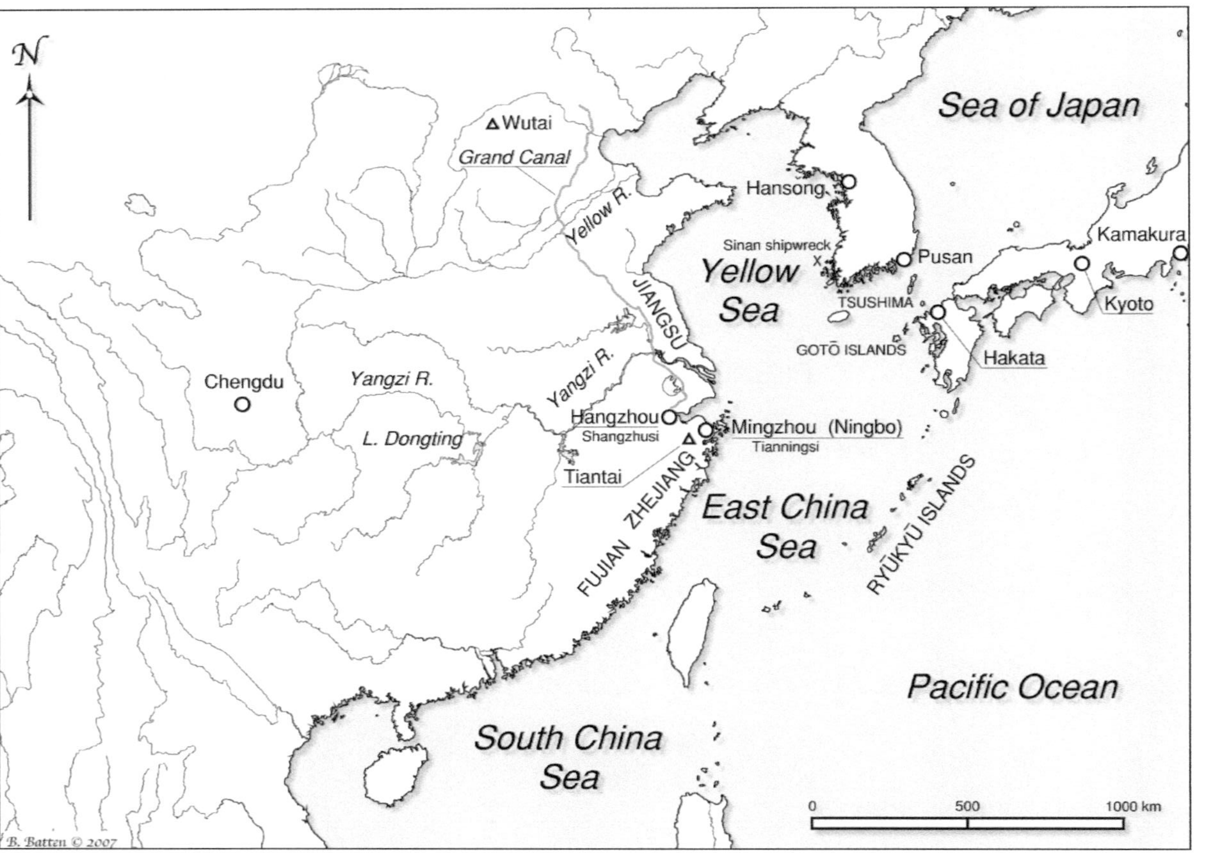

Map: East Asia. Courtesy of Bruce Batten.

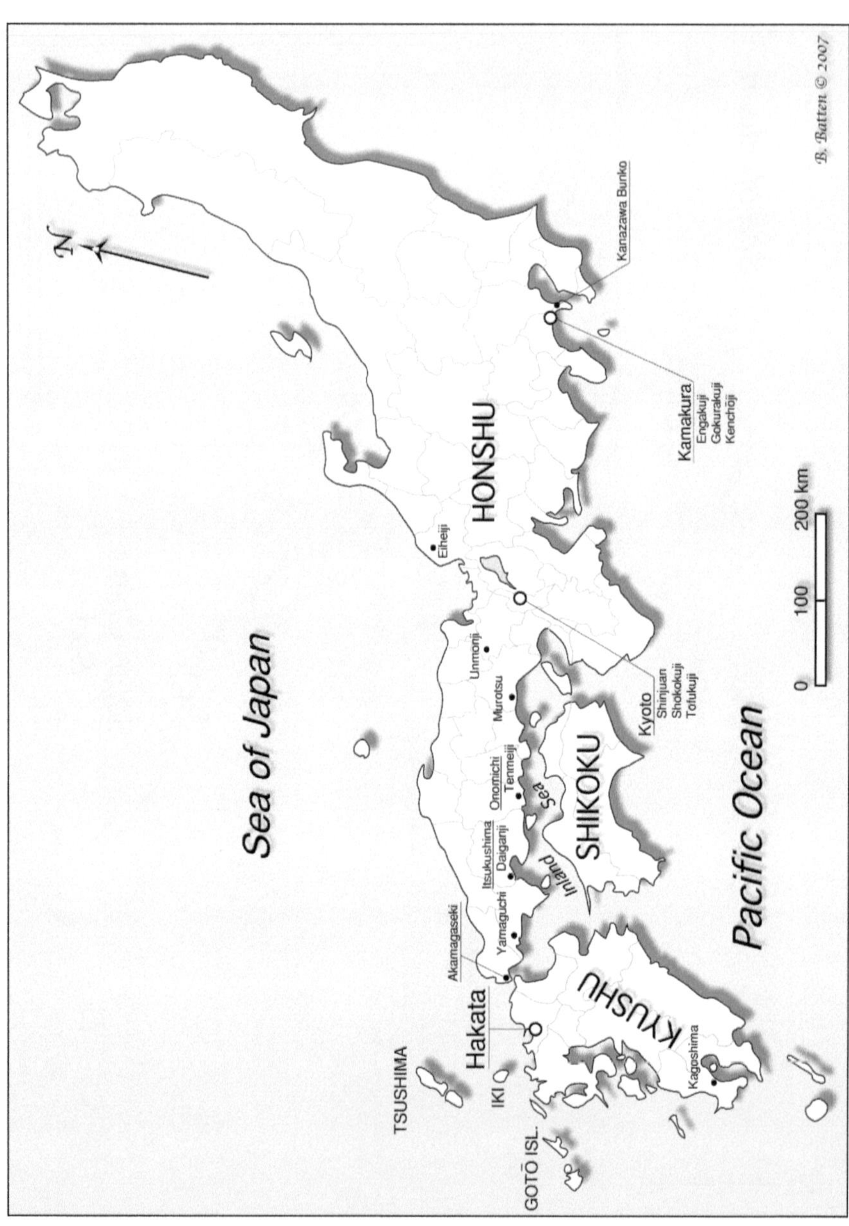

Map: Japan. Courtesy of Bruce Batten.

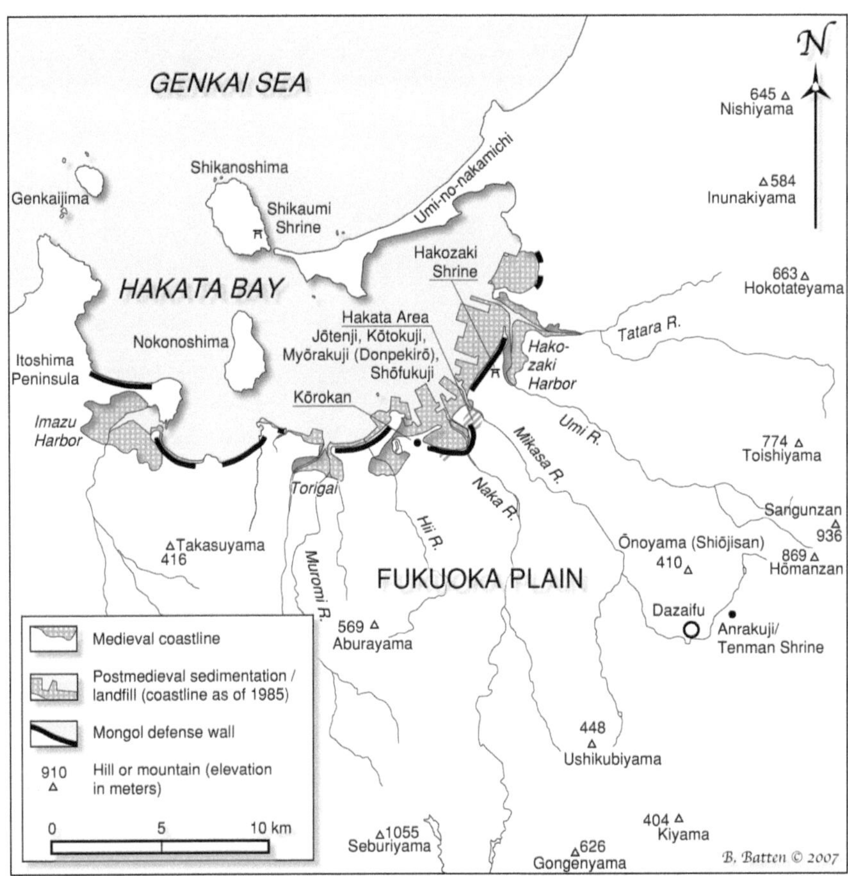

Map: Hakata Area. Courtesy of Bruce Batten.

Introduction: The Ubiquity of Interaction

**Andrew Edmund Goble, Kenneth R. Robinson,
and Haruko Wakabayashi**

This collection addresses aspects of Japanese human and material interactions in East Asia from the late eleventh century through the sixteenth century, a period coincident with Japan's late classical and medieval eras. Individually the papers provide context for and details of interaction rippling through Japanese society. Collectively, they display distinctions over time and geographical locations of contact.

At least two new perspectives on the study of these centuries emerge. The first relates to the general topic of overseas relations engaged in by the Japanese and Japanese institutions and by extension to the study of overseas contacts more generally in East Asia. The second relates to the understanding of what constitutes "Japanese history" and of what topics might fruitfully be engaged in studying that history.

On the first perspective, overseas relations, the collection departs from the overall thrust of much English-language scholarship, which has tended to look at overseas contacts and relations as extensions of the state and thus principally as diplomatic history.[1] Examples here are topics such as the licensed trade and tributary relations during the Muromachi period that occurred within a Sinocentric diplomatic framework or the treatment of "Japanese piracy," which involved the energies of East Asian regimes for centuries. Such scholarship also tended to make the general assumption that if there was little state to state contact then there could only have been little contact generally.

By contrast, while not ignoring state-level contacts, this collection looks foremost at factors and interactions that occurred beyond the state. Even when examining situations in which governments were involved, the focus here is on human and cultural aspects of these interactions. By utilizing a wide range of sources, the authors demonstrate the continuity and breadth of interaction across the seas of eastern Asia. Moreover, they highlight the fact that interaction, while not unaffected by the policies and actions of East Asian regimes, was propelled also by "non-state" interests. Indeed, the problematic nature of even the concept of "the state" as a tool for interpreting the premodern Japanese record attests to the diversity of that record. Accordingly, in order to provide a sense of the multiplicity of participants and their activities, the collection draws on contributions from scholars with training in a number of disciplines (history, art history, medical history, religion, literature), who specialize in different periods, and who are familiar with Chinese and Korean as well as Japanese sources.

On the second perspective, the notion of "Japanese history," the collection moves beyond land boundaries and notions of fixed administrative borders to embrace activities not readily incorporated in "nation-based" history. While it may seem intuitively obvious that, since Japan is an island country in close proximity to a continental landmass, the low-tide mark around its shores would not denote the end point of its history, this perspective still is not a common one in English-language studies of Japanese history. It is, of course, not inaccurate to note that the historical activity of most Japanese through the ages has occurred on the Japanese islands. Yet the coastline, while an obvious boundary, was not a barrier. The mounted warriors who dominated much of Japanese history did not ride their horses into the sea, but many were interested in what crossed the waters, and they did know that it was possible to regularly traverse these distances by boat. However, a land-focused approach to Japanese history has tended to marginalize those aspects of Japanese history that involved interaction between Japan and overseas regions and were by no means marginal. Moreover, that approach conveys a sense that contacts were episodic or sporadic rather than constant.

The land-focused approach to Japanese history has been undergirded by a further limiting perspective, one that has tended to focus on centrally based political, cultural, and religious elites. To be sure, it has long been appreciated that the rhythms and balances of central-local relationships have been crucial in the unfolding of Japanese history.[2] Nonetheless, until very recently,[3] scholarship has tended to invest meaning in other regions and non-elite social groups mainly insofar as they could be "fit" into a centrally focused framework. And, insofar as they might not fit, they have not been considered part of "the mainstream." These approaches constitute a "sedentary mapping" of history that elides the fluid dynamics of movement, both physical and cultural, in the premodern era. Such approaches, with their defined centers and peripheries, have also made it difficult to appreciate that areas and places "outside" the "center," such as the island of Kyushu, the city of Hakata,[4] or the island of Tsushima,[5] were peripheries only relatively. Indeed the center might usefully be regarded as their periphery. In other words, by recognizing wider horizons for Japanese history, this collection hopes to productively decenter some of the assumptions that have defined the understanding of what constitutes Japanese history.

In guiding Japanese history into the water, English-language scholarship is joining Japanese-language and recent Korean-language scholarship. However, the sea, and maritime history (e.g. J. *kaiikishi* and K. *haeyangsa*), should not be separated too cleanly from the land. Diplomatic travel, fishing, seaborne attacks, and the conveyance of objects, among many other activities and interactions, depended on vessels constructed from resources grown or produced onshore. States, individuals, and networks that resembled what Mary Elizabeth Berry has termed a "corporation" participated in maritime endeavors from urban or administrative centers.[6] In diplomatic settings in Ming China and Chosŏn Korea, both governments guided guests overland to and from the capital. Reception, entertainment, room and board, and sanctioned exchange consumed foods and other items collected as levies. On returning to Japan, the distribution, circulation, and consumption of goods from abroad followed.

Further, while it highlights interaction that was often conducted beyond the oversight of the Japanese state, the absence of barriers between land and sea reiterates the importance of foreign states. The "state" may have been a blurred entity in Japan during much of the period treated here, but the influence of Chinese and Korean governments on Japanese activities at sea and on land, at home and abroad, is becoming clearer, as, too, are activities beyond the control of governments in those two countries. Stated differently, the roles of Korean and Ryukyuan states in particular in inviting interaction and managing that contact should not be overlooked.

To reiterate, these essays firmly embed premodern Japanese history in eastern Asia. Events, structures, processes, and cultures rippled through the islands at varied intensities. The resulting expansions of macrocultures are emerging ever more visibly as sources produced elsewhere are mined. In short, the contexts of premodern Japanese histories increase, locations of those histories are found beyond the islands more readily, and those histories become shared with other "national" and regional histories. These national and regional histories require engagement in order to understand with greater subtlety the histories of Japanese and Japan in Asia.

As a review of the breadth of contact sites and interaction, and as a preview to the chapters that follow, one nexus of East Asian interaction invites introduction. The South China-Hakata concourse, more richly documented over several centuries and across diverse manners of exchange than other nodes that could be explored here (such as that between the Korean Peninsula and Hakata, and then Tsushima, or between Ryukyu and Kyushu), opens onto themes discussed in this volume. Trade, residence abroad, transmission of modes of thought and materials of pleasure, and passage to elsewhere, for example, brought consistent contact and confusion. We hope that this introductory exploration may also suggest the types of elements, sources, and themes that are awaiting study.

A Nexus of Interaction: South China through Hakata

The human, commercial, and intellectual routes that facilitated the movement of people, objects, and ideas in the period of our focus were part of broad, overlapping networks. Forms of trade and exchange were multifaceted, and the component parts of this system represented a range of interaction: formal state-to-state tribute-style exchanges; licensed trade; non-state exchange involving representatives of religious institutions; individual actors; "organized" and "random" piracy; movements occasioned by warfare; private exchange at locations away from major ports; direct trade as well as extensive transshipment enterprises; and natives, residents, and sojourners of numerous heritages. Interactions and exchanges ultimately linked objects and ideas all the way from the east coast of Africa; the Horn of Africa; the Red Sea littoral; the Arabian Peninsula; Iraq; Persia; various regions of India and Burma; the coasts and hinterlands of the Malayan Peninsula; Sumatra, Java, Timor, and other "Spice Islands"; the Philippine Islands, Taiwan, Ryukyu, various areas of China, the Korean Peninsula, the Japanese archipelago, and, perhaps finally, the Kurile Islands and maritime Siberia.

The interest of people separated by time and geographical distance in acquiring goods, learning about exchanges, or traveling to observe peoples and locales is well attested. We may note the observations on objects acquired from a distance in such Chinese works as Ji Han's fourth-century *Nanfang caomu zhuang* (Plants of the Southern Regions)[7] and Zhao Rukuo's (fl. ca. 1250) thirteenth-century *Zhufan zhi* (Records of Foreign Nations),[8] in the Arab physician Al-Kindī's (ca. 800–870) *Aqrābādhīn* (Medical Formulary),[9] or in the thirteenth–century *Āthār wa ahyā'* (Installations and Living Things) of the Jewish convert to Islam and a leading figure in the Mongol Il-Khan empire of Persia, Rashid al-Din (1248–1318).[10] And, if there is any doubt about the possibility of undertaking a journey through this vast region, we need only recall some of those who recorded their impressions. Examples include the Chinese Fa Xian's fifth-century *Foguoji* (A Record of Buddhist Kingdoms);[11] the Chinese Xuanzang's seventh-century *Da Tang Xiyuji* (The Great Tang Record of the Western Regions);[12] the Japanese Ennin's (793–864) ninth-century *Nittō guhō junrei kōki* (Record of a Journey to the Tang in Search of the Dharma);[13] the Venetian Marco Polo's (1254–1324) thirteenth-century *Il Milione* (Travels);[14] works of the fourteenth century, represented by the Japanese Sesson Yūbai's (1290–1346) poetic impressions of his years in Sichuan, the *Bingashū* (Collection from the Min and Emei Mountains),[15] or the Moroccan-born Ibn-Battuta's (1304–1377) *Tuhfat al-nuzzar* (Travels);[16] and works of the fifteenth century such as the Korean Song Hŭigyŏng's (1376–1446) *Nosongdang Ilbon haengnok* (Record of a Journey to Japan).[17]

In East Asia, trade and exchange were heavily dependent on, or securely managed by, Chinese merchants and overseas sojourners, who had from an early date developed what we might call a transnational trading community. To be sure, Chinese, by which we mean people from coastal South China, were not the only "nationality" to be involved in trade and exchange, and they did not necessarily control a majority of trade between all places and at all times. Yet the role of these Chinese seems to have been predominant, and it was primarily they who created networks that joined otherwise separate coastal communities.

Connections to places in Japan (where there are many place-name references to Kara, i.e. "China") were with harbors in Kyushu and its offshore islands;[18] ports along the Inland Sea; Tsushima, lying between Kyushu and Korea; and Wakasa Bay on the western coast of Honshu. Those places were linked, for example, to the open ports in Chosŏn, Naha harbor in Ryukyu, and such southern Chinese ports as Hangzhou, Mingzhou (Ningbo), and Quanzhou. These latter, officially designated trading locations were in turn connected to the world beyond the East Asian littoral.[19] The construction of the Shengyou mosque in Quanzhou around 1010 for the mainly Arab and Persian Muslim community,[20] and the Hindu temples constructed for the South Indian Tamil community, attests to those links.[21]

Southern Chinese cities were so prominent in trade and exchange that it is not unlikely that for many Japanese in the premodern era South China *was* China. It was not the only part of China known, and some Japanese had the opportunity to travel to such places as Changan or Beijing or to sail along the Grand Canal. Yet it was southern China that was broadly identified with Chinese culture, and people from there were the major cultural transmitters. A clear preponderance of the Chinese monks who traveled to Japan from the mid-twelfth century came either from the Zhejiang coastal areas near Hangzhou and Mingzhou or from the Yangzi hinterland, which extended as far as Chengdu in Sichuan. Sichuan was also the site of the first large-scale printing of the Buddhist canon, the *Tripitaka*, and the birthplace of the monk most responsible for implanting monastic Rinzai Zen Buddhism in Japan, Lanxi Daolong (Rankei Dōryū, 1213–1278).

Furthermore, people in southern China appear to have regarded Japan and the Japanese as familiar, not as distant and unknown. It is surely no coincidence that the first Chinese map depicting Japan was produced in South China, and it is not surprising to learn that a copy was acquired by a Japanese priest who had lived in China for fourteen years, returning in 1279 just as the Mongols finally vanquished the Southern Song.[22] Moreover, as we can see from the return from Japan of, for example, the Zen monk Wuan Puning (Gottan Funei, 1197–1276), or the discussions between Mingji Chujun (Minki Soshun, 1262–1336) and other monks prior to going to Japan, travelers knew that it was physically possible to return.[23] Even in the case of people whose departure was consciously permanent, they were going to a place where they might make use of institutional linkages or personal contacts to build their lives anew. For example, the Chinese woodblock carvers Yu Liangfu, Chen Mengrong, and Chen Boshou, who arrived in 1367 as political refugees after the fall of the Yuan, quickly went to work in the Zen monastic publishing industry, where they made significant contributions.[24]

Another example is that of Chen Zongjing (Chin Uirō) (?–1395) and his descendents.[25] Zongjing, a specialist in medicine in Mongol/Yuan service, fled to Hakata with his brother Yanyou following the triumph of the Ming. His reputation for medicine, for trade links with both China and Korea, and no doubt for bilingualism, recommended him to political figures like Ashikaga Yoshimitsu (1358–1408). Zongjing's Japanese-born nephew Zongshou (1372–post-1419) was sent as an interpreter on the 1404 mission to Ming China. He brought back with him a number of medicines, including one for disorders of the digestive organs, *Reihō-tan* or *Tōchinkō*, which, under the name Uirōyaku, became one of the most noted patent medicines of Japan's pre-modern era.[26] Zongshou was granted residential land in Kyoto by Yoshimitsu, was known as a man of learning, and supplied medicines (such as the patent medicine *Juntai-en* and the aromatic stomachic *Sogō-en*) to aristocrats.[27] Zongshou's son Changyou (1392–1461), a medical specialist and a poet of Chinese verse, was also tapped for diplomatic service. Sent as Vice Envoy on a sensitive mission to Korea in 1419, on the return voyage he served as the official escort for the Korean envoy Song Hŭigyŏng.[28] He also arranged for Song to meet Zongshou in Hakata.[29] The family retained its reputation (and an extensive library) at least through the lifetime of the next family head Zutian (1438–1514).

Other areas of material culture, such as painting, also benefited from the possibilities of movement and exchange. As one illustration, three portraits of the Zen monk Kokan Shiren (1278–1346) were commissioned by a Japanese supporter and painted by a Yuan Chinese artist in South China, most likely from a sketch done in Japan and provided to the painter for reference. Shiren added his own inscription to the completed portraits after they were sent back to Japan. He was thereby able to complete a spiritual journey to a land that he had planned to visit but had postponed due to the death of his mother and had never had further opportunity to make in person.[30] In another vein, we note the group of Ningbo literati artists who, perhaps wanting to expand their horizons in the broader East Asian macroculture, provided a vibrant intellectual home to a number of Japanese visitors. It is easy to imagine these friends banqueting together, enjoying seasons and the arts, inscribing comments on paintings, or even composing poems as mementos.[31] These personal contacts were maintained over many decades and through more than one generation, and the Japanese visitors were instrumental in introducing the works of their hosts to Japan.[32]

Ningbo, in fact, was the center of Buddhist art production throughout the Song and Yuan periods and catered to a widespread clientele. Ningbo workshops produced paintings for the temples and secular communities in the immediate vicinity and for Chinese temples in Zhejiang, Jiangsu, and Fujian. They also catered to the great demand for Buddhist paintings from Japan such as that for the genre of the Ten Kings of Hell.[33] The Ten Kings of Hell had been a popular iconography in Chinese temples and homes since the tenth century, and during the twelfth and thirteenth centuries these paintings were produced in large quantities in Ningbo. Such images also were exported to both Korea and Japan, and they became the main prototype for the Japanese depictions of the Ten Kings (not coincidentally, the earliest known copy of the painting produced in Japan in the late Kamakura period is at Seiganji near Hakata). Some of these were clearly influenced by Northern Song conventions, while others, quite distinct, were also introduced into Japan.[34] Some Ningbo artists, such as Lu Xinzhong (fl. 1195–1277), a number of whose sets have been preserved, appear to have become specialists in the genre.[35]

The Ten Kings genre provides even further nuance for our understanding of influence and exchange. Traditionally, Japanese connoisseurs had assumed that such imported paintings were, irrespective of the location of actual production, a product of China (hence the appellation "Chinese painting," *kara-e*). However, recent research has demonstrated that a number of the Ten Kings paintings preserved in Japan are more properly identified as works produced in Koryŏ or Chosŏn by Korean artists.[36] Thus, the East Asian macroculture both facilitated exchange and influence in a shared tradition and on occasion served to obscure issues of provenance.

Another painting theme was more specifically Japanese-oriented. This theme is the Totō Tenjin (Tenjin visiting China), which represents the ninth-century Japanese Confucian scholar Sugawara no Michizane (845–903, Tenjin) transposed to a Chinese environment; Michizane stands with a branch of plum blossoms in his hand and wearing Chinese scholar's robes.[37] These paintings are based on a legend created in the fourteenth century that Tenjin, advised by the thirteenth-century Japanese Zen priest Enni Ben'en (1202–1280), visited the Chinese Zen master Wuzhun Shifan (1177–1249) to receive his teachings, as certification of which he was given a monk's robe.[38] Paintings of Totō Tenjin made in Japan were taken to China to have Chinese monks and literati write poems on them. Ningbo artists were not slow to recognize opportunities, and we know that they produced Totō Tenjin paintings in order to serve a Japanese market that was eager to collect a variety of Chinese products (*karamono*).

It has been argued that the "artistic quality" of some objects obtained from Ningbo was not overly great and that the social status of many of the Ningbo literati contacts was not of the first order. Indeed, Ningbo artists such as Lu Xinzhong do not even appear in any of the official histories of Chinese artists.[39] However, these points simply underscore the range and depth of the contacts outside the usually valorized circles of elite cultural transmission. Clearly the cultural impact on Japan was by no means minimal.

The impression we have of broad contacts taking place in an eclectic milieu is also highlighted by evidence that comes not from people but from an item without which those contacts would never have occurred, a ship—or, more accurately, the wreck of a ship that foundered off the southwest coast of Koryŏ in 1323. The cargo, weighing at least twenty-eight tons, included pottery, Chinese coins, and aromatics and drugs such as pepper, croton, betel nut, jasmine, and sandalwood. The owner of the ship was most likely either a Chinese merchant resident in Hakata or Hakozaki or a Japanese merchant connected with the Zen monastic institutions (the *gozan*) of central and eastern Japan. The freight was owned by more than one owner, including the Kyoto Zen temple Tōfukuji, which was using the consignment to gain rebuilding funds in the wake of a fire in 1319 and was working through its branch temple of Jōtenji in Hakata. The actual shipper was probably a Chinese merchant. The items of daily use recovered from the wreck (such as Japanese swords, Korean pottery, and Chinese cooking utensils) indicate that the crew was most likely of mixed "nationality."[40] This information suggests a broader point as well, namely, that in looking at exchange and interaction we confront a milieu in which "affiliation" and "belonging" was determined as much by circumstances and activity as it was by accidents of birth and a priori assumptions of heritage.

Indeed, it is easy to get a sense that many lives enjoyed overlapping senses of affiliation and belonging. There were, of course, occasions when formal determination of primary association was required, as in the case of the altercation in China (Ningbo?) in 1191 between two Chinese ship captains, the Japanese-born Yang Rong and the Chinese-born Chen Qitai. Chinese officials, acting within the general parameters of their overseas trade regulations,[41] needed to determine whether Chinese or Japanese authorities had competent jurisdiction over the Japanese-born offender. The resolution was that "national jurisdiction" took precedence.[42]

On other occasions issues of home, or belonging, straddled borders and seem to have been simple acknowledgments of lives themselves rather than overt statements of where people might fit. One example of this is provided, in 1167, by three Chinese merchants—Ding, Zhang Ning, and Zhang Gongyuan, the latter identified as a native of Fujian—all of whom were residents of Hakata. During a trip to "home soil" in Mingzhou (Ningbo), Ding and Zhang Ning had inscribed markers seeking the general protection of the gods and Buddhas for their ventures. Much more personally, Zhang Gongyuan, evidently moved by filial devotion and perhaps his own sense of "native place," offered funds in order to purchase merit for the deceased Zhang Liulang (his father? his brother?) and his mother, the third daughter of one Mr. Huang, in the hope that they would be thereby assisted in rising to the top rank of living beings, those residing in the Buddha Realm.[43]

Another Chinese Hakata resident also left a carved record of memory and hopes for family. In 1220 one Ms. Zhang had inscribed on a sutra stele a document commending land to a temple in order that the former Munakata shrine head, Ujikuni, and his mother, Ms. Wang, might enjoy rebirth in the Land of Utmost Bliss; that Ms. Zhang herself might enjoy a peaceful life; and that her children and grandchildren might also enjoy a peaceful existence. The family relationships alluded to throw light on the marriages in at least two generations between members of the Munakata shrine family and Chinese women, who were most likely daughters of resident Chinese merchants. First, the daughter of a Mr. Wang married the twenty-fifth shrine head, Ujizane, and produced two sons, Ujitada and Ujikuni, both of whom later served as shrine heads. Then the daughter (our Ms. Zhang) of a Mr. Zhang married Ms. Wang's eldest son, the twenty-sixth shrine head, Ujitada, producing from this union four sons and one daughter, one of whom, Ujinaka (later Ujishige), alternated with Ujikuni as shrine head for some time. Ms. Zhang and her property appear in later records as part of the type of inheritance disputes that seem to have been almost ubiquitous in northern Kyushu.[44]

Indeed, there is much evidence that in the vicinity of this international port city of Hakata there were few "national barriers" that would have prevented "overseas Chinese" from becoming well integrated into local Japanese society, holding positions, owning property, or producing offspring. And, of course, that meant that at times they would be involved in various types of disputes. Sometimes the involvement was indirect, as when it emerged in an exceptionally complicated inheritance dispute that one of the early property owners was the son of a Chinese sea captain and, it appears, a Japanese mother.[45] Sometimes a dispute might turn violent, as when Zhang Kuan'an—a Hakata ship-captain, interpreter, and purveyor to the local temple Daisenji—was killed in 1218 by one Gyōben, Gyōben's son, and some other people affiliated with Hakozaki shrine. This set off disputes at the highest levels of the religious world that had to be mediated by the imperial court, and at the local level occasioned by a claim that the property at the site of the killing be made property of the Kanzaki farming estate with which Kuan'an had been affiliated.[46]

In another case, the dispute was "routine." The Japanese widow of one Xie Guoming was sued by Munakata shrine for the return of a title to land. The outcome is unknown, but it sheds light on the holdings of Guoming, one of the most prominent and successful Hakata area Chinese merchants and international traders of the entire thirteenth century. A patron of religious institutions in both China and Japan, his personal backing and financial support for the noted monk

Enni Ben'en on the latter's return from seven years of Zen training in China resulted in the construction of the Chinese-style Zen temple Jōtenji. This temple appears to have been the first such in Hakata, and in Japan, and was the model for the celebrated Tōfukuji.[47]

The image we have is that physical contact in northern Kyushu between Japanese and people we might refer to using terms or combinations of terms such as expatriates, sojourners, immigrants, people born in Japan or overseas, or people of mixed ethnic or cultural background was probably regarded as not exceptional. Indeed, the contacts may have been seen as positive and desirable, especially from an economic standpoint. Marriage, or at least the production of offspring from transnational unions, seems not to have been uncommon, as we might expect in the vicinity of a trading port. Indeed, the Hakata region was in any event well known for having a range of offspring-producing relationships.[48] And, without wishing to cast aspersions on any of the people referred to or named above, we might also note that the Hakata area was known for its opportunities for casual sexual relationships. It is probably no coincidence that, according to the most comprehensive medical work of the entire medieval era, the *Man'anpō*, compiled in Kamakura in the early fourteenth century, one type of genital sore was popularly referred to as the "Kyushu affliction" (*Tsukushi byō*).[49]

In short, contacts and movements encompassed a range of human association that was both a remarkable and ordinary phenomenon and integral to Japanese history in this era. The essays in this collection will explore this through an examination of religion, visual images, literature, medicine, material objects, and varieties of human movement. A brief overview of these essays follows.

The Essays

The essays in this volume have been organized under three themes. Part One, "Inscriptions and Interactions," examines ways in which the written word served as a vehicle of interaction. Part Two, "Arts and Aesthetics," focuses on the influences of intellectual, material, and visual cultures on the development of medieval Japanese culture. Part Three, "Prescribing and Prescriptions," refers to the possibilities for defining and engaging knowledge and physical artifacts (books and crude drugs) that embodied knowledge and that were presented as a result of the rise of print culture in Song China.

Part One: Inscriptions and Interactions

The three essays in Part One by Robert Borgen, Murai Shōsuke, and Kenneth R. Robinson examine a variety of written sources that in different ways attest to the importance of the written word. Yet these sources do not just record information. They also convey some of the ways in which the use of written Chinese was an embodiment of a world of civilized interaction throughout East Asia. While Borgen and Murai display technology and literary styles as common features of a shared culture, Robinson depicts cultural separation between social elites in Japan and Chosŏn Korea. Through the diary of a Heian monk on pilgrimage in Song China, Borgen interprets that individual's reactions to Chinese technology, medical practices, and other examples of applied knowledge known and unknown in that monk's eleventh-century Japan. Murai reads several centuries of poetry written by men serving states or local elites in contexts of diplomatic interaction. Robinson, too, focuses on a Japanese Buddhist monk's diary of travel abroad and seeks to link that mission sent by Ōuchi Yoshitaka (1507–1551) to patterns of Japanese-Korean and Korean-Japanese interaction.

Borgen follows one of the many Japanese who journeyed on Chinese junks, the monk Jōjin (1011–1081), who traveled to China in 1072 and left a detailed diary of his observations there. He examines how certain forms of Chinese scientific and technological knowledge, such as transportation through the man-made canals, architecture (monasteries, bridges, urban buildings, and the imperial palace), water-powered dolls, and camera obscura, were new and awe-inspiring to Jōjin. At the same time he shows that other aspects, such as the prediction and interpretation of heavenly phenomena, were familiar aspects of Japanese monastic life and went relatively unremarked. In some cases, Jōjin suggested that Japanese "technology" was more effective, as in the case of a Buddhist rainmaking ritual that was undertaken on behalf of the Chinese court in order to end a drought. In other cases there was useful exchange: Jōjin sent back to Japan as many books as he had brought with him to China. Among those latter books was Genshin's *Ōjōyōshū*, which impressed the Chinese monks to whom he lent the copies. Overall, Borgen suggests that Jōjin and the Chinese who received him regarded themselves as equals engaged in reciprocal exchange. However, assessing the legacy in Japan of Jōjin's interactions is more problematic.

Murai recovers poetry written in Chinese as a vehicle for intellectual exchange and diplomacy in Northeast Asia. Envoys of emperors, kings, and local Japanese elites enjoyed good company, negotiated with their hosts, and complained about their treatment through verse. Those men, whether officials who had passed civil service or military examinations to serve in the government or Buddhist monks, shared a common knowledge of poetic form if not always of the other's culture. Poetry might also be read as measures of a person and his country. Verse written by envoys while abroad also transmitted information and impressions of a foreign land. Such details could be retrieved subsequently for conversations, negotiations, or other purposes.

At the Chosŏn Korea court literary skill could trump other factors when the king and his officials selected men for diplomatic interaction with Japanese elites. Such talent, though not emphasized in the military examination, could earn appointments for military officials. Civil officials serving in low-ranking posts might be chosen ahead of men holding ministerial office. Officials in obscure posts might even be summoned solely for a gathering that would include the exchange of poems. In Japan, by contrast, the Muromachi bakufu did not rely on samurai officials. Rather, samurai officials turned to monks serving, especially, in Rinzai Zen temples. Such monks were associated with favored teaching lineages or Shōkokuji in Kyoto, a Rinzai temple that also played a large role in administering the Muromachi bakufu's policies toward Zen temples.

Yet Zen monks were active in their own sphere of intellectual engagement as well as in the world of state-level diplomacy. Murai also explores the tableau of poetic exchanges between Zen monks themselves, most particularly those between Japanese Zen monks and their Chinese teachers whose institutions were centered in South China. A particular characteristic of Chinese Zen Buddhism was the development of poetry as a vehicle for expressing personal understanding of doctrine, demonstrating familiarity with traditions, and providing verbal portraits for the rich symbols and imaginations that pervaded the fundamental quest to understand the cosmos. That use of poetry not only yielded evocative imagery but helped shape an entire genre of Japanese literary expression, the so-called Literature of the Five Mountains.

Robinson also deals extensively with movement. He attempts to situate a 1537 trade mission sponsored by Ōuchi Yoshitaka in the broader contexts of Korean reception, entertainment, travel, and trade regulations and changing Japanese trade patterns. This mission originated in the desire of a small temple to acquire a complete set of the printed Koryŏ *Tripitaka*. The temple's request for assistance provided Yoshitaka with an opportunity to trade in Chosŏn, and Robinson speculates that Yoshitaka may have sought to profit from the trade, which saw silver mined in western Honshu exported to Chosŏn.

A monk at Daiganji who served as the mission's envoy while in Chosŏn left an account of that mission. In its extant form, the account concentrates on the sutras and rarely mentions trade and thus is more a recounting of the temple's interests than of the mission as a whole. Unfortunately for the temple, the monks' desire for sutras collided with both a kind of donor fatigue in the wake of some one hundred (recorded) Japanese and Ryukyuan requests since the late 1380s and the deepening ideological commitment of Korean officials to Confucian government and their disdain for Buddhism. The account, written on the back of the folding screen, nonetheless provides substantial information on Korean management of Japanese travel.

Part Two: Arts and Aesthetics
The three essays in Part Two, by Haruko Wakabayashi, Martin Collcutt, and Saeki Kōji, explore the nature of cultural and intellectual exchange and the impact this exchange had on the shaping of medieval Japanese culture. Wakabayashi's essay illustrates one legacy of the contact occasioned by the Mongol Invasions launched from China and Korea. Her examination of one religious and artistic response to these invasions demonstrates that battles had a significant impact on Japanese visual culture. Martin Collcutt's examination of the Chinese Zen monk Lanxi Daolong shows yet another facet of the contribution of monks to the development of a new culture. The dissemination of Chinese religion and culture in the political capitals of Kyoto (Heian) and Kamakura contributed greatly to an enhanced interest in material goods from China. As Saeki Kōji demonstrates through his study of archaeological findings, as well as written documents, pottery was one such commodity.

Wakabayashi's exploration of aspects of the visual cultural legacies of interaction focuses on a fourteenth-century painting from Shikanoshima, where a battle took place during the second Mongol Invasion in 1281. The painting, known as *Shikaumi Jinja engi,* is one of the earliest illustrated accounts of the legendary conquest of the kingdoms of Silla, Paekche, and Koguryŏ by Empress Jingū in the third century.

Wakabayashi pays particular attention to the representation of foreign enemies depicted in the battle scene. They are portrayed in ways strikingly similar to the Mongols in other contemporary Japanese sources known for their vivid description of the battles, adding realism to the legendary event. The two isolated events, the Mongol Invasions and Empress Jingū's expedition, were synthesized into the battle scene, and the analogy between the two battles created an effective metaphor for propagating the power of the god Hachiman (manifested as Emperor Ōjin, who fought the battle while still in Empress Jingū's womb). By the sixteenth century, the painting gained a reputation such that Hideyoshi viewed it before his invasion of Chosŏn. The *Shikaumi Jinja engi* and other narratives composed after the Mongol Invasions suggest that the hostile encounter with the foreign other in the late thirteenth century made it possible for Japanese to create images of alien enemies that had not been visualized before. More important, this image became a fixed iconography used to depict the foreign other in later literary and illustrated works.

Collcutt's essay, a discussion of the Chinese monk Lanxi Daolong, elucidates in detail the type of intellectual and cultural exchange that was at the core of the Zen enterprise. He elucidates the transmission of what was regarded by those involved as authentic Chinese Chan monastic practice, thought, and culture to Japan in the thirteenth century by a trained and experienced Chinese monk.

Although Zen teachings had been known in Japan for some centuries, and from earlier in the thirteenth century we note the growth of some Zen culture in the imperial capital of Kyoto (e.g. Eisai's [1141–1215] temple of Kenninji and the building of Tōfukuji for Enni Ben'en in the 1240s), Zen in Kyoto was mixed with prayers and exoteric ritual, and the establishment of an independent and pure authentic Chan center in Kyoto under a Chinese master would have encountered hostility from the established Buddhist institutions. However, with the patronage and full support of warrior elites such as the Hōjō, who believed that Zen could develop as an ideological basis for warrior culture as a counter to Kyoto court society, Lanxi Daolong found in Kamakura a place in which to transmit authentic Chan Buddhism.

Yet he was certainly not free of challenges. During the times of the Mongol Invasions, he was accused of collaboration with the Mongols and was banished for several years. Also, in some cases, he made compromises with local customs and practices, as in keeping the Jizō image of Shinheiji in his monastery. However, his and his successors' contributions to the shaping of a new culture were immeasurable, as they filled the monasteries with Chinese goods, which provided major stimulus for Japanese artists and craftsmen. They had turned Kamakura into a center for Chan and Chinese learning and culture. The effort to create an authentic Chinese environment was so successful that within a few decades they could assert that it was no longer necessary to travel to Song China for authentic Chan training.

Saeki's essay builds on this fascination with things Chinese and explores more extensively and comprehensively the reception and circulation of one particular form of *karamono*, namely, ceramics. As Saeki notes, interest in *karamono*, and use of that term, can be traced back into the Heian period. However, from the thirteenth century on a new level of interest in *karamono* in general, and in pottery in particular, emerges in conjunction with the growing popularity of tea. Tea connoted more than the beverage and stood for a broader aesthetic built around stylized imbibing in social settings.

Appreciation of the "tea experience" spread from Zen monasteries to the elite members of the warrior class who were their supporters and patrons, and in time it came to constitute the core of medieval aesthetic culture. Indeed, so important was the aesthetic that it became highly formalized, even ritualized, and detailed manuals for the use and appreciation of *karamono* were compiled by leading aesthetes, acknowledged masters of the cultural form. Appreciation of pottery moved in new directions, including even the acquisition and appraisal of old pottery. That is, there was a Japanese market for antiques. The great demand for Chinese objects and how they were obtained could be seen through documents sent by absentee proprietors in the capital requesting the residents in their estates in Kyushu to acquire and send the objects to them.

Saeki also explores the nature of pottery trade through the use of archaeological findings. The Sinan shipwreck discovered off the southwest coast of South Korea in 1976, for instance, is known to have been a ship dispatched in 1323 to acquire products of China in order to raise funds for the repair of Tōfukuji. From this and other excavations, he concludes that there were wide-ranging networks of distribution and exchange with China and other East and Southeast Asian countries, that there were linkages between trade pottery and Japanese ceramics production, and that there were various trends in ceramic imports. The trade pottery unearthed from Hakata also shows that the port city was a major center of trade with China, Korea, Ryukyu, and Southeast Asia.

Part Three: Prescribing and Prescriptions

The three essays in Part Three, by Ivo Smits, Kosoto Hiroshi, and Andrew Edmund Goble, take up issues of the acquisition of knowledge and its physical embodiments. A common thread in the essays is the access to information that was facilitated by the Song revolution in printing technology, which moved the creation, dissemination, reproduction, and preservation of information away from an older technology of copying by hand to a newer one of readily reproducible woodblock printing. This created new possibilities for prescribing knowledge. Smits notes the development by Japanese aristocrats, in particular Fujiwara no Yorinaga (1120–1156), of a prescriptive canon of knowledge about classical China that formed the basis for a new tradition of writing in Chinese (*kanbun*). Kosoto examines the printing of medical texts undertaken during the Song period. Goble delves further into medical writings and prescriptions and examines how access to the medical and pharmaceutical knowledge in Song printed medical works helped prescribe a new body of medical knowledge in medieval Japan.

Smits's careful study of the book collections of two scholar-politicians of the twelfth century, Fujiwara no Yorinaga and Fujiwara no Michinori (1106–1159), elucidates the types of Song period Chinese works that were read and collected by Japanese courtiers. His study elaborates the social and political contexts that made it possible for leading members of the aristocracy to create their own intellectual salons and establish the agendas for inquiry and discussion for their groups. In the case of Yorinaga, a widely read Sinophile whose erudition was acknowledged as being of the highest order, his passion for the works of Chinese antiquity, the classics, went hand in hand with his desire as an avid bibliophile to establish a preeminent library. Fortuitously, the appearance of Song printed editions of the early classics (which, while not taken up in the essay, were the product of Song efforts to define the classics) facilitated his endeavors.

Smits shows that these courtiers evinced little interest in literary works produced by Song period authors. Rather, they were more interested in reference works, commentaries, and annotated editions of the classics, particularly those that were produced in the Tang period. Significantly, many of the Song printed works were editions of works that were already known in Japan and had long been the core of a classical education there. Thus, newer works were less familiar and enjoyed little prominence in courtiers' cognitive maps. He concludes that by the eleventh and twelfth centuries the Japanese elite had constructed a self-contained image of the Chinese literary canon and in so doing had established an indigenous tradition for the study and practice of *kanbun*. Some Japanese "Chinese classics," it appears, were not Chinese classics in China.

Kosoto addresses some of the impact of the Song revolution in printing on the field of medical writing in the Northern and the Southern Song eras. In the Northern Song the printing of texts was primarily undertaken by official government agencies that were charged with making medical knowledge widely available to the populace. This effort initially was directed to producing definitive, standardized versions of older texts and in effect defined a classical canon. Kosoto makes the important point that absent this effort the knowledge that is the foundation of Chinese medicine would have been lost: the printed Song versions of pre-Song texts are, in fact, the oldest extant editions of these works.

The Southern Song witnessed a "highly democratized information revolution" in which the printing of medical works was carried out primarily under private auspices. Some of these works achieved great stature within the medical tradition. Many, however, enjoyed a much shorter life span. Primarily pharmaceutical handbooks directed to the general population and intended for ready reference, these works represented an enormous range of medical knowledge practiced by people of diverse educational and social backgrounds. While receiving little, if any, official imprimatur, they provide a valuable window into nonelite medicine. Kosoto notes that these works, produced as working ephemera rather than "library editions," were handbooks of "the best" contemporary Chinese medicine.

Goble's essay addresses the impact of this Song medical knowledge in Japan. He begins by noting that, whereas civil aristocrats rarely traveled and had only limited knowledge of Chinese publishing (a point made clear by Smits), in this era Chinese and Japanese Buddhist monks traveled frequently between the two countries and readily acquired printed works. Goble examines the impact of this on Japanese medicine through an examination of the writings of the monk–physician Kajiwara Shōzen (1265–1337). He examines the titles to which Shōzen had access, and the ways in which the new information influenced medicine are illustrated through examples of Shōzen's comments on the failings of existing knowledge and the benefits of newer understandings.

Goble also examines the evidence for significant changes in the pharmaceutical regime from the Tang through the Song era, the fruits of which were also disseminated to Japan and utilized by Kajiwara Shōzen. By examining prescriptions, commenting on the changes in Chinese medicine from Tang to Song that are evident in Chinese medical writings, and examining the enhanced range of *materia medica* (crude drugs) that are noted in the various works, we are able to observe the range of factors that contributed to significant changes in the practice of Japanese medicine. Finally, Goble offers evidence that medical knowledge, crude drugs, and prescriptions originated as far away as the Islamic world and were brought to Japan via what we may describe as a Medical Silk Road.

Notes

[1] For a brief survey of this topic, see the section "Overseas Contacts" in Andrew Edmund Goble, "Medieval Japan." For a study of trade over the premodern period, see Charlotte von Verschuer, *Across the Perilous Sea: Japanese Trade with China and Korea from the Seventh to the Sixteenth Centuries.*

[2] The classic elaboration of the central-local relationship is John Whitney Hall's *Government and Local Power in Japan, 500–700: A Study Based on Bizen Province.*

[3] The collection edited by Mikael Adolphson, Edward Kamens, and Stacie Matsumoto, *Heian Japan: Centers and Peripheries*, represents a concerted effort to address the issue of how a centrally focused approach has obscured many aspects of the Heian historical experience.

[4] See Bruce Batten, *Gateway to Japan: Hakata in War and Peace, 500–1300.*

[5] In English, see Kenneth R. Robinson, "The Tsushima Governor and the Regulation of Japanese Access to Chosŏn in the Fifteenth and Sixteenth Centuries;" and "An Island's Place in History: Tsushima in Japan and in Chosŏn, 1392–1592."

[6] Mary Elizabeth Berry, *The Culture of Civil War in Kyoto*, pp. xxix–xxxii.

[7] Hui-Lin Li, *Nan-fang ts'ao-mu chuang: A Fourth Century Flora of Southeast Asia.*

[8] Frederick Hirth and W. W. Rockhill, *Chau Ju-Kua: His Work on the Chinese and Arab Trade in the Twelfth and Thirteenth Centuries, Entitled Chu-fan-chï.*

[9] Martin Levey, *The* Medical Formulary *or* Aqrābādhīn *of Al-Kindi.*

[10] A. K. S. Lambton, "The *Āthār wa ahyā'* of Rashīd al-Dīn Fadl Allāh Hamadānī and His Contribution as an Agronomist, Arboriculturalist and Horticulturalist." Our thanks go to Professor Timothy Gianotti for suggesting the English translation of *Āthār wa ahyā'.*

[11] Herbert A. Giles, *The Travels of Fa-hsien (399–414 AD)*; James Legge, *A Record of Buddhistic Kingdoms.*

[12] Li Rongxi, *The Great Tang Record of the Western Regions*; Samuel Beal, *Si-Yu-Ki: Buddhist Records of the Western Worlds Translated from the Chinese of Hiuen Tsiang (AD 639).*

[13] Edwin O. Reischauer, *Ennin's Diary: The Record of a Pilgrimage to China in Search of the Law.*

[14] Ronald Latham, *Marco Polo: The Travels*; Henry Yule and Henri Cordier, *The Travels of Marco Polo: The Complete Yule-Cordier Edition.*

[15] Our thanks go to Professor Ina Asim of the University of Oregon for suggesting the English translation of *Bingashū*. For a discussion of Sesson Yūbai and his travels, and a modern retracing of his steps, see Imatani Akira, *Genchō Chūgoku tokōki: Ryūgakusō Sesson Yūbai no suki na unmei*.

[16] H. A. R. Gibb, *The Travels of Ibn Battūta*. See, too, Ross E. Dunn, *The Adventures of Ibn Battuta, Muslim Traveller of the Fourteenth Century*.

[17] Song Hŭigyŏng, *Nosongdang Ilbon haengnok*.

[18] For one informative study, see Yanagihara Toshiaki, "Chūsei zenki minami Kyūshū no minato to Sōjin kyoryūchi ni kansuru ichi shiron."

[19] For particularly good guides to the official trading locations, and the city of Quanzhou in particular, see Hugh R. Clark, *Community, Trade, and Networks: Southern Fujian Province from the Third to the Thirteenth Century*; Billy K. L. So, *Prosperity, Region, and Institutions in Maritime China: The South Fukien Pattern, 946–1368*; and Angela Schottenhammer, *The Emporium of the World: Maritime Quanzhou, 1000–1400*.

[20] Clark, *Community, Trade, and Networks*, pp. 122–123, 128–129.

[21] See John Guy, "Tamil Merchant Guilds and the Quanzhou Trade."

[22] The map was acquired by Busshō Zenshi (Hakuun Keigyō) on behalf of the Kyoto Zen temple Tōfukuji. For a black and white reproduction, see Nanba Matsutarō, Muroga Nobuo, and Unno Kazutaka, *Nihon no kochizu*, p. 158. For discussions of the map and its provenance, see Aoyama Sadao, "Ritsukyokuan shozō no *Yochizu* ni tsuite," particularly pp. 68–69; and Ōji Toshiaki, "Echizu ni arawareta sekaizō," p. 315.

[23] See Nishio Kenryū, "Kamakura jidai ni okeru torai sō o megutte," p. 55; Murai Shōsuke, "Torai sō no seiki;" and Nishio Kenryū, *Chūsei Nitchū kōryū to Zenshū*.

[24] See Kawase Kazuma, *Gozanban no kenkyū*, pp. 142–160, particularly pp. 151–157. Kawase provides information on the arrival of eight Chinese (Tōjin) in Saga, near Kyoto, in 1267 and provides information on Chen Mocai and Chen Boshou.

[25] Fujiwara Shigeo, "Chin Uirō kankei shiryōshū (kō), kaidai: Kyoto Chin Uirō o chūshin ni;" Sugiyama Shigeru, "Chūsei Nissen kōeki ni okeru Uirō (Sōju, Jōyū) no katsuyaku."

[26] See Sugiyama Shigeru, *Kusuri no shakai shi: Uirō, Tōchinkō*.

[27] For his contact with Yamashina Noritoki, who laid the basis for a family specialty in medicine and pharmaceuticals that lasted at least 200 years, see *Noritoki kyōki*, Ōei 16 (1409).6.5 (3.143), 6.16 (3.147), 6.24 (3.152).

[28] Song Hŭigyŏng, *Nosongdang Ilbon haengnok*, section 48, entry for 1419.3.2 (Murai Shōsuke, *Rōshōdō Nihon kōroku: Chōsen shisetsu no mita chūsei Nihon*, no. 48, p. 52, and note 3 pp. 52-53, and p. 199).

[29] Song Hŭigyŏng, *Nosongdang Ilbon haengnok*, section 107, entry for 1419.4.21 (Murai Shōsuke, *Rōshōdō Nihon kōroku*, no. 107, pp. 101-102, 209-210).

[30] These portraits of Kokan Shiren are now held in Tōfukuji. See Ebine Toshio, "Kaizō-in zō Kokan Shiren zō."

[31] See Xu Ben's poem, "Saying Goodbye to a Monk from Japan," in Victor Mair, *The Columbia Anthology of Traditional Chinese Literature*, pp. 262–263.

[32] Ebine Toshio, "Neiha [Ningbo] no bunjin to Nihonjin: 15 seiki ni okeru."

[33] Suzuki Kei, "Riku Shinchū hitsu Jūō-zu;" Ide Seinosuke, *Nihon no Sōgen butsuga*.

[34] Cheeyun Lilian Kwon, "The Ten Kings at the Seikadō Library," pp. 1–7. See, too, Stephen F. Teiser, *The Scripture on the Ten Kings and the Making of Purgatory in Medieval Chinese Buddhism*, pp. 57–62, for comments on Japan. Parenthetically, the first Japanese known to have had contact with the Ten Kings was the monk Jōjin.

[35] Nakano Teruo, *Enma, Jūō-zō*; Ide Seinosuke, "Sakuhin no kosei to aidentitii: Neiha butsuga to chiiki shakai," Ide Seinosuke, *Nihon no Sōgen butsuga*. Lu Xinzhong's signed sets (ten hanging scrolls, each portraying one king) are presently kept at Nara National Museum, Zendōji (Fukuoka Prefecture), Eigenji (Shiga Prefecture), Jōdoji (Hiroshima Prefecture), Hōnenji (Kagawa Prefecture), and Shōmyōji Kanazawa Bunko (Kanagawa Prefecture).

[36] Ide, *Nihon no Sōgen butsuga*, pp. 17–22; Kwon, "The Ten Kings at the Seikadō Library;" Miyazaki Noriko, "Seikadō Bunko Bijutsukan zō 'Jūō-zu, ni shisha-zu' ni tsuite."

[37] Suzuki Hiroyuki, "Ōkan suru kaiga: Jugo seiki kanji bunkaken no naka no kara-e no igi." For Michizane, see Robert Borgen, *Sugawara no Michizane and the Early Heian Court*.

[38] See Shimao Arata, "Sesshū to Totō Tenjin;" Takahashi Noriko, "Banri shūkyū no san no aru nifuku no 'Totō Tenjin zō';" Imaizumi Yoshio, "Baigai san no Totō Tenjin zō."

[39] See Ebine, "Neiha no bunjin to Nihonjin;" and Ide, *Nihon no Sōgen butsuga*, pp. 20–22, 36–55.

[40] See Murai Shōsuke, "Chūsei ni okeru Higashi Ajia sho chiiki to no kōtsū;" Kawazoe Shōji, "Kamakura makki no taigai kankei to Hakata: Shin'an chinbotsusen mokkan, Tōfukuji, Jōtenji;" and Matsuki Satoru, "Chinsen wa kataru."

[41] See So, *Prosperity, Region, and Institutions in Maritime China*, pp. 42–49, and chap. 10.

[42] *Gyokuyō*, Kenkyū 2 (1191).2.19 (3.661).

[43] See Gu Wenbi and Lin Shimin, "Neiha [Ningbo] ni genzon suru Nihon koku Dazaifu Hakata tsū no kakyō kokuseki no kenkyū," pp. 103–104, for the inscriptions.

[44] Mori Katsumi, *Zoku Nissō bōeki no kenkyū*, pp. 364–367; Saeki Kōji, *Mongoru shūrai no shōgeki*, pp. 28–30, with a picture of the sutra stele on p. 29. For a transcription of the commendation, see Jōkyū 2 (1220).2.12 Chōshi kishinjō (*Kamakura ibun komonjo hen*, vol. 4, document 2576, hereafter cited as *KI*, 4:2576). For later disputes over property with which Ms. Zhang had been associated, see Bun'ei 5 (1264).6.27 Kantō hikitsukeshū renshō hōsho (*KI*, 13:10266); Bun'ei 5 (1264).7.3 Shami Jōkei (Munakata Ujinari) ukebumi (*KI*, 13:10274); and Bun'ei 6 (1265).2 Azukari dokoro kudashibumi (*KI*, 14:10390).

[45] See Antei 2 (1228).3.13 Kantō gechijō (*KI*, 6:3732). The complex and fascinating inheritance dispute is discussed in Jeffrey P. Mass, *The Development of Kamakura Rule, 1180–1250*, p. 96ff; and in greater detail in Hyungsub Moon, "Matsura-tō: Pirate Warriors in Northwestern Kyushu, Japan, 1150–1350," pp. 44–61.

[46] See Saeki Kōji, "Tairiku bōeki to gaikokujin no kyoryū," pp. 109–110.

[47] The definitive treatment of Xie Guomin is Kawazoe Shōji, "Jōtenji no kaisō to Hakata gōshū Sha Kokumei [Xie Guomin]: Kamakura chūki no taigai kankei to Hakata." For a photograph of the statue of Xie Guomin held in Jōtenji, see Nishioka Reizō and Yanagita Yoshitaka, *Genkō to Hakata: Shashin de yomu Mōko shūrai*, p. 19; and Mori, *Zoku Nissō bōeki no kenkyū*, pp. 261–262. See, too, Kenchō 5 (1253).7.12 Kantō gechijō (*KI*, 10:7458); and Kenchō 5 (1253).5.3 Hōjō Nagatoki kakikudashi (*KI*, 10:7551).

[48] An inheritance dispute involving the legacies of a father and his three sons who had been killed during the Mongol invasion of 1274 reveals that the three sons had been born to three different mothers. See Kenji 3 (1277).10.24 Shōni Tsunesuke shojō an (*KI*, 17:12888); Kōan 2 (1279).10.8 Kantō gechijō (*KI*, 18:13730); and Kōan 2 (1279).10.8 Kantō gechijō (*KI*, 18:13731).

[49] *Man'anpō* index (Kagaku shoin edition, 1986, p. 16, sec. M, leaf 64, hereafter cited as *Man'anpō* index [*KS*, p. 16, M–64]).

Part One

Inscriptions and Interactions

1

Jōjin's Discoveries in Song China
Robert Borgen

Members of the Heian elite left many diaries. Best known are those written in Japanese, usually by women, and prized for their literary qualities. Men typically kept their diaries in classical Chinese. Those diaries are more factual and less literary than those in Japanese and hence of particular value to historians. A very small subset of the men's diaries in Chinese consists of those kept by Buddhist monks who made pilgrimages to China. Although these works describe events and conditions in China, they also offer insights into the concerns and attitudes of their Japanese authors, making them important sources for the study of both Chinese and Japanese history.

One such diary is *The Record of a Pilgrimage to the Tiantai and Wutai Mountains* (*San Tendai godaisanki*) kept by the monk Jōjin (1011–1081) during sixteen months of his pilgrimage to China in the years 1072–1073.[1] Jōjin was a devout Buddhist, and so, as one might expect, he gave considerable attention to religious matters. More surprisingly, however, he also left detailed descriptions of man-made wonders and unfamiliar natural phenomena, suggesting an interest in what today might be termed technology and science or at least their precursors. Jōjin thus offers insights into the state of Chinese technology and science and, at the same time, into how at least one Japanese monk viewed them. Whereas once scholars writing in English were apt to condemn Heian courtiers as being somehow more "superstitious" than their presumably more "scientific" neighbors, Jōjin's observations suggest that the difference may have been much exaggerated.

In an age that valued hereditary status, Jōjin had been born to parents descended from key figures at court. Unfortunately, when he was still young his father died. Since that left his prospects at court uncertain, his mother entrusted him to a Buddhist monastery, where he became the disciple of a distinguished cleric. As he rose in the Buddhist hierarchy, he developed close ties to both the emperor and his Fujiwara regent. Thus, though a monk, he was also a man of the court. His clerical career was highly successful but unremarkable until 1069, when, at the age of fifty-eight, he informed his aged mother that he intended to make a pilgrimage to China's Buddhist holy mountains. The following year he petitioned the court for permission to travel.

Jōjin began his diary in the third month of 1072, when he and seven disciples boarded a Chinese merchant ship in Kyushu. After six days at sea, they arrived near the modern city of Ningbo. Jōjin and his entourage first visited the nearby Tiantai Mountains, where his sect of Buddhism, Tendai in Japanese, had been founded. Jōjin also sought to worship at the Wutai Mountains, another holy site far to the north. He petitioned the central government for permission to make that journey, but when the reply came it made no mention of Wutai. Instead it ordered him to the capital as a guest of the Chinese government with his travels generously subsidized. Jōjin had become a guest of state and subsequently traveled in style with official escorts. He went to the Song capital of Kaifeng, where he was greeted at an imperial audience and met Buddhist monks from throughout Asia. He was also granted permission to visit Wutai, a two-month journey through the northern mountains that he completed in the dead of winter.

Afterward, he arranged to dispatch five of his disciples home to Japan and to return to Tiantai with his remaining two followers. He also gathered many unfamiliar Chinese texts to send to Japan. Before he could depart, however, he was again summoned to the palace, this time to say prayers to end a drought. When rain fell, he was given credit and rewarded with a distinguished Chinese Buddhist title. He then proceeded to the coast and entrusted his diary to his returning disciples, who brought it safely back to Japan. Jōjin's subsequent activities are virtually unknown. One year later he sent a letter to a disciple in Japan encouraging him to disseminate the texts he had sent there. Jōjin is said to have died in 1081 at a monastery in Kaifeng.[2] Mostly, we know him from what he recorded in his diary.

Transportation

Jōjin was traveling during forty percent of the period covered in his diary. He covered great distances by various means, principally boat and horseback plus an occasional palanquin. Getting from one place to another does not seem to have been a serious problem. Once he got to China, government involvement was pervasive. On the one hand, the government maintained the domestic transportation systems that facilitated his travel; on the other hand, government regulation was the usual cause of any delays. Jōjin shows that Chinese methods of transportation were well developed and efficient. He took frequent notice of them, occasionally because of their novelty and always for their central importance to him as a traveler.

Crossing the Sea

Jōjin's diary begins the day he boarded a Chinese ship in Kyushu. For four days he and his party waited for a favorable wind, although neither the Chinese crew nor the Japanese passengers waited passively. On the second day, when an east wind blew momentarily, the ship set sail, only to return to port when the wind shifted. This failed departure inspired religious rites to improve the situation. The Chinese made offerings of chicken and wine, burned paper money and pennants, and said prayers, followed by a banquet. These familiar Chinese practices must have seemed exotic to the Japanese passengers, who recited esoteric Buddhist formulas to ensure a safe voyage. An ocean crossing was dangerous, and so all turned to religious rites that promised a favorable wind and safe passage. Early on the fifth day the wind again shifted. The following entries recount the voyage to China.

The Nineteenth Day:

The weather was clear and at 4:00 am a strong favorable wind blew from the northeast. First, the ship's launch went to observe beyond the point of land. It reported that the waves, too, were favorable, and so the ship was rowed out to sea. At 6:00 am the crewmen raised the sail amid wild shouts and beating of the drum. Thereupon the east wind began to blow fiercely and the waves grew high and turbulent. We were terrified. Although we were unable to perform the ceremonies, in our hearts we prayed to the Buddhas. The ship was tossed about at the mercy of the rising and falling waves. One rose so high that it injured a man atop the ship's launch. [The launch was carried onboard the ship and was five feet in depth; from the surface of the sea to the deck of the ship was another six feet.] Words cannot describe the scene. On this day, I could not eat at all. My disciples Seishū, Shinken, and Chōmei were completely overcome by seasickness. The others, however, were quite well. I reclined on a large sack and suffered through all the day and all the night. As a form of abstinence, for five years I have refrained from lying down to sleep, but now I found myself on the verge of breaking my vow.

The Twentieth Day:

Clear skies. Wind filled the sail, and the ship sped across the ocean. Since the clouds and waves blocked our view, we saw only the vast ocean; we could not see the mountains and islands of our native land. At noon, we passed T'amna Island of the country of Koryŏ. I felt quite well and ate a little, but the other three remained very ill, as they were yesterday. At 4:00 pm, light rain began to fall, and at nightfall the skies were still not clear. Since the stars could not be seen, the boat was allowed to sail where the wind blew it. We did not know the direction. According to the Chinese, the rain would fall all night without dispersing, but we should be glad it was not a great storm. The sound of the wind and waves was like thunder.

The Twenty-first Day:

The wind blew as before; the rain had not let up. At 8:00 am the sun became faintly visible. From it we determined our course and learned that the wind had not shifted. At noon the sky cleared and a light wind blew from the northwest. The sailors made a great commotion as they prayed to the gods and performed divination. The wind shifted to the northeast. Unperturbed, I meditated on Mañjuśrī and the ten thousand Bodhisattvas of the Wutai Mountains, and also on the five hundred Arhats of the Stone Bridge at Tiantai Mountains. I recited their names tens of thousands of times. At 8:00 pm I began to repeat the Acalanātha mantra ten thousand times. By 2:00 am I had finished six thousand of them and had an auspicious dream. At 4:00 am I completed the ten thousand and had a good dream.

The Twenty-second Day:

The weather was clear, and the Chinese were very pleased because a strong northeast wind blew. I thought this must be the result of the force of my ten thousand repetitions. I told this to the navigator, Lin Gao, who informed me that yesterday at 2:00 pm we had entered Chinese waters. This was established by throwing into the sea a piece of lead tied to a rope. In Japanese waters, the depth is fifty fathoms and the bottom is covered with rocks and sand; in Chinese waters, the depth is thirty fathoms and the bottom is muddy with no rocks. Yesterday when the measurement was taken I was in my cabin and did not witness it. Lin Gao is the son of Lin Yang, a Chinese from Tajima Province. I gazed in all four directions but saw neither islands nor an end to the sea. The three monks were still seasick. All day and throughout the night, wind filled the sails and sped the ship across the sea. I repeated my prayers several tens of thousands of times without interruption. Today two beach sparrows appeared on the ship, just as described in *The Record of a Pilgrimage*.[3]

The Twenty-third Day:

Rain fell. A strong northeast wind blew, and the waves were high. At noon the sky cleared and the wind ceased. In the middle of the sea, the ship stopped and waited for a favorable wind to blow. A man was ordered to climb the mast and make observations. He reported absolutely no mountain or island. At 8:00 pm we obtained a favorable wind and it set the ship sailing. All through the night we sailed. The sparrows were still there.

. . .

The Twenty-fifth Day:

The weather was clear, and a northeast wind blew. We were greatly pleased as the ship advanced, but after 10:00 pm the sky in all directions became cloudy and we could not determine our course. At noon it cleared and the favorable wind blew as before. At 2:00 pm we first saw Shifan Island of Suzhou. It was an enormous rock with no human habitations. The sailors were overjoyed. At 2:00 am we arrived at Daqi Island in Suzhou and stayed there overnight. From Japan to Suzhou in China is three thousand *li*. (Kōbō Daishi stated that the sea route to Suzhou is three thousand *li*).[4]

Jōjin had arrived not at Suzhou but among the Zhoushan Islands in the mouth of Hangzhou Bay. The voyage to China had taken only six relatively uneventful days, in marked contrast to the protracted and treacherous passages of earlier Japanese who had visited Sui and Tang China on more primitive Japanese ships. If the crossing to China had been expeditious, covering the short distance from the mouth of Hangzhou Bay to the city of Hangzhou itself, paradoxically, took a full eighteen days. One reason was that, as Jōjin noted, winds and tides made for difficult sailing in a bay dotted with treacherous rocks and islands. Eventually, a local pilot was recruited, and the following day a "river boat" was hired to carry some of the ship's crew and cargo. Although Jōjin's account stresses navigational difficulties, another concern may have been the urge to avoid officialdom and its tax collectors. Normally, a ship from Japan would have arrived in Mingzhou, the modern Ningbo. Jōjin's ship, however, appears to have taken some trouble to avoid that city, possibly in an effort to elude its customs office. Government policies would continue to complement technological issues in setting the course of Jōjin's travels in China.

Jōjin's account reveals his interest in technological details. He notes that the ship carried a launch. He explains how the Chinese determined whether they were in Japanese or Chinese waters, apparently after inquiring about this point, as the reasoning behind the method used could not have been simply observed. He describes how sailors climbed the mast to see a more distant horizon, presumably without realizing that this technique revealed the earth to be a sphere. Since this was a century before the invention of the compass, a cloudy day made navigation particularly difficult. Jōjin also shows that when conventional technology could not solve a problem all parties appealed to the supernatural. Jōjin's tone suggests a disdainful attitude toward the boisterous Chinese prayers and an immodest confidence in the effectiveness of his own. Modern readers, however, are more likely to be struck by the similarity of Japanese and Chinese attitudes.

Although Jōjin offers no further descriptions of sea travel, he does demonstrate that ships and people sailed between China and Japan regularly, if not necessarily in great numbers. After he arrived in Hangzhou, while he was waiting for permission to travel to Tiantai, he met two men who had been to Japan. One was the merchant Chen Yong, who was to accompany Jōjin throughout his travels as his interpreter (I/4/20). Three days later he met a Korean who knew Japanese (I/4/23). Furthermore, an officer on the ship that brought him to China also knew enough Japanese to serve as an interpreter (I/4/29; VIII/5/24), so we can assume that he, too, had been to Japan frequently. When Jōjin passed through Hangzhou the following year on his way to see off those of his disciples who were returning to Japan, he was greeted by another of his followers who now had previously seen him off in Kyushu and now had recently arrived in China (I/3/15; VIII/5/21, 26). In Mingzhou, the returning disciples had no trouble finding a merchant ship to take them home. Travel between China and Japan was not itself remarkable.

Inland Waterways

Jōjin's sea crossing took only six days, but he spent approximately 130 days traveling by boat within China. This included most of the distance between Hangzhou and Tiantai and the whole journey from Hangzhou to Kaifeng. Although the route to Tiantai included naturally flowing rivers, most of this impressive distance was traversed on a man-made canal, an ancestor of the still-functioning Grand Canal. Canals were unknown in Japan until the early Edo period, but the control of water for irrigation was a familiar technological problem in Heian Japan, and the fundamental issues involved in getting water to flow where people can use it are similar. Furthermore, one cannot preclude the possibility that even an aristocratic monk such as Jōjin might have been interested in such problems. For example, Kūkai (774–835), an earlier pilgrim to China whom Jōjin referred to as Kōbō Daishi, is credited with the construction of Mannō Pond in his home province of Sanuki, where it remains Japan's largest irrigation pond.

Whatever the reason, Jōjin took a great interest in the workings of China's canals, which offered amazing sights. Most notable were the systems that got boats safely from one water level to another, sometimes using ox-powered windlasses to pull them over dams, at other times using canal locks, then a relatively new invention for which Jōjin offers some of the earliest detailed descriptions. The comprehensive study *Science and Civilization in China,* by Joseph Needham et al., offers a detailed discussion of these features, including valuable insights into the significance of what Jōjin observed.[5] Needham explains the technique of hauling boats over dams as follows.

> [The Chinese] must have . . . realised that if the ramp of a spillway was made to slope at a reasonably gentle gradient it would be possible to drag canal-boats up and over it to the higher level, wastage of water at the same time being prevented. In this manner there arose the double slipway, a pair of inclined stonework aprons over which boats were hauled, generally in China with the use of capstans, from a waterway at one level to a waterway at another. . . . The Greeks called this a *diolkos.*[6]

The earliest unambiguous Chinese reference dates a *diolkos* to 384, and Needham even includes a photograph of one that was still in use circa 1926.[7]

Jōjin confirms the use of the *diolkos* in eleventh-century China. Although Needham's two illustrations show people turning the capstans to pull boats over dams, he also notes that oxen were commonly used, as Jōjin confirms when he first encounters a *diolkos* while traveling to Tiantai on a rented boat.

> After traveling fifty *li* from Wuyunmen, at 2:00 pm we reached the Chianqing dam. Oxen pulled the ropes through winches and hauled the boats over it. It was most unusual. Two head of oxen each on the left and right cranked the boats over the land. (I/5/6)

Five months later he traversed the same *diolkos* on his way to Kaifeng, now as a guest of state on his way to an imperial audience.

> At 6:00 am, eight water buffalo were attached to a windlass and the rope pulled the big boat over the dam. The boat was one hundred feet long, its cabin eight feet high, its width twelve feet. Because of the Japanese monks' journey to the capital, Yuezhou was freshly decorated. It was splendid. (III/8/20)

Note the increased number of oxen. Either Jōjin's improved status earned him better treatment or he was now traveling on a grander boat that required more oxen power to get over the dam.

Later, on the Grand Canal, the Song version of which ran from Hangzhou to Kaifeng, Jōjin encountered even more imposing examples.

> At 6:00 am, we crossed a dam. On each bank are five windlasses, and there are sixteen water–oxen, eight each on the left and right banks. (III/9/9)

And four days later:

> At 6:00 am, we crossed a dam. There were twenty-two oxen, eleven each on the left and right banks. We were pulled up and entered the upper stream. (III/9/13)

If the *diolkos* was new only to Jōjin, the canal lock of the familiar modern sort was a relatively recent Chinese innovation as yet unknown elsewhere in the world. The Chinese had begun using simple locks with only a single gate before the end of the first century B. C. E., but the origins of the two-gated canal lock are more controversial. Although foreign travelers on the Grand Canal in the seventeenth to nineteenth centuries noted only the *diolkos* and single-gated lock, in fact the Chinese had invented two-gated locks as early as 984. The first in Europe did not appear until 1375. Needham speculates that China abandoned the two-gated lock after the Yuan dynasty established its capital in Beijing and began shipping goods northward by sea. As the need to carry heavy cargoes by canal declined, the simpler yet still functional locks proved adequate.[8]

When Jōjin arrived in China, the use of two-gated locks was not quite a century old, but only one earlier description survives, which Needham characterizes as "more poetical than precise."[9] Jōjin offers several detailed, thoroughly prosaic descriptions. The most detailed is:

> Clear skies. At 6:00 am., the boat set forth. At noon, we reached Chang'an dam in Yanguan District. At 2:00 pm, the district magistrate came and prepared tea at the Chang'an pavilion. At 4:00 pm, two water gates were opened to let in the boat. The boat entered. A wooden bolt was drawn to close the gate. Then the bolt on the third water gate was opened and the boat was released. The surface of the river ahead was about five feet lower than the original level. After the gate was opened, the river ahead fell and the surface of the water became level. Then the boat left. (III/8/25)

Later, he describes another three-gated lock (III/9/14; VIII/5/1). To explain them, Needham speculates, "Either there was fear of too great a head of water at the gates, or some auxiliary supply fed one or both of the gate basins."[10] Eleventh-century China's canal system set the world standard, as confirmed by Jōjin's account.

Not only was the system advanced, but it was also well maintained. On his way to the capital, Jōjin tells us:

> At 10:00 am, we crossed Shangting dam and entered the territory of Changzhou. The dam, water gate, and windlasses are all dilapidated and old. (III/9/6)

The comment is striking because elsewhere all appears to be in good working order.

Two final issues concerning the canal system deserve brief comment. The first is Jōjin's emphasis on technology. Although at one lock he did describe worship of a god of the river crossing, it is a unique example of faith becoming an issue in inland waterways (III/9/14). A second issue is the scale of the enterprise. Both the distances covered and the amount of waterborne traffic were enormous. The distance from Hangzhou to Kaifeng was about a thousand kilometers. When gates were kept closed, presumably to regulate water levels, Jōjin noted the resulting traffic jams, one of over a hundred boats (III/9/17), another of several hundred boats (VIII/4/23). The scene at the capital was even more astounding.

> Countless boats were moored ahead of us on the left and right of the Bian River. Vessels of ten thousand *koku*, others of seven to eight *koku*, were numerous and imposing. I do not know how many great boats were there. In the past two days, I saw a thousand—even ten thousand—boats moored three or four deep. (IV/10/12)

Overland Travel

Water transport, whether on sea or canal, required a considerable degree of technological sophistication, most of which was novel to Jōjin. On land, Jōjin often went about carried in a palanquin or rode a horse, both commonly used in Japan. The palanquin received little comment from Jōjin and will be similarly slighted here. Although the horse, too, was hardly a novelty, it deserves brief comment. The first time Jōjin rode a horse was when he stopped to do some sightseeing on his way to Kaifeng and observed:

> We crossed the river and headed back to the pavilion to rest. Because the tide was low, we could not use a boat, so the district magistrate sent two horses and, together with the Chongban [the title of his Chinese escort], I rode back. Today I rode a Chinese horse for the first time; it is just like a Japanese horse. A saddle cover is placed on the saddle frame, and the stirrups are hanging metal rings. (III/9/10)

Jōjin reveals that Chinese equine technology (if such is the term) was similar to that of Japan. More significant, he reminds us that horsemanship was a common skill among men of the court. Jōjin's lack of comment about the horse itself is also revealing. Earlier, when he had just arrived in Hangzhou, he observed:

> I saw two donkeys: one was carrying goods, and the other had a rider. Their size was that of a two-year-old Japanese colt, only about three feet high and four feet long. Their ears were about eight inches long and in the shape of rabbit ears. (I/4/17)

As will be discussed later, unusual animals fascinated Jōjin and had the breeds of horses he rode in China been significantly different from those he knew in Japan, he would have let us know.

If the horses themselves were unremarkable, the government institutions that controlled them were. As early as the Qin dynasty, the Chinese had begun to establish systems of roads and relay stations for official transportation and communication. The Japanese began adopting these systems as part of the Taika Reforms, begun in 645, and the *ritsuryō* codes of the eighth century prescribed the workings of the Japanese version in detail. At least for a while, it functioned. Historical records note that messages from Dazaifu might reach Nara in as few as four days, and in 1986 archaeologists discovered the site of a relay station in modern Hyogo Prefecture. By the Heian period, however, the system was in decline and its last vestige disappeared in 1019, over fifty years before Jōjin's pilgrimage.[11] He may have been familiar with the concept of a government-run system of relay stations but not with their actual functioning.

On his pilgrimage to Wutai, Jōjin was traveling as a guest of state and so was permitted to use the relay stations and their horses. Before departing, he purchased two horses to carry his personal goods at a price of nearly twenty strings of cash (including tax), but only five days into his journey he sold them, taking a loss of five strings of cash in the process, "because feeding them while on the road was a great nuisance" (III/10/30; IV/11/5). Although Jōjin does not say so, another reason may have been that he had come to find them unnecessary. By his second day on the road, he had fallen into a comfortable routine.

> Clear skies. At 6:00 am., ten horses came from Xindian Stable and we departed. Proceeding fifteen *li*, we reached Bajiao Stable, where we exchanged the ten horses. Proceeding fifteen *li*, at noon, we reached Cugou Stable, where we exchanged the ten horses. [And so forth, changing horses three more times.] Proceeding twelve *li*, at 6:00 pm, we reached Baisha Stable, where we stopped for the night. Today we traveled seventy-three *li*. (V/11/2)

The ten horses were for Jōjin, his seven disciples, his interpreter, and his official escort. Stables were maintained at regular intervals, and most were able to provide Jōjin and his party with the horses they needed. Although this would remain the standard pattern, as they got farther from the capital, occasionally they did run into problems.

> Because there were no horses at the relay station, we kept the horses from Chengsi Stable overnight and fed them. Mounting them, we went twenty-five *li* to Xiaoyi Stable, where they only had two horses of poor quality, so, lacking fresh horses, we continued on our original ones. We did, however, employ ten bearers to carry our miscellaneous goods. After twenty-five *li*, we reached Jiulong Stable at Mount Jiulong, where five horses were provided. For the rest, we used the original horses. . . . Proceeding fifteen *li*, we arrived at Ziyansi, a magnificent, immense monastery at Mount Ziyan. As we were about to stop for the night, a corpse was carried from the monastery. Startled, we left the monastery and proceeded five *li* to Zhiting Relay Station, where we stopped for the night. (V/11/14)

Days such as this, however, were the exception. In general, Jōjin offers us a detailed picture of a smoothly operating system of relay stations.

Overall, China's systems of communication reveal impressive technology and strong social organization, all backed by government support. Jōjin's meticulous descriptions of the canal locks suggest that to him they were an impressive and new sight. In contrast, Jōjin did not marvel at the efficient relay system he saw in China. For whatever reason, he simply noted the distances between stations and the numbers of horses available at each. He expressed gratitude that the Chinese government made such facilities available to him but did not suggest that the Japanese should revive their own version of the system. Both the canal and relay station systems were quite rationally organized, but, when Jōjin's ship briefly faced difficulties in its voyage to China, both Jōjin and the Chinese crew resorted to prayer to ameliorate conditions. The supernatural will become increasingly important in the next group of topics to be addressed.

Heavenly Phenomena and Calendars

This section considers a seemingly disparate group of topics: eclipses, rain, and calendars. They have been placed together because the first two are heavenly phenomena and the third essentially calculations intended to predict heavenly phenomena. Furthermore, these are again areas of concern to both the Chinese and Japanese governments.

From the perspective of a Confucian government, eclipses and calendars were particularly important. Calendars were intended to predict heavenly phenomena. Some—the phases of the moon, the changes of the seasons—were easily calculated. Others, such as eclipses, were not. Since Chinese believed eclipses to be reflections on the quality of imperial rule, they could not be treated lightly. Solar eclipses, less obviously periodic than lunar eclipses, were viewed with special concern, and eventually Chinese learned to predict the appearance of both. Japanese adopted Chinese beliefs regarding the human significance of natural phenomena along with Chinese methods of reckoning calendars. The key difference is that Chinese constantly improved their calendars' reliability in predicting heavenly phenomena, whereas Japanese persisted in using the Chinese calendar they adopted in 862, when it was already forty years old. By the time they finally abandoned it eight centuries later, it was nearly two days off the mark. Modern critics lament that Japanese used the calendar primarily as a fortune-telling device and so neglected to observe the phenomena that might have prompted them to improve it or maybe even develop their own tradition of astronomy.[12]

Jōjin showed no evidence of being a calendar expert, although by his day monks, too, were involved in calendar making.[13] In passing, however, he touches on the issues outlined above. The first reference to a calendar appears on the day Jōjin arrived at Tiantai, an emotional highlight of his pilgrimage. The abbot who greeted him immediately consulted his calendar to find out if the day was auspicious. It was not, and so Jōjin and his companions were taken to burn incense, presumably to pray for good fortune (I/5/13). Calendars again appear in the diary with the arrival of the new year, 1073, when Jōjin had just returned to Kaifeng after his visit to Wutai. On each of the first three days of the year, he sent disciples out to buy new calendars, one of which he specifies was in two fascicles and cost sixty cash, another in only one fascicle (VI/1/1–3).

Later in the month, on the twenty-third day, he made arrangements to send the various texts he had acquired in China back to Japan. He sent calendars to three important officials, one of whom would shortly become chancellor (*kanpaku*) and another being one of his own uncles (VI/1/23). Although the Japanese may have continued using the same calendar for over eight centuries, Jōjin put some effort first into acquiring new Chinese calendars and then into sending them back to key government figures. We have no way of knowing whether he did this out of a scientific desire to improve the precision with which the calendar could predict natural phenomena or out of a hope that they would assist in divining human events more accurately, but he must have assumed that Japanese leaders would be interested in the latest Chinese calendar.

During his stay in Kaifeng, Jōjin reported an incident that showed how calendars were used. On the first day of the year, the grand astrologer had reported that the calendar foretold a solar eclipse. In an edict shown to Jōjin in the third month, the emperor acknowledged this to be the result of his own failings, and so, to atone, he proclaimed an amnesty for all criminals except those charged with the most serious crimes (VII/3/16). The edict does not give a date for the eclipse, but two weeks later Jōjin noted that government business had ceased because the eclipse was expected the following day. Officials stayed home, devoting themselves to literary pursuits, while the emperor himself sat on the floor rather than his usual dais, presumably as a form of penance. Jōjin himself prayed for rain to obscure the anticipated eclipse, as he was readying himself for his return to Tiantai and feared that were the eclipse to be observed the resulting special rites would interfere with his plans. His prayers proved effective, for rain clouds obscured the sun and the court resumed its normal routines (VII/3/30; VIII/4/1). The prediction by the court astrologers in fact was accurate, and an eclipse did occur over China on the date specified, although it would not have been visible in Kaifeng even without the rain. Two points need to be stressed. The Chinese knew enough astronomy to predict an eclipse, but they regarded it as an omen, not simply a natural occurrence.

The eclipse was not the only time Jōjin prayed for rain, another heavenly phenomenon. On the first day of the third month, just before he first learned of the predicted eclipse, he received a summons from the imperial palace. There had been no rain in the first two months of the year, and so the emperor wished Jōjin to participate in Buddhist rituals to end the drought. He obeyed the command, and his prayers proved to be so effective that eventually he was asked to pray for an end to the rain. For his efforts, the emperor awarded him an imposing title, Shanhui Dashi (J. Zen'e Daishi, VII/3/1–6, 13, 22, 28; VIII/4/4).

This episode is fascinating from several points of view. First, Jōjin revealed the importance of sectarianism in Japanese Buddhism by performing the Lotus Rite associated with his own Tendai sect. He noted that the more common rite for producing rain was in the domain of the esoteric Shingon sect and hence he did not perform it (VII/3/7). He also showed his national pride by resolving to produce a substantial downpour by the third day of the rites, which had been scheduled to last seven days, explaining that, first, he wanted to demonstrate the miraculous power of the *Lotus Sutra;* second, he wanted to repay the generosity of the Chinese; and, third, although many Japanese monks had previously visited China, none yet had been commanded to pray for rain. If his prayers were to fail, it would be a great embarrassment for the Japanese nation (VII/3/3). Finally, the rites themselves were highly irregular, as they were Buddhist, conducted in the emperor's private quarters, and not recorded in sources that would normally note droughts and rites to alleviate them. Although Jōjin offers the only account of the event, its accurate description of the palace suggests its authenticity.

Here the most notable point is that rain was like an eclipse, a natural phenomenon believed to be affected by the emperor's personal and political behavior. In an edict that would proclaim an amnesty in response to the predicted eclipse, the emperor also noted that water shortages had threatened the harvest. These heavenly phenomena were all related to human activities. The only unusual feature of Jōjin's prayers for rain is that they were of a Buddhist, not Confucian, nature. An eclipse and a drought were similar problems calling for ritual responses.

Other Sciences and Technology

Natural History

Unfamiliar plants and especially animals fascinated Jōjin. Samples of his vivid descriptions follow. "Natural history" seems an appropriate designation for these interests since more modern terms suggest too scientific an approach to something that was then not yet recognized as a branch of learning. Jōjin himself lacked an analytical framework. He simply offered careful, precise descriptions of flora and fauna that were new to him.

The lure of the exotic may have been one reason for his interest, but it should not be dismissed as idle fancy. Exchanges of rare gifts were a key feature of traditional East Asian diplomacy (and modern diplomacy, too). The Japanese commonly received such creatures as parrots from foreign representatives. Before Jōjin met the Chinese emperor, he was asked what beasts there were in Japan, and he replied, "My land has no lions, elephants, tigers, sheep, peacocks, or parrots, but it has all the other varieties" (IV/10/15). Furthermore, strange plants and animals also might have more mundane value. The donkeys Jōjin observed were useful beasts of burden; unfamiliar fruits might serve as pleasing additions to the Japanese diet. In one case, religion may have spurred his interest. Elephants were a familiar element in Buddhist iconography, since the bodhisattva Samantabhadra was traditionally portrayed riding a white elephant, and in that context they are often mentioned in the diary. As Jōjin was approaching Kaifeng, he had a chance to see some elephants and left a detailed description. Although he did not mention Samantabhadra, surely the popular bodhisattva was on his mind. Possibly he was the first Japanese ever to see a real elephant.

> In one stable were three elephants, in another four. First we looked at the three elephants. The man who cared for them explained to the elephants that foreign monks had come to see them and so they should bow. The first elephant bowed, bending its hind legs and lowering its head. Then he indicated that it should greet us, and it immediately bellowed. The elephant was about twelve feet tall and sixteen feet long. Its nose was six feet long. Its tusks were seven feet long and curved upward. It wrapped its nose around hay, picked it up, and ate it. I gave the elephant trainer fifty cash. [The second and third elephants are similar.] These three elephants were all males.
>
> Next I went to the stable with four elephants. [Three female elephants are briefly described.] The fourth elephant was a female. I paid fifty cash. The final elephant trainer climbed from the tusk to the top of the elephant, which raised its tusk and allowed the man to climb it. It was amazing! The elephant was about fourteen feet high and eighteen feet long. Just as before, it bent its hind two legs to bow and bellowed. All of these were black elephants. Their two hind legs were bound with rope. Here and there, a mountain of hay was piled up. Each day's fee was fifteen catties per animal. The hay is about seven or eight feet in length.
>
> I was told that originally the great king of Guangnan kept the elephants in his fortress for use in battle, but after Guangnan was defeated they were kept here. The elephants have no hair. The color of their skin resembles that of a Japanese black ox. When their hair falls off, their color is dull gray. The location and shape of their sexual organs resembles those of a horse. The nipples on the female elephants are like those of a pig. (III/10/7)

On his way to Wutai, Jōjin also saw camels.

> Every day for the past six or seven days I have seen camels, altogether thirty or forty of them, and have observed the form of their bodies carefully. Their heads are like those of a horse, and, like oxen, they have ropes attached to their noses. They lack upper teeth, and their eyes resemble those of an ox. Their long, narrow necks with hair above and below are always curved and hold up their heads in

the manner of a crane's neck. Their hooves, like those of oxen, are divided in two. Their tails are like pig's tails. On their backs are two humps one foot high. Their hair is long, and they always lay down as oxen do. They are ten feet tall and twelve or thirteen feet long. Their sins in former lives must have been great indeed! (V/11/17)

Novel fruits and vegetables, too, attracted his attention. For example:

Lin Gao gave us some cherries. They were the size of a jujube; their flavor was like that of cherry-peach fruit, as was their color. At 2:00 pm, the helmsman Chen Cong gave me a stalk of sugarcane about four feet long and one inch in diameter. The segments are about three and a half inches long and are all equal. You cut them into thin slices and suck the juice. Apparently it was not boiled, but it was very sweet. After you have sucked out the juice, you throw it away. (I/4/15)

And:

[A Chinese monk] also sent an apple. It looks like a Japanese green pear, and its taste, too, resembles that of a pear. (II/6/13)

Apples and surely sugarcane may have been unknown in Heian Japan, but Jōjin's reaction to the cherry is more surprising. If Jōjin were noting only an unfamiliar variety of cherry, one would have expected him to compare it with the cherries he knew from home, not with totally different fruits. Apparently, the poets who praised the blossoms were ignorant of their fruits.

Architecture

Chinese skills at building made a deep impression on Jōjin. For obvious reasons, he offered particularly loving and detailed descriptions of Buddhist monasteries, of which the following is but a brief example.

At noon, . . . I boarded a small boat and crossed the Yangzi River to visit Jinshansi. Also known as Fuyu [Floating Jade] Island, it is a solitary mountain in the middle of the river. Women are forbidden to enter it. I worshipped and burned incense at each of the halls, all of which are within a corridor that encircles the island. The decoration is splendid. It is just like the Castle of Many Fragrances.[14] Everything is completely covered with paintings in noble hues: blue, green, and vermilion. The high railings here and there are painted either with black lacquer or vermilion and glitter as if mirrors had been fastened to them. An area of two *li* is completely paved with stone. The corridors, halls, towers, and terraces glisten, reflecting the bright sunlight. Even Dongtai of the Liang Court (502–557) or Yongning of the Wei dynasty (386–535) could not possibly match this.[15] The Great Buddha Hall with its sixteen-foot Buddha, the other buildings, the stone grottos—more than ten of them—and the stupas all are most splendid. The *Tripitaka* Repository is truly precious. In the monks' hall, bowls and two or three quilts are arranged at each of the over eighty places where monks sleep. The other monks' cells are all very beautiful. In the Sutra Reading Cloister were more than eighty monks, each studying the *Tripitaka*. In the Fanhai Tower is a life-size image of Śākyamuni. What I have seen today seems the most magnificent of all monasteries. The great master who serves as abbot prepared a vegetarian feast of rare dishes and fine delicacies. It was most splendid. (III/9/10)

Clearly Jōjin's principal interest was in the edifices as expressions of faith, not examples of technology. Still, Needham's discussion of Chinese architecture cites Jōjin twice.[16] In addition to the monasteries, Jōjin also describes various types of bridges, occasional urban buildings, and even the imperial palace.

Artificial Wonders

This short category consists of three man-made curiosities that Jōjin described. The first was part of his description of a night market he visited shortly after his arrival in Hangzhou.

At one place various water-powered dolls danced, beat drums, or spouted water. Two of them spun around like wizards, two spewed water from their mouths a height of four or five feet, two sprayed water five feet from their elbows, and two galloped on horseback. In all, there were more than one hundred dolls. They were displayed on a high stage, and each was about five inches tall. I cannot possibly describe all of their marvelous tricks. Every person who watched was given a cup of tea and had to pay one copper coin. (I/4/22)

Although Jōjin surely did not think of the scientific principles behind the devices, they demonstrated what could be done with waterpower. The two that sprayed water from their elbows presumably were spinning around, illustrating the principle of jet propulsion.

On his way to Kaifeng, Jōjin visited a grand monastery, on which he lavished one of his most detailed descriptions. Among the wonders he observed there was a camera obscura.

I entered another structure and in its southwest corner were two holes about one inch in size. After removing their covers, images of the pagoda appeared on a white board two feet long and about one inch thick that faced the holes about two feet from them. Matching the number of holes, two pagodas appeared, both upside down. This is a rare thing. All thirteen stories are reflected on the board. (III/9/21)

The camera obscura in fact had been invented centuries earlier in China.[17]

Jōjin saw a final wondrous object while he was in the capital, where he met monks from various parts of Central and South Asia, one of whom had:

> A "water-filtering bag" [part of a monk's paraphernalia] from the land of Purusapura. It was shaped just like a pagoda bell. When you poured water into a small opening, it did not fall out the bottom. It was most amazing. (VI/1/5)

Presumably, this was a device in which air pressure somehow kept the water from escaping. To Jōjin, it was a wonder.

Medicine

In traditional East Asia, medicine was one of the principle branches of learning among those that today might be considered scientific.[18] Heian medicine and its Chinese models involved a wide range of treatments. Some—acupuncture, massage, and medicinal herbs, for example—were the domain of secular doctors; others—notably incantations—belonged to the realm of Buddhist monks. Jōjin himself, shortly before making his pilgrimage, had been a key leader in praying for the health of both an ailing retired emperor and his chancellor.[19] In other words, medicine of a sort was among his professional skills, and references to it appeared often in his diary.

Jōjin was constantly using medicinal products of one sort or another, although definition is a problem, for example, in the case of tea. Although the drink had been introduced to Japan in the ninth century, it was not yet popular. Nonetheless, Jōjin appears to have been familiar with it, mentioning it frequently without explanation or comment. Occasionally, instead of taking simply "tea," he states he had "tea-medicine" (*chayaku*; see I/4/29 for a day on which he used both terms), but he never explains why he uses different terms. The actual infusions may have been different or he may have been simply using a different term for the same drink. He does, however, mention some products that were unambiguously medicines (II/6/7; VI/2/16; VII/3/10, 11, 14). He also mentions a few medical texts. One would seem to be a Daoist work on sexual hygiene that he bought and later sent to the minister of the left in Japan (VI/1/2, 23). Another was an herbal that his interpreter gave him. In return, Jōjin gave what would appear to be a book concerning health and noted that the interpreter knew "the way of medicine" (VI/1/6). Jōjin also acquired a sutra that promised to cure haemorrhoids (I/5/13). Once he prayed for a monk who suffered from the palsy (II/6/19); another time he himself caught a cold and in the following days is sent medicines and foods that perhaps were thought to have medicinal benefits (VI/2/13–19). On the whole, Chinese medicine seems to have made little impression on Jōjin. Since he commented on remarkable things he encountered, be they canal locks or camels, his apparent lack of interest in Chinese medical practice suggests that what he saw of it may have been similar to what he knew from Japan and hence merited nothing more than passing mention.

Books

"Books," here, will be loosely defined to include various types of written texts, printed and hand-written. Whatever their form, books had always been a key element in Japan's efforts to learn from the Chinese, and the rise of vernacular literature in Japan did not mean the demise of interest in Chinese learning. Times, however, had changed, and with increasing self-confidence, Heian intellectuals had come to seek a Chinese audience for their own writings. Jōjin's persistent interest in books thus casts light on many broader issues in late Heian Sino-Japanese cultural exchange.

First, Jōjin reminds us of an often overlooked detail in the history of Japanese technology: early in the eleventh century, Heian aristocrats had begun to sponsor the publication of Buddhist sutras in woodblock print editions as a form of religious devotion.[20] Accordingly, printing was no novelty to Jōjin, and so, when he saw an image of the five hundred arhats, he simply borrowed the block to print it and had his disciples make copies (VI/1/25; also see VI/1/28). He also expressed no great wonder on discovering that the Chinese government was not only sponsoring new translations of Buddhist sutras but also producing a printed edition of them. Indeed, the mechanics of printing were of less interest to Jōjin than acquisition of the end product. The sutras were available to foreigners only on special petition. Jōjin noted that a century earlier a previous Japanese pilgrim, Chōnen, had been given a complete set of the *Tripitaka* plus 286 fascicles of newly translated sutras, all of which where carefully preserved at Hōjōji, the splendid monastery that Fujiwara no Michinaga (966–1027) established when he took Buddhist vows as his health began to decline. Jōjin's request for copies of the latest sutras was granted. Subsequently, the monastery responsible for printing them had trouble figuring out exactly which ones he wanted, but after an exchange of documents the matter was straightened out and he got exactly the texts he sought (VI/3/18, 23–25).

If printing was nothing new to Jōjin, many of the books he found in China were. As noted in the discussion of calendars, Jōjin did not simply accumulate writings; he sent them back to Japan addressed to specific individuals and institutions. Altogether, Jōjin acquired well over 600 fascicles of books in China: 412 fascicles of newly translated sutras the emperor granted him, 102 of new translations that he purchased and over 90 of Tendai texts, plus various other works that Chinese acquaintances gave him or he purchased himself.[21] Along with the calendars, he sent other secular works to the three high officials noted above. Religious texts, which made up the overwhelming majority of the works, he divided between his home monastery, Daiunji, located just northeast of the capital in Iwakura, and Byōdōin in Uji. Presumably, all these texts arrived safely in Japan with Jōjin's disciples. Once there, some appear to have been transferred to Onjōji (Miidera), the headquarters of Jōjin's lineage within the Tendai sect. What became of them subsequently is not known.

Jōjin took with him to China over six hundred fascicles of books (I/6/2), by coincidence approximately the same number he sent home. Most were religious works associated with his Tendai sect, some of Chinese origin, others Japanese. Although many cannot be identified precisely, among them were the famous *Ōjō yōshū* (Essentials of Salvation) by Genshin and four works apparently by Jōjin himself. Genshin (943–1017) was an early advocate of faith in Amitābha, and *Essentials of Salvation*, completed in 985, was his most influential work. Genshin himself entrusted a copy to a Chinese merchant to take to Tiantai, where, according to Japanese legend, both monks and laymen were so impressed that they built a hall of fifty bays to enshrine it. Although the subject of Genshin's work did not come up while Jōjin was at Tiantai, in Kaifeng Jōjin lent his copy of *Essentials of Salvation* to two Chinese monks, who were so impressed that they proposed to make copies for themselves. Jōjin, however, was disappointed.

> I was told *Essentials of Salvation* had not been disseminated to Guoqingsi [the principle monastery at Tiantai] nor to any other prefecture or monastery. Perhaps it was received at Wuzhou but had not been disseminated. This is totally contrary to what I had heard in Japan. (IV/10/25)

Conclusions

What do these details gleaned from Jōjin's diary reveal? First, they suggest something of Jōjin's personality or at least his personal interests. He was not the only Heian monk who went to China and left a diary recounting his travels. In addition to Jōjin's, five are known today, although only one of them survives intact, *Nittō guhō junrei kōki* (The Record of a Journey to the Tang in Search of the Dharma), by Ennin (794–864). Unlike Jōjin, Ennin gave scant attention to novel devices or unfamiliar flora and fauna that he, too, surely encountered in China. Jōjin's interests were broader. This contradicts some conventional views of both Heian monks and aristocrats, which Jōjin also was.

Scholars have observed that later Heian monks who traveled in China went merely as pilgrims to worship at holy sites, unlike the monks of earlier times—and later ones, too—who went in search of new knowledge, new teachings, or new sectarian identities. The very titles of their diaries reflect this distinction. Whereas Ennin's diary was "*a Journey . . . in Search of the Dharma*," Jōjin's was "*a Pilgrimage to the Tiantai and Wutai Mountains.*"[22] In fact, however, the differences between the two are not that simple. By Jōjin's day, the tradition of pilgrimage was well established, and Jōjin was following a set pattern. Observing tradition, however, did not preclude an interest in the new. Jōjin was an enthusiastic collector of unfamiliar books and carefully sent them all back to Japan, where presumably he expected them to find an audience. In this respect, the most obvious difference between him and earlier pilgrims is that they left catalogues of the books they brought back; he did not.

A more conspicuous difference between Jōjin and earlier pilgrims is that Jōjin took with him to China as many books as he sent home. Furthermore, he expected his Chinese hosts to be familiar with the most famous of them. Times had indeed changed. Unlike Japanese monks of an earlier day, Jōjin regarded himself as a participant in a two–way intellectual exchange, and in fact his Chinese hosts did show an interest in the Japanese books Jōjin showed them. One sees, at least within the Buddhist community, a sense of intellectual equality. Jōjin was not a humble seeker of religious teachings but a respected and knowledgeable member of the Buddhist clergy who seems to have fit easily into the Chinese religious community. If he was anxious to acquire the latest translations of sutras, his hosts sought to learn a ritual he performed that was unfamiliar to them (VI/6/24) and eagerly borrowed books he brought with him. Although the connection may be difficult to prove, curiosity about Jōjin's Buddhism could be related to the "rhetoric of lesser empire" that has been noted in Song China's diplomacy.[23] The relatively weak Song dynasty could not afford to be as arrogant in its dealings with its neighbors as were stronger dynasties. Perhaps this attitude was shared by monks of the period. Furthermore, they must have been aware that in China theirs was a foreign religion and so did not choose to look down on other foreign believers. Finally, by Jōjin's day Japanese Buddhism may have reached such a degree of sophistication and creativity that it offered new insights to the Chinese.

Unlike Buddhism, science and technology in early Japan have received little attention from scholars. The few studies available in English argue that in the Nara period Japanese adopted elements of China's sophisticated science and technology but in the Heian these traditions at best atrophied or, at worst—at least in the realm of science—degenerated into superstition.[24] Indeed, Heian aristocrats did not make noteworthy contributions to our understanding of the physical world or develop any new technology as important as a canal lock, but Jōjin's observations suggest that one cannot make a simple contrast between "scientific" Chinese and "superstitious" Japanese. Although the Chinese had learned to make relatively safe and swift passages between China and Japan, before embarking on their voyage both the Chinese sailors and the Japanese monks performed religious rites to ensure a safe passage. Both assumed that prayer, "superstition" in the view of critics, was a valuable supplement to mere seamanship. The Chinese did correctly predict an eclipse, demonstrating the accuracy of their calendar, but they related the event to the emperor's moral qualities. Their fastidiousness over calendrical precision was closely tied to the belief that heavenly irregularities were a reflection of the human moral order. Japanese do not seem to have shared the Chinese avidity for that Confucian theory. Jōjin took the trouble to send new calendars to political figures in Japan, but they do not appear to have been inspired to update the ones already in use. To some this may prove that Heian Japanese were "unscientific," but alternatively one might argue that it suggests the Japanese were less "superstitious" than the Chinese. If Japanese were less convinced of the moral or political implications of an eclipse, they may not have felt compelled to predict them accurately. The calendar they knew was adequate for their purposes. Jōjin took an interest in the natural world and offered reasonably precise, "scientific" descriptions of, for example, the camels he saw. His religious explanation for their strange appearance proves him only a man of his time.

Unfortunately, Jōjin's diary only tells us what he did in China, not how Japanese responded, which is difficult to assess. One monk was inspired by Jōjin's deeds to make his own pilgrimage to China. Furthermore, Fujiwara no Munetada (1062–1141) noted in his diary, *Chūyūki*, on the nineteenth day of the sixth month, 1102:

> I spent the whole day serving before his majesty Emperor Horikawa. His father, Retired Emperor Shirakawa, presented him twelve folding screens illustrating the late Jōjin Ajari's journey to China [lit., "the Tang"] from the time he left Japan through his visit to the Chinese court. It was truly wonderful.[25]

Since a typical folding screen consisted of six panels, this must have been an exceptionally detailed visual re-creation of the diary. Clearly, some people in the highest places were deeply impressed by Jōjin's achievement. But what became of the books he sent back? Their known impact consists of a single book with a colophon indicating that it was copied from a text Jōjin sent to Japan.[26]

Jōjin witnessed and recorded in his diary striking scenes illustrating the advanced state of eleventh-century Chinese science and, in particular, technology, for which it is a valuable resource. He also acquired many new books, especially of a religious nature. All of this information he carefully sent back to Japan, where it impressed at least a few members of the court elite. The later centuries of the Heian period may not have been an age of seclusion, but they were a time when the Japanese felt content to work within the familiar elements of Chinese civilization they had already mastered. Although critics may be right in their judgment that Heian courtiers failed to expand on the scientific knowledge that had been introduced from China, differences between the two countries cannot be explained merely by labeling one scientific and the other superstitious.

Notes

[1] As of this writing, the best edition of the diary remains that edited by Takakusu Junjirō in *Dai Nihon Bukkyō zensho*, first published in 1917 and reprinted many times, with the diary appearing in different places depending on the reprint. To facilitate use of the alternate reprints and editions, references to the diary are in the form volume (*kan*), number, month, and day and are placed parenthetically in the text of the essay. By the time this appears in print, Takakusu's edition will probably be out of date. Wang Liping 王麗萍 has a better edition of the text ready for publication. Fujiyoshi Masumi has already published the first volume of his annotated translation (*San Tendai godaisanki*); the second and final volume should appear shortly. For a general introduction in English, see my "Jōjin's Travels from Center to Center (with Some Periphery in Between)."

[2] *Tendai kahyō*, p. 108; *Honchō kōsō den*, p. 850.

[3] That is, Ennin's diary, discussed below.

[4] A *li* is just under four kilometers.

[5] Joseph Needham with Wang Ling and Lu Gwei-djen, *Science and Civilization in China*, vol. 4, pt. 3, *Civil Engineering and Nautics*, pp. 211–378.

[6] Ibid, p. 363.

[7] Ibid., plate 925.

[8] Ibid., pp. 346–360.

[9] Ibid., pp. 352–353.

[10] Ibid., p. 353. Note that Needham and his collaborators get some of their details wrong because apparently they looked only at Jōjin's account of his trip to Kaifeng, ignoring his trip back. For example, contrary to their claim, he did not use technical terms consistently, as alternate terms are used to describe the same lock when he returned to Hangzhou.

[11] Takahashi Zenshichi, *Tsūshin,* pp. 18–27.

[12] Shigeru Nakayama, *A History of Japanese Astronomy*, pp. 65–73.

[13] Masayoshi Sugimoto and David L. Swain, *Science and Culture in Traditional Japan, A.D. 600–1854*, pp. 125–127; Nakayama, *A History of Japanese Astronomy*, pp. 75–76, 203–207.

[14] This probably is Gandharva's Castle. Gandharva was a heavenly musician who lived on fragrance, not food, and whose name is translated as "Seeking Fragrance." Gandharva became a nickname for itinerant performers from Central Asia who, it

is said, did not work for their food. Instead, when they smelled food, they would perform in exchange for a meal, and hence they, too, lived by seeking fragrance. Their skills included the ability to produce illusory castles, which were known as Gandharva's Castle. As a result that term came to refer to a mirage, and so Jōjin is telling us that Jinshanci was "fantastic" in both the literal and colloquial sense of the term.

[15] Emperor Wu (r. 502–549), founder of the Liang dynasty, became a great patron of Buddhism and took religious vows himself. In 521, he established Tongtai monastery, and it became the principal center for his many religious activities. In 516, during the Northern Wei, Empress Dowager Ling sponsored the construction of Yongning monastery in the capital of Loyang.

[16] Needham, pp. 105–106, 141.

[17] Joseph Needham, *Science and Civilization in China,* vol. 4, pt. 1, *Physics,* pp. 97–99.

[18] Sugimoto and Swain, *Science and Culture in Traditional Japan, A.D. 600–1854,* pp. xxvii–xxviii.

[19] This information is also found in his mother's "diary." See Ii Haruki, *Jōjin no Nissō to sono shōgai,* pp. 9–12; also see *San Tendai godaisanki,* I/6/2.

[20] Shōji Sensui, *Insatsu bunkashi: Insatsu, zōhon, shuppan no rekishi,* pp. 38–41.

[21] Unless otherwise noted, material in this section is based on Fujiyoshi's valuable study, "Jōjin no Motarashita Higa no Tenseki," in his *San Tendai godaisanki no kenkyū* pp. 402–443. For this reference, see pp. 436–437.

[22] Mori Katsumi stresses this point in his pioneering study "*San Tendai godaisanki ni tsuite,*" pp. 278–282.

[23] Wang Gungwu, "The Rhetoric of a Lesser Empire: Early Sung Relations with Its Neighbors."

[24] The best study in English of early Japanese science remains Nakayama, *A History of Japanese Astronomy in Traditional Japan, A.D. 600–1854.* For comprehensive overviews, see Sugimoto and Swain, *Science and Culture;* and Hideomi Tuge, *Historical Development of Science and Technology in Japan.* An early work that remains quite interesting is David Eugene Smith and Yoshio Mikami, *A History of Japanese Mathematics.*

[25] *Chūyūki,* vol. 2, p. 192; Ii, *Jōjin no Nissō to sono shōgai,* pp. 239–242.

[26] Fujiyoshi Masumi, *San Tendai godaisanki no kenkyū,* p. 442.

2

Poetry in Chinese as a Diplomatic Art in Premodern East Asia

Murai Shōsuke

Translated and adapted by Haruko Wakabayashi
Poems translated by Andrew Edmund Goble

On sending Song Hŭigyŏng as a Reciprocation Envoy (K. *Hoeyesa*) to Japan in 1420, King Sejong (r. 1418–1450) of Chosŏn Korea reminded him, "One must compose poems when visiting a foreign country [as an envoy]." To this Song responded, "I shall record everything I hear and see as poems, from the day I leave Hansong until the day I report my mission, heedless of my poor talents."[1] The reason why Song chose to record his travels to and in Japan, *Nosongdang Ilbon haengnok* (Nosongdang's Record of a Journey to Japan), not as an ordinary travel diary but as a collection of poems with a long preface, lay in the unique function of Chinese poetry (C. *hanshi*; J. *kanshi*; K. *hansi*) in diplomacy in East Asia.[2]

Similarly, in 1544, Im Kwŏn, the Special Participant in the Office of the Royal Lectures (K. Kyŏngyŏn T'ŭkchingwan), in a conversation with King Chungjong (r. 1506–1544) stated, "The ruler and the subject must treat each other with proper rites (K. *ye*). In the past, the lord offered a poem to send off his subject as an envoy and offered another poem to reward his services [upon his return]."[3] The "rites," as described in the first part of this comment, taken from the *Analects*,[4] have no diplomatic context. However, Im Kwŏn consciously reinterpreted this passage to place "poetry" at the heart of diplomacy.

In this way, in diplomacy in East Asia, poetry was emphasized in the relationship between the ruler and envoys. Poems were frequently exchanged between the envoy and those greeting him in the country to which he traveled as well. Pak Sŏsaeng, who visited Japan in 1429 as a Korean envoy, is known for his keen observations of Japan. which appear in the *Sejong sillok*. He also wrote, in a format similar to that of the *Nosongdang Ilbon haengnok*, the *Pak P'ansa Ilbon haengnok* (Pak P'ansa's Record of a Journey to Japan). Unfortunately, this latter record has been lost except for a postscript written by Yi Sŏm. In this we are fortunate, since the concluding passage of that postscript expresses well the role of poetry in foreign diplomacy.

> Because I studied poetry, my verbal expression had improved, and because I
> could skillfully express myself in words, I could serve as an envoy to various
> countries. This is according to reason, since songs and poems have the power
> to move things. It has been more than a thousand years since Japan broke off
> diplomatic relations with our country. That Japan today has offered to return
> captives to Chosŏn and reestablish diplomatic relations all began with the
> master's mission. [This is not a historically accurate account.] Ah, his way of
> poetry must have deeply impressed [the Japanese].[5]

Hence, the exchange of Chinese poetry, which originally was a means of socializing among intellectuals in China, spread to various regions that were constituent parts of the Chinese cultural sphere. Poetry was not limited in those places to simply serving as a literary embellishment. Rather, well before these fifteenth–century interactions between Koreans and Japanese, verse had become an accepted and expected form of interaction between guests and hosts. Those participating might be of varied social positions and included officials, Buddhist monks, aristocrats, and members of local elites.

Even at times when political circumstances and exigencies weighed heavily on parties with different national affiliations and agendas, Chinese poetry composed using common ideographs and common rules of composition established a foundation for mutual understanding. Reflecting on this issue, we must certainly come to appreciate the aspect of Chinese poetry that produced a "direct and human communication and solidarity beyond political discrimination and conflict."[6] However, we must not overlook the fact that the skills of composing poetry, the use of words, and even personal demeanor had a direct bearing on the assessment of the individual and the reputation of his country.

The relationship between Chinese poetry and diplomacy was not limited to diplomatic negotiation in its narrow sense. Some poems composed during diplomatic missions were composed when envoys reached their official destination and exchanged poems with their hosts or else expressed among themselves their relief at having arrived safely. Other poems that originated during a mission were simply the product of daily literary activity. Yet we should not draw too clear a line between diplomacy and literary activities. The literary record of Japanese Zen monks (the Gozan, or Five Mountains literature), for example, contains a large number of diplomatic sources and poems relating to diplomatic activity. The reason for this is that, with diplomacy not established as a separate governmental skill, Zen monks of the officially recognized Gozan institutions had, because of their collective familiarity with the East Asian macroculture, taken on diplomacy and as a matter of course incorporated it into their daily literary activities.[7] In this essay, I wish to examine the role of Chinese poetry as one of the skills that supported diplomacy and intercourse among East Asian countries and people. I will illustrate the exchange of poetry in a number of locations and between individuals of diverse social statuses who came from a number of backgrounds.

The Spectacle of "Harmony" in Chinese Poetry

Why did Chinese poetry become a tool for communication among those who were involved in diplomacy and whose perspectives were based on different standpoints? While it is evident that much Chinese poetry was composed by individual authors, it is also the case that much was also composed in response to a poem offered by another or even produced as a chain composition by several authors. As I have noted, these were produced using a common script and syntax, and following an accepted set of rules of composition. Communication was thus made through the brush and the need for verbal communication obviated; conversely, lack of verbal facility with a foreign vernacular was not an impediment to communication. The exchange of poems in these circumstances was referred to as "harmony" and very much resembles the Japanese linked verse meetings (J. *rengakai*). We can characterize this tradition using a medieval Japanese expression, "the literary art produced by assembly" (J. *yoriai no bungei*).

Early examples come from the eighth to the tenth centuries, when envoys from Parhae frequently visited Japan. Since persons who were talented in poetry composition were chosen as envoys, poetry parties often livened up the proceeding, and at the same time produced heated competition on the Japanese side. Pae Chŏng, who was sent to Japan twice as an ambassador toward the end of the Parhae kingdom (it was destroyed in 927 by the Liao), was so talented that he is said to have composed one poem every seven steps. Some sense of the cultural significance of poetic exchanges may be gained from a consideration of the poetry meeting held during his first visit, in 883, which lasted from the twenty-ninth day of the fourth month to the first day of the fifth month.[8]

Participants exchanged poems among themselves according to established protocols of composition. Eight-line poems were composed in accordance with strict conventions. Each line should contain seven Chinese characters; the final characters in lines 1, 2, 4, 6, and 8 must rhyme; in each poem the same five characters must be employed by each poet at the end of the lines; lines three and four, and five and six, should be couplets; and the couplets should employ words that are either opposite to or similar in meaning. In translation it is not possible to convey fully the artistry and talents of the authors as they followed these conventions. But, remembering that in Chinese poetry characters themselves are often intended to convey rich, evocative, and layered imagery, we can try to convey the tone of the verses and the emotions they intended to elicit.

Participants also took into account informal considerations, such as seating arrangements and order of presentation, so that all would be equally highlighted. Indeed, as is clear from the preface to the poetic record (containing a total of fifty-nine poems) that Sugawara no Michizane later compiled from the collective effort, concerns about not being shown in a bad light on more than poetic skills. According to Michizane's preface, Michizane and Shimada no Tadaomi (his father-in-law) had planned ahead of time not to compose poems unless they were seated together because they would be in trouble if Pae had prepared a poem in advance.[9] Clearly, poetry parties were not simply a place for literary exchange but a battleground where the country's dignity was on display.

Unfortunately Pae's poem, composed in response to the initial poems of Sugawara no Michizane and Ki no Haseo, has not survived. But we gain some sense of the meeting from the poems composed in response to Pae by Tadaomi and Michizane, which are preserved independently in the respective family literary collections of Tadaomi and Michizane. Tadaomi's poem to the envoy from Parhae reads:[10]

> The lone true blade is as the keen-edged frost white
> Piercing through foe, reaching slanting rays of light.
> So, too, is creativeness the messenger of the heart unfettered
> And youth the unadorned mien of those yet unlettered.
> Reputation follows on the blowing wind, fanning among the vulgar herds
> A well-versed envoy dispels the thunder, refrains, composed are the words.
> A precious treasure it is to commune in a place of cultured release
> Next month a missive, the autumn flocks of geese.

Michizane's poem to the envoy reads:[11]

> Enduring, the enwintered pine defies frost's foliate embrace
> The salutary mien awaits not dappled light's fleeting face.
> Wellsprings tended in the royal glade, a cultivated talent I am made
> Peripatetic in my whim, a searching counsel I am him.
> Be it one thousand years, how could it make my own heart terse
> Be it ten thousand miles, would I not but hold to that verse.
> Yet ear-full of others' stories and riant bonhomie
> Yours our tear-full parting cloaks my journey.

Multiple Facets of Poetry and Diplomacy

There were diverse facets to the relationship between poetry and diplomacy. Let us examine this relationship through the case of Japan and Chosŏn. I will note three contexts: poetry used as a means of direct communication, the content of poems causing problems, and occasions where diplomatic contact was a venue for testing poetic skills.

Let me first offer one example of poetry used as a means of direct communication. After the Ōei attack in 1419, in which the Korean government attacked Tsushima because of recent pirate raids, the Muromachi bakufu sent a mission to probe the intentions of Chosŏn under the pretext of requesting the *Tripitaka* and appointed the monk Mugai Ryōgei, of Myōrakuji in Hakata, as Envoy. He reached Hansŏng in the first month of 1420 and chose poetry as the vehicle for communicating with King Sejong. He first apologized, noting, "Since I cannot express myself fully in words, I humbly depict my heart by composing a poem." He then offered this one.

> Cultivating widely mountain and stream, the tributes of Yu[12] we return in plenitude
> This Sage King Yao we exalt and esteem, with sun and moon in celsitude
> How can our virtued Court *this* perfect rule repay?
> Upright, I three times hail, "Your Reign for aeons and aeons, I pray!"

The king, having read this, expressed his intentions, stating, "The relationship between the two countries shall be lasting, solid, and unchanging," and giving the "reasons for the punishment of Tsushima the previous year."[13]

The second context relates to diplomatic problems that could be caused because so much emphasis was placed on poetry as a diplomatic medium. In 1466, when the envoy of the deputy shogun Hatakeyama Yoshinari arrived at Hamch'ang in Kyŏngsang Province, on his way to Hansŏng he was scheduled to stay in the upper east room of the guesthouse. However, because Yi P'yŏng, an aide to the Military Records Officer (K. *Kunjŏksa Chŏngsagwan*), who was already in the guesthouse, had refused to leave, the envoy had no choice but to stay in the upper west room. Yi P'yŏng also sent a poem to the guest, but the guest was angered, claiming that there was an expression of insult in the poem. The Office of the Inspector General (K. *Sahŏnbu*) reported this incident to King Sejo (r. 1455–1468), and the king sent a letter to Yi P'yŏng, reproaching him: "What you did regarding the lodging and poetry were thoughtless acts with no concern for the reputation of the country. From now on, you must never send poems to a guest."[14]

Similarly, in 1542, a poem composed in Chosŏn by a Japanese shogunal envoy, the monk Anshin Tōdō, who had come seeking permission to engage in trade on behalf of the Sō family of Tsushima, became an issue. At the time of this visit, the major issue of debate within the Korean government was whether or not to allow the monk to trade the eighty thousand *ryō* of silver he had brought and, if allowed, what amount and at what rate the silver should be exchanged.[15]

Frustrated by the protracted negotiations, Anshin Tōdō expressed his disdain through insolent words and in the end composed a poem that scoffed at the attitude of the Koreans.

> Though the politics of the world shift the vulgar with celerity
> Yet the commands of the Son of Heaven are removed from veracity.

This poem caused a scandal because it was taken as depicting the incident as "not having followed the proper way to receive an envoy, not having taken the proper measures regarding the silver trade, having deliberated over the matter reported by the envoy only to renew the argument, and, finally, not having been able to make a decisive order." In short, "There has never been an incident in the past in which a Japanese person was treated falsely as such."[16] Anshin's poem appears to have been effectively deployed, for over the next ten years he made four more visits in a successful effort to facilitate trade.

The third context is where, since advanced skills in composing poetry and literature were demanded of a diplomat, diplomatic relations became a venue for testing literary skills. Since this was a matter not only relative to the diplomat's personal reputation but to the prestige of the country he represented, selecting a suitable person was taken seriously. The following four cases reflect this.

First, in 1479, in order to select a military officer to accompany the envoy to Japan, King Sŏngjong (r. 1469–1494) sponsored an arrow-shooting contest in the rear garden. Thirty men, including Kim Chinsŏk, were divided into left and right groups to demonstrate their archery skills. Sŏngjong suggested, "Today's selection should be based not only on military skills. Select and recommend a person who is also well versed in poetry." The First Royal Secretary of the Royal Secretariat (K. *Sŭngjŏngwŏn Tosŭngji*) nominated Cho Chisŏ, a First Copyist in the Office of Diplomatic Correspondence (K. *Sŭngmunwŏn Chŏjak*), and Pak Kyegan, a Chief in the Office of Sacrifices (K. *Pongsangsi Chikchang*). The two men were asked to compose a single–stanza Chinese-style poem of eight lines (K. *yulsi*) entitled "Huwŏn kwansa" (Viewing Arrow-Shooting in the Rear Garden) and a long poem (K. *changsi*) entitled "Pongsa Ilbon" (Mission to Japan). Cho Chisŏ was able to compose and present both poems and thus was chosen for the post.[17] This episode reveals that even for military officers literary skills were emphasized more than military skills when they were sent on a diplomatic mission.

Second, in 1487, a Japanese monk who arrived at the capital asked for poems. King Sŏngjong ordered the Office of Special Counselors (K. *Hongmungwan*) to compose poems and, as he did so, reminded the officials, "This person is asking for poems in order to test our country's men of talent. Do not compose them in haste. Be sure to choose from among the civil officials of ministerial and nonministerial rank those who are skilled in poetry and literature."[18]

Third, in 1562, hearing that a recently arrived Japanese envoy that had just arrived was talented in literary arts, the Board of Rites (K. Yejo) told King Myŏngjong (r. 1545–1567), "The Reception Official (K. *Sŏnwisa*) Yi Yon is not sufficient in ability and talent to receive a diplomatic envoy. If the envoy is talented in exchanging poetry and composes too many poems, then he might be at his wit's end. The former Chinese Language Clerk (K. *Hanihakkwan*) Kwŏn Ŭngin stands unrivaled in his literary skills. Shall we summon him from his residence, provide him with a fast horse, and send him to serve with the reception official?"[19]

Fourth, in 1587, King Sŏnjo (r. 1567-1608) issued a special order: "The duty of receiving envoys from neighboring countries should be taken seriously. Japanese, especially, are skilled in poetry, and if the talents of our men do not match theirs at times of exchange, we will be ridiculed in that country. Since this is an extremely serious matter, we must choose the best man of writing as reception official, regardless of his post and rank."[20]

Japanese Zen Monks in China

From the mid–thirteenth century onward, the sea route between Japan and China became extremely busy, and monks, especially Zen monks, frequently traveled between the two countries. Their interactions were extensive and covered many different areas of activity. Communication was often in writing (*hitsuwa*, "brush talk") rather than spoken words, and exchanges by poem were central to that effort, including one poem that laments, perhaps unnecessarily, the poor state of the author's spoken and written Chinese.[21]

The poetry (and, more broadly, essays and other writings) that was produced as a result of these interactions involving Zen monks constitutes its own literary genre, the literature of the Five Mountains. This poetry, written in Chinese, constituted a new style of poetry in Japan. It drew on a new epistemology that embraced the rich symbolism of mind and experience and contained images and memories of scenes and places throughout East Asia. That is, it evoked a collective memory and culture shared by Zen Buddhist monks and, as we shall see, many of these who interacted with them. To be sure, Japanese Zen monks occasionally expressed nativist reactions to the cosmopolitan, and to images not part of the native landscape,[22] but that response was more idiosyncratic than representative.

The immense corpus of Gozan literature produced throughout East Asia has, in comparison with study of distinctly national literatures, barely been studied let alone sufficiently annotated. The examples, then, will serve to provide a sense of the range of the poetry written in Chinese, some of it easily graspable, some less so, and some of it not at all "familiar." Yet, it is worth recovering.

I will start with four examples of poetry that celebrated the presence of Japanese Zen monks in China. It is apparent that their presence and successful engagement of the Zen tradition were appreciated and that poetry was the form in which that recognition was most permanently inscribed. A further shared thread is that these poems were constituent parts in the building of a new transnational Buddhist subculture.

The first example is the poetry of Nanpo Jōmin (1235–1308), who was to produce what some regard as the most important lineage in Japanese Rinzai Zen. Originally a student of Lanxi Daolong (1213–1278) in Kamakura, Nanpo entered Song China in 1259, where he studied for eight years under the guidance of Xutang Zhiyu at Jingshan in the suburbs of Hangzhou. On the occasion of his return to Japan in 1267, he requested some parting words from Xutang, who was eighty–three years old at the time. Xutang bestowed on him the gift of the following poem.[23]

> Once knocking at every door and gate, now done with your own burnishing
> No more path to tread nor answer to await, just those steps returning
> This Xutang has transmitted without surcease, knowledge a gleaming
>   coruscating ray
> Disciples and progenies in Eastern Seas, shall now increase day by day.

Inspired by Xutang, forty-three Chinese monks who were Nanpo's colleagues and friends sequentially composed poems of their own, thus producing a scroll of farewell poems that is an expression of their wishes for his safe return home. This scroll, titled *Yifanfeng* (J. *Ippanfū*), or "Full-Sail Wind," was presented to Nanpo, who took it back with him to Japan. We do not know what other material items Nanpo took back with him, but this scroll no doubt was valued greatly by him as a cultural and intellectual memento of his sojourn and intellectual development. And Xutang's faith in his disciple proved to be well placed, for Nanpo's return to Japan did indeed result in an increase in disciples and progenies.

From 1271, Nanpo was in residence in Hakata, first at Kōtokuji and then at Shōfukuji, where he remained until 1304. His location meant that he was well placed to meet people coming and going to China. One of those with whom he interacted, through poetry, was Chao Liangbi. Liangbi, a Jurchen and formally the Shanxi Circuit Pacification Commissioner (C. *Shanxi-lu xuanfushi*), arrived in Japan in 1271 and again in 1272 as the personal envoy of the Mongol Yuan emperor Khubilai Khan (1215–1294). Chao was lodged at a guard station not far from Nanpo's Kōtokuji, but it can hardly have been a coincidence that he came into contact with one of the most well-versed Zen priests in Japan, whose own teacher, Lanxi Daolong, was adviser to the bakufu leader Hōjō Tokimune (1251–1284). For Nanpo's biographers, what was important to record about their meeting was that

Nanpo offered, in response, "To the Mongol Envoy Pacification Commissioner Chao, two poems on the topic of Donlin Yuan." The first poem is based on the old story of "Huiyuan and the Three Laughers of Tiger Gorge."[24] That poem reads:

> Oh why did Yuan Gong [Huiyuan] from Tiger Gorge not emerge?
> If not Tao Qian then from whom would comprehension surge?
> I beg to know the deepest thoughts within
> When will that silent rush-wrapped wheel ever reach Yunlin?

The second poem, more reminiscent of a comment on a concrete issue, reads:

> A man of foreign eminence has to Japan brought his presence
> Well met, conversations all pleasant parts, therein we reveal our true hearts
> When all is said and done, of divided paths to other regions there are none
> Yet to know at a glance that there is a Way, whom among us can that assay?

It is not known what Chao made of these poems. However, it is clear that even in a time of tension, with the Mongol invasion of Japan in 1274 on the horizon, poetry was central to communication.

The second example is the poetry of Yūzan Shisai (1301–1370), who entered Yuan China in 1328 and during his sixteen-year sojourn (he returned to Japan in 1344) paid visits to famed monks throughout the country. Included in the third and last volume of his collected writings, the *Yūzanroku* (Records of Yūzan), is a series of Buddhist verses (C. *jiesong*) written by Kuzhi Qingzhe, Yuejiang Zhengyin, Bingshi Ruzhi, Qiaoyin Wuyi, Nanqu Shishuo, Dingmen Shixi, Mengtang Tan'e, Fulong Xingyi, and Liaoan Qingyu. Of those, the verse composed by the seventy–three–year-old Yuejiang in 1339 expresses well the universe of a traveling monk: his journey quest, his achievements, some memories, and his destination in life.[25]

> Companion of the dragon clouds, o'er-striding whales and Atlas-turtle
> Cintamani jewel 'midst my shrouds, my spirits lofted high they hurtle
> Unicorn awe of eastern waters oceanic, thrusting horn like a gem iridescent
> Lion roar of southern mounts titanic, rippling mane of gold resplendent
> With their visits I am replete, those Good Friends of Jiangsu and Zhejiang
> With this sight I am complete, surging August waves of moon-festival Qiantang
> In memory now of no account, a road to a birthplace I did once inhabit
> Fond of temple and of mount, in any place I harbor those of kindred habit.

The third example is the poetry of Muga Shōgo (fl. mid-1300s), who entered Yuan China in 1348. After visiting a number of famed Zen masters, he paid his respects to Xutang Zhiyu's memorial pagoda. On that occasion, three Chinese Zen priests, Yuejiang Zhengyin, Liaoan Qingyu, and Chushi Fanqi, dedicated to him a series of Buddhist verses entitled "On Sending Off Our Japanese Superintendent of the Sutra-Storehouse, Paying Respects at the Tower of Our Founder Xutang."[26]

> Waves from celestial streams debouch in Eastern Seas
> Founding their own teachings those disciples and progenies
> Replete is the country with golden treasure,
>   yet of none of it can he take the measure
> For a third time at the temple he aspires, of the venerable master he inquires.
>
> (Yuejiang Zhengyin)

> Setting forth from mulberried Yamato's East
> Crossing seas deep and mountains steep,
>   upon the first teachings you sought to feast
> Mount Xiang's black beans: round like pop beans are so small
> Our lineage life and all it means: like to a venerable deaf master being in thrall.
>
> (Liaoan Qingyu, signed as Nantang Qingyu)

> "The sun rises from the west and at night sinks into the east"
> What teaching is it that does not know these words, at least?
> "Does hair grow on the back of Space Void or Emptiness?"
> Each head gets it, the vision of our teacher his venerableness.
>
> (Chushi Fanqi)

The fourth example is an exchange between a Zen monk and a Chinese emperor. Zekkai Chūshin (1334–1405), who entered Ming China in 1368, was summoned to meet the founding Ming emperor, Hongwu (Taizu, r. 1368–1398), at the Yingwulou pavilion. There he was asked about a site in his island country, the ancient shrine at Kumano. Chūshin responded with a poem, to which Hongwu penned his own reply, thus giving Chūshin the unique distinction of being the only Japanese monk ever to be graced with a poem from a Chinese emperor. Oddly, however, scholars of Japanese literature often comment on, or even acknowledge, only Chūshin's poem, despite the fact that the significance of the poem lies as much in it being part of an exchange as it does in the fact that Zekkai wrote it. In any event, the exchange was as follows.[27]

First, Zekkai wrote:

> Afront of Kumano's rocky peaks, Xu Fu shrine of ancient story
> Luxuriant from rain's cascade creeks, medicinal herbs a mountain glory
> Seas tranquil for the while, the cresting waves me will not harry
> Fair wind for ten thousand amile, returning home I dare not tarry.[28]

The Emperor Taizu responded:

> At Kumano's soaring craggy tines, a shrine that descendents will so nourish
> At roots of clinging gnarled pines, the precious amber will so flourish
> That year Xu Fu had but one urge, of finding that Immortal Potion
> From then 'til now the present verge, of returning there is no notion.

These poems were much talked about in later ages. For example, in a preface to a poem under the date 1474 in Ōsen Keisan's *Ho Ankei kazen shū* (Supplemented Collection from the Hermitage Afront the Splendoured Capital) we find the comment "When the old master Shōken [Zekkai] visited Ming China, the Venerable Emperor [Hongwu] summoned him to the Yingwulou pavilion and asked him to compose a poem about the three mountains of Kumano. In return, he received a poem composed by the emperor himself. This is a rare event." The same preface notes that Zekkai "also exchanged poems with great elders such as Jitan and Qingyuan. This is an admirable tale of a thousand ages,"[29] thus suggesting that Zekkai also had exchanges with Jitan Zongle and Qingyuan Huaiwei.

Zekkai returned to Japan with a distinguished reputation. He was to rise to the pinnacle of the Gozan organization and was a trusted adviser on foreign relations.[30] In that capacity, as will be seen, his poetic skills continued to be on display.

Exchanges with Chinese Envoys

In the medieval period, official Japanese contact with foreign countries might take place in either the absence or the presence of official diplomatic relations. Key here, of course, is that the presence or absence of diplomatic relations did not preclude the Chinese or Korean governments from dispatching envoys to address matters of pressing importance. Envoys, of course, had their official schedules, but opportunities for establishing personal contacts while staying away from complex international affairs were an "unofficial" but integral part of the interaction. I will note some examples of interaction with Chinese ambassadors at times when there were, and were not, official relations.

In the Ōan period (1368–1375) a number of Ming envoys journeyed to Japan, as part of the broader diplomatic effort of the new Ming emperor, Taizu, to establish formal relations with neighboring countries. This was a complicated period internationally, and at the time Japan was in the midst of a civil war, which had implications for matters of diplomacy.[31] Under these circumstances, poetry enabled a leavening cultural exchange.

One example is the exchange of poems between the Ming envoys Zhongxian Zuehan, Wuyi Keqin, Chao Zhi, Zhu Ben, and others, who were in Japan from 1373 through the following year, and the Zen priest Shun'oku Myōha (1311–

1388), a disciple of and successor to Musō Soseki. Poetic exchange was nothing new to Shun'oku, and as recently as 1367 he had been involved in diplomatic matters with the Koryŏ envoy Kim Yong, as part of which he had sent a poem to Kim Yong and an official accompanying Kim.[32] In 1373, however, Shun'oku, his disciple Santo, and others had temporarily retired to Unmonji temple in Tango Province due to a falling out with Deputy Shogun Hosokawa Yoriyuki (1329–1392). However, Shun'oku was close to the young shogun Yoshimitsu (1358–1408, who rehabilitated him soon afterward), and so the Chinese envoys were given leave to visit Shun'oku unofficially. The legacy of the visit is a collection of the linked poetry exchanged between hosts and guests, the *Unmon ikkyoku* (Unmon Composition). Yet, just as the exchange of poems was not just about poetry, neither is the collection: the preface, commenting on the background to the compilation, directly touches on some diplomatic matters.[33]

In a different vein, a temple in Hakata became famous as a "must visit" site for religious and official travelers from China. The Donpekirō (Azure Tower) pavilion on the grounds of Myōrakuji was known even in China as a scenic spot overlooking Hakata Bay. The wall was a spectacle, filled with poems by famed wise men of Yuan and Ming China such as Liaoan Qingyu, Chushi Fanqi, Yuanpo Liangqi, Xueshan Wenxin, Fuxun Shouren, Tanyai Chongshu, and Qingyuan Huaiwei. The Ming envoys that came to Japan during the Ōan period also visited this place and inscribed poems on the pavilion's wall. The authors included Zhongxian Zuehan, Wuyi Keqin, and Zhu Ben (who later visited Shun'oku Myōha), as well as Wang Youqian, Zhan Yu, an émigré literatus named Lu Ren, and Japanese monks such as Dokuhō Seidon, Daihon Ryōchū, Chintei Kaiju, Chūken, Jorin Myōsa, and Ichigen Keisho.

Let us engage a poem by Zhongxian.[34] The poem is laden with allusions that require further study in order to elicit a full reading (and possible political references). But it is easy to recognize long-standing images of voyaging across the seas,[35] acknowledgment of long-term flows of culture and interests, the integration of the Mongol Invasion era's defensive wall around Hakata Bay and the Donpekirō into the image of Hakata ("Stone Fortress"), and, of course, the view from the Donpekirō pavilion.

> Surmounting Stone Fortress by emerald clouds brushed,
>> Azure Tower into heaven's vault thrust
> Earthen firmament, Kyushu near-shrinking and the Gotō's linking
> Acqueous filament, past Paekche flows then to Eastern reaches goes
>> The majestic whale swallowed it all, the exposed corals did appear
> The golden Garuda flapped its wings, the Puffing Sea became nought but sere
> The great river has a source and a destiny, a history that pervades
>> And ere evening tides raise the moon 'top these balustrades.

Formal travel of official envoys between China and Japan recommenced a few decades later (and for the first time in some centuries) after the Ming Chinese emperor Jianwen (r. 1398–1402) invested Ashikaga Yoshimitsu as king of Japan in 1402. At that time, Zekkai Chūshin, who had now become the abbot of Shōkokuji and thus the head of what we may describe as the Zen diplomatic service, exchanged poetry with the visiting imperial envoys Tianlun Daoyi (chief priest of Tianningsi, a Chan temple in Mingzhou) and Yian Yiru (chief priest of Shangzhusi, a Tiantai temple in Hangzhou). These envoys may or may not have been aware of Zekkai's exchange with the founding emperor of the Ming dynasty (though it is hard to believe that they would not have known), but Zekkai would surely not have forgotten. Zekkai's poem, written to fellow Buddhists and students of Chinese history, evoked notions of tranquil exchange between good friends with shared traditions.[36]

> A temple deep away and in the quiet of the day, those who come are few
>> Chrysanthemum beautiful at the garden's fore, petals couch the dew
> If not for these divine masters whose legs have bent this way
>> Then as I sweep the unkempt mossy path, it would be for who?
> Ere long have I worshipped the guiding brushes of Huailian and Qigao
>> Overjoyed I commune with the legend talents, Sima Qian and Ban Gu
> Mountains and rivers of this country ours majestic in their powers
>> I see you off on your return, ten days of zephyrs pleasing and true.

In the following year, 1403, Yoshimitsu, in response to the visit by these envoys, sent an embassy to Ming China with Kenchū Keimitsu serving as envoy. Zekkai's disciple, Ryūkei Tōbun, was also a member of this embassy, and in order to encourage his disciple on his departure Zekkai composed a verse as a Zen precept (*kyōsaku*).[37]

> On Austral voyage of myriad mile, 'tis with the envoys you will have hewed
> Imbibing scenery all the while, comporting with the Pacific dragon
>> oh! beatitude
> Stone Fortress Hakata, tiger crouches waiting, mountains and rivers emanating
> Yishui where the Celestial dragon soars, by those vapors are the climes renewed
> Step by step to meet the master you essay, scholars past have paved the way
> The Imperial envoy his country repays with gratitude, a man of ample fortitude
> Your duty done and business met you might go whither,
>> but on your return you dare not dither
> Scratching back in casual mood, of future gravitude is this one imbued.

At the end of the mission in China, Ryūkei showed this poem to Rulan, of Zhongzhusi, a temple in Hangzhou, as he prepared to return to Japan. Rulan presented him with a poem, which we may read in part as a report to Zekkai on the mission and his disciple's performance, entitled "In Harmony with the Rhymes of Shōken Daishi [Zekkai], I Send this Poem with Ryūkei Chizō upon His Return to Japan."[38]

> In the infinite heavens and on earth's reaches far,
>> none but are subject to rule compleat
> Upward gazing, in cluster pivoting on the Boreal Star,
>> a twinkling astral fleet
> Windswept billows on miasmic seas,
>> driven to where they ebb, gain their ease
> Prized robes soaked by rain and dew in surfeit,
>> new ones bestowed and again made meet
> Upholding the envoys in their mission,
>> fulfilling well the sovereign commission
> Turning for the while to Zen retreat,
>> "let me lodge as a guest" he did entreat
> In the Eastern country where it has been nourished,
>> I learn that literature long has flourished
> To say there are none enough lettered for one to greet,
>> surely this would be false conceit.

The Korean Envoy Song Hŭigyŏng in Japan

By entering into Ming China's tribute system in 1402, Japan also established official relations, fundamentally a relationship of equality, with Chosŏn, and embassies traveled between these two countries. Song Hŭigyŏng, the reciprocation envoy that King Sejong dispatched to Japan, traveled to Kyoto under conditions shaped by a sudden resurgence of piracy by Tsushima islanders in 1418, the Korean government's attack of Tsushima in 1419.6, rumors in Japan of another Mongol invasion, and the Muromachi bakufu's dispatch of an envoy to Chosŏn later in 1419. King Sejong sent him to Japan approximately six months after the Korean forces had withdrawn from Tsushima. Accompanying the shogunal envoy, Song represented Chosŏn at a delicate moment.

Song departed the Korean capital on the fifteenth day of the intercalary first month in 1420, and arrived in Kyoto on 4.21. From Pusan he sailed with the Japanese to Tsushima, and after spending two weeks there continued to Hakata, where he stayed two and one-half weeks. Progress through the Inland Sea to Kyoto took one month. The king of Chosŏn's envoy spent more than two months in the capital. He met the shogun on 6.16 and left Kyoto on 6.27.[39]

Included in Song's *Nosongdang Ilbon haengnok* are many poems that were exchanged with Japanese. Song's companions in poetry were not only the shogunal envoy, the monk Mugai Ryōgei, but also Monkei Shōyū and Kōzan of Hakata, who was an elder monk at Eifukuji in Akamagaseki, and Eisei and Kazō, both priests from Kyoto. If we include those to whom poems were sent, there are even more, including laypeople. Let me give four examples from Song's record.

(1) Ryōgei and Monkei discoursed with me at my Myōraku[ji] residence, and we boiled tea; following on from their verses (At Myōrakuji in Hakata):[40]

Mount Penglai's[41] distant placement, to the Milky Way adjacent
Gone myriad miles in Land of Mulberry, I am become a traveler carefree
I have known you masters for but the nonce, yet such fortune comes only once
Sitting facing each other our poems reciting, in this farthest land a spring
     so inviting.

(2) A priest, Unsui, and Shamon all come to see him, but because of his ongoing affliction he did not meet with them. Following on from those verses, two verses (At Akamagaseki):[42]

Confucian scholars Practical Learning have conveyed
Sakyamuni in the teaching of Emptiness is engaged
As distant as Heaven and Earth are their Truths, by any measure,
Yet both in the presence of the heart see true pleasure.

In pointless wandering I did roam, until I found the Buddha Home
By illness made prostrate, now I face the Dragon Gate
Though the truths that He did teach are difficult near beyond reach
Reading the poem again and again, I know the Way is within my ken.

(3) Piling up stones and making a mountain in the garden, re–creating in the image of the Yangzi River and Lake Dongting; following on from verses on the wall (At Amidadera in Murotsu):[43]

In planting pines and setting stone, those talents were not wanting
Now made the temple's own, Yangzi River vista and scenic Lake Dongting
Chanting poems 'neath these eaves is a thirst I cannot slake
'Tis as though my body of mountains and seas truly does partake.

(4) First day of the fifth month, following on from the verses by Shinrei-in Eisei.

The temple is next to Shinjuan in the west, separated by a fence. Atop the rocks outside of the western building is a small arbor without a name. Master Eisei asks for a name. I named it with an upright mind (At Shinjuan in Kyoto):[44]

> Tho' sunny heat through heaven passes, this arbor yet retains some chills
> Past the bamboo grasses, those yonder rolling verdant hills
> This master I envy and praise, the vulgar world ne'er in his mind scene
> Now and then an outward gaze, those uplifting crests his dividing screen.

These poems, selected from the many in Song's diary, are a guide to some of the ways in which communication was enhanced through the exchange of Chinese poems. We see that poetry and tea came as a set for mediating friendship; that priests might gather and ask for poems from the reciprocation envoy; that travelers quite unknown to each other, yet forming a community of letters, might inscribe poems on the walls of major temples (including the previously noted Donpekirō) along the travel route; and that a poem might serve as the fitting capstone and memorial for Song Hŭigyŏng to give a name to a small arbor in a temple.

What made this possible was the universality of poetry, which surpassed differences of ethnicity and ideas. As Song noted in the first of the poems he wrote at Amagasaki, "Although as a Confucian it is difficult for me to accept Buddhist norms, I can tell when I read the poem that there exists a common Way between the two teachings." A similar view is expressed in the preface of a poem that Song sent to the priests Shūben and Bondō of Tenneiji, in Onomichi, on his return trip.[45]

> Since my first meeting with the two masters on my embassy to establish harmony between the two countries, I felt as if we were old acquaintances, and, although our language was different, we could have a deep understanding of each others' feelings and intentions. Therefore, we visited each other at the meditation hall or the boat almost every day for several days. At times we sang of pine trees and bamboo, at other times we looked over the seas and the mountain, burned incense or boiled tea, composed poems and recited them together, and enjoyed together the peaceful autumn days.

Conclusion

The examples above have shown situations in which the poetic exchanges involved people from two countries. But it also might be noted that there were occasions when the poem as communicator was on display among individuals from more than one political entity. Two examples follow.

In the entry for 1540.4.4 in *Shotoshū*,[46] a record of Sakugen Shūryō's (1501–1579) visit to Ming China as vice envoy, there is this passage: "A Ryukyuan brought forth a fan and asked for a poem." At the time, the Japanese mission had completed the presentation of the shogunal letter and tribute gifts to the emperor and was staying at the Yuheguan residence hall in Beijing. This residence hall was full of tributary envoys from Chosŏn and Ryukyu and representatives from Mongol leaders. On the twenty-seventh day of the third month, at the lodgings of Diaoyun, a Chinese monk who had accompanied the Japanese mission, Sakugen, met with "Kawakami, the Senior Clerk, from Ryukyu" and "made a vow over drink." This Kawakami seems to have been of the same family as the boatman of the second embassy ship, Kawakami Mokuzaemon.[47] The Ryukyuan who asked Sakugen for a poem on his fan must have been this Senior Clerk Kawakami, too. This anecdote displays human networks between Japan and Ryukyu with Beijing as a contact point and, again, the important social role that poetry played in interaction.

Another instance of "multilateral poetry" is found in southern Japan. During the fourth month of 1575, Shimazu Yoshihisa (1533–1611) sponsored an exhibition of the sport of mounted archery with dogs as targets (J. *inu oi mono*) in honor of the Ryukyuan envoy, the monk Nanshuku of Tenkaiji, who was visiting the Satsuma capital of Kagoshima. In the spectator's seat, Nanshuku composed poems. Nanshuku exchanged a total of ten poems with his Satsuma counterpart, the monk-envoy Sesshin Shinkō, and with the Chinese visitor, Dongyun from Luoyang. Yoshihisa and his family members for their part composed Japanese poems (J. *waka*), an indication perhaps of their pride and training in Japanese poetry.[48]

These two examples involving Ryukyuans abroad point to other aspects of verse in foreign interaction. First, the poem also was a gift and a reminder of a congenial meeting abroad, in this instance in civilization's center. Second, the gathering in Kagoshima reminds us of the possibility of excluding people from "harmony" because they might not be able to produce poetry in Chinese. Yet it should not be forgotten that Japanese shoguns in Ming China and Chosŏn were represented by monks and not by other samurai. Moreover, while a local style of verse, such as Japanese *waka* or Korean *sijo* (or *tanga*), could not ascend into poetic exchange in part because its usage required knowledge of that other's language, use of it may be seen as a challenge to the conventions of diplomatic engagement that were embodied in Chinese poetry. Significantly, however, poetry was still the form of choice for making statements about culture and relationships.

As we have seen, Chinese poetry, though not as direct as interviews and diplomatic documents written in Chinese, was an important means of communication in East Asian diplomacy and cultural contacts more generally. The poetry banquet, or other occasions when individuals communed in verse, was a place where the level of cultivation of the diplomatic representatives was tested and also a place where people from different ethnic groups could express their feelings. In other words, diplomacy was a womb that gave birth to Chinese poetry.

Notes

[1] Song Hŭigyŏng, *Nosongdang Ilbon haengnok*, no. 196, pp. 187, 235.

[2] Although primarily a study of a later period, the sixteenth to nineteenth centuries, the reader is also directed to Liam C. Kelley's *Beyond the Bronze Pillars: Envoy Poetry and the Sino-Vietnamese Relationship*, which highlights roles of poetry in state-level interaction between China and Vietnam.

[3] *Chungjong sillok* 104:57b–59a [1544.9.27].

[4] The reference is taken from *Analects* III.19. For translations, see Roger T. Ames and Henry Rosemont Jr., *The Analects of Confucius*, p. 86: "Rulers should employ their ministers by observing ritual propriety;" James Legge, *The Confucian Analects,* book III, chapter XIX: "A Prince should employ his ministers according to the rules of propriety;" and D. C. Lau, *Confucius: The Analects*, p. 70: "The ruler should employ the services of his subjects in accordance with the rites."

[5] Yi Sŏm, "*Pak P'ansa Ilbon haengnok* pal," 103:17b–18b.

[6] Ishimoda Shō, "Shi to bankaku," p. 358.

[7] On the topic of Zen monks and Sino-Japanese relations in the medieval era, including their role in the diplomatic sphere, see Nishio Kenryū, *Chūsei Nitchū kōryū to Zenshū.*

[8] For further discussion of the event and its context, see Robert Borgen, *Sugawara no Michizane and the Early Heian Court*, pp. 231–240.

[9] Kawaguchi Hisao, *Heianchō Nihon kanbungakushi no kenkyū*, vol.1, p. 193. For a translation of the preface, see Borgen, *Sugawara no Michizane and the Early Heian Court*, p. 236.

[10] *Denshi kashū*, p. 350. See, too, Murai Shōsuke, *Higashi Ajia ōkan*, pp. 8–9. For another of Shimada Tadaomi's poems, see Borgen, *Sugawara no Michizane and the Early Heian Court*, p. 234.

[11] *Kanke bunsō*, no. 105, in *Kanke bunsō Kanke goshū*, ed. Yamaguchi Hisao, p. 191. See, too, Murai, *Higashi Ajia ōkan*, p. 9. For another of Sugawara Michizane's poems see Borgen, *Sugawara no Michizane and the Early Heian Court*, p. 234.

[12] See the "Tribute of Yu" chapter in the *Book of Xia* section of the *Shujing*; and James Legge, *The Chinese Classics,* vol. III, *The Shoo King or Book of Historical Documents*, "The Tribute of Yu," pp. 92–151.

[13] *Sejong sillok* 7:4a [1419.1.6]. See, too, Murai, *Higashi Ajia ōkan*, p. 37.

[14] *Sejo sillok* 38:1b–2a [1466.1.2].

[15] Murai Shōsuke, *Chūsei Wajinden*, pp. 161–163.

[16] *Chungjong sillok* 98:57b–58a [1542.6.19]; 99:2a–3b [1542.8.5]. See, too, Murai, *Higashi Ajia ōkan*, p. 119.

[17] *Sŏngjong sillok* 100:7a–b [1478.1.19].

[18] Ibid. 204:6b–7a [1487.6.9].

[19] *Myŏngjong sillok* 28:43b [1562.11.6].

[20] *Sŏnjo sillok* 21:16b [1587.10.22].

[21] See the poem by Chūgan Engetsu, in which he notes that "my Chinese still sounds as bad as it did before. My clumsy poems produce ridicule," in David Pollack, *Zen Poems of the Five Mountains*, p. 76.

[22] For a discussion of this phenomenon, see David Pollack, *The Fracture of Meaning*, pp. 111–133.

[23] *Ippanfū*, p. 925. See, too, Murai, *Higashi Ajia ōkan*, p.15. For a different translation, see Heinrich Dumoulin, *Zen Buddhism: A History*, vol. 2, *Japan*, p. 39.

> To knock on the door and search with care
> To walk broad streets and search the more
> Old Hsü-t'ang taught so clear and bright
> And many are the grandchildren on the eastern sea who
> received [this dharma].

[24] For these two poems, see *Entsū Daiō kokushi goroku*, p. 125, third register, and p. 126, first register. See, too, Murai, *Higashi Ajia ōkan*, pp. 24–25, and Nishio, *Chūsei Nitchū kōryū to Zenshū*, pp. 34–37. For the "Three Laughers of Tiger Gorge," see John M. Rosenfield, "The Unity of the Three Creeds," pp. 208–217.

[25] *Yūzanroku ge*, pp. 102–103. See, too, Murai, *Higashi Ajia ōkan*, pp. 15–16. Helpful suggestions regarding lines 5 and 6 were made by participants in the Classical East Asian Buddhist Texts Workshop, University of Oregon, June 30–July 4, 2005.

[26] *Shūkoroku*. See, too, Murai, *Higashi Ajia ōkan*, pp. 16–17.

[27] *Shōkenkō*: *Shōkenkō zenchū*, ed. Kageki Hideo, pp. 142–144; and *Gozan bungaku shū*, ed. Iriya Yoshitaka, nos. 80 and 81, pp. 140–141. See, too, Murai, *Higashi Ajia ōkan*, pp. 17–18.

[28] For two other translations of Zekkai's verse, see (1) Marian Ury, *Poems of the Five Mountains*, p. 87.

Rhyme Describing the Three Mountains, Composed in Response to the Imperial Command

Before Kumano's peak is Hsu Fu's shrine
The mountains are rich with herbs grown lush after rain.
And now upon the sea the billowing waves are calm
Kind winds a myriad miles will speed him home.

and (2) Donald Keene, *Seeds in the Heart*, p. 1074.

Before the peak of Kumano stands Hsu Fu's shrine;
The mountains abound in herbs thanks to the rains
Now the billowing waves of the sea are calm;
A favorable wind blows ten thousand miles; it's time he went home.

[29] *Ho Ankei kazen shū*, p. 235. Thanks to Xia Yun for the sense of splendoured.

[30] For a discussion of Zekkai as a diplomat, see Nishio, *Chūsei Nitchū kōryū to Zenshū*, pp. 190–210.

[31] For a brief overview of the circumstances, see Kawazoe Shōji, "Japan and East Asia," pp. 423–440.

[32] Murai, *Ajia no naka no chūsei Nihon*, pp. 318–319.

[33] See ibid., pp. 250–258, 264–267, 275–279, 301, 308–309.

[34] For this poem, see Murai, *Higashi Ajia ōkan*, p. 26.

[35] Some of the imageries and tropes in poetry in Chinese related to voyaging to Japan, and of the imaginary lands that populated the "eastern seas," are treated in Edward H. Schafer, "Fusang and Beyond: The Haunted Seas to Japan."

[36] *Zekkai oshō goroku*, p. 754, first register. See, too, Murai, *Higashi Ajia ōkan*, p. 26.

[37] *Zekkai oshō goroku*, p. 754, second register. See, too, Murai, *Higashi Ajia ōkan*, p. 28.

[38] *Zekkai oshō goroku*, p. 754, second register. See, too, Murai, *Higashi Ajia ōkan*, p. 28.

[39] See Murai, *Rōshōdō Nihon kōroku*, pp. 288–291.

[40] Song Hŭigyŏng, *Nosongdang Ilbon haengnok*, no. 63, pp. 67–68, 202.

[41] For more on the locations of Penglai and the Land of Mulberry (used also as an appellation for Japan), see Edward H. Schafer, *Mirages on the Sea of Time*, esp. pp. 51–60, 103–107; and "Fusang and Beyond."

[42] Song Hŭigyŏng, *Nosongdang Ilbon haengnok*, no. 76, pp. 77–78, 204.

[43] Ibid., no. 101, pp. 94, 208–209.

[44] Ibid., no. 115, pp. 113–114, 214.

[45] Ibid., no. 157, pp. 150, 223.

[46] *Shotoshū*, in *DNBZ*, vol. 116.

[47] Fujita Motoharu, *Nisshi tsūkōshi no kenkyū: Chū-kinsei hen*, p. 170.

[48] See *Kyūki zatsuroku kōhen*, vol. 1, p. 416 [1575.4.21].

3

A Japanese Trade Mission to Chosŏn Korea, 1537-1540: The *Sonkai tokai nikki* and the Korean Tribute System

Kenneth R. Robinson

In the summer of 1539, a Japanese monk named Sonkai reached Hansŏng, the capital of Chosŏn Korea. Two years earlier, his superiors at Daiganji had approached Ōuchi Yoshitaka, who governed Suō and Nagato Provinces and administered Hakata in western Japan, for assistance in obtaining a set of the Koryŏ *Tripitaka* (K. *Koryŏ taejanggyŏng*), then the largest collection of printed Chinese-language sutras in the world, from the king of Chosŏn. Yoshitaka expanded their request into a trade mission that would seek scriptures. The mission departed from Yamaguchi in 1538.5. However, delays, including the sudden resignation of the envoy in Tsushima, slowed its progress. Sonkai became the new envoy in Tsushima, but he returned to Yamaguchi without sutras.

Yoshitaka's efforts on behalf of Daiganji came during a period of transition in Korean-Japanese/Japanese-Korean interaction. The Chosŏn court stopped fulfilling requests for sutras, and Japanese had recently begun trading silver in the peninsula. Seen in a longer time frame, however, this trade mission was but one among the thousands that Japanese based in western provinces sent to Chosŏn between 1392 and 1592. Further, the Korean government's treatment of this mission followed regulations already in place for more than half a century. While not a unique enterprise, it is the earliest for which a Japanese participant's account of travel in Chosŏn is extant. That record offers a window on to the regularities of state-supervised interaction in Chosŏn.

Daiganji preserves the account. Attributed to Sonkai, it is found on the back of a folding screen bearing a Korean landscape painting. Today called the *Sonkai tokai nikki*, this diary follows the mission from Daiganji to Yamaguchi, Hakata, Tsushima, and the Korean port (K. *p'o*) of Pusan, up to Hansŏng and through the guest ritual up to the King of Chosŏn. The text does not relate the return to Pusan or to Japan.

The diary is not particularly intriguing, though, and its information about Chosŏn, Sonkai's activities there, and the mission's activities after reaching Pusan is sparse. On the other hand, the record provides detailed information about the Korean government's treatment of Japanese tribute missions. Offering a view of the diplomatic rites designed for Japanese elites, the *Sonkai tokai nikki* displays

Korean regulations through which Japanese retinues moved in the fifteenth and sixteenth centuries. While satisfying those regulations and rites, Japanese received bestowals, traded metals and Southeast Asian goods for cloth and other items, negotiated with Chosŏn government officials, and, among still other forms of interaction with Koreans, engaged in smuggling.

As the envoy, Sonkai represented Yoshitaka, for whom trade was the mission's principal goal, to the king of Chosŏn. As a Daiganji monk, he also carried the hopes of temple superiors for the Koryŏ *Tripitaka*. Of these two purposes, the *Sonkai tokai nikki* treats the hope for scriptures almost exclusively. The diary is primarily an account of the sutra request, of Daiganji's priority, and implicitly of the envoy's appropriate performance of diplomatic rituals in Chosŏn. It rarely records the broader responsibilities borne by the mission and the envoy. A brief description and an annotated translation of the *Sonkai tokai nikki* will introduce a discussion of sutras, silver, and reception in Korean-Japanese/Japanese-Korean relations.

Sonkai and the *Sonkai tokai nikki*

During the second half of the fifteenth century and the first half of the sixteenth, temples in Japan frequently asked provincial governors or shoguns and retired shoguns to approach the Korean government for a set of the Koryŏ *Tripitaka*. The Ōuchi petitioned the Chosŏn court on behalf of specific temples on at least five occasions from 1473 on.[1] On Miyajima island, in the Inland Sea, Daiganji is to the west of the Itsukushima shrine. The temple possessed a set of sutras in the early sixteenth century, but the volumes had become tattered over time. Sonkai's superiors sought this largest set of Chinese-language sutras and contacted Yoshitaka. Their representative, a monk named Inkan, soon received from Yoshitaka documentation required for his reception in Chosŏn and departed.

Little is known of Sonkai. Born near Itsukushima, the monk joined the mission in Hakata and became envoy after Inkan quit in Tsushima. At some point after the mission, he seems to have been appointed as the temple's chief monk (J. *jūji*); by 1547 documents were being issued under the name Sonkai. Assuming this individual to be the monk that went to Chosŏn, Sonkai retired from official duties because of old age and health concerns in 1550.[2]

The *Sonkai tokai nikki* appears on the back of a landscape painting called the *Sosang p'al kyŏngdo*, the "Eight Views of the Xiao and Xiang Rivers." The "Eight Views," which depict these rivers in southern China, is a representative image in Southern Song landscape painting. The image was produced by painters in Koryŏ, and paintings also were executed and images commented on by Koreans in the fifteenth, sixteenth, and seventeenth centuries.[3] The popularity of the "Eight

Views" extended to Muromachi Japan, and by the late fifteenth century four complete Chinese sets were in Japan.[4] The folding screen at Daiganji is 116.0 cm x 494.0 cm, and each of the eight panels is 98.3 cm x 49.9 cm.

Sekino Tadashi believed the painter of "Eight Views" to have been the Korean landscape painter Yang P'aengson (1488–1545).[5] Takeda Tsuneo suggested that the screen reflects the style of painters such as Yang P'aengson; Ahn Hwi-joon considers the landscape the work of a Korean painter other than Yang P'aengson.[6] In terms of style, for Ahn Hwi-joon the Daiganji holding is one of several Korean renditions of the "Eight Views" that belong to the An Kyŏn school and dates to the first half of the sixteenth century.[7] Itakura Masaaki has divided renditions of the "Eight Views" composed in the early Chosŏn period into three groups. He places the Daiganji holding in the second group, paintings that bear a striking affinity with images of the Li Guo school in late Yuan China. These Korean works were clustered in the first half of the sixteenth century. Itakura, too, believes that Yang P'aengson did not paint the "Eight Views" held by Daiganji.[8]

The Chosŏn court and Japanese elites frequently exchanged art objects in the fifteenth century and the early sixteenth. Japanese shoguns and other elites included Buddhist paintings, folding screens, and fans among their gifts to Korean kings.[9] The Ōuchi, in particular, often sent folding screens as gifts in the late fifteenth century.[10] Korean monarchs bestowed or granted Japanese requests for landscape paintings and other images.[11] If Daiganji's "Eight Views" was a gift from the King of Chosŏn, the bestowal to a Japanese individual or an institution was not unique. It is not known whether Sonkai received the painting in Chosŏn as a personal gift, on behalf of the temple, or on behalf of Yoshitaka or whether the Ōuchi received the screen at another time. The writing of Sonkai's travels onto the folding screen, though, may suggest a commemoration of Yoshitaka, Daiganji, or Sonkai having received the painting in Chosŏn or of Daiganji or Sonkai having received the painting from Yoshitaka.

The title *Sonkai tokai nikki* probably was created when the Japanese government conferred National Treasure status on the account and the screen in 1910.[12] Written vertically, the diary is read from right to left and from the second panel of the screen to the seventh panel. Interlinear comments and intralinear comments, both written in smaller script, add further detail. In addition, the text provides *furigana* transliterations of place-names, personal names, government posts, and other Korean words. The transliterations of place-names as spelled in *katakana* are reproduced in parentheses within the translation below. Hyphens separate each *kana* in the diary's transliteration of the place-name.

The translation is from Nakamura Hidetaka's typeset text in volume 1 of his *Nissen kankeishi no kenkyū*.[13] Dates in the account follow the Japanese calendar. Interlinear text is marked by parentheses, intralinear text by brackets. Sonkai's progress through Chosŏn may be followed on three maps adapted from province maps in the *Sinjŭng Tongguk yŏji sŭngnam*, a Korean state gazetteer completed in 1531[14] (see maps 3.1, 3.2, and 3.3). The comprehensive legend provides the county names.

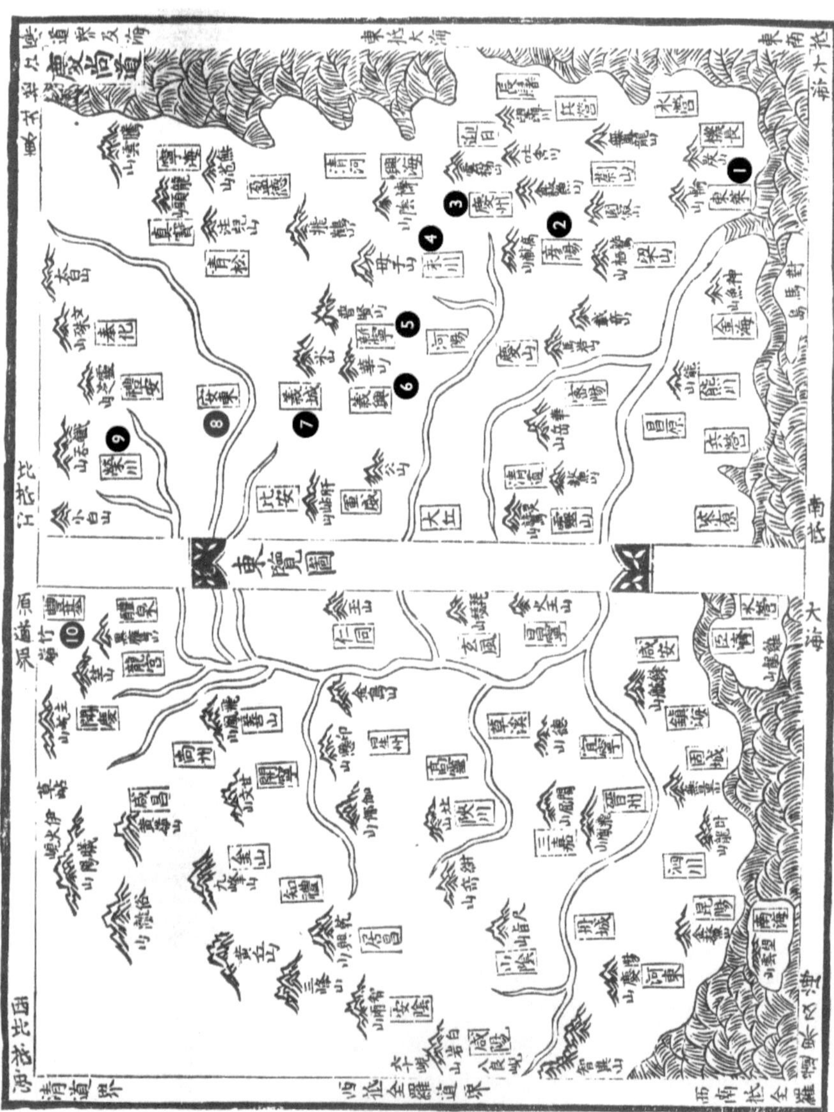

Map 3.1: Sonkai's Route through Kyŏngsang Province. Based on the map "Kyŏngsang-do," in the *Sinjŭng Tongguk yŏji sŭngnam*. Reproduced with the permission of the publisher, Myŏngmundang.

Map 3.2: Sonkai's Route through Ch'ungch'ŏng Province. Based on the map "Ch'ungch'ŏng-do," in the *Sinjŭng Tongguk yŏji sŭngnam*. Reproduced with the permission of the publisher, Myŏngmundang.

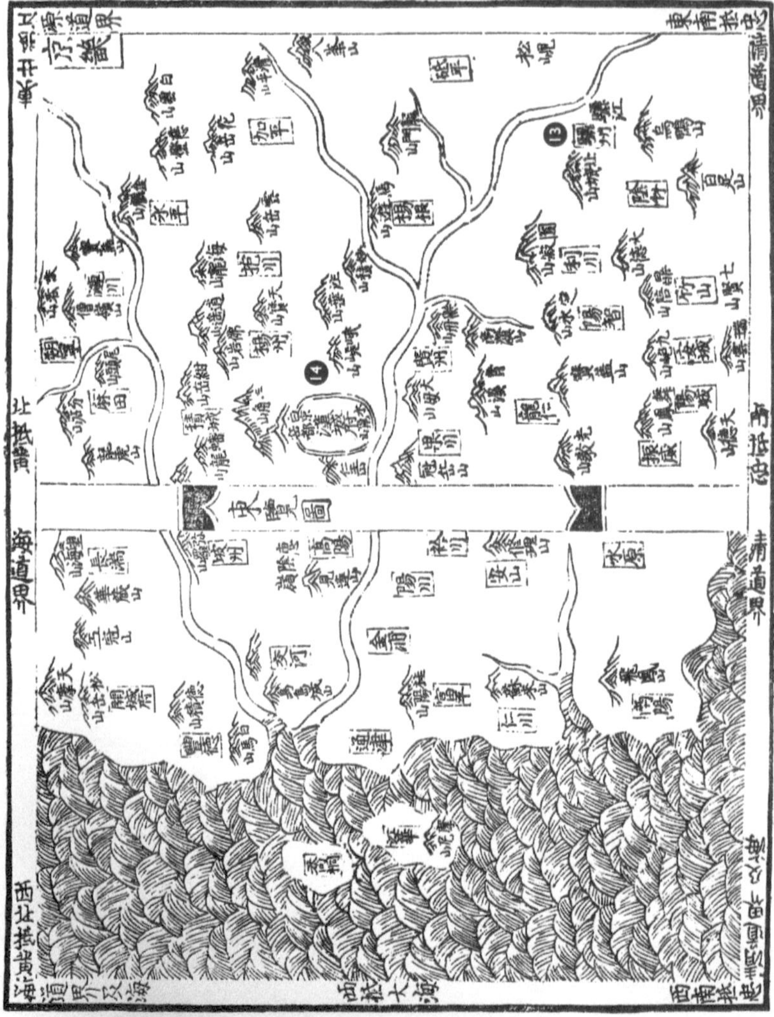

Map 3.3: Sonkai's Route through Kyŏnggi Province. Based on the map "Kyŏnggi," in the *Sinjŭng Tongguk yŏji sŭngnam*. Reproduced with the permission of the publisher, Myŏngmundang.

Comprehensive Legend (Maps 3.1–3.3):

1. Tongnae County	6. Ŭihŭng County	11. Tanyang County
2. Ŏnyang County	7. Ŭisŏng County	12. Ch'ungju County
3. Kyŏngju County	8. Andong County	13. Yŏju County
4. Yŏngch'ŏn County	9. Yŏngch'ŏn County	14. Hansŏng-bu
5. Sillyŏng County	10. P'unggi County	

A Translation of the *Sonkai tokai nikki*

At the bottom right of the second panel is written "Sonkai of Daiganji," followed by what Nakamura suggests may have been Sonkai's monogram (J. *kaō*).[15] Two lines are written on the third panel. The first line reads, "The entrance gate nameboards of Chosŏn's Kyŏngbok Palace are as follows." The next line reads, "The Tongdae Gate is the Hŭngin Gate.[16] The first gate of Kyŏngbok Palace is the Kwanghwa Gate.[17] Next is the Hongye Gate.[18] Next is the Kŭnjŏng Gate.[19] (The color of the Kŭnjŏng Hall nameboard is gemstone blue.)[20] The Kŭnjŏng Hall." The account continues on the third panel:

(Regarding Inkan, he was a generous person who gave much to people and had a heart as broad as the great ocean. Securing his status suddenly, Inkan's position was higher than even the peaks of Mount Sumeru. Dōhon entrusted the mission to this sort of person. Making many excuses, Inkan abandoned the mission in Tsushima.)

Regarding the monk Yudono Dōhon of Daiganji, on the island of Itsukushima,[21] Aki Province: Although Daiganji possessed the Buddhist scriptures (*Issaikyō*), the texts were old and only fragments remained. In order to secure a complete collection for future generations, Dōhon came to the temple and became one of its monks. There also was a monk named Inkan. Dōhon entrusted Inkan with this wish and dispatched him [on 1537.8.2] to Suō Province. Inkan received documents from Ōuchi Yoshitaka, organized the gifts for the King of Chosŏn,[22] and departed for Hakata. [The date was 1538.5.12.]

At Daiganji there was a person named Sonkai, who was from Hera estate[23] in Aki Province. He was appointed to accompany Inkan and subsequently joined him in Hakata. They boarded a ship on 7.1 and arrived at Iki on 7.8. Setting sail the next day, 7.9, they arrived at Fuchū, in Tsushima,[24] before dawn on 7.10.

In Tsushima, the ship captains could not be decided upon, but on 9.2 the mission settled on two ship captains. One was a man from Tsushima [Sō Magozaburō Nagayuki],[25] the other a man from Yamaguchi, in Suō Province [Watanabe Uemonnosuke]. These two men were the ship captains.[26]

[It was the spring of 1539.] Meanwhile, Inkan said, "One night I had a dream. Although we went to Chosŏn, they had a reason for why the sutras were not available." He visited the Hachiman shrine in Fuchū and drew a fortune. The fortune stated that there would be no scriptures. Inkan subsequently spoke to the two captains. Blaming "official matters," he told them to drop this pursuit and halted the mission.

(On 1539.3.5 there was a large fire in Fuchū. It seemed as if there were thousands of fires all at one time. Inkan and the two captains did not contact each other for more than twenty days.)

As the mission had been interrupted, before this news reached others, Sonkai assumed responsibility and continued to Chosŏn to determine whether the scriptures were available or not. [At this time I became Envoy,[27] and I led the mission from Izu(hara). On 4.14] we departed Fuchū, and arrived at the port of Pusan (Fu-sa-n-ka-i), in Chosŏn, on 5.9.

(At their departure, I said to Inkan, "I hope you will pray that we obtain the sutras." Inkan grew angry and said, "Both ships should meet with disaster and I curse the attainment of sutras." This occurred on 3.20.)

5.12	Pusan and Tongnae (To-ku-ne-gi) officials[28] met us at the [Japan House's] main hall[29] and served various drinks.
6.8	A court interpreter arrived from Hansŏng. [His name was Secretary Chang.][30] We were provided envoy meals[31] from 6.11.
6.12	There was a banquet.[32]
6.14	There was a banquet.[33]
6.15	Seven persons departed on the water route.[34] [There were ninety-three *t'a* of baggage.][35]
6.18	Eight persons departed on the overland route. [There were one hundred persons.][36] Both officials accompanied us, and there were drinks and a sendoff. We arrived in Yangsan (Ri-ya-gu).
6.19	We arrived in Ŏnyang (O-i-ni-ya-gi).
6.20	We arrived in Kyŏngju (Ke-gu). There is a large bell here.[37]
6.21	There was a banquet.[38]
6.22	We arrived in Yŏngch'ŏn (E-gu-se-n).
6.23	We arrived in Sillyŏng (Shi-ne-gi).
6.24	We arrived in Ŭihŭng (U-i-fu-gu).
6.25	We arrived in Ŭisŏng (U-i-se-n).
6.26	We arrived in Andong (An-to-gi).
6.27	There was a banquet.[39]
6.28	We arrived in Yŏngch'ŏn (E-gu-se-n).
6.29	We arrived in P'unggi (Fu-n-gu-i).

Intercalary 6.1

    We arrived in Tanyang (Ta-i-ni-ya-gi). [Here the official in charge of the baggage[40] returned to his home.]

Intercalary 6.2

    We arrived in Ch'ungju (Chi-gu).

Intercalary 6.3

> There was a banquet.[41] [From here, we traveled by boat on the river.][42]

Intercalary 6.4

> We arrived at Kahŭng (Ka-wa-gu).

Intercalary 6.5

> We arrived at Hŭngch'ang (Ho-a-ku-sa-n).[43]

Intercalary 6.6

> We arrived in Yŏju (Re-i). There was a banquet.[44]

Intercalary 6.7

> We arrived at Taet'an (A-ne-ri).

Intercalary 6.8

> We passed through Pongan (Ho-a-n) and arrived at Tumo-p'o (Tsu-mu-su-ka-i).[45] On this day, we entered the capital[46] and lodged at the Hall of Eastern Peace.[47]

Intercalary 6.13

> We presented gifts and offered our greetings.[48]

Intercalary 6.16

> There was a banquet conducted by the Board of Rites.[49]

[On this day, I presented the letter from Yoshitaka. When I requested the sutras, the Board of Rites replied, "This country does not revere the Buddha. We have burned pagodas, and thus there are no scriptures."][50] We received alcohol and fruits three times from the King of Chosŏn and three times from the Board of Rites, as well as midday drinks.[51] This was repeated every fifth day.

8.13[52]   [We were greeted by the King of Chosŏn at the Kyŏnghoe Pavilion.[53] It was difficult to put into words.] We received gifts. [All fifteen of us were in attendance.][54]

8.15   [There was an imperial procession. It is called *aseri*.][55] The imperial procession was held at the Kŭnjŏng Hall.

8.23   There was an audience with the Board of Rites. [On this day, we appealed for the sutras. Although the appeal touched the hearts of the Minister and the Second Minister of the Board of Rites,[56] yet again it was not granted. All will be completely forgotten.]

8.28   [There was a farewell audience with the king. This audience is called *ateki*.][57]

> 9.4 [We received return gifts for the gifts we brought.] Also, among our requests,[58] these were met as presented.[59] [In Chosŏn there is an intercalary seventh month.]
>
> 9.13 [We departed the capital[60] and proceeded southward along the river by boat.] We received farewell gifts from the Board of Rites.
>
> 1539.9.10 Sonkai (*in*)
> Held by Daiganji, Itsukushima

The Mission Concluded

Inkan's prediction came true. Daiganji did not obtain sutras. Sonkai reported to Yoshitaka in 1540 and presented the King of Chosŏn's gifts. These included eight bolts (K. *p'il*; J. *hiki*) each of white cotton thread, white linen, and black fine linen; one tiger pelt; one leopard pelt; two catties (K. *kŭn*; J. *kin*) of white ginseng; and three measures (K. *tu*; J. *to*) of honey.[61] The monk then returned to Daiganji and reported to Dōhon. Yoshitaka later ordered Sonkai to survey the sutra holdings of temples in the provinces that he governed. Based on the monk's report, Yoshitaka transferred sutras from another temple to Daiganji.[62]

The Mission's Purposes

The *Sonkai tokai nikki* presents Korean tribute system procedures ranging from documentation, greetings, banquets, and other gatherings to travel within the peninsula. Specifically, Sonkai detailed regulations designed for contacts whom the Chosŏn court assigned to the second of the four hierarchical reception grades for Japanese and Ryukyuans. He also depicted the process by which envoys delivered their sponsors' petitions for sutras. On the other hand, the text written on the back of the folding screen obscures Yoshitaka's interests in trade by not specifying the goods brought or acquired and not discussing negotiations. Consideration of recent changes in Japanese trade in Chosŏn may, however, permit speculation about the cargo. The following sections will situate the mission in currents of Korean-Japanese/Japanese-Korean interaction. They review royal releases of sutras to Japanese, speculate about the trade conducted for Yoshitaka, and trace the rites and routes through which the Chosŏn court channeled Japanese envoys to and from Hansŏng and the king of Chosŏn.

Seeking Sutras

Japanese had been asking Korean kings for Buddhist scriptures since 1388.[63] Monarchs fulfilled more than fifty of the slightly more than one hundred known requests from Japanese and Ryukyuans. Approaches made on behalf of Japanese temples that had petitioned the sponsor were common in the late fifteenth century.[64] The Ōuchi were an excellent choice for sponsorship, though Daiganji's superiors had no other choice given their temple's location in Ōuchi territory.

This family, and especially the Sō, had helped the Korean government steer Japanese from piracy to trade in the 1390s and the early fifteenth century. The Ōuchi also escorted royal embassies from Akamagaseki (today Shimonoseki) to Kyoto and back, thereby protecting royal letters, gifts, and envoys from pirates active in the Inland Sea. Korean kings released scriptures to the Ōuchi and the Sō as rewards for such assistance during the Chosŏn government's first decades. The court continued to so favor the Ōuchi, the Sō, and the sitting and retired shoguns into the late fifteenth or early sixteenth century. These royal bestowals came to be based over time more on past practice than on current contributions to security, trade, and state-level diplomacy.

Korean officials and their kings, especially monarchs from King Sŏngjong (r. 1469.11–1494.12) on, displayed less affinity for Buddhism than had their predecessors. On the enthronement of the youthful Sŏngjong, whose grandfather, King Sejo (r. 1455.Intercalary 6–1468.9), had supported the religion through policy, piety, and performance, court officials rescinded many of Sejo's policies and ensured that the youthful ruler received a Confucian education. In 1490, as it gathered texts for a bestowal to Ōuchi Masahiro, the Board of Rites wrote to Masahiro, "The King does not believe in the Buddha's teachings."[65] The constant requests may have grown tiresome.

Sonkai received an even stronger denunciation of Buddhism. In one of its replies to him, the Board of Rites stated that Chosŏn did not follow the Buddha's teachings, pagodas had been burned, and no more scriptures remained. Though an exaggeration, the comment underlined the firmness of the refusal. The Chosŏn court may also have been telling Japanese to stop requesting sutras.

Trade, Silver, and Smuggling
Obtaining sutras was not the sole intention of the Japanese that sponsored those requests. Trade goods accompanied the missions. The Ōuchi and Ashikaga (as the King of Japan, the King of Chosŏn's diplomatic status equal) often appointed a monk from the temple desiring scriptures as the envoy. In such instances, another member of the mission probably managed the trade in Chosŏn. This likely was the case with the mission led by Sonkai. The monk did note that the Korean government had responded favorably to the mission's "requests." This likely referred to exchange with the Board of Rites.[66]

The Sonkai account is silent regarding the specific items in the cargo, but information in the diary and recent trends in trade may help in speculating about the objects carried to the peninsula. In Chosŏn, Korean porters and ships moved ninety-three horse loads (K. *t'a, ta*; J. *da*) of goods from Pusan to the capital. Weights used in the early Chosŏn period require further clarification, and the calculations here should not be considered conclusive, but ninety-three horse loads may have exceeded six tons.[67]

The veritable records for King Chungjong's reign (r. 1506.9–1544.11) typically do not identify the gifts and trade goods carried to the capital. From the late fourteenth century on, Japanese exchanged Southeast Asian goods such as dyes, medicines, and spices for cotton, various cloths, and other items. Through networks that extended from Southeast Asian polities into Chosŏn, Japanese traders acquired these goods in Ryukyu and then exchanged them in Japan and/or Chosŏn. Items from Japan, with the exception of copper, other metals, and inkstones, attracted less interest. However, trade patterns changed in the late 1520s.

The Ōuchi regained control of Hakata in 1479, after having been pushed out of the port city early in the Ōnin War, and without doubt maintained close relationships with the city's merchants. In the 1520s the Hakata merchant Kamiya Jutei helped introduce to the Iwami area a silver extraction technique learned from Koreans, one the Koreans had learned from Chinese.[68] By 1528 Japanese were trying to trade silver for immense quantities of cotton and cloth. Silver also fueled a lively smuggling trade with Korean officials and merchants.[69] A memorial to the king submitted by eleven high-ranking officials on 1538.8.19 stated that they had heard that "the Japanese who have now come to Chosŏn brought only silver."[70] Two months later the court permitted the Shōni to trade 375 catties of the metal.[71]

Illicit trade in silver between Japanese and Koreans was of such concern that Korean officials were discussing how to prevent smuggling two months after Sonkai left the capital. The court had just learned that two officials had gone to Che-p'o (in Ungch'ŏn County, Kyŏngsang Province), which also was open to Japanese trade, and obtained silver. They then forwarded the silver to an individual in the capital who would facilitate its exchange in China.[72] When in 1542 an imposter shogunal envoy outfitted almost certainly in Hakata and Tsushima wished to trade 80,000 *yang*, or perhaps nearly 3.33 tons, of silver, a long discussion at court about how to respond ensued.[73] Might the potential profits from trading silver in Chosŏn in the late 1530s have contributed to the decision to stay in Tsushima for nine months, from 1538.7 to 1539.4? Perhaps the ships were waiting for a delivery from Iwami or elsewhere along the western coast of Honshu or via Hakata.

Regardless of what the cargo may have been, by continuing on to Chosŏn after Inkan's desertion of duty, Sonkai fulfilled Yoshitaka's interest in trade and his temple's desire for the sutras. Of course, the mission could not have but proceeded to Chosŏn. Trade must have been an important consideration, for it was to be conducted on behalf of the sponsor of the mission and the sutra request.

Proceeding Up to the King of Chosŏn

Identification, Status, and Banquets

The King of Chosŏn interacted with Japanese and Ryukyuan elites through their envoys according to a carefully organized complex of regulations and rites. Specifics of interaction differed per the four reception grades and per diplomatic statuses within reception grades. The court placed the Ōuchi in the second reception grade and later added Muromachi bakufu contacts. Only "kings," or Japanese shoguns, a retired shogun, and monarchs of Ryūkyū ranked higher.[74]

The envoy and the letter addressed to the Second Minister of the Board of Rites represented Yoshitaka to the Korean government. Royal recognition initiated the sequence of bestowals that permitted the contact to move through the tribute system. When Yoshitaka's ships arrived at Pusan-p'o, local officials reviewed the documents and reported to the provincial governor, who then informed the Board of Rites. On bestowing recognition to Yoshitaka, whose letter bore the imprint of a copper seal that the King of Chosŏn had given the family in 1453, the monarch ordered the Board of Rites to send a court interpreter (K. *kyŏng t'ongsa*) to the port. In Pusan-p'o was the Japan House (K. *Waegwan*), a compound where embassies and trade missions stayed at Korean government expense. The court interpreter conveyed the royal welcome in the compound's main hall (K. *taech'ŏng*). The communication of the mission's arrival to Hansŏng, administrative processing, and the court interpreter's travel to Pusan-p'o accounts for the time between Sonkai's meeting with local officials on 5.12 and the royal greeting on 6.8.

The King of Chosŏn interacted directly and symbolically with maritime elites at these state functions in the provinces. Though absent in body, he was present in status, authority, and power. At the banquets and the royal audience for tributary contacts, too, the court reconstituted power relationships between the king and the contact, the king and the envoy and his assistants, the king and his officials, and his officials and the guests.

The regulations for interaction reduced the privileges at each reception grade and diplomatic status. For example, the number of banquets held on the journey from the port to the capital and back decreased per reception grade.[75] The Korean government prepared the most banquets for Japanese "kings" and Ryukyuan kings. En route to the capital, officials prepared three banquets at the Japan House, three in Kyŏngsang Province (one province banquet hosted by the provincial governor and two county banquets hosted by magistrates), one province banquet in Ch'ungch'ŏng Province, and one province banquet in Kyŏnggi Province. The envoys of the King of Chosŏn's diplomatic equals within the Ming China–centered tribute system participated in a total of eight banquets.

Envoys representing contacts in the second reception grade attended two fewer gatherings from the port to Hansŏng. Government officials hosted two at the Japan House, two in Kyŏngsang Province (one province banquet and one county banquet), and one province banquet each in Ch'ungch'ŏng Province and Kyŏnggi Province.[76] The court interpreter led the two gatherings at the Japan House. Sonkai's banquets matched the schedule for contacts of the second reception grade.[77] After departing the Japan House, the monk participated in the county banquet in Andong, which the Special City Magistrate (K. *Taedohobusa*, senior third grade) hosted.

In Ch'ungch'ŏng Province, the governor hosted the gathering at the provincial capital of Ch'ungju. The governor of Kyŏnggi Province, though, was to meet Sonkai at Yŏju, which was not the capital but a city (K. *mok*). The multiple diplomatic travel routes that passed through this province complicated the geography of diplomatic ritual there. Kwangju, the provincial capital, was on a different route from Pusan to Hansŏng than that which Sonkai traveled. If the Governor of Kyŏnggi Province met Sonkai, he traveled to Yŏju. If he did not attend, the Yŏju City Magistrate likely presided.

From Yŏju, Sonkai sailed the Han River to Tumo-p'o on the north shore of the Han River and in the Hansŏng Magistracy (K. Hansŏng-bu). The manner in which he entered the capital is not related in the account or generally in Korean records, but an official escorted the retinue from Tumo-p'o through the East Gate (K. Tongdaemun) into the city and then to the Hall of Eastern Peace (K. Tongp'yŏnggwan), where Japanese and Ryukyuan embassies and missions stayed. Within the Hansŏng Magistracy, the royal welcome of contacts at the second, third, and fourth reception grades occurred at the Hall of Eastern Peace, not at Tumo-p'o as for the King of Chosŏn's diplomatic status equals.[78]

In the capital, the calendar featured gatherings with the King of Chosŏn and the Board of Rites. As the court did not restrict the number of days that missions could spend in Hansŏng, there was no time frame within which the rites had to be conducted. Thus could Chungjong's meeting with Sonkai be postponed due to hot weather and held one month later.[79]

At the banquet presided over by the Board of Rites, Japanese guests bowed before Korean officials. They performed at least two types of bows. In one written script, the Envoy of the King of Japan placed his knees and hands on the floor and touched his head to his hands (K. *kongsu chaebae*) before the banquet's convenor (K. *Abyŏngwan*) and the Minister of the Board of Rites. Prostrating more deeply before these two officials, the envoy's assistants touched their heads to the floor (K. *tonsu chaebae*). The form of bodily reply by Korean officials varied depending on the diplomatic status of the contact.[80]

The meeting with the King of Chosŏn was the culmination of the series of diplomatic rites, which also included a banquet with the Board of Rites. Envoys representing contacts of the second reception grade and lower presented the letters and tribute offerings (K. *chohŏn*) according to procedures designed for Korean officials' appearances before the monarch.[81] With the royal audience completed, the court and the guests turned toward another item on the ritual calendar, supplementary trade.

For Japanese such as Yoshitaka, the supplementary trade more likely was the culmination of the ritual calendar. During the one or more such meetings with officials of the Board of Rites and the Board of Taxation (K. Hojo), Sonkai or, more likely, others in the mission negotiated exchange values for the goods transported northward. Guests did not leave the capital until the supplementary trade and the open market trade that followed were concluded.[82] After the last meeting with the Board of Rites, at which the Japanese received farewell gifts, a court interpreter would have escorted Sonkai back to Pusan.[83]

Diplomatic Travel Routes

The route that Sonkai traveled to Hansŏng originated in the 1420s and 1430s. The systematization of diplomatic travel routes at that time contributed to the Chosŏn court's sharpened oversight of interaction in the peninsula. Guests now moved along roads that passed through local government seats, post stations (K. *yŏk*), and water transport stations (K. *such'am*). The courses from the ports to the capital (and back) were unique to diplomatic relations, but their component sections were not traveled solely by foreigners. The guests proceeded along roads that also conveyed Korean officials, written communications, supplies, taxes, and other matters. Domestic administration contributed to the management of diplomacy.

During the Chosŏn government's first decades, Japanese departed from the ports for Hansŏng when they wished, were not escorted by Korean officials along the paths that they chose, and often injured people and stole objects. In the early 1420s, the court was channeling retinues departing from the open ports of Che-p'o and Pusan-p'o along two overland routes and one river route (K. *suro*), selecting the road based on the quantity of goods to be carried northward. The river route was designed in order to reduce damage along the overland routes, but progress by river had to continue overland while still in Kyŏngsang Province because the capital could not be reached by water. In 1432, the court specified one overland route each from Che-p'o, Pusan-p'o, and Yŏm-p'o. Although the number of courses varied over the fifteenth and sixteenth centuries, retinues departing from Pusan-p'o passed through government installations on the routes outlined in 1423 and 1432.[84]

As noted, the Korean government absorbed the economic costs associated with reception, entertainment, trade, transportation, and lodging. The court also ordered Koreans living along the routes to assist in moving guests and their baggage. These impositions were heavy and unceasing. During the first ten-plus months of 1447, for example, Koreans transported northward some two thousand horse loads of Japanese baggage.[85]

The pace through the provinces added to the cumulative burden that interaction imposed on local residents and the provincial and local economies. Travel to Hansŏng in the first half of the fifteenth century could consume, with delays, thirty or forty days, as well as the requisite food, water, and other supplies.[86] In 1471.4 the court squeezed travel time to between thirteen and twenty-one days depending on the port of departure, the type of route, and the specific route.[87] These calendars proved optimistic, though, and several years later the court extended each by five days.[88] Sonkai's retinue reached Hansŏng at this slower pace.

En route to the capital, the Korean government tried to prevent guests from straying off course or lingering at pleasurable locations such as hot springs. To avoid still further mischief, Japanese were not to spend evenings in villages. Care also was taken to prevent the ransacking of post stations.[89]

In 1438 the court modified the diplomatic travel routes because more Japanese missions were arriving at Che-p'o than at the other two ports. Two tracks now connected the monarch and this port, one of them being the course from Pusan-p'o charted in 1432. Retinues departing from Pusan-p'o and Yŏm-p'o, which were east of Che-p'o, followed the Yŏm-p'o–Hansŏng course recorded in 1432.[90] By funneling groups proceeding from Pusan-p'o and Yŏm-p'o along a single road the court narrowed the geographic range of impositions on villagers and enhanced oversight. An intention behind adding a second path from Che-p'o may have been to spread impositions in that area more broadly. The Korean government used these channels for more than thirty years. The ensuing discussion of diplomatic travel routes will focus on Pusan-p'o.

Korean officials divided Sonkai's retinue into two groups at Pusan-p'o. The first group accompanied the goods upriver. It rejoined the second group, which had moved overland and included Sonkai, near Sangju, Kyŏngsang Province, beyond which ships carrying Japanese goods sailed no farther.[91] This course resembled the Yŏm-p'o river designated route set in 1471,[92] and the banquets for Sonkai matched those scheduled in that route's itinerary.[93]

Leaving Pusan-p'o, the court interpreter led Sonkai to Yangsan and then northward to Ŏnyang and Kyŏngju. From Kyŏngju the retinue continued overland to Ch'ungju. From Ch'ungju these Japanese traveled by river to Tumo-p'o, Kyŏnggi Province.

The river route from Pusan-p'o, as preserved in the 1585 edition of a 1554 Korean text of which no printings or manuscript copies are extant, helps chart the monk's progress between Ch'ungju and Hansŏng. The *Kosa ch'waryo* shows a passage from Mowŏl to Kŭmch'ŏn, Kahŭng, Hŭngwŏn, Yi-p'o, Taet'an, Pongan, Amhoesa-ch'am, and Tumo-p'o. In his diary, from Ch'ungju, Sonkai named Ch'ungju, Kahŭng, Hŭngwŏn (incorrectly listed as Hŭngch'ang),[94] Yŏju, Taet'an, Pongan, and Tumo-p'o. According to this itinerary, the province banquets for foreign rulers and contacts of the second reception grade were held in Ch'ungch'ŏng Province at Mowŏl, which was within the jurisdiction of Ch'ungju, and in Kyŏnggi Province at Yi-p'o, which was within the jurisdiction of Yŏju.[95] As Sonkai attended banquets in Ch'ungju and Yŏju, these gatherings may have been held at Mowŏl and Yi-p'o. That is, some of the identifications of counties in the diary may refer to the county rather than the site where the retinue lodged. Or the retinue may have stayed at several county seats en route. In the itinerary for the Left Road (K. *Chwano*) recorded in the 1585 edition are included thirteen county seats. The account records eleven of those seats. Among the eleven, Kyŏngju was only in the Left Road's itinerary. Regardless of where, specifically, the retinue lodged in each county, the diplomatic travel route on which the court interpreter guided Yoshitaka's mission as recorded by Sonkai closely resembles the Left Road as it was known in 1585.

The overland path on which the court interpreter led Sonkai indicates that the court had restored at least one overland route used prior to 1510 after the reopening of Pusan-p'o in 1521. From 1471.4 on, the second Pusan-p'o overland route and the single Yŏm-p'o overland route matched.[96] That route closely resembled the 1438 Pusan-p'o–Yŏm-p'o route. Sonkai's course even more closely resembled the 1438 Pusan-p'o-Yŏm-p'o route, which the court had modeled largely after the 1432 Yŏm-p'o route. That is, the overland route from Pusan-p'o that Sonkai followed originated in the 1432 Yŏm-p'o itinerary (if not in a path that the court introduced on opening Yŏm-p'o to Japanese trade and residence in 1427). As for the river route taken in 1539, the three 1471 river routes all proceeded from Ch'ungju through Kwangju, a city in Kyŏnggi Province.[97] As Pongan, through which Sonkai passed, was within the jurisdiction of Kwangju, it is probable that the river route preserved in the 1585 text was similar to that followed by Sonkai.

The overland route that Sonkai followed also closely resembled the Left Road, one of the three overland routes—the Central Road (K. *Chungno*), the Left Road, and the Right Road (K. *Uro*)—followed from 1547. These three overland routes recombined the paths that had linked the capital with Yŏm-p'o, Pusan-p'o, and Che-p'o. In addition, a river route also extended from Pusan-p'o. That course closely resembled, if it was not the same as, the itinerary set in 1471 for the Pusan-p'o river route (see table 3.1).[98]

Table 3.1: Diplomatic Travel Routes from Hansŏng to Pusan-p'o as Recorded in 1585

Central Road	Left Road	Right Road	River Route
Kwangju-mol	P'yŏnggu-yŏk (Yangju)	Yangjae-yŏk (Kwach'ŏn)	Tumo-p'o (Yangju)
Kyŏngan-yŏk (Kwangju)	Pongan-yŏk (Kwangju)	Aksaeng-yŏk (Kwangju)	Amhoesa-ch'am (Kwangju)
Yich'ŏn-bu**	Yanggŭn-gun	Yongin-hyŏn	Pongan (Kwangju)
Mugŭk-yŏk (Ŭmjuk)	Yŏju-mok**	Yangji-hyŏn	Taet'an (Yanggŭn)
Ŭmjuk-hyŏn	Anp'yŏng-yŏk (Yŏju)	Chuksan-hyŏn**	Yi-p'o** (Yŏju)
Ŭmsŏng-hyŏn	Kahŭng-yŏk (Yusin)	Chinch'ŏn-hyŏn	Hŭngwŏn (Wŏnju)
Koesan-gun**	Yusin-hyŏn**	Ch'ungju-mok**	Kahŭng (Ch'ungju)
Yŏnp'ung-hyŏn	Hwanggang-yŏk (Ch'ŏngp'ung)	Munŭi-hyŏn	Kŭmch'ŏn (Ch'ungju)
Anbo-yŏk (Yŏnp'ung)	Susan-yŏk (Ch'ŏngp'ung)	Okch'ŏn-hyŏn	Mowŏl** (Ch'ungju)
Mungyŏng-hyŏn	Tanyang-gun	Yŏngdong-hyŏn	Anbo (Yŏnp'ung)
Yugok-yŏk (Kaegyŏng)	P'unggi-gun	Hwanggan-hyŏn	Yugok-yŏk (Kaegyŏng)
Hamch'ang-hyŏn	Yŏngch'ŏn-gun	Ch'up'ung-yŏk (Kŭmsan)	Hamch'ang-hyŏn
Sangju-mok*	P'yŏngŭn-yŏk (Yŏngch'ŏn)	Kŭmsan-gun	Naktong (Sangju)
Sŏnsan-bu	Ongch'ŏn-yŏk (Andong)	Puyŏ-yŏk (Sŏngju)	Wŏlp'a-jŏng** (Sŏnsan)
Haep'yŏng-hyŏn (Sŏnsan)	Andong-taedoho-bu**	Sŏngju-mok**	Haep'yŏng (Sŏnsan)
Indong-hyŏn	Unsan-yŏk (Andong)	Mugye (Sŏngju)	Yangmok (Indong)
P'algŏ-hyŏn (Sŏngju)	Ŭisŏng-hyŏn	Hyŏnp'ung-hyŏn	P'algŏ (Sŏngju)
Taegu-bu**	Ch'ŏngno-yŏk (Ŭisŏng)	Ch'angyŏng-hyŏn*	Tong-wŏn (Sŏngju)
Kyŏngsan-hyŏn	Ŭihŭng-hyŏn	Yŏngsan-hyŏn	Habin (Taegu)
Sŏnghyŏn-yŏk (Ch'ŏngdo)	Sillyŏng-hyŏn	Yŏngp'o-yŏk (Ch'irwŏn)	Hwawŏn (Sŏngju)

Central Road	Left Road	Right Road	River Route
Ch'ŏngdo-gun	Yŏngch'ŏn-gun*	Ch'angwŏn-bu**	Kayi (Sŏngju)
Yuch'ŏn-yŏk (Miryang)	Ahwa-yŏk (Kyŏngju)	Chayŏ-yŏk (Ch'angwŏn)	Sangsan (Hyŏnp'ung)
Miryang-bu**	Muyang-yŏk (Kyŏngju)	Kimhae-bu	Kaesan (Koryŏng)
Mugŏl-yŏk (Miryang)	Kyŏngju-bu**	Yangsan-gun	Samak** (Ch'ogye)
Hwangsan-yŏk (Yangsan)	Cho-yŏk (Kyŏngju)	Yongdang (Yangsan)	Magu-wŏn (Ch'angnyŏng)
Yangsan-gun	Kuo-yŏk (Kyŏngju)	Pusan-p'o (Tongnae)	Kisan (Sŏllyŏng)
Sŏsan-yŏk (Tongnae)	Ulsan-gun		Puldang-wŏn
Pusan-p'o (Tongnae)	Kangok-yŏk (Ulsan)		Yogwang (Yŏngsan)
	Awŏl-yŏk (Kijang)		Chumulyŏn (Ch'angwŏn)
	Sŏsan-yŏk (Tongnae)		Susan (Miryang)
	Pusan-p'o (Tongnae)		Toyojŏ (Kimhae)
			Yongdang (Yangsan)
			Kamdong-p'o (Tongnae)
			Pusan-p'o (Tongnae)

Source:

Ŏ Sukkwŏn, *Kosa ch'waryo*, 11a–12b.

Notes:

The itineraries begin with the place closest to the capital, thus identifying the location of the king as the beginning of these routes. The travel traced began in Pusan, though, and the title of this section in the *Kosa ch'waryo*, "Waein chogyŏng toro," or "Routes to the Capital for Japanese," reflects the departure from Pusan-p'o. Within the itineraries is an instance of inconsistent editing, presumably from after 1567.10. The Left Road has the retinues stopping at Yusin, Ch'ungch'ŏng Province, but the River Road pauses at Ch'ungju. As outlined in note 93, the Chosŏn court changed the name of Ch'ungju to Yusin and reduced the county's administrative status in 1549. The court renamed the county Ch'ungju and restored its earlier administrative status in 1567.10 (*Sŏnjo sillok*, 1:2a–b [1567.10.12]). As Yusin was the county name when Ŏ Sukkwŏn completed the *Kosa ch'waryo* in 1554, the listing of "Ch'ungju" in the River Road itinerary may indicate an instance of editing after 1567.10. Further, that Yusin appears in the 1585 text indicates that the Chosŏn court had designed these diplomatic travel routes prior to 1567.10. I have added the county names identified in parentheses.

A single asterisk indicates the site of a banquet for "kings" as recorded in the *Kosa ch'waryo*. Two asterisks indicate the site of banquets for "kings" and contacts of the second reception grade as recorded in the *Kosa ch'waryo*.

The following administrative terms are used.

Bu (or Pu)	Special Capital
Taedohobu	Special City
Mok	City
Gun (or Kun)	Great County
Hyŏn	County or Small County
P'o	Port
Yŏk	Post Station
Wŏn	Rest Station
Ch'am	Water Transport Station

En route to the capital Sonkai stayed in or passed through centers at several levels of Korean administration. He encountered officials at the following hierarchy of administrative seats: provincial capital, Special Capital (K. *pu*); Special City (K. *taedohobu*); City; Great County (K. *kun*); County and Small County (K. *hyŏn*); port; post stations; and water transport stations. The last two facilities were especially important in the coordination of official travel as well as the conveyance of taxes and other objects. Less numerous on the Central Road and the Right Road, these stations totaled seventeen of the thirty-one stops on the Left Road.[99]

The Board of Military Affairs (K. Pyŏngjo) oversaw the post stations, and the Board of Taxation and the Bureau of Ships (K. Chŏnhamsa) managed the Han River water transport stations. The stations performed several roles. They were links in official communications networks and were lodgings and supply depots for official travel.[100] The government organized the post stations into circuits (K. *yŏkto*); these were composed of from four to twenty-nine stations. Each station belonged to a county magistracy, and one station in each circuit served as the circuit's administrative center.[101] Sonkai entered at least four circuits en route to Hansŏng.

Water transport stations dotted the shores of the Han River. The court used them for moving goods into Hansŏng and Korean officials to and from the capital.

Two of the post stations that Sonkai noted, Hŭngwŏn and Kahŭng, also belonged to the network of water transport stations in the Left Circuit of Ch'ungch'ŏng Province (K. Ch'ungch'ŏng Chwado such'am).[102]

Among the post stations along the Left Road after 1547, three identified in the account were located on rivers. These were Yangsan, where Sonkai spent an evening; Kahŭng, where he also spent an evening; and Pongan on the Han River between Taet'an and Tumo-p'o. Yangsan was near the junction of the Hwangsan and Naktong rivers in Kyŏngsang Province.

Kahŭng also was the site of the Han River storehouse (K. *ch'ang*) for Ch'ungch'ŏng Province's Left Circuit. Tax goods from the Left Circuit and both circuits in Kyŏngsang Province were sent to and stored at Kahŭng. They were then delivered to the capital through water transport stations.[103] Include the Japanese retinues that passed through and Kahŭng becomes an even more vital intersection of administrative, communication, tax, and transportation networks.

Conclusion

Daiganji's wish for the Koryŏ *Tripitaka* provided Ōuchi Yoshitaka with another opportunity to trade in Chosŏn. The *Sonkai tokai nikki* relates the request for sutras and indicates that the Chosŏn court regularly implemented the tribute system regulations. The supervision of diplomatic travel also demonstrated the overlap of diplomacy and domestic administration. The monks of Daiganji probably judged the mission's success or failure by the request for sutras and Yoshitaka by the items traded, items acquired, and benefits achieved. But the diary does not detail the acquisition, transport, or exchange of goods. The *Sonkai tokai nikki* is an account of Daiganji's participation more so than a record of Yoshitaka's trade. The mission, though, was a Yoshitaka trade enterprise more so than a dispatch on behalf of the temple. That point is underscored if the wait in Tsushima was indeed related to the preparation of silver or other cargo for exchange in Chosŏn.

The "Eight Views of the Xiao and Xiang Rivers" and Sonkai's diary form a pair even as they remain distinct texts. Each is a representation of a foreign landscape, and each of a foreign landscape composed in Chosŏn. The painting is a Korean (re)production of a Chinese landscape in a Chinese style inflected with Korean accents. Like Chinese renderings of the Xiao and Xiang rivers,[104] this painting invited imaginary travel. The *Sonkai tokai nikki* is a written account of physical travel to the Chosŏn capital. The viewer of the Korean artist's painting and the reader of the Japanese monk's diary encountered foreign places made imaginable through visual and verbal projects. These two possibilities for travel intersected with the recording of Sonkai's travels on the back of the folding screen.

Notes

I wish to thank James B. Lewis and Leo Hanami for reading earlier drafts of this essay.

[1] *Sŏngjong sillok* 33:9b–10b [1473.8.9]; 103:7b [1479.4.7]; 183:6a–7a [1485.8.30]; 204:13b [1487.6.16]; 256:11b [1490.9.18].

[2] 1547.9.25 Daiganji Sonkai bugakuryō sōbun an narabi ni shake sanbō seishu uragaki an (*Daiganji monjo*, doc. 48, p. 1207); 1550.5.26 Daiganji Sonkai yuzurijō narabi ni Ōuchi-shi bugyōnin rencho uragaki (*Daiganji monjo*, doc. 55, p. 1215).

[3] Ahn Hwi-joon, "Two Korean Landscape Paintings of the First Half of the Sixteenth Century," pp. 36–37.

[4] For English-language comments on the Korean paintings, see ibid., pp. 36–40; and Ahn Hwi-joon, "Korean Landscape Painting of the Early and Middle Chosŏn Period," p. 9. For the "Eight Views of the Xiao and Xiang Rivers" landscape paintings in Japan in the fifteenth and sixteenth centuries, see P. Richard Stanley-Baker, "Mid-Muromachi Paintings of the Eight Views of the Hsiao and Hsiang"; and Carolyn Wheelwright, "A Visualization of Eitoku's Lost Paintings at Azuchi Castle," pp. 91–93, 305–306, notes 12–17. Wheelwright translated the title as *Eight Views of Hsiao and Hsiang*.

[5] Sekino Tadashi, *Chōsen bijutsushi*, pp. 257–258.

[6] Takeda Tsuneo, "Daiganji zō Sonkai tokai nikki byōbu," p. 130; Ahn Hwi-joon, "Two Korean Landscape Paintings of the First Half of the Sixteenth Century," pp. 37–38.

[7] An Hwijun, *Hanguk hoehwa ŭi chŏnt'ong*, pp. 176, 178.

[8] Itakura Masaaki, "Kankoku ni okeru Shōshō hakkei zu no juyō, tenkai," pp. 15–29.

[9] *T'aejong sillok* 17:27a [1409.Intercalary 4.11]; *Sejong sillok* 29:7a [1425.7.15]; *Sejong sillok* 52:23b [1431.5.21]; *Sejong sillok* 127:36a [1450.2.16]; *Sŏngjong sillok* 256:2b–3a [1491.8.4]; *Sŏngjong sillok* 289:5b–6a [1494.4.10]; *Yŏnsangun ilgi* 43:24a–b [1502.4.20].

[10] *T'aejong sillok* 16:2b [1408.7.6]; *Sejong sillok* 102:35b–36a [1443.12.11]; *Sŏngjong sillok* 158:14b [1483.9.13]; *Sŏngjong sillok* 182:10a–b [1485.8.30]; *Sŏngjong sillok* 244:11b [1490.9.18]; *Sŏngjong sillok* 281:22a–b [1493.8.11].

[11] *T'aejong sillok* 16:6a [1408.8.1]; 34:30a [1417.11.5].

[12] Nakamura Hidetaka, *Nissen kankeishi no kenkyū*, vol. 1, p. 729.

[13] *Sonkai tokai nikki*, in Nakamura, *Nissen kankeishi no kenkyū*, 1, pp. 730–732.

[14] *Sinjŭng Tongguk yŏji sŭngnam* (hereafter cited as *STYS*).

[15] Nakamura, *Nissen kankeishi no kenkyū*, 1, p. 730.

[16] *STYS* 1:15a; Nakamura, *Nissen kankeishi no kenkyū*, 1, p. 747, note 23. Nakamura suggests that this likely was the gate through which Sonkai entered the capital.

[17] *STYS*, 1:15a.

[18] Ibid., 1:17a.

[19] Ibid., 1:17a.

[20] Nakamura, *Nissen kankeishi no kenkyū*, 1, p. 742.

[21] Today this is Miyajima in Hiroshima Prefecture.

[22] The king of Chosŏn was King Chungjong. The text repeatedly refers to Chosŏn as Kōrai. Japanese often used this term in the fifteenth and sixteenth centuries. See Tanaka Takeo, *Taigai kankei to bunka kōryū*, pp. 336–342, for a discussion of the term during this period.

[23] Hera no shō (estate) was located in Sasai district of Aki province on the northwest coast of Hiroshima Bay and north of Itsukushima. The present city of Hatsukaichi, Hiroshima Prefecture, is located on the site. (*Nihon chimei daijiten* 34: *Hiroshima-ken*, Hera, p. 723; Sasai-gun, p. 390; Hatsukaichi, p. 646).

[24] The administrative center of Tsushima was called Fuchū from 1486 and was moved to Izuhara sometime between 1467 and 1492 (*Nihon chimei daijiten* 42: *Nagasaki-ken*, p. 856).

[25] He may have been Sabuei-dono Fukkan-no-hito Taira Nagayuki, who appears in the Korean veritable records in 1553.11 and 1554.3. See Nakamura, *Nissen kankeishi no kenkyū*, 1, p. 745, note 7; *Myŏngjong sillok* 15:58b [1553.11.30]; and *Myŏngjong sillok* 16:23b [1554.3.10].

[26] The cooperation of Tsushima islanders was essential for missions bound for the peninsula. This was another instance in which an islander served as ship captain. (Takahashi Kimiaki, "Jūroku seiki no Chōsen, Tsushima, Higashi Ajia kaiiki," p. 167).

[27] *Jōkanshi*. The religious names (J. *hōmyō*) of the envoys from before and after Inkan's resignation are not clear. Court officials referred to Ryūon Tōdō as Envoy (*Chungjong sillok* 91:53b [1539.8.13]). Nakamura suggests that Inkan was Ryūon Tōdō (Nakamura, *Nissen kankeishi no kenkyū*, 1, p. 735). Tanaka Takeo believes that Ryūon Tōdō became the envoy in Tsushima but does not specifically link the name with Sonkai (Tanaka Takeo, *Wakō to kangō bōeki*, p. 147).

[28] Nakamura believes that these officials were the Kyŏngsang Left Province Navy Deputy Commander, Pusan garrison (K. *Kyŏngsang Chwado Sugun Ch'ŏmjŏlchesa* [junior third grade {*Kyŏngguk taejŏn,* 4:8a (hereafter cited as *KT*)}]), and the Tongnae County Magistrate (K. *Tongnae Hyŏllyŏng* [junior fifth grade {*KT,* 1:46b}]). (Nakamura, *Nissen kankeishi no kenkyū,* 1, p. 735; *STYS,* 23:1b, 23:5a–b.) The Tongnae County Magistrate at this time was Chŏng Sup'aeng (*Tongnae-bu ŭpchi,* vol. 3, p. 358).

[29] *Teki,* or *taech'ŏng* in Korean. This term likely refers to one of the two types of *taech'ŏng* buildings within the hostel compound, the administrative halls and the residences (Nakamura, *Nissen kankeishi no kenkyū,* 1, p. 746, note 12).

[30] *Chaku semisemi* or the Sayŏgwŏn Ch'ŏmjŏng Chang (Nakamura, *Nissen kankeishi no kenkyū,* 1, p. 735). This may be Chang Sŏkchi (*Chungjong sillok,* 101:70a–b [1544.1.20]). *Sayŏgwŏn* refers to the Bureau of Interpreters, *Ch'ŏmjŏng* to the junior fourth grade post glossed here as "Secretary" (Nakamura, *Nissen kankeishi no kenkyū,* 1, p. 735; *KT,* 1:28b; *T'ongmungwan chi,* 1:1b; Ki-Joong Song, "The Study of Foreign Languages in the Yi Dynasty (1392–1910)," p. 33).

[31] *Kekki* or *kyŏkki* (*kyŏnggi*). This term is *idu.* It referred to the four meals served each day to the envoys (Nakamura, *Nissen kankeishi no kenkyū,* 1, p. 736; Sin Sukchu, *Haedong chegukki,* 113a–b [hereafter cited as *HC*]; Chang Chiyŏng and Chang Segyŏng, *Idu sajŏn,* p. 226).

[32] *Ihachi* or *ibachi* in dictionaries of modern Korean. This banquet corresponds to the first of the two port banquets to be held at the open ports for contacts of the second reception grade (Nakamura, *Nissen kankeishi no kenkyū,* 1, p. 736; *HC* 104a–b; *KT* 3:33a).

[33] This banquet corresponds to the second of the two port banquets to be held at the open ports for contacts of the second reception grade (*HC* 104a–b; *KT* 3:33a).

[34] If these individuals followed the route prescribed in 1471, they sailed the Hwangsan River and then entered the Naktong River (*Sŏngjong sillok* 10:4a–b [1471.4.9]).

[35] *T'a* refers to the amount of baggage carried by a horse. See note 67.

[36] This figure probably included the Korean escorts and porters, as well as the entourage of fifteen Japanese (Nakamura, *Nissen kankeishi no kenkyū,* 1, p. 737).

[37] This bell may be the Pongdŏksa bell, National Treasure no. 29, preserved today at the Kyŏngju National Museum. It is also known as the King Sŏngdŏk bell (K. *Sŏngdŏk taewang sinjong*) in honor of this Silla king, who ruled from 702 to 737. Cast in 771, this bell, according to its inscribed text and the *Sinjŭng Tongguk yŏji sŭngnam,* weighs 120,000 *kŭn,* and its peal is audible "100 *ri*" away. In 1460

the bell was moved to Yŏngmyosa, in Kyŏngju, and then to outside the southern gate of the city wall after a fire destroyed that temple. See *STYS*, 21:28a–29b; Yŏm Yŏngha, *Hanguk chong yŏngu, chŭngbop'an*, pp. 143–46, 161; and Lee Jang Moo, "The Divine Bell of King Sŏngdŏk," p. 271. For color photographs, see *Kungnip Kyŏngju Pangmulgwan*, pp. 30–31.

[38] *Ihachi*. This banquet corresponds to the first of the two to be held in Kyŏngsang Province. If the Chosŏn government required that Korean officials hold banquets for envoys of contacts of the second reception grade at the same locations, then, according to the *Haedong chegukki*, this first Kyŏngsang Province banquet was to be hosted by the Governor (K. *Kwanch'alsa*) of Kyŏngsang Province (*HC* 115a–b; *KT* 3:33a; Ŏ Sukkwŏn, *Kosa ch'waryo* [1585 ed.], B:41b). Kim Chŏngguk was appointed Governor of Kyŏngsang Province seven days before this province banquet. He arrived in Kyŏngju in the eighth month (*Chungjong sillok* 89:29a [1539.7.14]; *To sŏnsaeng an*, in *Kyŏngju sŏnsaeng an: Ojong*, p. 92). Prior to Kim Chŏngguk, Kang Hyŏn served as Governor from 1538.6. As Kang Hyŏn left Kyŏngju during the eighth month, he likely hosted this event (*Chungjong sillok* 87:53b–54a [1538.6.24]; *To sŏnsaeng an*, p. 92).

[39] This banquet corresponds to the second of the two to be held in Kyŏngsang Province. Following the *Haedong chegukki*, this county banquet was to be hosted by the Andong Special City Magistrate (K. *Taedohobusa*). See *HC* 115a–b; *KT* 3:33a; Ŏ Sukkwŏn, *Kosa ch'waryo* [1585 ed.], B:41b; and *STYS* 24:1a–2b. That official was either Yu Sŏng, whose appointment as Special City Magistrate ended in 1539, or Kim Malson, who began his term as Special City Magistrate in 1539 (*Yŏngga chi*, in *Chosŏn sidae sach'an ŭpchi 18, Kyŏngsang-do 3*, p. 293).

[40] *Sosoon*, or *ch'awŏn*.

[41] This banquet corresponds to the province banquet to be held in Ch'ungch'ŏng Province (*HC* 115a–b; *KT* 3:33a; *Kosa ch'waryo* [1585 ed.], B:41b). The Governor of Ch'ungch'ŏng Province in early 1539, intercalary 7, almost certainly was Ch'ae Segŏl. He had been appointed in 1539.2 (*Chungjong sillok* 89:49b [1539.2.9]).

[42] Han River. Travel on the Han River started at Ch'ungju (*HC* 121b). Sonkai had been led along the left road from Pusan as far as Tanyang.

[43] Hŭngch'ang was a mistake for Hŭngwŏn-ch'ang (Nakamura, *Nissen kankeishi no kenkyū*, 1, p. 731). Ŏ Sukkwŏn identified this stop as Hŭngwŏn (*Kosa ch'waryo* [1585 ed.], B:42b).

[44] This banquet corresponds to the province banquet to be held in Kyŏnggi Province (*HC* 115a–b; *KT* 3:33a; *Kosa ch'waryo* [1585 ed.], B:41b).

[45] See *Hanyang to*, in Hŏ Yŏnghwan, *Chŏngdo 600 nyŏn Sŏul chido*, p. 33, map 10. Tumo-p'o also was a site for departures by boat along the river (Kim Chongjik, "P'alwŏl ch'o kuil Tumo-p'o tŭngju," in *Chŏmp'ilche chip*, p. 300).

[46] Sonkai completed the trip from Pusan to Hansŏng within the prescribed twenty-one days (Nakamura, *Nissen kankeishi no kenkyū*, 1, pp. 737–738; *Taejŏn songnok*, in *Taejŏn songnok–Hu songnok*, 2:1b–2a).

[47] *Tongp'yŏnggwan*. On this day the envoy was to be greeted by the Ritual Guest Agency (K. *Yebinsi*), an office under the Board of Rites that was responsible for the entertainment of foreign guests (*KT* 3:33b; *STYS* 2:26a). See also *Sejong sillok* 22:22b [1423.12.20]; and *Sejo sillok* 24:23a [1461.6.8], for the Ritual Guest Agency at work in this capacity. This banquet was to be held on the envoy's arrival at the "*kwan*," which was the *Tongp'yŏnggwan*, where Japanese and Ryūkyūans stayed while in Hansŏng (*HC* 115b–116a). Sonkai does not refer to this banquet.

[48] *Shiffui*, or *sukpae*. This audience with the monarch corresponds to that prescribed in the *Haedong chegukki* and the *Kyŏngguk taejŏn* for contacts at the second reception grade (*HC* 117b; *KT* 3:33b). Nakamura suggests that Sonkai, as the envoy of Ōuchi Yoshitaka, presented two documents during this audience, which was held at the Kyŏngbok Palace. One document was the letter that Yoshitaka had addressed to the Second Minister of the Board of Rites (J. *Chōsen-koku Reiso Sanpan*; K. *Chosŏn-guk Yejo Ch'amp'an* [junior second grade {*KT* 1:11a}]). The other document was the list of Yoshitaka's gifts [J. *beppuku*]. That list is not extant (Nakamura, *Nissen kankeishi no kenkyū*, 1, pp. 733–734, 743). Nakamura believes that the *Geihan tsūshi* includes what may have been that letter from Yoshitaka. See Rai Kyōhei, *Geihan tsūshi*, vol. 1, pp. 399–400, for the text and the notice of the appended list of gifts; Nakamura, *Nissen kankeishi no kenkyū*, 1, pp. 733–734; and Kondō Seiseki, *Ōuchishi jitsuroku*, pp. 91–92.

[49] Reisu, or Yejo, the Board of Rites. This banquet corresponds to the banquet prescribed in the *Haedong chegukki* and the *Kyŏngguk taejŏn* for contacts at the second reception grade (*HC* 118a–b; *KT* 3:33b).

[50] Kang Hyŏn, now the second minister of the Board of Rites, explained in a written reply to Yoshitaka that the monarch had turned to Confucian writings and did not follow Buddhist teachings (*Geihan tsūshi*, vol. 1, p. 400). Kang's letter is dated 1539.9.[unspecified]. The ninth month in the Korean calendar corresponded to the eighth month in the Japanese calendar. Kang became Second Minister on 1539.7.25 and was reappointed Second Minister on 8.5 after the monarch had named another official to that post on 7.30 (*Chungjong sillok* 91:34a [1539.7.25]; *Chungjong sillok* 91:35b [1539.7.30]; *Chungjong sillok* 91:51a [1539.8.5]; Nakamura, *Nissen kankeishi no kenkyū*, 1, p. 748, note 29).

[51] *Chikunboi* or *chubongbae*. This follows the prescription in *HC* 119a–b.

[52] This audience was to have been held on 7.11 (Korean calendar: Intercalary 7.11), but the king postponed it because of the extreme heat (Nakamura, *Nissen kankeishi no kenkyū*, 1, p. 739; *Chungjong sillok* 91:43b [1539.Intercalary 7.11]). Ryūon was treated to drinks at this gathering, and each of the Japanese received gifts (*Chungjong sillok* 91:53b [1539.8.13]).

[53] Sonkai refers to the Kyŏnghoe Pavilion (K. *Kyŏnghoe-ru*), which was a common site for royal audiences with envoys during the spring and summer as the "Hasu no dairi." For such audiences, see *Sejo sillok* 12:18a [1458.5.15]; *Sejo sillok* 43:13b [1467.7.17]; *Sŏngjong sillok* 104:6a–b [1479.5.7]; *Sŏngjong sillok* 118:12a [1480.6.13]; *Sŏngjong sillok* 204:16b–17a [1487.6.27]; *Sŏngjong sillok* 205:12b [1487.7.21]; *Sŏngjong sillok* 256:17b [1491.8.28]; *Yŏnsangun ilgi* 43:22b [1502.4.12]; *Chungjong sillok* 54:37a–b [1525.6.1]; and *Chungjong sillok* 54:50a [1525.6.28]). According to the *Sinjŭng Tongguk yŏji sŭngnam*, "To the west of Sajŏng Hall is a pond that surrounds the pavilion. The pond is deep and wide. Planted in the pond are lotus flowers. There also are two islands in the pond" (*STYS* 1:18b). More specifically, Chungjong held the greeting at the Kyŏnghoe Pavilion (*Chungjong sillok* 91:53b [1539.8.13]).

[54] This was the number of Japanese in the retinue. It matched the regulation for contacts of the second reception grade (*HC* 114a).

[55] A ceremony was held on this day, the day of the harvest moon, or *ch'usŏk*. Nakamura suggests that *aseri* was a corruption of the Korean "*hajŏl*" (celebration) and referred to *ch'usŏk*. If envoys were in the capital on that day, the Chosŏn court invited them to participate in the ceremony (Nakamura, *Nissen kankeishi no kenkyū*, 1, p. 742; *Chungjong sillok,* 91:54a [1539.8.15]).

[56] The two terms in the text are *seikan* (K. *chŏnggwan*) (Minister [K. *P'ansŏ*, senior second grade]) and *fukkan* (K. *pokkwan*) (Second Minister [K. *Ch'amp'an*, junior second grade]). The Minister at the time of both meetings was Yi Kwiyang (*Chungjong sillok* 91:16b–17a [1539.6.10]; 91:47b–49b [1539.8.4]; 92:68b [1540.1.18]). The Second Minister was Kang Hyŏn. The Minister typically handled Chosŏn court contact with the Ōuchi (and the other Japanese contacts at the second reception grade) in the mid–fifteenth century (Takahashi Kimiaki, "Gaikō girei yori mita Muromachi jidai no Nitchō kankei," pp. 75–79). By 1485.10.8, the Second Minister had become the official responsible for written communication with the Ōuchi (*Sŏngjong sillok* 184:5a–b [1485.10.8]).

[57] This audience corresponds with the audience prescribed in the *Haedong chegukki* and *Kyŏngguk taejŏn* for the second reception grade (*HC* 117a; *KT* 3:33b). *Ateki* may be a rendering of the Korean *hajik* (Nakamura, *Nissen kankeishi no kenkyū*, 1,

p. 739). This Korean term appears in *HC* 117b–118a. According to Arai Hakuseki, the *hajik* took place when the Japanese envoy was preparing to leave and thus was the farewell audience with the king (*Chōhei ōsetsuki*, p. 690).

[58] *Kussegi,* or *kuch'ŏng.*

[59] Nakamura dates the letter from Kang Hyŏn addressed to Ôuchi Yoshitaka to this entry (Nakamura, *Nissen kankeishi no kenkyū*, 1, p. 743). Kang's letter is dated 1539.9.[unspecified]. See Nakamura, *Nissen kankeishi no kenkyū*, 1, p. 744, for the full text; and *Geihan tsūshi*, vol. 1, 400, or Kondō, *Ōuchishi jitsuroku*, p. 94, for Nakamura's source.

[60] Similar to the envoy's arrival in the capital, a reception was to be held on the envoy's departure (Nakamura, *Nissen kankeishi no kenkyū*, 1, p. 739; *HC* 115b–116a; *KT,* 3:33b). See *Sejong sillok* 23:13a [1424.2.4], for an example of the Ritual Guest Agency providing a meal at the Han River for a departing Japanese envoy. Also see *Sejong sillok* 6:15a [1419.12.14], for the greeting of an arriving shogunal envoy. Tumo-p'o also was the site of farewell gatherings for officials assigned to governor, magistrate, and other posts outside the capital (Sŏ Sŏngho, "Chosŏn-ch'o Han-gang ŭi uisang kwa yŏnan chiyŏk ŭi hyŏnhwang," pp. 7–8).

[61] *Geihan tsūshi*, vol. 1, p. 400.

[62] Nakamura, *Nissen kankeishi no kenkyū*, 1, p. 744; Undated Daizōkyō mokuroku-ko kakiutsushi (*Daiganji monjo*, doc. 41, pp. 1197–1198).

[63] For sutras in Korean-Japanese/Japanese-Korean interaction, see Kenneth R. Robinson, "Treated as Treasures: The Circulation of Sutras in Maritime Northeast Asia from 1388 to the Mid–Sixteenth Century," pp. 33–54.

[64] *Sŏngjong sillok* 33:9b–10b [1473.8.9]; 103:7b [1479.4.1]; 202:15a [1487.4.26]; 204:13b [1487.6.16]; 244:11b [1490.9.18].

[65] Ibid., 246:8a [1490.10.14].

[66] See Nakamura, *Nissen kankeishi no kenkyū*, 1, p. 743.

[67] The account is not clear whether this unit of weight followed the Korean measure or the Japanese, assuming these differed. In the early Chosŏn period one *t'a* equaled 100 *kŭn* (*KT* 3:32a, 4:23b). One *kŭn* equaled 16 *yang* (*KT* 6:2a). One *yang* may have been equivalent to 37.30 grams, but this particular calculation introduces a Chinese measure for *yang* into the equation (Wang Yi-t'ung, *Official Relations between China and Japan, 1368–1549*, p. 117). One *kŭn* by this calculation was equivalent to 596.8 grams. Multiplied out, 100 *kŭn* and 1 *t'a* were each equivalent to 59,680 grams or 131.45 pounds. By this method of calculation, the 93 *t'a* equaled 12,225 pounds. Calculating from the *kŭn* and its conversion into

kilograms as provided in an article on a Silla period bell, the weight of the goods transported to Hansŏng becomes 3,487.5 kilograms or 7,682 pounds (see Lee Young-bae, "The Bell of Sangwonsa Temple," p. 87). Wang Yi-t'ung calculated one Japanese *da* at 193.65 pounds. (Wang, *Official Relations between China and Japan, 1368–1549*, p. 117). At this rate, 93 horse loads total 18,009 pounds. In his translation of the Japanese poet Sōchō's diary from the 1520s, H. Mack Horton assesses 1 Japanese *da* at 133 kilograms or 36 *kan* (H. Mack Horton, *The Journal of Sōchō*, p. 292, note 246). Multiplied out, 93 Japanese *da* total 12,369 kilograms or 5,611 pounds. Thirteen years later, the Chosŏn court changed or introduced regulations that limited the weight of goods that the King of Japan, the Ōuchi, and the Shōni could forward to the capital. From 1552.4, the court permitted the King of Japan 150 horse loads and the Ōuchi and the Shōni 70 horse loads. Each bundle was to weigh 50 catties or 29,840 grams or 65.79 pounds (*Kaksa sugyo*, pp. 34–35).

[68] Kobata Atsushi, *Nihon kōzanshi no kenkyū*, pp. 51, 110; Kobata Atsushi, *Kingin bōekishi no kenkyū*, pp. 110–114, 227.

[69] Yi Ŏnjŏk, *Hoejae sŏnsaeng pyŏlchip*, 1:20a–21a; Murai Shōsuke, *Umi kara mita sengoku Nihon: Rettōshi kara sekaishi e*, pp. 160–175.

[70] *Chungjong sillok* 88:10b–11b [1538.8.19].

[71] Ibid., 88:64b–65a [1538.10.29].

[72] Ibid., 92:30b–31a [1539.10.23]; 92:31b–32a [1539.10.24]; 92:32a–33a [1539.10.24].

[73] Yongho Ch'oe, "Precious Metals," pp. 597–600.

[74] *Sejong sillok* 124:19a [1449.6.14]; *HC* 111b.

[75] The banquet schedules in this and the next two paragraphs are from *HC* 115a–b.

[76] Ibid., 115a–b.

[77] *Ibid.,* 114a–115a; Nakamura, *Nissen kankeishi no kenkyū*, 1, p. 736.

[78] *HC* 115b–116a. This gathering also was to be held as the envoy was leaving. On one occasion the veritable records identify the site of the gathering for the departing Japanese envoy as the Chech'onjŏng, a pavilion on the north side of the Han River (*Sŏngjong sillok* 80:10a [1477.5.29]; *STYS* 3:24b).

[79] *Chungjong sillok* 91:43b [1539.Intercalary 7.11]; 91:53b [1539.8.13].

[80] *Sejong sillok* 133:49a–50a; *HC* 124b–125a.

[81] *Sejong sillok* 132:23a–b; 132:24a–b; 133:47b–48b.

[82] For an example, see ibid., 98:9b–10a [1442.11.20].

[83] *HC* 115a–b.

[84] Nakamura, *Nissen kankeishi no kenkyū*, 1, pp. 500–506; *Sejong sillok* 19:24a–b [1423.3.12]; *Sejong sillok* 55:4a [1432.1.8].

[85] *Sejong sillok* 118:11a–b [1447.11.26]. This calculation also causes concern.

[86] Ibid., 10:4a–b [1471.4.9] for travel requiring up to thirty or forty days; *Munjong sillok* 5:51b [1451.1.20] for comments on the provision of food.

[87] *Sŏngjong sillok* 10:4a–b [1471.4.9]; *HC,* 121a–122a.

[88] *Taejŏn songnok* 3:1b–2a.

[89] *KT* 3:33b.

[90] *Sejong sillok* 55:4a [1432.1.8]; 80:21a [1438.2.15].

[91] Nakamura, *Nissen kankeishi no kenkyū*, 1, p. 737. Nakamura suggests that missions probably came ashore at the Naktong Station near Sangju (1, p. 507).

[92] *Sŏngjong sillok* 10:4a–b [1471.4.9]; *HC* 121a–122a; *Taejŏn songnok* 3:1b–2a.

[93] *Kosa ch'waryo* (1585 ed.), B:41b. There is one difference between the Sonkai account and this Korean source. Whereas in 1539 Sonkai participated in a province banquet at Ch'ungju, the capital of Ch'ungch'ŏng Province, the *Kosa ch'waryo* placed that gathering in Yusin. This seeming discrepancy may be explained by an administrative change. In 1549, the court renamed Ch'ungju as Yusin and reduced the county's administrative status from City to Small County (*Myŏngjong sillok* 9:47a [1549.5.21]). Ŏ Sukkwŏn completed the *Kosa ch'waryo* in 1554, but the earliest extant text contains information probably no older than 1585, hence the title of table 3.1.

[94] See note 43.

[95] *Kosa ch'waryo* (1585 ed.), B:42a–b; *STYS* 7:4a–b.

[96] *Sŏngjong sillok* 10:4a–b [1471.4.9]; *HC* 121a–122a; *Taejŏn songnok* 3:1b–2a.

[97] *Sŏngjong sillok* 10:4a–b [1471.4.9]; *HC,* 121a–122a; *Taejŏn songnok* 3:1b–2a.

[98] *Kosa ch'waryo* (1585 ed.), B:11a–12b; *Sŏngjong sillok* 10:4a–b [1471.4.9]; *HC* 121a–122a.

[99] *Kosa ch'waryo* (1585 ed.), B:11a–12b.

[100] For post stations in the early Chosŏn period, see Cho Pyŏngno, "Chosŏn chŏngi yŏngno chŏngbi wa yŏngma kakpo," pp. 233–280; Ch'oe Wangi, "Kyot'ong-Unsu-T'ongsin: Toro ŭi chŏngbi; Yŏk-wŏnje ŭi chŏngbi; Susang kyot'ong kwa

choun," pp. 495–538; and Rokutanda Yutaka, "Chōsen ōchō jidai no kōtsū seido to shukuhaku shisetsu," pp. 6–9.

[101] Yukkun Ponbu, ed., *Hanguk kunjesa: Kŭnse Chosŏn chŏngi p'yŏn*, pp. 552–554; *KT,* 1:46b–49a.

[102] Rokutanda Yutaka, "Richō shoki Kan-kō no sutan seido ni tsuite," pp. 90–96.

[103] Rokutanda Yutaka, "Richō shoki no denzei unsō taisei: Kakudō tani ni mita sono seibi hensen katei," pp. 115–119.

[104] See Valérie Malenfer Ortiz, *Dreaming the Southern Song Landscape: The Power of Illusion in Chinese Painting*, pp. 6–7; and Alfreda Murck, *Poetry and Painting in Song China: The Subtle Art of Dissent*. Murck emphasizes political dissent in her reading of the "Eight Views." She writes, "For scholar-officials cast out of the center, the Eight Views became a painted equivalent to the poetry of complaint, the visual counterpart to the melancholy literature written in and about the XiaoXiang" (p. 3). Elsewhere, she states that painters "intended their paintings, like their poems, to have more meanings than were accessible to an uninitiated viewer" (p. 61). Murck's argument invites consideration of how Korean elites, and government officials in particular, interpreted Chinese and Korean representations of the "Eight Views" in the Koryŏ and Chosŏn periods.

Part Two

Arts and Aesthetics

4

The Mongol Invasions and the Making of the Iconography of Foreign Enemies: The Case of *Shikaumi jinja engi*

Haruko Wakabayashi

In 1592, while preparations for his invasion of Chosŏn Korea were under way, Toyotomi Hideyoshi summoned the priest of Kisshōji of Shikanoshima of Chikuzen Province to his palace, Jurakutei, in Kyoto. The priest brought three scrolls that depicted the legendary conquest of the three ancient Korean kingdoms of Silla, Paekche, and Koguryŏ by Empress Jingū and presented them to Hideyoshi. The chronicler in the *Taikō gunki* notes that "it was as if signs of auspices that he shall achieve his goals had been unfolded before his eyes."[1] Hideyoshi rewarded the priest with garments, gold, and silver.

Kisshōji was a shrine-temple (*jingūji*) of the Shikaumi shrine, located on the island of Shikanoshima in Hakata Bay.[2] The island is known for the discovery in 1784 of the gold seal granted by the Chinese emperor to "King Nu of Wa" in 57, as the site from which Empress Jingū and her troops set out for the Korean Peninsula in the third century, and as a battleground during the second Mongol Invasion in 1281. The Shikaumi shrine enshrines the three gods of the sea, Nakatsuwatatsumi no kami, Sokotsuwatatsumi no kami, and Uwatsuwatatsumi no kami. Ancient records identify these gods and Azumi no Isoramaru, the god of Shikaumi who served as the captain of the ship on which Empress Jingū sailed, as the ancestral gods of the Azumi clan.

It is quite possible that the three scrolls that the priest brought are the same Hachiman *engi* scrolls that are presently possessed by the Shikaumi Shrine, known as the *Shikaumi* (or *Shikanowata*) *jinja engi* (fig. 4.1). The above anecdote in the *Taikō gunki* suggests that the reputation of the scrolls of Shikanoshima had reached the capital by the late sixteenth century. It also reflects the popularity of Empress Jingū and her child, Emperor Ōjin (who was believed to be an incarnation of Hachiman) in the face of foreign battles, and it provides an example of how paintings depicting the conquest were perceived.

This essay explores the significance of the *Shikaumi jinja engi* as an example of how medieval Japanese perceptions of the foreign other were constructed after the Mongol Invasions. This particular set of scrolls is historically notable for the following three reasons. First, dated by art historians to the Nanbokuchō period (1336–1392), it is one of the earliest of the surviving illustrated accounts of Empress Jingū's expedition. Second, it is important that this early Hachiman *engi-e* was handed down in a shrine in Kyushu, where contacts with the continent were most frequent and direct. Indeed, the legends of Empress Jingū and the birth of Hachiman both take place in Kyushu, and specific local sites are identified in each scene. This point is especially important when thinking about the impact of the Mongol Invasions on the shaping of the medieval accounts of the Jingū legend.

Third, the enemy warriors depicted in the painting are strikingly similar to the Mongols that are illustrated in the *Mōko shūrai ekotoba*. Although art historians have touched on this fact, its significance in the context of the development of the medieval mentality remains unexplored. Illustrated accounts of the legend of Empress Jingū appear only after the Mongol Invasions, and, needless to say, the Mongol Invasions took place in Kyushu. It is therefore worthwhile to investigate how this experience of direct confrontation with foreign aggressors led to the construction of an iconographic tradition of "foreign enemies."

Through a study of the *Shikaumi jinja engi*, I wish to examine the early stage of the visual representation of the legend of Empress Jingū, especially the iconography of the foreign enemies, the significance of its production site, Kyushu, and the influence of the Mongol Invasions in the process.

The Illustrated Hachiman engi from the Post-Mongol Invasions Era

The story of Empress Jingū and her conquest of the Three Kingdoms first appears in the *Kojiki* and the *Nihon shoki* and has been repeatedly told at moments of national crisis and resurgent patriotic sentiments. According to the *Nihon shoki*, Empress Jingū, upon the death of her husband, Emperor Chūai, went to sea to conquer the kingdoms in the west. Because she was pregnant at the time, she placed a stone in her womb so the baby would wait to be born until she completed her expedition. As soon as she left the harbor, a strong wind blew, the waves rose high, and a big fish appeared from the sea to push her ship, enabling her to reach the kingdom of Silla swiftly and with ease. The king of Silla, having witnessed this miracle, immediately surrendered, and the kings of Koguryŏ and Paekche followed. The empress thus successfully subjugated the Three Kingdoms. On returning to Japan, she gave birth to the prince, who later became Emperor Ōjin.[3]

Throughout the ancient and medieval periods, Hachiman shrines promoted the cult through their histories, *Hachiman engi*, asserting their god's contribution to the defense of the country from foreign intrusions and victory over enemies of the imperial house, which included the "rebels" in northeastern Japan. The Mongol Invasions of 1274 and 1281, especially, gave Hachiman shrines all over

Japan the opportunity to emphasize the power and virtues of Hachiman. Many shrines that offered prayers for conquering the foreign enemies regenerated their histories so that they could be used to demand rewards from the bakufu. The most famous Hachiman *engi* from the post–Mongol Invasions period is the *Hachiman gudōkin*, written in the late thirteenth to early fourteenth centuries. Its author is believed to have been closely associated with the Iwashimizu Hachiman shrine and its involvement in the war efforts against the Mongols.[4]

A number of illustrated Hachiman *engi* (Hachiman *engi-e*) were also produced during the centuries following the invasions, among them the scrolls of Shikanoshima. Consequently, many of the surviving Hachiman *engi* are dated from the late Kamakura and early Muromachi periods.[5] These Hachiman *engi-e* have been categorized by the art historian Miya Tsugio into two groups according to their style and content:[6]

Group A
San Francisco Asian Art Museum copy (1389)[7]
Tomofuchi Hachiman Jinja copy [Wakayama][8]
Itsuō Museum copy [Osaka][9]
Akagi Bunko copy [formerly the property of Ena Hachimangū] (1402)
Hachiman Natanomiya copy [Ōita] (1421)
Kokubungaku Kenkyū Shiryōkan copy (1466)
Hama Tenjin copy [Hyōgo] (1527)
Tenri Library copy (1531)
[In addition to the above, the recently discovered Idemitsu Art Museum copy (1322) should belong to group A.][10]

Group B
Iwashimizu Hachimangū copy [lost due to fire] (1433)
Honda Hachimangū *Jingū Kōgō engi* (1433)[11]
Tōdaiji copy (1535)[12]
Yusuhara Hachimangū copy (1549?)[13]

Of the group B scrolls, both the Iwashimizu Hachimangū and Honda Hachimangū copies were produced under the commission of the sixth Ashikaga shogun, Yoshinori. According to records, he commissioned three scrolls— Iwashimizu, Honda, and Usa—in 1433 and offered each to the corresponding shrine. These scrolls are believed to have been the prototypes for the Tōdaiji and the Yusuhara copies.

Miya discusses the differences and similarities between the motifs and texts of the two groups. He notes several significant stylistic differences in both text and painting, three of which are as follows.

> 1. The literary texts of the scrolls belonging to group A use *katakana* and are based on a *kanbun*–style literature, whereas group B texts use *hiragana*. This suggests that the texts of the two groups come from different prototypes.
> 2. The texts of group A scrolls have stronger regional qualities, suggesting that they may be closer to the archetypal text derived from Kyushu legends.
> 3. The artistic skill of group A scrolls is cruder and more amateurish. It is a style that emerged in the Nanbokuchō period and is different from the traditional elitist *Yamato-e* style. The prototype was probably not done by a professional painter but by a talented amateur. On the other hand, the more detailed and colorful paintings of the group B scrolls, all of which were commissioned by courtiers, can be placed along the lines of the aristocratic *edokoro* (workshop).

Miya concludes that the group A scrolls came first, and the group B scrolls were produced based on the former. During the process, the verbal texts were revised in accord and with the text of the *Hachiman gudōkin*.

Miya's studies have been regarded as the preeminent work on Hachiman *engi-e*. However, it is important to note that regardless of the fact that some of the Kyushu paintings are dated earlier than any of those mentioned above, and Miya himself suggests that the earlier, group A paintings reveal regional qualities, he downplays these Kyushu paintings as a mere variant version that comes not in horizontal, hand scroll form but in a vertical, hanging scroll (*kakefuku*) format. There are a number of noteworthy medieval Hachiman *engi* paintings in Kyushu. Of these, the *Shikaumi jinja engi-e* and *Tamataregū engi* were produced earlier than or roughly in the same period as the scrolls in group A.

Kyushu Paintings
Shikaumi jinja engi-e (early to late fourteenth century)
Tamataregū engi (1370)[14]
Kōra Taisha engi (late Muromachi)[15]
Chiriku Hachimangū engi-e (around 1590)[16]

These Hachiman scrolls, all of which come in the vertical, hanging scroll format, come in pairs, with one scroll depicting the shrine complex and the other the Jingū legend. The *Shikaumi jinja engi* is unique in that it uses two scrolls to depict the legend.

Watanabe Yūji conducted a close study of the Hachiman *engi* in Kyushu and compared them with the hand scrolls.[17] He concludes that the Kyushu scrolls more faithfully depict the tale of Emperor Ōjin's birth (including Empress Jingū's conquest of the Three Kingdoms) as it is told in the *Hachiman gudōkin*. In this sense, the Kyushu paintings may be associated in terms of both period and region with the development of the *Hachiman gudōkin*, which was composed relatively soon after the Mongol Invasions. He further suggests that the *Hachiman gudōkin* is heavily based on regional legends and myths of Kyushu.

With the above studies in mind, let us now move on to study the *Shikaumi jinja engi* and examine where this painting can be placed among the surviving medieval Hachiman *engi-e*. One aspect that I wish to emphasize is the significance of the place of its transmission, Kyushu. Both Miya and Watanabe overlook this point, having worked under the assumption that information travels from the center to the periphery. In the case of the visual iconography of foreign enemies, however, the situation may have been otherwise. The alien aggressors were first witnessed in Kyushu, where their imagery was produced, and then transmitted to the capital through such works as the *Mōko shūrai ekotoba* and the Hachiman *engi-e*.

The *Shikaumi jinja engi* and the Narratives of Empress Jingū's Expedition

The *Shikaumi jinja engi* is a set of three scrolls that are done in color on silk, each roughly 155 x 85 cm in size. Of the three, the one that illustrates the shrine complex is dated to the Kamakura period. It is likely that this first scroll, painted in a style clearly different from that of the other two scrolls, was originally produced independently as a *keidai ezu* (illustrated map of the shrine complex) or *miya mandara* (shrine mandala).[18] The other two scrolls, dated to the mid– to late fourteenth century, illustrate the legendary conquest of the three ancient kingdoms of the Korean Peninsula by Empress Jingū. Both Fukushima Tsunenori, who has conducted the only close study of the *Shikaumi jinja engi* as of today, and Watanabe Yūji think that all three scrolls were produced in the central Kinai region by a professionally trained Yamato-e artist and that the latter two were produced sometime in the mid–fourteenth century. This makes the Shikaumi scrolls distinct from the other *kakefuku*-style Hachiman *engi-e* in Kyushu, the earliest dated being the scrolls at Tamataregū (1370), which are known for their crude and regional quality and are assumed to have been produced by local artists.

The history of Shikanoshima well attests to its intimate relations with the capital. From the late Heian to Nanbokuchō times, Shikanoshima is known to have belonged to a group of *shōen* estates collectively called the "Chōkōdō-ryō." Chōkōdō was a private Buddhist sanctuary (*jibutsudō*) built by Emperor Go-Shirakawa (1127–1192) in his own residence. The number of *shōen* donated to it totaled 180 in provinces from Dewa in the northeast to Higo and Hizen in the southwest, and it was one of the largest clusters of imperial estates.[19] It is therefore not surprising that as an imperial estate Shikanoshima had close contacts with the people and culture of the central Kinai region and that the scrolls illustrating the shrine and legends pertaining to it were made by a court artist. At the same time, the resemblance of the scrolls' motifs and narrative to the other Kyushu scrolls, as shown below, suggests that the Shikaumi scrolls are clearly a product of an amalgam of regional and central cultural traditions.

Although there is no verbal text to the *Shikaumi jinja engi,* inscriptions on the painting, possibly used as a reference for *etoki* storytelling, give us an idea of its narrative content. The narrative can be recounted as follows (by following the numbers in Figure 4.1).[20]

Screen One

1. At the time of Emperor Chūai's death, Empress Jingū climbed Mount Shiōji in Chikuzen (in present-day northern Fukuoka Prefecture), attached a golden bell to the *sakaki* tree, and prayed to the gods of heaven, earth, and the sea so that she would successfully conquer the foreign land. In the painting, the empress is attended by the gods Kōra and Sumiyoshi.

2. At Kashii, she made a coffin of gold for Emperor Chūai and placed the coffin on top of a pasania tree (*shii*).[21]

3. She also performed two rituals as told by Amaterasu. First, she dipped her hair in the river and waited for the daughters of the water god and the Dragon King to come and divide her hair in two.

4. Then she caught a meter-long *ayu* fish with a straight needle and no bait.

5. *Kagura* dances and songs were performed to invite Azumi no Isora (a manifestation of the god Shikaumi).

6. Isora appeared, exposing his ugly form.[22] In the painting, Isora is depicted with a white cloth that covers his face, riding on a turtle.

7. The empress was pleased to see Isora. She then went to Toyora (present Shimonoseki) and logged trees for her ships from Funakiyama. In Usa (present Ōita Prefecture), she built forty-eight ships and brought them to Shikashima. She appointed Isora captain of her ship.

8. Toyohime (Empress Jingū's sister) returned from the Dragon King's palace with the magical *kanju* (tide-ebbing jewel) and *manju* (tide-raising jewel).

9. The empress found a white stone, cooled her womb with the stone, and placed a rock between her legs so that the baby would wait to be born until the expedition was completed.

10. The empress put on armor made of gold and set out for the peninsula.

Figure 4.1: Screen One: A numbered guide to the *Shikaumi jinja engi*

Screen Two

11. The Japanese force consisted of only forty-eight ships and 375 men. The empress threw the *kanju* into the sea, and the sea suddenly dried up. The enemy forces were elated to see this; they descended from their ships and attacked on foot.
12. The enemy consisted of 108,000 ships and more than 496,000 men.
13. When the *manju* was thrown into the sea, the sea again filled with water and the enemy soldiers were drowned.
14. The foreign king and his ministers pledged that, since Japan is protected by Heaven, no one would ever attack her. Then Kashii Daibosatsu engraved the words "the King of Ko[gur]yŏ is Japan's dog" on a rock along the coast.
15. Ten days after her return to Japan, the empress gave birth to a prince on Mount Shiōji. The prince, who later became Emperor Ōjin, is the Hachiman Daibosatsu.

To examine where the *Shikaumi* text can be placed among other narratives of the same legend, let us now compare the above with the texts of other medieval Hachiman *engi*. Chart 4.1 shows the variations in the narrative as seen in medieval Hachiman *engi-e* texts and the *Hachiman gudōkin*. The prototype of the above narrative can be found in the *Kojiki* and the *Nihon shoki*.[23] Some significant differences between the *Shikaumi jinja* narrative and the *Kojiki* and *Nihon shoki* versions are as follows.

   1. *There is no mention of Kyushu gods in the* Kojiki *and the* Nihon shoki. The two texts do not mention the regional gods that play important roles in the *Shikaumi jinja engi,* including Kōra Daimyōjin, Kashii Daibosatsu, and Azumi no Isora (Shikaumi Daimyōjin). The rituals performed by the empress prior to her departure for Silla in the Shikaumi text are also locally specific. First, she climbs Mount Shiōji, attaches golden bells to the *sakaki* tree, and prays to the gods. Then she places Emperor Chūai's gold coffin on top of a pasania tree at Kashii. Next she dips her hair in Kashii Bay and fishes for *ayu* in the Tamashima River in Matsura, Hizen Province (in present-day Saga and Nagasaki Prefectures). Each of these rituals is associated with a particular location in northern Kyushu, and it is not surprising to see them depicted in these Kyushu paintings. While the gods Kōra, Kashii, and Shikaumi do not appear in the *Kojiki* and *Nihon shoki*, all of the rituals described here are included in both. This suggests that the *Shikaumi* text is based on local legends, some of which are old enough to be included in the *Kojiki* and *Nihon shoki*.

   2. *There is no battle scene in the* Kojiki *and* Nihon shoki. According to the *Kojiki* and *Nihon shoki,* as Empress Jingū's troops set off for the peninsula, a strong wind blew and a big fish came out of the sea and pushed the empress's

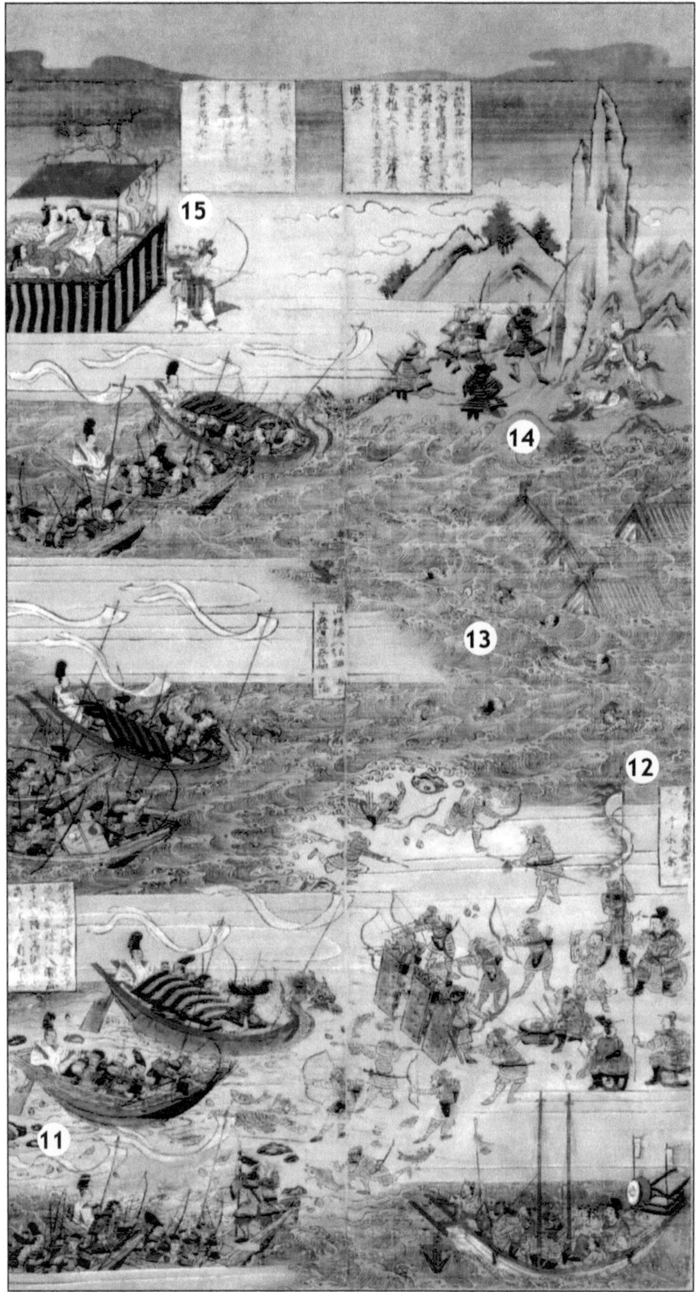

Figure 4.1: Screen Two: A numbered guide to the *Shikaumi jinja engi*

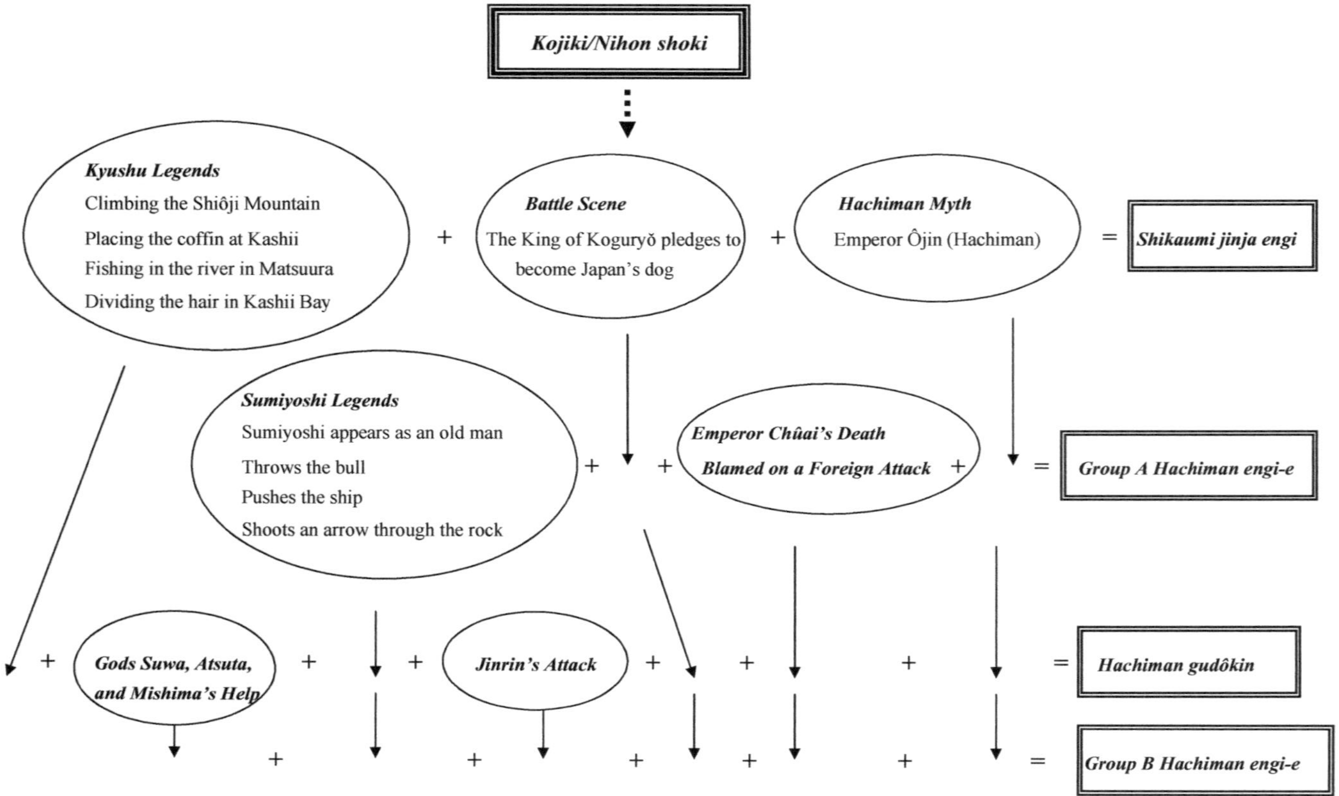

Chart 4.1: Narratives

boat. Having witnessed this miracle, the kings of Silla, Koguryŏ, and Paekche immediately surrendered and pledged to send tribute to Japan. In other words, there is no detailed and vivid description of the battle like that found in the *Shikaumi* narrative, nor is there any mention of the miraculous jewels borrowed from the Dragon King. Nor is the king of Koguryŏ degraded as "Japan's dog" in the *Kojiki* and *Nihon shoki* texts (although the king of Silla pledges to become the royal stable groom and Paekche pledges to accept imperial rule).

3. *There is no connection made between the Great Bodhisattva Hachiman and Emperor Ōjin in the* Kojiki *and* Nihon shoki. The connection between Hachiman and Emperor Ōjin is believed to have been made later in the Nara period.[24]

4. *The main target of subjugation in the* Kojiki *and* Nihon shoki *is Silla, whereas in the* Shikaumi *narrative it is Koguryŏ, referred to as Koryŏ.* It is highly possible that the middle character, *gu*, was intentionally dropped to represent Koryŏ, which was founded in 918 and continued until 1392 and from which the Mongol forces sailed, instead of Koguryŏ, one of the three ancient kingdoms.

The narratives of the group A and group B scrolls, and the *Hachiman gudōkin*, tell versions of the legend that differ slightly from the *Shikaumi* text.

A. *While the Shikaumi text does not explain why or how Emperor Chūai died, group A and group B scrolls and* Hachiman gudōkin *blame the death of Emperor Chūai on a foreign attack.* Whereas both the *Kojiki* and *Nihon shoki* describe his passing as a "sudden death due to divine punishment," later medieval texts specify different causes of the emperor's death. The group A scrolls, for example, explain that Emperor Chūai died in Kyushu while confronting the forces from Silla.[25] The *Hachiman gudōkin* and group B scrolls state that the emperor was shot by a stray arrow after having slain an eight-headed demon, Jinrin, which flew from Silla to attack Japan.[26] Neither the *Kojiki* nor the *Nihon shoki* associate the death of Emperor Chūai with any of the Three Kingdoms. The idea of a foreign invasion that killed Emperor Chūai and thus induced Empress Jingū's expedition is a later addition that became extremely popular after the Mongol Invasions. In this sense, the narrative of the *Shikaumi jinja engi*, which mentions no foreign invasion, is closer to the *Kojiki* and *Nihon shoki* texts than any other medieval versions of the legend.

B. *The gods Kōra, Kashii, and Sumiyoshi are important in the Shikaumi narrative, Sumiyoshi plays a central role in both group A and group B scrolls, and Suwa, Atsuta, and Mishima are mentioned, among others, in the* Hachiman gudōkin *and the group B scrolls.* The key deities in the *Shikaumi* narrative are Kōra and Sumiyoshi, who appear when Empress Jingū climbs Mount Shiōji; Azumi no Isora (the god of Shikaumi), who acts as the captain of the empress's ship; and Kashii, who engraves the words "the King of Ko[gur]yŏ is Japan's dog" on the rock along the coast. Kōra, Sumiyoshi, Shikaumi, and Kashii are worshipped at major shrines in northern Kyushu.[27] The central god in both group A and group B is Sumiyoshi, who appears as an old man constantly demonstrating his power. For example, a large bull suddenly appears offshore and attacks the empress's ship. At that moment, the old man grabs the bull's horns and throws it into the water. At a place called Ōegasaki, the water suddenly dries up and the ship is stranded. At that time, too, the old man pushes the ship offshore, all alone. Furthermore, on their way to the peninsula, the old man shoots an arrow through a rock, again impressing the empress with his extraordinary power. This old man is also the one who tells Empress Jingū about the Dragon King's jewels and summons Azumi no Isora to the empress. Today there are three major Sumiyoshi shrines—in Fukuoka, Shimonoseki, and Ōsaka. The one in Fukuoka claims to be the oldest, and the Ōsaka Sumiyoshi Shrine is known today as the head shrine (*sōhongū*). At this point, it is difficult to ascertain whether it was the cult in the Kyushu or the Kinai region that prompted the development and spread of the Sumiyoshi episode in the Jingū legend. It is highly possible that the legend had its origins in Kyushu but was propagated by the central authorities, which venerated Sumiyoshi.[28] Finally, the gods Suwa, Atsuta, and Mishima are mentioned, among others, in the *Hachiman gudōkin* and group B scrolls. The author of the *Hachiman gudōkin* is believed to have been associated with the Iwashimizu shrine in Kyoto, and the first copies of the group B scrolls, as mentioned earlier, were commissioned by the Ashikaga shogun in the capital. Hence, we naturally encounter gods from regions other than Kyushu.

As seen in chart 4.1, medieval narratives of the Hachiman *engi* developed as new legends pertaining to regional and central shrines and locations were added to the earliest surviving tale from the *Kojiki* and *Nihon shoki*. The chart shows that the *Shikaumi* text is a relatively early and simple version of the narrative. The variance among the texts reflects the differences in the interests of the commissioners and producers of each narrative. Judging from the format, the hanging scrolls of Kyushu were most probably used for *etoki*, to be narrated to a popular audience. In this sense, they must respond to the interest of their local audience and therefore include legends from the vicinity and mention the achievements of gods who were worshipped at local shrines. Compared to the *Kojiki* and *Nihon shoki* texts, the *Shikaumi* text, for example, more specifically relates an event to a local site. Scrolls belonging to group A and group B have less inclination toward Kyushu myths but stronger emphasis on the god Sumiyoshi and his achievements. Group B scrolls and the *Hachiman gudōkin* mention gods and shrines from regions other than Kyushu, reflecting the centrality of their production site. Furthermore, episodes about the invasion of the Three Kingdoms and the humiliating pledge made by the Koguryŏ king become standard events in the narratives produced after the Mongol Invasions. This suggests that the experience of Mongol aggression had an impact on the development of the hostile attitude toward Koryŏ that is reflected in the narratives.

The *Shikaumi jinja engi* and the Mongol Invasions

On looking at the *Shikaumi jinja engi,* one would soon notice the striking resemblance of its portrayal of the enemy troops to the depiction of Mongols in the *Mōko shūrai ekotoba.*[29] This is important since we do not necessarily see this resemblance in the other Hachiman *engi* scrolls. In many of the other scrolls, enemies are demonized. They are depicted standing behind shields bearing the faces of demons or are even disfigured into demonic figures. In contrast, the enemies in the *Shikaumi jinja engi* are depicted "accurately" as humans and foreign warriors. In this section, I wish to look into surviving texts that are known for vivid accounts of the battles fought between the Mongol and Japanese forces, namely, the *Mōko shūrai ekotoba* and the *Hachiman gudōkin.* I will then compare their depictions of the Mongols with the enemies depicted in the *Shikaumi jinja engi* and examine the significance of any resemblance.

The illustrations of the *Mōko shūrai ekotoba* give a clear visual representation of the Mongol forces and in many ways are comparable to those found in the verbal account of the *Hachiman gudōkin.* In describing the physical features of the Mongols, for example, the *Hachiman gudōkin* says:

> [The messenger] was accompanied by the black Mongol and the white Mongol (*kuro mōko, shiro mōko*). The white Mongol's body was white, and even his hair was white. The black Mongol's body was dark, and all of his features were dark.[30]

Indeed, looking at the *Mōko shūrai ekotoba,* some of the Mongols are depicted as light colored, and others as dark colored (fig. 4.2). The artist deliberately made a distinction between *kuro mōko* and *shiro mōko.*

The Mongols also wore distinctive armor, described in the *Hachiman gudōkin* as "light so that they can easily mount the horse."[31] From what we see in the *Mōko shūrai ekotoba,* the Mongols wore a heavy garment (not a piece of armor) and a distinctive helmet with a furlike decoration on the sides and a featherlike ornament

Figure 4.2: Scene from the Mongol Invasion scroll (*Mōko shūrai ekotoba*)

on the top. Other types of armor are also depicted—more armorlike uniforms that protect the wearer's whole body and helmets with flaps on both sides that cover and therefore protect the neck and shoulders (fig 4.3 and 4.4).[32]

Figure 4.3: Scene from the Mongol Invasion scroll (*Mōko shūrai ekotoba*)

Figure 4.4: Scene from the Mongol Invasion scroll (*Mōko shūrai ekotoba*)

From the portrayal of the Mongols in the *Mōko shūrai ekotoba*, we can also speculate that the Mongols were fierce and well-equipped soldiers. They surprised the Japanese soldiers by fighting in a manner quite different from the way in which the Japanese were accustomed to fighting.[33] In fig. 4.3, for example, arrows and spears are being discharged. The uniquely shaped bows and the cone-shaped bow and arrow case especially catch the eye of the viewer. The bows that have a grip in the middle are Song-style short bows.[34] Long bows without the grip were used as well, but their principal weapons were the short bows, which had a range of about two-hundred meters, and the soldiers who carried the short bows carried many short arrows in the arrow case. The number of these short arrows, which they discharged in rapid succession, determined their combat strength.[35] These depictions correspond to the verbal description of the first invasion in the *Hachiman gudōkin*.

> The Mongol arrows were short, yet they poisoned the tips of the arrows; therefore, those who were shot by the arrows were affected by the poison. Several tens of thousands shot arrows and threw spears in array, so that they were discharged at us like rain.[36]

Most important, this scene depicts the famous iron bombshell labeled *teppō*. According to Joseph Needham, this is the only surviving picture of the thirteenth-century explosive known in Chinese records as the "thunder-crash bomb."[37] *Hachiman gudōkin* describes its effects.

> Our soldiers were frightened out of their wits by the thundering explosions; their eyes were blinded, their ears deafened, so that they could hardly distinguish east from west.[38]

Other notable props are the gongs and drums that were used to coordinate their units (fig. 4.3). According to the *Hachiman gudōkin*:

> They beat their drums and gongs . . .[and] the loud noise scared the Japanese horses [so] that they could not move forward or backward . . . . The commanding general kept his position on high ground and directed the troops with signals from hand drums.[39]

Battles were fought on land as well as at sea. In fig. 4.4, we see the Mongols on their elaborately decorated ships. Their ships, according to the *Yoshōki*, were huge, with a lofty structure of gold and silver and banners fluttering in the wind.[40] Shields, spears, and drums were lined up along the edge to protect the ships. The unique shape of some of the shields is noteworthy (fig. 4.5). The upper part looks like a three-pointed crown, and inscribed on its surface is the Buddhist swastika character (*manji*), which was frequently used on Chinese military devices.[41]

Figure 4.5: Scene from the Mongol Invasion scroll (*Mōko shūrai ekotoba*)

We must, of course, treat these visual materials with care when using them as historical sources. We must remember the context in which the sources were produced. Scholars have suggested that the *Hachiman gudōkin* was written to emphasize the contributions made by the Iwashimizu Hachiman shrine to the Japanese victory and thereby to ask the bakufu for rewards. Takezaki Suenaga, as he produced the *Mōko shūrai ekotoba*, highlighted his own achievements in the battles. For these reasons, some exaggerations in figures and enemy description are inevitable. Furthermore, we also find similar expressions (such as the short bows and three-pointed shields) in earlier paintings that describe the "foreign," or alien, such as the *Kibi daijin nittō ekotoba* and the *Kitano tenjin engi-e*, suggesting that icons symbolizing "foreignness" or "otherness" that predate the Mongol Invasions were used to depict the Mongols in the *Mōko shūrai ekotoba*.[42] The narratives should be read with these contexts in mind. Yet, at the same time, Chinese military sources, such as the *Wujing zongyao*, suggest that these are relatively accurate descriptions of the Mongol/Song troops.[43] Both texts were produced by persons who either actually witnessed and experienced the Mongol invasions or had access to firsthand accounts of the battles. In this sense, they are invaluable, primary records of the battles fought against the Mongols.

Now, let us return to the *Shikaumi jinja engi* and examine its battle scene (fig. 4.6). We now notice that there are significant similarities between the enemy soldiers in this painting and the Mongol forces depicted in the *Mōko shūrai ekotoba*. Some are darker in skin color while others are lighter. This reminds us of the *shiro mōko* and *kuro mōko*, described in both the *Hachiman gudōkin* and the *Mōko shūrai ekotoba*. Their armor, characterized by horizontal lines, and helmets with side flaps and a featherlike decoration on the top, are comparable to those worn by the soldiers on the ship in the *Mōko shūrai ekotoba* (fig. 4.4). Many of them carry short bows and cone-shaped bow and arrow cases. Some are throwing spears. There is one soldier beating a drum that is placed on the ground. Another soldier is holding a red banner. Their ship, with a small hutlike structure at the back, a drum, and banners, is also similar to the ones depicted in the Mongol Invasion scroll. In sum, the artistic conventions used in the *Mōko shūrai ekotoba* to represent the Mongols are deployed to represent the Korean forces in the legend of Empress Jingū's battle illustrated in the *Shikaumi jinja engi-e*. How can this phenomenon be explained?

The two isolated events—the Mongol Invasions and Empress Jingū's expedition—were synthesized in the battle scene in the *Shikaumi jinja engi-e*. There are a few obvious similarities between the two battles: both were fought

Figure 4.6: Scene from *Shikaumi jinja engi*

against foreign enemies, the enemies came from the continent, and northern Kyushu was an important site related to both battles. However, these similarities would not have been enough to link the two events so closely as to depict the Koreans as Mongols. Most narrative texts of the illustrated Hachiman *engi* from the late Kamakura and Muromachi periods make no reference to the Mongol Invasions, nor does the *Mōko shūrai ekotoba* make any reference to Empress Jingū's expedition. In other words, there was no natural and immediate connection between the two: the connection had to be made. The analogy had to be constructed, mapping the similarities between the two events, and during the process some similarities were inevitably *created*. Only when we understand this process of analogy can we perceive the double meaning behind the battle scene.[44]

Analogy: Empress Jingū's Expedition and the Mongol Invasions

According to the *Hachiman gudōkin*, the Mongol Invasions took place "at a time when people were becoming more and more dependent on reason, that religious rituals had come to be neglected, and there remained no sincere veneration toward the gods." On the fifth day of the tenth month, eleventh year of Bun'ei (1274), the people of Tsushima saw the Hachiman shrine suddenly burn in flames. Soon they realized that it was an illusion. Yet not long afterward 450 foreign ships with thirty thousand men appeared on the western shores of the island. On the fourteenth day, more Mongol forces landed on the island of Iki. Prayers for subduing foreign enemies began to be recited at the Iwashimizu Hachiman shrine on the twenty-ninth day. The first invasion ended with the burning of the Hakozaki Hachiman shrine and the unexpected withdrawal of the Mongol troops due to strong winds. The *Hachiman gudōkin* attributes the first victory to the god Hachiman of Hakozaki. The second invasion took place in the summer of 1281. This time the Mongols attacked with 108,000 ships and several million men, including Chinese and Korean soldiers. Again, prayers and rituals were carried out to ask Hachiman to lead his divine expedition and quickly conquer the foreign enemy. Then a strong northwesternly wind blew and a blue dragon appeared from the sea to repel the Mongol forces. The Mongol ships were sunk, and several thousand men were drowned.

How are these incidents of foreign invasion in the late thirteenth century related to the earlier legendary conquest of the Three Kingdoms, which supposedly happened in the third century? The *Hachiman gudōkin* is an excellent example of the making of an analogy between Empress Jingū's conquest of Korea and the Mongol Invasions (see chart 4.2).[45] Other than the obvious similarity that both were fought against foreign enemies, the analogy is further enhanced in the *Hachiman gudōkin* by blaming Emperor Chūai's death on attacks from Silla. "Historically"

	Empress Jingū's Expedition	Mongol Invasions
Two Consecutive Foreign Attacks, and First Attack Won after Grave Sacrifice	Demon Jinrin sent by Silla → Death of Emperor Chūai. Amaterasu warns that the enemy has sent 108,000 ships to Japan	The first Mongol attack in 1274 → Burning of the Hakozaki shrine. The second Mongol attack in 1281
Enemy Size (larger)	108,000 ships + 496,000 men vs. 48 ships + 375 (1,375) men	70,000 ships + 3,700,000 men! (according to the *Taiheiki*)
Divine Oracles and Rituals	Empress Jingū hears an oracle from Amaterasu on Mount Shiōji. Empress Jingū divides her hair in the river and catches an *ayu* fish. Male gods and female dancers perform *kagura* to invite Azumi no Isora	Burning of the Hachiman Shrine in Tsushima is taken as an omen of foreign attack. *Kagura* and other performing arts are offered to the gods. Girl in arms and armor enacts the victorious battle fought by Empress Jingū
Japanese Victory with the Help of Divine Intervention	Strong wind pushed the empress's ship to Korea, etc.	Strong wind blew away the Mongol ships, etc.
Claim of Victory and Superiority Associated with the Battles	Hachiman is the son of Emperor Chūai and Empress Jingū. His father was killed by the foreign enemy. His mother conquered this enemy. Since the foreign country is the enemy of both his father and his mother, Hachiman has a strong ambition to conquer it and will protect Japan for ages to come. It is this very god that protected Japan from the Mongol Invasions and conquered the foreign enemy.	Japan is a divine country of prestige and wisdom. At the time of Empress Jingū's conquest, the Kolgulryŏ king swore that his people should become dogs for Japan. The Mongols are the descendants of these dogs; the Japanese are the descendants of the gods. The distinction between the high and low is clear. How can the gods and beasts be on an equal level?

Chart 4.2: Analogy

speaking, the earliest extant written texts, the *Kojiki* and *Nihon shoki*, relate nothing that suggests that the emperor was killed by Silla forces. Instead, his death is explained as the gods' punishment for not following their oracles, which told him to conquer Silla. According to the *Hachiman gudōkin,* however, a stray arrow killed the emperor when he was fighting the eight-headed demon, Jinrin, which had been sent by Silla to kill the people of Japan. This added detail of the earlier battle suggests that the event that killed the emperor was also a case of foreign invasion. In fact, the text implies that there were *two* consecutive foreign attacks before Empress Jingū planned her expedition: (1) the battle that Emperor Chūai fought, followed immediately by (2) Goddess Amaterasu's warning that the enemy had already sent 108,000 ships to attack Japan. In making the analogy, the *Hachiman gudōkin* elaborated on the death of Emperor Chūai to suggest that there were two attempted foreign invasions. The legendary invasions would hence correspond to the two invasions by the Mongols, bringing the events closer.

Second, in relation to the above, the *Hachiman gudōkin* draws a parallel between Emperor Chūai's death and the burning of the Hakozaki Hachiman shrine. In both cases, the first invasion could be hindered only through profound sacrifices: Emperor Chūai slew the demon, but he was killed by a stray arrow; the god Hachiman of Hakozaki repelled the Mongols, but the shrine was burned in the course of the battle.

Third, in both events, the enemy force was much larger in scale (at least, so say the narratives). In the case of Empress Jingū, the Japanese built 48 ships and took 375 gods along, whereas they confronted 108,000 enemy ships with some 496,000 men.[46] The *Hachiman gudōkin* explains that the Japanese forces were so small that it was like comparing a sparrow to a phoenix or gecko to the Dragon King and that fighting the enemy was more frightful than patting a dragon's whiskers or stepping on a tiger's tail.[47] Similarly, the first Mongol troops arrived at Tsushima aboard 453 ships carrying 30,000 men, whereas the *jitō* Sō Umanojō confronted them with only 80 mounted troops. The second Mongol attack was made with 108,000 ships and several million men. According to the *Taiheiki*, the enemy had 70,000 ships and 3,700,000 men.[48] Again, these numbers are clearly exaggerations. Yet the idea of a huge enemy force versus the small Japanese force was important in order to emphasize the miraculous victory.

Fourth, divine oracles and rituals were crucial factors in both battles. Empress Jingū received the first oracle from the goddess Amaterasu when she climbed Mount Shiōji. She was told that the enemy forces were already approaching Japan and therefore she must carry out the rituals to procure the gods' protection. Thereupon, she divided her hair in the river and caught a one-meter-long *ayu* fish. Musical performances were also part of the rituals. Five male gods and eight female dancers performed the *kagura* (a Shinto theatrical dance) to call for Azumi no Isora. Similarly, at the time of the Mongol Invasions, the Hachiman shrine in Tsushima suddenly burned, and this incident was taken as an omen of foreign invasion. Just as Amaterasu had advised the empress of the approaching enemy forces, Hachiman, too, was believed to have warned the people of Tsushima of the Mongol attack. Furthermore, the *Hachiman gudōkin* mentions that *kagura* and other performing arts were offered to the gods as Japanese awaited the invasions. Among the rituals was a performance by a girl who had been chosen to dress in arms and armor. The girl enacted the victorious battle fought by Empress Jingū against the foreign enemies.[49] Not only do we see a parallel in the rituals performed at the time of Empress Jingū's expedition and the Mongol Invasions. The *kagura* and the girl dressed as a male warrior suggest that rites in allusion to Empress Jingū's expedition were procreated at the time of the Mongol Invasions.

Fifth, the Japanese were able to win an impossible battle only with the help of the supernatural forces of the gods. According to the *Hachiman gudōkin,* the captain of Empress Jingū's ship was Shikashima Daimyōjin (who is also identified as Kasuga Daimyōjin), and the empress was accompanied by Great General Sumiyoshi Daimyōjin and Vice General Kōra Daimyōjin. The gods of Itsukushima, Munakata, Suwa, Atsuta, and Mishima were among those who supported the empress's expedition. The ship was also helped by a strong wind, which enabled them to swiftly reach the peninsula. Furthermore, the empress had the Dragon King's miraculous jewels, *kanju* and *manju*, which could cause the sea to rise or ebb. At the time of the Mongol Invasions, prayers were offered to gods to procure their protection. The dragon again appeared at the time of the second invasion, sinking the ships and drowning the foreign enemies. The most important of all gods in both events was, undoubtedly, Great Bodhisattva Hachiman, who avenged his father's death from within the empress's womb. The *Hachiman gudōkin* claims that Hachiman was ultimately responsible for the victory over the Mongols, too. He had caused the great winds that blew the enemy away.

Finally, two critical claims are made by the *Hachiman gudōkin* that bring the battles together.

> Great Bodhisattva Hachiman is the son of Emperor Chūai and Empress Jingū. His father, the emperor, was killed by a stray arrow shot by the foreign enemy. His mother challenged and conquered this enemy. Since the foreign country is the enemy of both his father and his mother, Hachiman has a strong ambition to conquer it and will protect Japan for ages to come. It is this very god that protected Japan from the Mongol Invasions and conquered the foreign enemy.[50]

> Although Japan is a small and inferior country, it is a divine country of prestige and wisdom. At the time of Empress Jingū's conquest, the Ko[gu]ryŏ king swore that his people should become dogs for Japan and protect Japan. The Mongols

> are the descendants of these dogs, whereas the Japanese are the descendants of
> the gods. The distinction between the high and low is clear and is separated as
> much as heaven and earth are. How can the gods and the beasts be at an equal
> level?[51]

These two claims tied the two events together with a strong sense of superiority over the Koreans and Mongols and a belief that Hachiman has protected Japan from foreign enemies throughout its history.

The analogy between Empress Jingū's conquest and the Mongol Invasions created an effective metaphor through which to propagate the power of Hachiman, as can be seen in the *Hachiman gudōkin*. The same is true in the *Shikaumi jinja engi-e*. Although the exact date is unknown, the *Shikaumi jinja engi-e* is the earliest of the known extant works of illustrated Hachiman *engi,* possibly produced around the same time the *Hachiman gudōkin* was written. It is important to note that it is a product of Kyushu, the site where the actual battles against the Mongols took place. The people who were involved in producing this work most probably had access to firsthand accounts of the invasions—they may even have witnessed the Mongol troops. In this sense, it is not surprising that the foreign enemy is a lifelike depiction of the Mongol warriors. The Mongol Invasions provided Japanese (in Kyushu) with vivid images of foreign enemies and gave them the incentive to put into drawing one of the most famous battles against foreign enemies in their "history." The application of the Mongol motif made the realistic portrayal of the battle possible and added realism to the legendary event. At the same time, although there is no explicit verbal reference to the Mongol Invasions, it is highly likely that the viewers of this painting were aware of the analogies, like those in the *Hachiman gudōkin*. They could therefore also read this painting as a depiction of the Mongol Invasions and the divine participation that brought victory to Japan. In this sense, the painting had a double meaning. First, it was a "realistic" and lively depiction of Empress Jingū's conquest of the three Korean kingdoms and the miraculous birth of Hachiman, which told the history and significance of the shrine and the gods worshipped at Shikanoshima. Second, it was a metaphoric depiction of the Mongol Invasions, which reminded the audience that a perilous event could be overcome only with the help and support of the gods.

The meanings that were assigned to the scrolls were perhaps the very reasons why Hideyoshi chose this particular painting among others to be brought to him before he set out on his own expedition. Three years after viewing the illustrated scrolls, he sent a vermillion seal document to the shrine.[52] Kobayakawa Takakage (1533–1597), to whom Hideyoshi entrusted the province of Chikuzen and portions of Higo and Hizen after his subjugation of Kyushu, repaired some of the buildings of the Shikaumi shrine in 1590, and Kuroda Nagamasa (1568–1623), who was placed in charge of the province of Chikuzen after the battle of Sekigahara, did the same in 1609. Both warriors had fought in Hideyoshi's invasion of Korea.

The image of the Mongol forces became a fixed icon for depicting enemy forces in the post–Mongol Invasion accounts of Empress Jingū's expedition. In the *Kōra Tamataregū goengi*, an Edo period copy of the narrative that is believed to have accompanied the hanging scroll *engi-e,* dated 1370, in the Tamataregū shrine in Fukuoka, the enemy forces are described as follows (emphasis added).

> As they left their ships and stood on the tideland, they *beat the drums,* blew the flute, *shot poisonous arrows*, and *threw their spears.*[53]

As noted earlier, the drums, the poisonous arrows, and the spears that are thrown are all major battle strategies used by the Mongols as described in the *Mōko shūrai ekotoba* and the *Hachiman gudōkin*. None of the earlier, pre–Mongol Invasions narratives of the legend of Empress Jingū's expeditions contains such a vivid portrayal of the ways in which the enemy forces fought. We may, therefore, conclude that the Mongol Invasions had a significant influence on the visual representation of the empress's conquest of the Three Kingdoms. The Mongol warriors and their war strategies were juxtaposed with the Jingū myth, synthesizing a new literary and visual text for representing the legendary battle scene. This new analogy allowed for the Shikaumi shrine and other shrines associated with gods pertaining to Empress Jingū's expedition to assert its importance in the face of a foreign threat.

Conclusion

The enemy forces depicted in the *Shikaumi jinja engi* represent an early stage of the iconographic development of the foreign enemy immediately following the Mongol Invasions. One clear indication lies in the striking similarity between the Koreans depicted in the *Shikaumi jinja engi* and the Mongols in works such as the *Hachiman gudōkin* and *Mōko shūrai ekotoba, which* are known for their accurate depictions of the Mongol Invasions. The resemblance is less evident in the later Hachiman *engi-e* produced in Central Japan, in which the foreign warriors tend to be represented as subhuman or demonic.

Certain images of foreign enemies had emerged from the experience of direct contact with the Mongol warriors were carried on to later periods to depict the Mongols, Koreans, and eventually alien enemies in general. In the *Yuriwaka daijin,* originally known as a chanted narrative piece (*kōwakamai*) from the Muromachi period, the Mongols are described as follows (emphasis added).

> The Mongols arrived on forty thousand ships . . . and landed at Hakata in
> Tsukushi . . . . They *shot poisonous arrows like spring rain*, and *dispatched iron
> bombshells* to all directions and disturbed Heaven and Earth as they attacked.[54]

Furthermore, by the Muromachi period, Empress Jingū's successful conquest
of the Three Kingdoms, by then juxtaposed with the Mongol image, had become
a standard metaphor for foreign battles in general. The Korean/Mongol motif
became a fixed icon for depicting not only the Mongols but any foreign or alien
foe. In the *Taishokan*, for example, the battle between Tang and the Asura is
described as follows.

> According to the customs of Tang battle . . . they attacked and retreated with
> signals sent through the beat of the *drums* . . . . When they saw that odds were
> against them, they *dispatched iron bombshells to all directions* . . . . The Asura
> shot flames like rain, blew evil wind . . . *threw spears, and shot poisonous
> arrows.*[55]

These motifs were also used in visual texts such as the *Kiyomizudera engi*,
produced in the early sixteenth century.[56] The Emishi subjugated by Sakanoue no
Tamuramaro, who are depicted in this scroll carry short bows and three-pointed
shields. Their ships are huge, with a lofty structure and banners fluttering in the
wind. Shields, spears, and drums are lined up along the edges of the ship. These
features remind us of the Mongol troops. The Emishi are eventually defeated by
a thunderstorm caused by the gods, and the verbal text accompanying this scene
makes reference to Emperor Chūai's battle against the Koreans.

Clearly, the Mongol Invasions (or perhaps we should say the shrines that
wished to take advantage of the event to propagate their worthiness) reminded
the people of an earlier legendary battle in which the gods similarly participated
in defeating foreign aggressors. More important, this immediate hostile encounter
with the foreign other made it possible for Japanese to create an image of alien
enemies that had never been visualized before. This study suggests just some
of the reasons why the *Shikaumi jinja engi* and other Hachiman *engi-e* from the
Kyushu region deserve more scholarly attention. Though regional and not as
sophisticated as the paintings done in Central Japan, they are examples of an early
style of Hachiman *engi-e* in which we can see a direct and immediate response to
the actual historical encounters with foreign aggressors.[57] The Mongol Invasions
proved to be an ideal analogy that could be used to more vividly describe the
Jingū legend, and this very analogy helped in the making of a new iconography of
the foreign other that would be rehearsed over and over again thereafter.

Notes

[1] *Taikō sama gunki no uchi*, pp. 205–206.

[2] The *Shikaumi jinja engi* is presently kept at the Fukuoka City Museum. I wish to express my gratitude to the Museum and its curator, Mr. Sueyoshi Takeshi for allowing me to see and photograph the paintings, to Mr. Azumi Isokazu at the Shikanoumi Shrine, Mr. Ashizu Akihiko at the Hakozakigū Shrine, and Kumadaki Ryūzō at the Kōra Taisha for allowing me to see the *Hachiman engi-e* at the respective shrines, and to my friends, Kimuro Akihiro at the Fukuoka City Hall and Kevin Gray Carr for assisting me during my research trip in Fukuoka. Reproductions of the *Shikaumi jinja engi* can be found in Miyaji Naokazu and Fukuyama Toshio, *Jinja kozushū*, p. 65, and Ōita Kenritsu Usa Fudoki no Oka Rekishi Minzoku Shiryōkan, *Jishae no sekai: chūseijin no kokoro o yomu*, pp. 48-49. Also see Fukushima Tsunenori, "Shikaumi jinja engi-kō"; and Watanabe Yūji, "Kyūshū no Hachiman engi-e: Kakefukusō keishiki o chūshin to shite."

[3] Jingū's umbilical cord for Ōjin is 'said to be' at the Hachiman shrine in Fukuoka today. In front of the shrine building is a tree surrounded by a fence, and, according to the sign on the fence, the umbilical cord is underneath the tree (Kenneth R. Robinson, personal communication). The passage on Empress Jingū, according to the *Nihon shoki*, is from Nakano Hatayoshi, *Usa jingūshi shiryō-hen* vol. 1, pp. 13–17.

[4] In this essay, I will mainly use the so-called *kō* copy of the *Hachiman gudōkin*, in *Jisha engi,* pp. 170–205.

[5] For *Hachiman engi*, I have consulted Abe Yasurō, "Hachiman engi to chūsei *Nihongi*," Kawazoe Shōji, "Mōko shūrai to chūsei bungaku;" Shinjō Toshio, "Chūsei Hachiman shinkō no ichi kōsatsu;" and Tada Keiko, "Chūsei ni okeru Jingū kōgōzō no tenkai." For reprints of texts related to the Jingū legend, see Nakano Hatayoshi, *Usa jingūshi shiryō-hen*, vol. 1, pp. 13–82.

[6] Miya Tsugio, "Hachiman Daibosatsu goengi to Hachiman engi;" Watanabe, "Kyūshū no Hachiman engi-e."

[7] Reproduced in *Tenjin engi emaki, Hachiman engi, Amawakahiko zōshi, Nezumi zōshi, Bakemono zōshi, Utatane zōshi*, pp. 30–37.

[8] Reproduced in Kameda Tsutomu, "Tomofuchi Hachimansha no hakubyō engi," in his *Bukkyō setsuwa-e no kenkyū*, pp. 229–237.

[9] Partially reproduced in Miya, "Hachiman Daibosatsu engi to Hachiman engi," *Bijutsu kenkyū,* part 3.

[10] Partially reproduced in Shibuya-ku Shōtō Bijutsukan, ed., *Chūsei shomin shinkō no kaiga: Sankei mandara, jogoku-e, otogizōshi*, pp. 64, 84.

[11] Partially reproduced in Nara Kokuritsu Hakubutsukan, *Shaji engi-e,* p. 21.

[12] Reproduced in ibid., pp. 25, 116–125.

[13] Reproduced in Watanabe Fumio, "Den Tosa Mitushige hitsu *Ōita Yusuhara Hachimangū engi emaki* ni tsuite."

[14] Reproduced in *Chūsei shomin shinkō no kaiga*, pp. 40–41.

[15] Reproduced in Ōsaka Shiritsu Hakubutsukan, *Shaji sankei mandara*, pp. 212–213.

[16] Reproduced in ibid., pp. 210–211.

[17] Watanabe, "Kyūshū no Hachiman engi-e."

[18] This painting is done on a better quality silk than the other two. Furthermore, an additional band of silk about 9 cm wide was added to the top portion of each of the latter two scrolls in order to match the height of the first scroll. This suggests that not only its style but its size, too, were initially different and that the three were deliberately made into a "set" at a later date.

[19] The Shimada family documents presently kept at Kyoto University provide detailed accounts of the Chōkōdō estates (including reports on Shikanoshima) during the medieval period. The documents are introduced in Ōyama Kyōhei, *Chōkōdōryō mokuroku to Shimadake monjo*.

[20] Figure 4.2 is from Watanabe, "Kyushu no Hachiman engi-e."

[21] This legend tells the of the origin of the name Kashii (fragrant pasania). The emperor's coffin, which had been placed on top of the pasania tree, is said to have released a sweet scent. A shrine was later built at the site, and the place came to be called Kashii.

[22] According to the legend, all sorts of shells were attached to Isora's face, since he had lived under the sea for a long time. Ashamed of his appearance, he had initially hesitated to present himself to the empress.

[23] Nakano Hatayoshi, *Usa jingūshi shiryō-hen*, vol. 1, pp. 13–29.

[24] For the Hachiman cult, see Miyaji, *Hachimangū no kenkyū*; Nakano Hatayoshi, *Hachiman shinkō*; and Nakano Hatayoshi, *Hachiman shinkō*.

[25] This is also the version told in the Tamataregū scroll.

[26] Similarly, the Edo period copy of the *Kōra Tamataregū goengi* and a surviving *etoki* text, both of which are believed to have accompanied the *Tamataregū engi*, explicitly mention that the emperor was killed while fighting the Silla forces. "*Kōra Tamataregū goengi*" and the *Etoki-bun* are reprinted in Kikutake Jun'ichi,

"Kyūshū no engi-e;" and Chikushi Yutaka and Nakano Hatayoshi, *Shintō taikei jinja-hen*, vol. 44, *Chikuzen, Chikugo, Buzen, Bungo no Kuni*, pp. 195–198.

[27] Kōra Taisha is located on Mount Kōra in Kurume city, and Kashii Jingū is in Fukuoka city.

[28] The Sumiyoshi shrine in present-day Ōsaka had intimate relations with the court. For eight years beginning in 1360, Emperor Gomurakami of the Southern Court built his residence at Sumiyoshi and established his headquarters there.

[29] See *Mōko shūrai ekotoba*. Also see Ishii Susumu, *Kamakurabito no koe o kiku;* Ōta Aya, *Emaki Mōko shūrai ekotoba;* and Satō Tetsutarō, *Mōko shūrai ekotoba to Takezaki Suenaga no kenkyū*. For a translation of the scrolls, see Thomas Conlan, *In Little Need of Divine Intervention: Scrolls of the Mongol Invasions of Japan*.

[30] *Hachiman gudōkin*, p. 181.

[31] Ibid., p. 184.

[32] The exhibition "Hōjō Tokimune to sono jidai ten," held at the Edo-Tokyo Museum in 2001, displayed a number of armors and helmets that were identical to the ones depicted in the *Mōko shūrai ekotoba* such as the leather armor that was described as being more suitable for shooting arrows on horseback and helmets with bird feathers of animal fur attached on the top for decoration. NHK and NHK Promotion, *Hōjō Tokimune to sono jidai ten*, pp. 212–214 (plates, pp. 91–111).

[33] The Mongols were a combined force consisting of Mongols, Chinese, and Koreans. On weapons depicted in the *Mōko shūrai ekotoba*, see Yoshida Mitsukuni, "Mōko shūrai ekotoba ni okeru buki ni tsuite."

[34] Shimizu Hisao, in "*Mōko shūrai ekotoba* no rekishi shiryō to shite no kachi: Yumi no keitai o megutte," argues that, since these bows are also depicted in earlier scrolls, the bows depicted in the *Mōko shūrai ekotoba* are not necessarily historically accurate and indeed may follow a Buddhist iconographic tradition of depicting "foreignness." I do agree that the short bow cannot stand alone to prove that the Mongols in the *Mōko shūrai ekotoba* are accurately depicted. However, other features mentioned below attest to the accuracy of its depiction.

[35] Ōta Kōki, *Mōko shūrai: Sono gunjishiteki kenkyū*, p. 23.

[36] *Hachiman gudōkin*, p. 184.

[37] Joseph Needham, *Science and Civilization in China,* Vol. 5, Pt. 7, *Military Technology: The Gunpowder Epic*, pp. 176–178. Bombshells were found among other artifacts from the battles offshore Takashima in Hakata Bay in 2001 (Saeki Kōji, *Mongoru shūrai no shōgeki*, pp. 150–155).

[38] *Hachiman gudōkin,* p. 184 (translation taken from Needham, *Science and Civilization in China,* Vol. 5, pt. 7, p. 176).

[39] *Hachiman gudōkin,* p. 184.

[40] The *Yoshōki* is a record of the Kōno family, a powerful clan of Iyo Province (Ehime Prefecture), whose members participated in both battles against the Mongols. An excerpt from the *Yoshōki* is in Nakano Hatayoshi, *Usa jingūshi shiryō-hen,* vol. 6, pp. 55–57.

[41] Yoshida Mitsukuni, "Mōko shūrai ekotoba ni okeru buki ni tsuite."

[42] Shimizu Hisao, in "*Mōko shūrai* ekotoba no rekishi shiryō to shite no kachi," pp. 13–30, emphasizes this point in his argument. For earlier images of the foreign other, see Haruko Wakabayashi, "Hell Illustrated: A Visual Image of *Ikai* That Came from *Ikoku*"; and "Sangoku shisō and Japan's Identity in the Buddhist Cosmology as Depicted in the *Konjaku monogatarishū.*"

[43] Yoshida Mitsukuni, "Mōko shūrai ekotoba ni okeru buki ni tsuite."

[44] On analogy and metaphor, I have consulted Keith J. Holyoak and Paul Thagard, *Mental Leaps: Analogy in Creative Thought*; and Victor Turner, *Dramas, Fields, and Metaphors: Symbolic Action in Human Society,* pp. 23–59.

[45] *Hachiman gudōkin.* The Jingū legend is described on pages 170–178, and the Mongol Invasions are described on pages 181–194.

[46] The number 108,000 is frequently used as an exaggeration to mean "very, very many." According to the *Sutra of King Asoka,* King Asoka is known to have killed 108,000 non-Buddhists (*gedō*). The monkey king Sun Wugong, in *The Journey to the West,* could fly 108,000 *li* (about 54,000 km) in one leap on his cloud.

[47] *Hachiman gudōkin,* p. 175.

[48] Both events are described in the *Taiheiki,* chap. 39 ("Taigen yori Nihon o semuru koto" and "Jingū Kōgō Shinra o seme tamau koto"): *Taiheiki, NKBT,* vol. 36, pp. 451–458.

[49] *Hachiman gudōkin,* p. 191.

[50] Ibid., p. 178.

[51] Ibid., p. 191.

[52] This is according to the *Banreki kanai nenkan,* pp. 125–148.

[53] *Kōra Tamataregū goengi.*

[54] *Yuriwaka daijin.*

[55] *Taishokan.*

[56] The *Kiyomizudera engi* is reproduced in *Zoku zoku Nihon emaki taisei denki/engi-hen,* vol. 5.

[57] As we examine the illustrated Hachiman *engi* of slightly later periods, we find that the image of the Mongols is transformed once it encounters the conventional Japanese image of the foreign other. Indeed, even within the *Shikaumi jinja engi-e,* we see that the standard codes for "foreignness" (such as those described in Kuroda Hideo, *Rekishi to shite no otogi zōshi*) had already been applied. The King of Koryŏ is depicted here just like any foreign king in other medieval texts portraying the foreign other such as the kings of the western kingdoms in the *Genjō Sanzō-e,* the King Enma in various paintings of Hell, including the *Kasuga gongen kenki-e,* or the Dragon King in the *Hikohohodemi no mikoto emaki.* These codes for foreignness came to be more widely applied in later Hachiman *engi* paintings. Furthermore, we begin seeing signs of the gradual demonization of foreign enemies, especially when the site of the production shifted from Kyushu to Central Japan and as the experience of the battle became an event of the remote past. The enemies depicted in the *Tōdaiji Hachiman engi-e,* for example, resemble the demons (*oni*) in numerous medieval Hell paintings.

5

Lanxi Daolong (1213-1278) at Kenchōji: Chinese Contributions to the Making of Medieval Japanese Rinzai Zen

Martin Collcutt

Stages in the Introduction of Chan Buddhism to Japan

The full and authentic transmission of Zen (Chan) Buddhist lineage transmissions, teachings, meditation techniques, *kōan* methods, and monastic practices came to Japan in several waves. The first wave was one in which knowledge of meditation and its techniques arrived in Japan as part of a larger "Buddhist package." Japanese monks, including Saichō (767–822), Kūkai (774–835), and Ennin (794–864), went to China during the early Heian period and brought back knowledge of the emerging Chan devotees and their meditative practices. The Tang Chinese monk of the Vinaya school, Ganjin (C. Jianzhen, 688–763), who came to Japan in 754, was experienced in meditation as well as the Vinaya precepts. Esoteric sects such as Tendai and Shingon also had their own meditative practices, known in Japanese as *shikan*. Hence, the forms of Chan meditation and *kōan* study developing in Tang China were not transmitted until several centuries later.[1]

The second wave of Chan transmission occurred in the late twelfth and early thirteenth centuries when Chan teachings were specifically sought and studied. The Japanese monks Eisai (alt. Yōsai, 1141–1215), Dōgen (1200–1253), and Enni Ben'en (1201–1280), who journeyed to Song China, recognized the vitality of Chan Buddhism and Chan masters in Chinese monasteries and brought back to Japan Chan teachings, practices, and texts.[2] In this second surge, during the late twelfth and early thirteenth centuries, Rinzai (C. Linji) Zen took root alongside more traditional Buddhist practices in Kenninji and Tōfukuji in Kyoto. Dōgen's Sōtō (C. Caodong) practice spread from Eiheiji in northern Japan. No doubt Rinzai Zen would have survived without further direct infusions from China—after all Sōtō Zen was able to do so—but it is unlikely that the transmissions by Eisai and Enni were sufficient to have allowed it to establish its own very strong character and identity vis-à-vis the older schools of Japanese Buddhism, especially in the Heian capital, the stronghold of Tendai and Shingon Buddhism.

The third wave took place beginning in the mid–thirteenth century, when Rinzai Zen in Japan was transformed and strengthened by the arrival in succession of more than twenty-five Chinese monks, all of them experienced in Chan monastic practice in China and several already recognized as distinguished masters.[3] Most of these Chinese monks quickly found their way to the warrior stronghold of Kamakura in eastern Japan, where they became tutors in Zen to their Japanese warrior patrons. Chinese-style Zen was already spreading in eastern Japan thanks to the efforts of Eisai, Dōgen, Enni, and their Japanese disciples. What the Chinese masters added was the confirmation of an authentic and complete Zen transmission of dharma lines, religious practice, monastic rules, art, and the whole panoply of Zen-related cultures and lifestyles. They were, of course, also patronized by members of the imperial court in Kyoto, but it is fair to say that their principal and most enthusiastic patrons were warriors, especially members of the warrior elite in Kamakura. This half century or so witnessed a remarkable encounter, one in which things Chinese, especially Zen-related things Chinese, flowed into Japan via Kamakura, and to a lesser degree Hakata and Kyoto, under the patronage of provincial warriors who saw Chan and Chinese culture as a way of asserting their cultural parity with the imperial court in Kyoto.

It has been argued by Tsuji Zennosuke and others that these Chinese monks fled to Japan to escape the Mongol invasion of China, and of Koryŏ, which was proceeding intermittently but violently throughout the thirteenth century. There is probably some truth in this, but the story is also more complicated. Murai Shōsuke's research has shown that Lanxi Daolong (1213–1278, J. Rankei Dōryū) and most of his successors came from the province of Sichuan (six monks) or from monasteries located in the coastal area around the port of Mingzhou and in the Yangzi Delta (fourteen monks). He suggests that Chinese monks were able to learn about the state of Buddhism in Japan from Japanese pilgrim monks who visited Chinese monasteries. Once Lanxi and one or two others had made the journey and found a warm welcome in Japan, they may have encouraged other monks to follow them. With a lively commercial trade developing among Chinese, Japanese, and Korean ports the journey, while still hazardous, was not too intimidating.[4]

This essay looks more closely at this remarkable transmission of Chinese Chan monastic practice, thought, and culture to thirteenth-century Japan by focusing on the life and travels of Lanxi Daolong, the first of the Chinese Chan monks to come to Japan, and the Kamakura monastery of Kenchōji, which he founded and guided for more than a decade (fig. 5.1).

Figure 5.1: Sculpture of Lanxi Daolong. Courtesy of Kenchōji Rinzai Zen Monastery, Kita-Kamakura, Japan.

A Note on Sources

Readers may wonder what documentary and other sources exist for the study of the transmission of Chinese Chan Buddhism to Japan and its vigorous development in that new environment. The surviving record is far from complete, but there are many documents and secondary studies that allow historians to recover the main outlines of the transmission with occasional vivid insights. None of the Japanese and Chinese monks involved in the transmission left detailed, candid diaries of their daily activities, thoughts, and personal contacts. However, those monks, like Eisai (Yōsai) or Lanxi Daolong, who attained prominent positions in the medieval Zen Buddhist world were honored with posthumous biographies, *goroku*, compiled by the temples they headed and their closest disciples. The temples and disciples treasured and preserved their writings and kept records of them, or relating to them, including lectures on the Buddha's teachings, Zen comments, and certificates and robes confirming the enlightenment of disciples and the dharma transmission. Thus, for Lanxi we have the *Daikaku Zenji goroku*. In addition, the monastery of Kenchōji has managed to preserve monastic regulations, samples of calligraphy, regulations for the monastic community, and portraits of eminent monks, *chinsō*, bearing inscriptions.

Temples also preserved documents related to their establishment, lay patrons, landholdings, and so on. Some were lost in fires over the centuries, but some have survived. For Kenchōji, for example, there are surviving records of early estate holdings and a plan of the early temple layout.

The patrons of Zen temples included nobles and leading warriors, including shoguns, regents, and provincial chieftains. Again, the documentation is sporadic, but records do survive allowing us to establish at least the outlines of Hōjō Tokiyori's patronage of Zen monks and monasteries. While we cannot answer all the questions we may have about the world of medieval Chan/Zen, we can at least provide an outline of its principal features, its great temples, its most eminent monks, and their lay patrons.

Lanxi Daolong: Carrying Authentic Chan Practice to Japan

In 1246 the thirty-four-year-old Chinese monk Lanxi Daolong reached Hakata after making the treacherous sea crossing from Ningbo in southern China. He was to spend the remainder of his life in Japan.[5] Though still quite young, Lanxi was a fully trained Chan monk when he set out for Japan, and he was the first recognized Chinese Chan (Zen) teacher to reach Japan. He became a major figure in the transmission of the doctrines and spirit of Rinzai Zen and the introduction of Chinese Song dynasty monastic practice.

It is not clear why he decided to make the long journey. According to Tsuji Zennosuke, he was invited by the warrior regent Hōjō Tokiyori (1227–1263), but there is no surviving record indicating that he was invited by Tokiyori or anybody connected with the bakufu in Kamakura or at the imperial court in Kyoto. It is possible, however, that he had heard from a Japanese pilgrim monk, perhaps Getsuō Chikyō, whom he had met in one of the Chinese monasteries, that Chan teachings were spreading in Japan under the patronage of nobles and warriors but there was still a great need for experienced Chinese masters to transmit an authentic Chan dharma and the detailed practice of monastic life.[6]

Lanxi was born in Sichuan Province in 1213, and at the age of thirteen he entered the Taci Buddhist monastery in the Chinese provincial capital of Chengdu. He later moved to the Hangzhou area, where several of the most distinguished masters resided at Chan centers. Traveling from one official monastery to another, he seems to have met most of these renowned religious masters, among them the revered abbot of Mount Jing, Wuzhun Shifan (1177–1249) and Beijian Jiujian (d. 1246). His enlightenment was recognized by Wuming Huixing (1160–1237) of the Songyuan lineage, whose direct disciple he became. After completing his studies under Wuming at the Yangshansi in Pingjianfu, he moved on to the famous monastery complex on Mount Tiantong.[7] Thus, although Lanxi had not held high office in a major Chinese monastery, he was a fully trained and experienced monk who had lived at Jingshansi, Tiantongsi, and other great Chan centers and whose spiritual attainment had been confirmed by a leading Chinese master.

After learning about the condition of Buddhism and Zen in Japan, Lanxi and three fellow monks—Yiweng Shaoren, Longjiang Yingxuan, and a monk known only as Faping—set out for Japan to guide monks and laypeople in Chan.[8] After a few weeks in Dazaifu (Hakata), the young Chinese monk made his way to Kyoto to visit Getsuō Chikyō at Sennyūji.[9] While in Kyoto, Lanxi also probably contacted Enni Ben'en (1202–1280) at Tōfukuji, near Sennyūji. They had both studied at different times under Wuzhun Shifan. From Getsuō and Enni, Lanxi would no doubt have learned something more of the vicissitudes of Zen in Japan up to that point. He would have been told that Eisai and Dōgen, as well as Enni, had brought Rinzai and Sōtō school teachings back from China in previous decades. They had each sought to establish Chan-style monasteries in the capital but had been put under great pressure from the Tendai establishment not to assert Zen exclusively but to blend it with other, more traditional, teachings. Dōgen had felt it necessary to quit the capital in 1243 and was leading a small isolated Zen community at Eiheiji in the mountains near the north coast of Japan. Chan-style meditation was being practiced in Kenninji and Tōfukuji in Kyoto, but it was mixed with prayers and esoteric rituals. These were far from being authentic Chan monasteries, and the support from nobles and townspeople was less than enthusiastic. Enni had courtly connections and was well respected, but the prospects for the advancement of Zen in Kyoto were not promising and Lanxi would have expected to encounter active hostility from Enryakuji monks.

Getsuō, and Enni, probably told Lanxi that his prospects for support and patronage would be better under the warrior regents in Kamakura than in Kyoto. When Eisai returned from four years of Chan practice in China in 1191, with his insight validated by a Chinese master, he had planned to teach Zen in Kyoto but was attacked for his unorthodox practice. He was, however, warmly welcomed to the warrior garrison town of Kamakura, headquarters of the bakufu, by the young shogun Minamoto no Sanetomo (1192–1219) and his mother, Hōjō Masako (1157–1225). Under their patronage he established the small Zen temple of Jufukuji in 1200. Eisai was probably welcomed in Kamakura more for his ability to lead esoteric rituals than for his guidance in Zen, and he did not stay there very long. He certainly did not put Zen on a very firm footing.[10] But Getsuō and Enni would also have told Lanxi that the current strong man in Kamakura, the regent Hōjō Tokiyori (1227–1263, regent 1246–1256) seemed to be deeply

Figure 5.2: Sculpture of Hōjō Tokiyori. Courtesy of Kenchōji Rinzai Zen Monastery, Kita-Kamakura, Japan.

interested in Zen (fig 5.2).[11] He had invited both Dōgen and Enni to Kamakura shortly after their return from China and urged them to stay and instruct monks in the new Chinese practices. Both soon left, however, Dōgen to head the Eiheiji community and Enni to establish Tōfukuji in Kyoto. A fully trained Chinese Chan monk such as Lanxi might be just the kind of spiritual guide Tokiyori was seeking for himself, warriors, and monks in the east.

In Kamakura, Lanxi was invited to Eisai's old temple, Jufukuji, by the Zen monk Daikatsu Ryōshin, who was friendly with Tokiyori.[12] The news of the presence of a Chinese Chan monk in Kamakura thus quickly came to the ears of Tokiyori, who met him and installed him in Jōrakuji just outside Kamakura. Jōrakuji was converted into a Zen monastery for Lanxi,[13] and he lived there until Kenchōji was completed in 1253. Its main sanctuary houses a statue of him, as well as the temple's principal statue of Amida Nyorai.[14] Jōrakuji had been established in 1237 by the monk Taikō Gyōyū, a disciple of Eisai and a teacher of Enni of Tōfukuji, under the patronage of the third regent, Hōjō Yasutoki. Prior to Lanxi's arrival, the monks of Jōrakuji practiced a mixture of Zen, Tendai, and Shingon doctrines and ceremonies. Lanxi quickly transformed Jōrakuji into much more of a Chan-style monastery centered on meditation practice and *kōan* interviews. He built a monks' hall, *sōdō*, for the growing number of Japanese monks who came to train under his guidance. He also issued Chan monastic rules for the community.

Tokiyori was clearly impressed by the transformation the Chinese master was making at Jōrakuji. He visited the Chinese monk frequently, practiced Zen under his guidance, and asked him about his life as a monk and his experience of Chan in Chinese monasteries. After consultation with Lanxi, Tokiyori decided on a more ambitious project: the building of a new and larger monastery, in the Song monastic style, modeled on the renowned center on Mount Jing, under his direct patronage and closer to the bakufu. Lanxi supervised the construction of this new monastery in Kamakura, Kenchōji, and on its completion in 1253 was installed as the founder-abbot (*kaisan*).[15] The site selected was a narrow valley to the north of the garrison town of Kamakura and separated from it by a steep and densely wooded hill. The site was not necessarily auspicious. It had once been a bloody execution ground. However, a small temple, the Shinheiji, had been erected on the site, and its principal image was a statue of Jizō Bosatsu (Ksitigharba), a compassionate boddhisattva who is believed to roam the realms of hell looking for repentant souls to lead to paradise. Tokiyori ordered several local families to move their homes and had what was left of the Shinheiji moved farther up the valley. However, in what we may see as a first compromise with local customs and practices, the image of Jizō was incorporated into the new monastery. Clearly Lanxi agreed with, perhaps even encouraged, the adoption of Jizō as the central image, a decision that was unusual in Zen monasteries of the day.

Why Did the Regent Hōjō Tokiyori Patronize Lanxi and Chan Buddhism?

Hōjō Tokiyori was clearly deeply impressed by the energy and dynamism of the young Chinese monk Lanxi Daolong. He not only prevailed on him to stay in Kamakura but engaged in Chan-style meditation and *kōan* study and installed him as the abbot of a new and impressive Chan-style monastery and generously endowed it with extensive landholdings. Tokiyori may not have been exclusively committed to Zen. He probably continued to patronize other schools of Japanese Buddhism. But until his death Zen seems to have been his most absorbing spiritual commitment. Beyond his obvious respect for Lanxi, what other factors might have impelled his support for Zen?

Tokiyori may have seen in Chinese Zen an ideological basis for a strengthened warrior culture. Soon after he became the shogunal regent in 1246, Tokiyori had expressed concern about both a decline in martial skills and the self-discipline of warriors in Kamakura. He also commented unfavorably on the fact that some religious in Kamakura flouted their priestly vows. The organized discipline of Zen was very well suited to respond to such concerns. Chinese Chan masters were well versed in Buddhist learning and the Chinese literary classics, but they were far from bookish. The Zen masters had a vigor and force that commended them to many Kamakura warriors, and the path they taught stressed discipline and strength of spirit. It was, moreover, a self-reliant path centered on meditation as a way of transcending the limited ego and awakening to one's innermost nature, thereby fostering a spirit of equanimity even in the face of death. The direct, practical teachings of Zen did not require the doctrinal and ritual sophistication of the Tendai and Shingon schools, nor did its followers have to leave the world for the monastery—"everyday mind is the Way," in the words of the great Chinese Zen master Mazu Daoyi (709–788).[16]

The ultimate goal of Zen is, of course, spiritual awakening and the attainment of Buddhahood, but the concentration and equanimity fostered by the practice were of great practical use even for provincial samurai. This is not to suggest that warrior families suddenly made an exclusive commitment to the new Zen teachings. Some samurai males with direct access to Zen temples and monks would have devoted themselves exclusively to Zen practice, but others would have combined Zen with their traditional devotion to local Shinto divinities and other traditions of Buddhism. Women in samurai families would have had less access to Zen, but we should not discount the fact that Zen nunneries were gradually established. In short, the growing number of Zen monasteries, and nunneries, in Kamakura, Kyoto, and throughout the provinces in the late thirteenth and fourteenth centuries is itself an indication that provincial warrior families were increasingly supportive of Zen, even if most did not accord it exclusive patronage.

We might also suggest another element that appealed to Tokiyori. By adopting the new Chinese Chan teachings, the leadership of the bakufu, and eastern warriors more generally, would gain greater access to Chinese learning, secular as well as Zen. They would also, perhaps, be able to develop cultural links more generally, and have greater access to Chinese *karamono* goods, and overall might be able to claim, in the sphere of Chinese culture at least, to be the peers of the old nobility in the capital.

Kenchōji and Lanxi

The new monastery was named Kenchōji, the "Temple of the Kenchō Era," after the era name, the use of which implied imperial recognition. Yet, despite the clear significance of the construction of this new temple, surviving records do not entirely agree on the dates of construction, dedication, and the like.

According to the *Kyofukusan Kenchō Kōkoku Zenji sōken nyūbutsuki*, a record of the matters relating to the principal image at Kenchōji, construction of the Buddha Hall began on Kenchō 1 (1249).11.1 and was completed two years later on 1251.11.21. The statue of Jizō was formally set in the hall in 1251.12.14. On 1253.2.24 a plaque asserting "Great Zen Temple of the Kenchō Era for the Protection of the Country" (*Dai Kenchō Kōkoku Zenji*) was formally raised above the great doors of the Central Hall, giving the temple official recognition. A few months later, in the seventh month, gifts of landholdings in various *shōen* were made to provide an economic base for Kenchōji. These included scattered but extensive rights to specified amounts of annual tax income, *nengu*, from the following holdings.

> 5,000 *kanmon* from Hekikai no Shō, Mikawa Province
> 7,000 *kanmon* from Yoshida no Shō, Mikawa Province
> 500 *kanmon* from Iwashiro no Shō, Mutsu Province
> 13,000 *kanmon* from Numazu no Shō and Ōtsu no Shō, Suruga Province
> 3,000 *kanmon* from Kosakuya no Shō, Kai Province

In addition to the *nengu* holdings for the general support of the monastery, land rights were also granted for annual ceremonies on the memorials days of members of the Hōjō regent family.

> 500 *kanmon* from Aota no Shō, Suruga Province

Also, land rights were granted as "abbot's domain" in several provinces.

> 5,000 *kanmon* from Tsukuba gun, Hitachi Province
> 3,000 *kanmon* from Nanbu no Shō, Hitachi Province
> 5,000 *kanmon* from Jina gun, Satsuma Province

In total forty-two-thousand *kanmon* in income from *shōen* holdings was awarded to the new monastery. This was very substantial economic base for a fledgling community and gives some indication of both the respect accorded to Lanxi and Hōjō Tokiyori's determination to promote Zen in Kamakura.[17]

According to the *Azuma kagami*, construction began in 1251 and was completed two years later.

> On the twenty-fifth day of the eleventh month of Kenchō 5 (1253.11.25) hail fell. After 8:00 am it rained a little, but the Kenchōji dedication ceremony was held. A sixteen-foot (*jōroku*) statue of Jizō Bosatsu was enshrined as the central image, and one thousand smaller images of the same deity were also dedicated. Sōshū [Hōjō Tokiyori] was especially sincere in his devotion. On the eighth day of the eleventh month of Kenchō 3 (1251) work had begun. Having completed the construction phase, this day the seat of the Buddha is expanded.[18]

Other records state that Kenchōji was actually dedicated two years earlier, in 1249. The chronology of the life of Enni Ben'en states explicitly that he went from Kyoto to Kamakura in 1249 for a dedication.[19]

Kenchōji was dedicated to "the longevity of the emperor, the welfare of the shogunal line and its ministers, peace under heaven, the repose of the souls of three generations of the Minamoto, of Masako, and other deceased members of the Hōjō family." Lanxi attracted numerous disciples, and Kenchōji soon had an enrollment of several hundred monks.

Although he had accepted the image of Jizō as the central icon of Kenchōji, Lanxi was clearly intent on establishing at Kenchōji the core of a Song-style monastery, the first of its kind in Japan, where communal *zazen* (seated Zen) would be the central practice for the monks. We can reconstruct something of the physical character of early Kenchōji (in the early fourteenth century) from a detailed ground plan known as the *Kenchōji sashizu* (discussed below). Construction buildings gradually spread up the valley and came to include most of the buildings that would have been part of the great monastic centers of Song China: a main Buddha Hall (*hondō*), Dharma or Teaching Hall (*hattō*), Zen Meditation Hall, monks' quarters, guest quarters, kitchens and storehouses, sutra repository, bell tower, great gate, front gate, midgate, refectory, and abbot's buildings.

Kenchōji was one of the first Zen monasteries in Japan to include among its buildings a communal meditation center or monks' hall (*sōdō*), a characteristic Chan building but one that was new to Japanese monastic experience. Lanxi stressed the importance of the *sōdō* and composed strict regulations for the mandatory four daily meditation sessions held there. His Zen emphasized meditation and discussion of *kōan* within the context of a monastic life based on strict observance of Chan regulations (*shingi*). "The practice of Zen and the pursuit of the Way is nothing other than grappling with the great problem of birth and death. Even on bath days or holidays do not allow your practice of Zen to relax for an instant."[20]

Unlike some of the Chinese monks who followed him to Japan, Lanxi did not encourage his disciples to indulge in scholarship or literary activity: "The practice of Zen (*sanzen bendō*) does not lie in the study of four- and six-character parallel prose."[21] He did, however, share with other Song dynasty Chan masters a willingness to accept, at a secondary level, the validity of the existing social order and the man-made law. After centuries of accommodation to Chinese society and interaction with Confucian thought, Chan teaching, while stressing the primary aim of individual enlightenment, sometimes couched this teaching in Confucian terms. Thus, Lanxi could say in one of his sermons that "faithful observance of the laws of the [secular] world does not differ from faithful observance of the laws of the religious world." Acceptance of the present world by Chinese Zen monks dovetailed with the contemporary teachings of Nichiren (1222–1282). Nichiren's appeal to "Attain Buddhahood in this very body!" (*sokushin jōbutsu*), for instance, was an assertion that salvation could be found in daily life, even in the pursuit of profit, if it were accompanied by genuine devotion to the *Lotus Sutra*. Approval of the political order and its laws by Zen monks naturally gave the sect an added attraction in the eyes of practical-minded warrior-leaders whose chief concerns were keeping the peace and holding, if possible increasing, the loyalty of their vassals.[22]

The completion of Kenchōji at midcentury marks an important stage in the development of the Zen schools in Japan. Unlike Kenninji and Tōfukuji in Kyoto, Kenchōji had no Tendai or Shingon building within its compound, nor was it a branch temple of any other established monastery. A plaque, said to have been written by Emperor Go-Fukakusa (1243–1304, r. 1246–1259), placed above the main gate publicly proclaimed its independence: "Kenchō Kōkoku Zenji" (The Kenchō [era] Zen monastery for the Prosperity of the Country). This would have been one of the first recorded public uses of the characters *zenji* (Zen monastery) in Japan and an implicit formal recognition of Zen as an independent branch of Buddhism. Kenchōji remained throughout the medieval era the leading Kamakura monastery. It served as a model for many subsequent Zen foundations in Japan, including a rebuilt Tōfukuji and a new Tenryūji; provided the base for the expansion of the Lanxi school and Song Zen in the Kantō region; and was designated as the senior Kamakura monastery in the administrative hierarchy of Rinzai temples known as the Gozan, or Five Mountains, system.

While Lanxi was training young Japanese monks at Kenchōji he must have been intensely aware that Mongol forces were making ever deeper inroads into northern China and the Korean Peninsula. Chinggis Khan's horsemen had captured the Jurchen capital of Zhongdu (Beijing) in 1215, twenty years before

Lanxi sailed for Japan. In 1252 Khubilai Khan led a Mongol force into Sichuan and Yunnan. The Mongols began pressing into the Korean Peninsula in 1218, and in 1259, after fierce resistance, they forced the Korean king to accept Mongol suzerainty. Japan then became an object of Mongol attention.

On four occasions (1268, 1271, 1272, and 1273) Khubilai Khan sent ambassadors to urge the Japanese to submit to Mongol authority. The demands of the Mongol envoys caused a flurry of dismay in the imperial court in Kyoto and angered the bakufu in Kamakura. The Hōjō regents, who dominated the bakufu, took a defiant line with Khubilai. In 1268 the bakufu ordered its vassals living in Kyushu to prepare for the defense of the country, and in 1271 it ordered all vassals, who held land in Kyushu but resided elsewhere in the country to proceed to the island to assist in defense preparations. Shrines and temples began to offer prayers for the safety of the country. Khubilai's demands were ignored or rejected, and his envoys were either executed or banished. Khubilai then resorted to direct action, and in the late summer of 1274 he dispatched a large invasion fleet to Japan. This attempted invasion was frustrated by Japanese warriors and "divine winds," but the Hōjō immediately began to brace for another attempt. The most visible effort was the construction of a defensive wall to protect the beaches lining Hakata Bay, which played a crucial role in the second Mongol Invasion in 1281.[23]

These broader currents also impacted Lanxi's life. In 1265 retired emperor Go-Saga (r. 1242–1246) invited Lanxi to Kyoto to serve as the eleventh-generation abbot of Kenninji. Three years later, in 1268, Lanxi returned to Kamakura. In 1272, religious rivals envious of his success in promoting Zen, among them monks from Enryakuji in Kyoto, accused him of secret collaboration with the Mongol regime, which by now was regarded as a significant threat to Japan. Despite the fact that Lanxi was Chinese and hailed from southern China, which was ruled by the Southern Song, whom the Mongols were trying to destroy, he was banished for several years to the mountainous province of Kai (north of Mount Fuji). Apparently undaunted by this setback, he used the Tōkōji temple as a base from which to establish several small Zen temples and propound his teachings among local warrior families.[24] Early in 1278 he was called back to Kamakura by Hōjō Tokimune (1251–1284), who wanted to appoint him founding abbot of a new Zen temple, Engakuji. However, Lanxi was at this point ailing. He died at Kenchōji on 1278.7.24, at the age of sixty-six, before the temple-building project was completed. In death he became the first representative of Zen in Japan to receive the honorary title Zenji (Zen master) and the imperial court bestowed on him the posthumous name Daikaku (Great Enlightenment).

Lanxi was followed by a succession of Chinese monks, some of whom he encouraged to come to Japan, but it is fair to say that his role in the transmission of an authentic Chan monastic practice to Japan was critical in laying the foundations for the future development of unadulterated Rinzai Zen monastic practice in Japan. He trained hundreds of Japanese monks, and many of the leaders of the proliferating Zen monasteries in Kamakura, Kyoto, and throughout the provinces were taught by him or his direct disciples.

What Did Lanxi Bring to Japan?

Let us now look more closely Lanxi's contribution to the growth of authentic Rinzai Zen in Japan. What did he bring with him to Japan? And how did he shape Kenchōji and the other temples he headed? For convenience we will look at things under the following headings:

1. The Chan mind-to-mind dharma transmission
2. Chan training methods, including intensive meditation and the use of *kōan*
3. Chan monastic codes and practices
4. The Chan monastery and monastic life: layout, architectural styles, building locations, functions, fixtures, ceremonies, and so on
5. Chan-related culture, including calligraphy, portrait paintings and sculpture, Zen-related art, landscape painting, ceramics, lacquer, and metal work.

The Chan Dharma Transmission

Although Lanxi was still in his early thirties when he reached Japan, he had been in training as a Chan monk for twenty years in such major Chinese monasteries as Jingshansi. He had lived and meditated in their monks' halls, studied in their common rooms, worked in their kitchens, prayed in their Buddha halls, listened to lectures in their dharma halls, and presented his understanding of *kōan* to such renowned masters as Wuzhun Shifan in their abbots buildings. His enlightenment had been recognized by Wuming Huixing, one of the leading Chinese Chan masters of his day, from whom he received a certificate of enlightenment (*inka*) and whose lineage transmission he carried to Japan. Lanxi was thus steeped in every aspect of Zen practice, teaching, training, organization, monastic life, and culture. Moreover, he was not a brief visitor to Japan. He spent more than thirty years training Japanese monks and lay devotees in Zen. For Lanxi and his Japanese disciples the certainty that he was the bearer of an authentic Chan transmission and that he could recognize and validate Zen insight and transmission in others was probably his most important contribution. His, of course, was not the first Chan dharma transmission. Eisai, Enni, and Dōgen had all been validated by Chinese masters, and the monks and laypeople recognized by them believed that they, too, were within the valid Chan transmission. In Lanxi's case, that assurance was even greater. There was no question that the monks and laypeople trained and recognized by him were in the mainstream of authentic Chan. Before long, his work, combined with that of other Chinese masters, would allow Musō Soseki and other Japanese monks to feel that they need not go to China to experience authentic Zen training, that Zen was now firmly rooted in Japan and they could receive the full Zen experience, and enlightenment, under a Chinese or Japanese master in one of the new monasteries there.[25]

Chan Training Methods, Including Zazen and the Use of *Kōan*

Lanxi was deeply experienced in the core practice of seated meditation. As part of his meditation practice and search for insight, he had worked on *kōan* and deepened this practice in Japan. *Kōan* were widely used in Chinese monasteries. The two great *kōan* collections known in Japanese as the *Hekigan roku* (*Biyanlu*, ca. 1130) and the *Mumonkan* (*Wumenguan*, 1228) were both compiled before Lanxi left China. Wumen Huikai (Mumon Ekai), the compiler of the *Mumonkan*, was active during Lanxi's lifetime. They may have known each other. Lanxi may have brought copies of these *kōan* collections with him to Japan or had them sent later. The Japanese monk Shinchi (Muhon) Kakushin (1207–1298), who went to China in 1249, practiced Zen, including *kōan* study, under Wumen for five years before returning to Japan in 1254. He is said to have introduced the *Mumonkan* to Japan. But Lanxi may well have been aware of it before he left China. And there were plenty of other monks going to and fro who would also have known of it. He may have used these *kōan* collections or he may have presented *kōan* not included in these collections and in an order he thought appropriate for the particular monk or layperson he was guiding. Even if he did not have a copy of the *Mumonkan*, there is no doubt that he had worked on many *kōan* with different masters in his itinerant practice in the great Chan centers. He used *kōan* to support *zazen* in his training of monks and laypeople. That he was punctilious about this is indicated by the survival of a document at Kenchōji recording the responses to various *kōan* on which different monks were working.[26]

Chan Monastic Codes and Practices

Chan monastic life in China was governed by distinctive monastic codes known as *jinggui* (*shingi*), meaning "pure rules," that aid monks in their quest for enlightenment. These monastic codes supplemented the Buddhist *vinaya*, the traditional disciplinary code that governs the behavior of all Buddhist monks and nuns.[27] One example of divergence is provided by the Zen monastic emphasis on manual labor. Whereas the *vinaya* forbids gardening and other such work because of the inevitable loss of life involved, the Zen monastic codes actually mandate such labor both as a means of providing for the monastery's needs and as a way of expressing the insights of meditation in the everyday activities of life. Such "working meditation" is known in Zen as *samu* (work duty).

The strict, active style of Zen practice introduced to Kenchōji by Lanxi is reflected in a short treatise of his, the *Hōgo kisoku* (Dharma Words and Regulations), a portion of which may be paraphrased as follows (fig. 5.3).[28]

A horse that runs only when shown the whip is not a good horse; a monk who practices only when admonished is not a good monk. None who live in this pure temple will suffer from hunger or cold. Reflect carefully on this while you are here. If one behaves in a way dismissive of this, the transgression is great indeed. An ancient said, "Though thoroughly versed in the teachings, you cannot realize liberation. Nothing surpasses mastery of the Buddha Way for benefiting all sentient beings." How does one master the Buddha Way? All day you drag around a corpse, laughing, shouting, and getting angry. Asked "Who are you?" those who can answer are few. Annoyed by some little thing, you lose your temper and depart. And this isn't just one or two of you. The purpose of Zen training is to resolve the Great Matter of life and death. You must never indulge your feelings and become neglectful, even when resting after the bath.

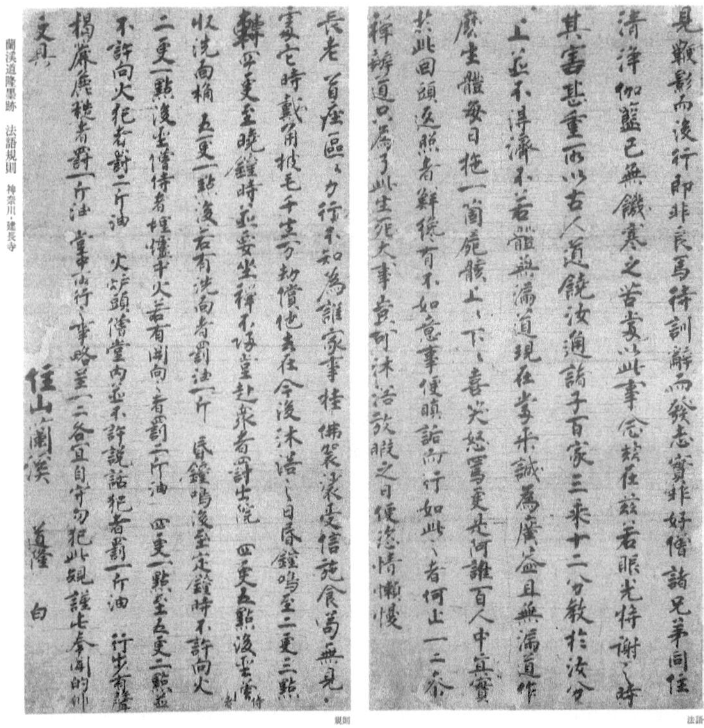

Figure 5.3: Lanxi Daolong's Calligraphy, Dharma Words, and Kisoku. Courtesy of Kenchōji Rinzai Zen Monastery, Kita-Kamakura, Japan.

The final line of this passage refers to the Zen monastic custom of bathing on dates that contain the numbers four and nine, that is, the fourth, ninth, fourteenth, nineteenth, twenty-fourth, and twenty-ninth of each month. On the fourteenth and twenty-ninth bathing takes place in the morning and the afternoons are free. Even then, Lanxi emphasizes, the monk must not relax his attention to the training.[29] He continues:

> Elders and head monks must attend carefully to their training without regard for the opinions of others. You wear robes and receive the donations of the faithful; if nothing comes of this, when can you repay the debt? From now on even on bath days *zazen* must be practiced in the evening and early morning; those who do not go to the meditation hall but head for their quarters will be punished by expulsion. Those washing their faces after 4:20 am are subject to a one-*kin* oil fine. Warming oneself by the hearth fire is forbidden between 6:00 and 10:00 pm. The hearth fire must be covered after 10:20 PM; opening the fire after this time is punishable by a two-*kin* oil fine. Warming oneself by the fire between 2:20 am and 3:40 am is punishable by a two-*kin* oil fine. Talking by the fire or in the *sōdō* is punishable by a one-*kin* oil fine. Speaking while walking and needlessly raising the screens [to the rooms] are punishable by a one-*kin* oil fine. These are several guidelines pertaining to behavior in the *sōdō*. Each monk should obey them and not break the regulations.[30]

The meaning of the "oil fine" referred to in this passage is unclear. According to one explanation it was a form of punishment in which minor offenders were required to sit *zazen* for the length of time it took to burn the stipulated amount of oil (one *kin* is approximately six hundred grams); another explanation is that the offenders were fined the amount needed to buy the oil, which was used in the votary lamps placed in front of the Buddha images. On ordinary days four sessions of *zazen* were held, at 4:00 am, 10:00 am, 4:00 pm, and 8:00 pm. On bath days some rest was scheduled, but Daolong did not permit this. One can only speculate on the extent to which Lanxi's strict and uncompromising Chinese style of Zen was followed by the Japanese assembly, accustomed as it was to a more relaxed approach.[31]

The Chan Monastery and Monastic Life: Layout, Architectural Styles, Building Locations, Functions, Fixtures, and Ceremonies, and So Forth

Although we do not know exactly what Kenchōji looked like at the time of Lanxi's death in 1278, there is no doubt that it was becoming a fully equipped Zen monastery in the basic Chan style with certain modifications to accommodate the terrain in which it was built and the residential preferences of its patrons. It incorporated the core Song Chan monastic features more fully than any other monastery in Japan in the thirteenth century, at least before the building of Engakuji.

We can probably provide a fair sense of Kenchōji in the 1270s by "placing" it in relation to two important documents. One of these is commonly known as the "Illustrations of the Five Mountains and Ten Temples" (*Gozan jissatsu zu*) the other as the "Kenchōji Ground Plan" (*Kenchōji sashizu*).[32]

Gozan jissatsu zu

Tōfukuji owns a copy of a fairly detailed thirteenth-century manuscript (a set of two scrolls) illustrating several major Song dynasty Chan monastery buildings and their furnishings. This is known as the *Daisō shozan zu* (Depictions of Great Song Monasteries). A slightly different version of the same document, known as the *Gozan jissatsu zu* (Illustrations of the Five Mountains and Ten Temples), is held by the Sōto Zen temple of Daijōji in Kanazawa. Each document consists of two long hand scrolls containing a total of about seventy individual drawings and textual units. These drawings include temple ground plans, building floor plans, building elevations, construction details, altar and interior furnishings, and seating arrangements for such important Chan monasteries as Jinshansi, Tiandongsi, Lingyinsi, and Wanniansi. For the investigation of both the Southern Song Chan monasteries and the early Japanese Zen temples modeled on them, these illustrations are invaluable.[33]

The surviving sets are probably fifteenth- or sixteenth-century copies of earlier versions of the scrolls. The authorship of the original manuscript is unknown. According to Tōfukuji tradition, the original was brought to Japan by Enni Ben'en when he returned from China in 1241. The Daijōji scrolls have been attributed to Dōgen Kigen, who supposedly made them when he studied in China from 1223 to 1227. They have also been attributed to Tettsu Gikai (1217–1309), Dōgen's disciple, who went to China in 1259 and later became the founding abbot of Daijōji. Japanese art historians have convincingly dated the information in the hand scrolls to about 1247 based on evidence indicating when certain buildings shown in the scrolls were built or burned. Assuming the author was recording extant structures, none of these Japanese could have made the drawings since they were not in China at that time. Either Enni or Dōgen might have requested the sketches be made and sent by acquaintances in China, but such a request does not seem to have been recorded anywhere. Another possibility is that Lanxi Daolong, who arrived in Japan in 1246, had them made and sent when he found the Japanese so anxious to duplicate the Chan models.

These illustrations of several major official Chinese Chan monasteries as they were around 1250, in providing a detailed blueprint for a traditional Chan monastery, would have been invaluable to the Japanese patrons, designers, and builders of Zen monasteries. We can't be sure that they were immediately available to Lanxi at the outset of the building of Kenchōji. But, even if he did not have them sent to him directly in Kamakura, he had close relations with Enni at Tōfukuji and would almost certainly have had access to them very shortly after they reached that shrine. On the basis of his personal experience, including direct experience of several of the great Chan monasteries illustrated in the scrolls, he would easily have been able to interpret the illustrations for patrons, monks, and carpenters.

Ground Plan of Kenchōji in 1331: The Kenchōji sashizu

It was probably in the realm of monastic life and organization that Lanxi was able to make the greatest contribution. Under his leadership and guidance, and with the enthusiastic support of his warrior patrons, Kenchōji became the first full-fledged "Chan" monastery in Japan and set the example for Engakuji and the dozens of Rinzai Zen communities that were to quickly follow (figs. 5.4 and 5.5). This is not to suggest that Kenchōji, or later Rinzai monasteries, were carbon copies of any particular Chinese monastery or that their layouts and buildings were necessarily "all Chinese." Each Japanese monastery would be shaped to some extent by its topography, and all retained some Japanese features, most often in the abbot's complex. But at the core of the monastery—in the monks' meditation hall, the monks' common room, the kitchen and office buildings, the latrines and bathhouses, and the great central buildings (great gate [*sanmon*], Buddha hall [*butsuden*], and dharma hall [*hattō*])—any Chinese monk would have felt immediately at home. The monastic day was organized as in China, the same chants and rituals were performed, and the sound signals regulating the timetable were all as they would have been in one of the great Chan monasteries.

In the early fourteenth century Kenchōji was considered the most "pure Zen" monastery in Japan, having been built under the direction of a Chinese monk and patterned after the Chan monasteries of the Southern Song.[34] Yet distinctly Japanese elements are evident in the architectural composition. We can visualize Kenchōji in the late Kamakura period from the *Kenchōji sashizu*, a copy of a ground plan for Kenchōji. The original drawing, now lost, was made in 1331 to serve as a reference for the rebuilding of Tōfukuji.[35] The extant version was made in 1732 for the archives of Kenchōji and was based on another copy held by a family of master carpenters who worked for Tōfukuji.

The Kenchōji illustrated in the *sashizu* clearly resembles the Chan monastery ground plans shown in the *Gozan jissatsu zu* in its functional organization, building conformations, and overall scale, but there are also significant differences. Kenchōji seems long and narrow in its north-south axis compared with the illustrations of Chan monasteries in the *Gozan jissatsu zu*, which seem to spread from east to west. This was partly due to the fact that Kenchōji was built in a long and narrow

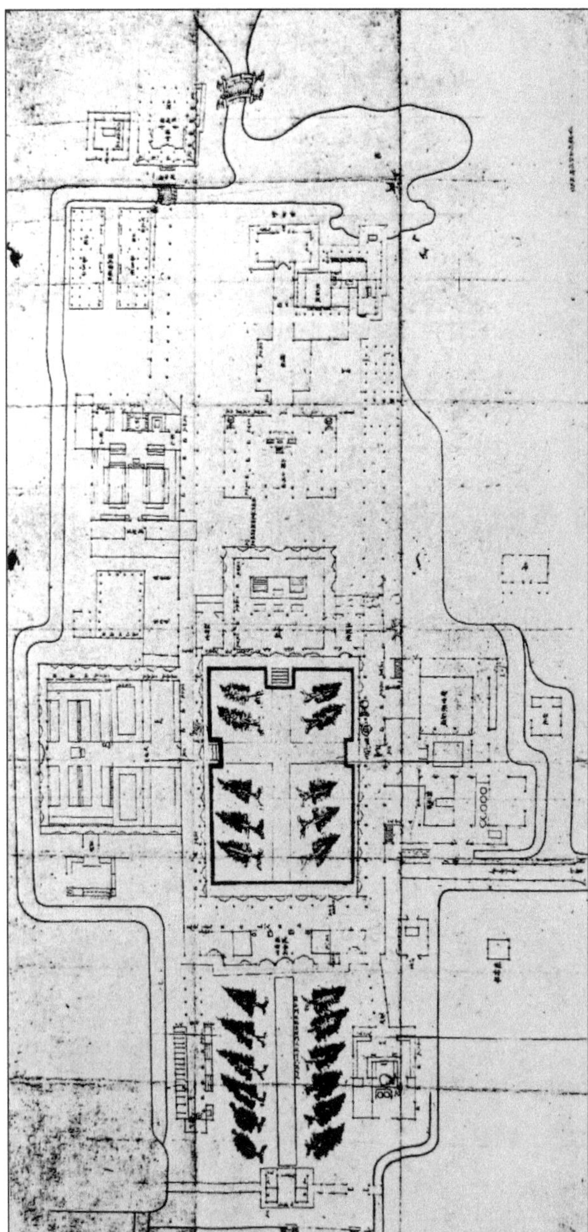

Figure 5.4: *Kenchōji sashizu* (ground plan of Kenchōji).
Courtesy of Kenchōji Rinzai Zen Monastery, Kita-Kamakura,
Japan.

Figure 5.5: Modern Kenchōji. Courtesy of Kenchōji Rinzai Zen Monastery, Kita-Kamakura, Japan.

valley in the hills to the north of Kamakura. We should also take into account that the scrolls on which the *Gozan jissatsu zu* were sketched were long and narrow, perhaps overemphasizing the east-west axis of the ground plans included there. The abbot's complex at Kenchōji was in the Japanese style, not Chinese. This was due to the fact that Hōjō Tokiyori made a gift of the residential buildings to the monastery. Allowing for these differences from the Chinese models, in all other areas of the monastery the buildings, their architecture, their layout, and their furnishings were very like those in Chan monasteries.

We know that Lanxi had the patronage, knowledge, and experience to oversee the building in Japan of a full-scale Chan monastery and that he may well have had detailed plans to remind him of important features. We know, too, that he stressed the strict practice of communal *zazen* and *kōan* interviews. We also have a ground plan that tells us that in 1331 Kenchōji had all the features of a Chan monastery (though accommodating topography and Japanese circumstances). However, we do not know exactly what Kenchōji was like at the time of Lanxi's death in 1276 or, indeed, at any time prior to 1331. In that interval it was burned and rebuilt, then shattered again by a major earthquake. The record suggests that its main public buildings, the monks' halls, and the service buildings were all in Chan style, but we do not know the details.

Chan-Related Culture, Including Calligraphy, Portrait Paintings and Sculpture, Zen-Related Art, Landscape Painting, Ceramics, Lacquer, and Metal Work

Lanxi was a fine calligrapher and has left many examples of Zen-related calligraphy, or *bokuseki*. He had received confirmation of his dharma transmission from his own teacher in the form of a portrait, *chinsō*, and gave such portraits of himself, painted and sculpted, to his own disciples. He knew all the prayers, texts, and ritual forms to be used in ceremonies in the Buddha hall or dharma hall. He was familiar with the fine ceramics used in monastic rituals and tea ceremonies. He knew all the bell, gong, and clapper signals that regulated monastic life. In all of these areas he was able to advise, correct, and introduce authentic Chinese practices.

Lanxi and Chinese Calligraphy: Bokuseki

In Zen practice, *bokuseki* are usually regarded as expressing a person's state of enlightenment, with the brushwork being at least as important as the content of what is written. The calligraphy of Zen masters, however, is hardly the untutored expression of Zen Mind that it is sometimes represented to be. Lanxi and the influential Chinese master Wuzhun Shifan, the teacher of Enni Ben'en and several Chinese priests later active in Japan, both studied the calligraphic style of the Southern Song calligraphy master Zhang Jizhi (1186–1263) while Daxiu Chengnian (Daikyū Shōnen, 1215–1289), the founder of Jōchiji in Kamakura, and Yishan Yining (Issan Ichinei, 1247–1315), the third abbot of Nanzenji in Kyoto, took as their model the Tang dynasty calligrapher Yan Zhenchung (709–784).

Among surviving fine examples of calligraphy, by Lanxi we might mention the following.

Colophon by Lanxi on a painting of a red-robed Bodhidharma. This designated National Treasure of the bearded Indian patriarch is one of the most famous Zen paintings in Japan. It was painted, at Lanxi's request, around 1271 (the date of the famous *chinsō*) as a gift for a lay patron (probably either Hōjō Tokiyori or Tokimune). The colophon reads:

> *He [Bodhidharma] was the youngest son of King Xiangzhi*
> *And a follower of Prajñâtâra's eminent line.*
> He studied [the tenets of] the Buddha,
> Destroying the heretical views of the Six Sects
> He came to China, and the marvelous five-petaled flower blossomed.
> The fragrant doctrine was transmitted to Japan,
> The auspicious signs like sands of the river.
> The original spiritual sprout of the Shao-lin flourished.
> And transplanted to the noble line abroad,
> An extraordinary flower grew.
> > Respectfully written for Rōnen-koji,
> > Lanxi Daolong of Kenchōji.[36]

Buddhist Chant. Another piece of calligraphy in Lanxi's hand contains the text of a Buddhist hymn he composed. The text has been translated as follows.

Great Buddhas of the Ten Directions, and all of you holy saints who have attained the Path, all who have attained Undifferentiating and Subtle Perception, we reverently raise our heads and beg you to bear witness.

May those who have attained the Four Fruitions, and those who have attained the Four Stages of Sanctity all favor us with their luminosity and extend to us their blessings.

To the Heaven of Mahābrāhman, To the Heaven of Indra, To the Eighteen Heavens of the Sphere of Form, where the True Law is protected, To the Tráyastrimsá Heaven, the Yâma Heaven, To the Four Meditations of the Sphere of Form, the Eight Concentrations of the Spheres of Form and Formlessness, To all the congregations of saints gathered in the Thirty-three Heavens, To all saints of all Heavens and Spheres,

We especially pray that our disciple Tokimune may always support the Imperial Throne, and protect, for many years, the doctrine of our sect; that the land within the Four Seas may live in peace and harmony without even one arrow being shot; that the host of demons may bow their heads and desist without so much as a tip of a lance having to be bared.

May we increasingly profit from Virtue and Benevolence; may Longevity and Happiness become ever stronger; may we hold up the torch of intelligence to illuminate the dark road of life; may we open our compassionate hearts to relieve those who are in peril and in want.

May all the Gods assist and protect us, may all the saints closely support us, and may all auspicious events come together and accumulate during the hours of night and day.

Also, we hope that tranquility may reign inside our temple gate; that peace may prevail inside as well as outside; may beneficence and faith be again venerated.[37]

Lanxi Daolong wrote these characters in a bold, vigorous style that is said to be reminiscent of that of the great calligrapher Zhang Jizhi. "That the host of demons may bow their heads" supposedly refers to the Mongol invaders. At that time, the imperial court was holding continuous services to pray for the safety of the country, and Lanxi may well have led his priests in chanting invocations such as this hymn.

Other examples could be introduced, but this should be sufficient to make it clear that Lanxi left his imprint on, and set high standards for, the whole range of calligraphy in Japanese Zen monasteries. Monks who studied under him and laymen and laywomen who had contact with him would have been exposed to the highest standards of Zen *bokuseki*. It is not hard to understand why his writings should have been treasured and preserved at Kenchōji.

Chinsō *Paintings and Sculptures*

There is in Zen a tradition of receiving, on completion of one's formal training, the portrait (*chinsō)* or surplice (*kesa*) of one's teacher as evidence of dharma transmission (*inka shōmei*). These often became cherished temple possessions, as did the portraits and sculptures of eminent priests who were associated with the temple and, in many cases, were buried on the temple grounds. From this evolved the genre of Zen *chinsō* art. Temples also possessed paintings of such figures as Sakyamuni (the historical Buddha), Bodhidharma (the sixth-century Indian monk said to have transmitted Zen to China), and the various bodhisattvas and arhats (enlightened Buddhist sages), as well as collections of flower vases, candle stands, censers, incense containers, and other accoutrements necessary for the performance of ceremonies. Important temples sought the highest quality in such objects, with the result that Song dynasty temples were filled not only with texts, paintings, and studies but also with artistic masterpieces made of celadon, red lacquer, and bronze.

The ideal in *chinsō* portraiture is not just to represent the physical features of the subject but to capture something of his personality and spirit as well. The painter or sculptor is, of course, simply an artist and cannot be expected to possess the same spiritual insights as a Zen master. Nevertheless, *chinsō* artists with a sincere desire to convey the inner qualities of their subjects have often succeeded in producing likenesses of striking insight and power. Needless to say, such renditions were possible only when artists could work directly with their subjects; otherwise they had to rely on sketches, which provided them with, at best, a secondhand sense of the masters' spirituality.

There are at least four surviving painted portraits of Lanxi and several portrait sculptures. Let me note three examples.

Portrait of 1271. Among the extant portraits or Lanxi Daolong that are dated Bun'ei 8 (1271) and inscribed by Lanxi himself, there is a particularly fine example of *chinsō*.[38] The portrait has a real sense of individuality. The Chinese monk is not presented as a physically imposing man, but the slim figure radiates energy and power. The piece was presented by Lanxi to a certain Layman Rōnen (thought to be the regent Hōjō Tokimune or his father Tokiyori) and thus appears not to have been a certificate of dharma transmission.

Lanxi's Portrait in Walking Meditation (*Kinhinzō*). The portrait shows an older Lanxi and does not have quite the force of the 1271 likeness, but it still conveys the strong presence of the Chinese monk.[39]

Seated Sculpture of Lanxi. Not all *chinsō* were painted. Some powerful images of Chan monks were modeled and sculpted, often from life. There seems to have been a vogue for sculpted *chinsō* in Kamakura. The seated sculpture of an emaciated Daolong, holding the whisk that symbolizes his mastership in Zen, in the possession of the Kenchōji subtemple Seirai'an, rivals the Bun'ei *chinsō* in its sense of vitality and concentrated energy.[40]

Conclusion: Kamakura as a Center of Zen and Chinese Culture

Lanxi and his Chinese monk successors, with the patronage of the Hōjō regents and other eastern warriors, turned the garrison town of Kamakura into a center of Chan practice and Chinese learning and culture in the second half of the thirteenth century. In addition to Song-style *bokuseki* and *chinsō*, Lanxi (and his Chinese successors) would have filled Japanese monasteries with the kinds of metalwork, ceramics, books, lacquerware, and so on with which they were familiar. Eager Japanese patrons would gladly have purchased goods from China, *karamono*, in enormous quantities to fill these monasteries. We do not know exactly what Lanxi brought with him, or had sent from China, but we do know, on the basis of documents such as the *Butsunichian kōmotsu mokuroku*, that Song wares of all kinds were imported to Japan in the thirteenth century. It is also fair to assume that Japanese copies of some of these items were being attempted. It is possible to include Song dynasty works of art that were *probably* at Kenchōji or other Kamakura monasteries before the end of the thirteenth century. It is, however, difficult to know exactly when and how they came to Japan. The Chinese metal, ceramic, lacquer, and wood wares that became available in these decades certainly provided a major stimulus for Japanese artists and craftsmen.

The many monks who came to practice Zen with Lanxi had few material possessions apart from their robes, eating bowls, and straw sandals, but they imbibed all the many Chinese-style practices and forms in use in the Kamakura monasteries and carried knowledge of them throughout the country. Within a few decades they could assert, with some confidence, that it was no longer necessary to travel to Song China to find authentic Zen practice and its traditional monastic receptacle.

Notes

[1] On Zen-style meditative practices in Nara and Heian period Japan, see Ibuki Atsushi, *Zen no rekishi*, pp. 173–186.

[2] This phase of Zen history in Japan is discussed in many books in Japanese and English. See, for example, Tsuji Zennosuke, *Nihon Bukkyōshi*, vol. 2.

[3] Murai Shōsuke has identified as many as twenty-eight Chinese monks (and one from Koryŏ) who came to Japan between 1228 and 1368. Some soon returned to China, but many spent the remainder of their lives in Japan. Of these, twenty-five arrived during the Kamakura period. Collectively they ensured a solid transmission of every aspect of Chinese Chan practice, monastic life, and culture. See Murai Shōsuke, "Toraisō no seiki," especially the chart on pp. 174–175. See also Murai Shōsuke, *Higashi Ajia ōkan*. Many entries on Lanxi and Kenchōji may be found in Asami Ryūsuke et al., *Zen no genryū*, a catalogue for an exhibition of art from Kamakura temples celebrating the 750th anniversary of the founding of Kenchōji in 2003.

[4] See Murai, "Torai sō no seiki."

[5] On Lanxi, see Tsuji, *Nihon Bukkyōshi*, 2; Murai, *Higashi Ajia ōkan*; and Matsuo Kenji, *Nihon Chūsei no Zen to Ritsu*, pp. 122–31.

[6] According to the monk Kokan Shiren, author of the 1322 *Genkō shakusho*, Lanxi made the trip because he had heard that the Japanese islands offered a promising mission field for Chan (*Genkō shakusho*, vol. 6, p. 78). For more on Shiren and his efforts to "bring the mainland to the islands," see Carl Bielefeldt, "Kokan Shiren and the Sectarian Uses of History."

[7] Tsuji, *Nihon Bukkyōshi*, 2, p. 125; *Daikaku Zenji goroku*, pt. 1.

[8] Yiweng, who came from the same part of China as Lanxi, later headed Kenninji in Kyoto and Kenchōji in Kamakura. He died in Japan in 1281. Longjian headed Jōmyōji in Kamakura. Little is known about the subsequent activities of Faping. See Murai, "Toraisō no seiki," pp. 174–175.

[9] Tsuji, *Nihon Bukkyōshi*, vol. 2, p. 125.

[10] For the history of Jufukuji, see Kamakura Shishi Hensen Iinkai, *Kamakura shishi, shajihen*, section on Jufukuji. See also *Azuma kagami* Shōji 2 (1200).intercalary 2.12. For more on Hōjō Masako, see Martin Collcutt, "'Nun Shogun': Politics and Religion in the Life of Hōjō Masako (1157–1225)," esp. pp. 180–183.

[11] *Kamakura Shishi Hensen Iinkai, Kamakura shishi, shajihen*, p. 290.

[12] Ibid., p. 213.

[13] *Daikaku Zenji goroku*, pt. 1.

[14] For a history of Jōrakuji, see *Kamakura Shishi Hensen Iinkai, Kamakura shishi, shajihen*, pp. 413–418.

[15] On the foundation and early history of Kenchōji, see ibid., section on Kenchōji.

[16] Asami Ryūsuke et al., *Zen no genryū*, p. vi.

[17] This information on Kenchōji's early landholdings is taken from Matsuo, *Nihon chūsei no Zen to Ritsu*, p. 129.

[18] Quoted in Daihonzan Kenchōji, *Kyofukuzan Kenchōji,* p. 48.

[19] *Shōichi Kokushi nenpu*, p. 61.

[20] *Kenchōji kishiki.*

[21] *Ikai gojō,* art. 4.

[22] Martin Collcutt, *Five Mountains*, p. 62.

[23] For more on this, see Thomas Conlan, *In Little Need of Divine Intervention: Scrolls of the Mongol Invasions of Japan.*

[24] Takagi Sōkan, *Kenchōji-shi Kaisan Daikaku Zenji den.*

[25] For more on Musō, see Martin Collcutt, "Musō Soseki."

[26] Asami et al., *Zen no genryū*, p. 197.

[27] See Collcutt, *Five Mountains*, pp. 133–165.

[28] Asami et al., *Zen no genryū*, pp. vi–vii.

[29] Ibid.

[30] Ibid., p. vii.

[31] Ibid.

[32] These are carefully analyzed by Bruce Coates in "The Architecture of Zen-Sect Buddhist Monasteries in Japan, 1200–1500;" see especially pp. 44–107 and 209–240.

[33] For illustrations of the *Gozan jissatsu zu*, see *Zengaku daijiten*, III, pp. 10–32; and Coates, "The Architecture of Zen-Sect Buddhist Monasteries in Japan, 1200–1500."

[34] Ōta Hirotarō, *Chūsei no kenchiku*, p. 229.

[35] Ink on paper, 175 x 83.5 cm. A detail of the original drawing is published in Daihonzan Kenchōji, *Kyofukuzan Kenchōji*, p. 120. A modern rendering of the plan is published in Sekiguchi Kin'ya, "Gozan to Zen'in," p. 155.

[36] Jan Fontein, ed., *Zen Painting and Calligraphy*, p. 51.

[37] Ibid., p. 52–53.

[38] For an illustration, see Asami et al., *Zen no genryū*, p. 36.

[39] For an illustration, see ibid. p. 37.

[40] Ibid., pp. 38–39.

6

Chinese Trade Ceramics in Medieval Japan

Saeki Kōji

Translated and adapted by Peter Shapinsky

Japanese people have treasured "Chinese goods," *karamono*, from ancient times. The term *karamono* originally applied to items associated with the Tang period but over time was applied more broadly to products that came to Japan from China. The term, which remained as standard usage for close to a thousand years, might thus refer either to products that were made in China or to objects from a variety of Asian lands that came to Japan through China. Most broadly, the term could indicate any goods originating overseas. Accordingly, a wide variety of goods and items are included in the category of *karamono*. Books, comestibles, condiments, fauna, flora, paintings, and pharmaceuticals are but a few that readily come to mind. What I would like to take up here are ceramics, which are representative of both the narrower and wider definitions of *karamono*. As such, ceramics provide us with a good example of how the circulation of material objects in East Asia, based on issues of demand and supply and inextricably linked to issues of reception and appropriation, shaped standards of fashion and aesthetics.

We may note three more specific reasons for taking up the topic of ceramics when considering the various issues involved in cultural exchange between Japan and foreign lands in the premodern period. First, ceramics are especially representative of those Chinese products exported in large quantities to many parts of the world over the centuries. The English-language terms *china* and *chinaware* are ready reminders of that. In Japan, many imported ceramics have survived as heirlooms, and written sources reveal the ways in which the Japanese imported and received trade ceramics. Second, vigorous archaeological excavations of medieval Japanese sites currently under way have discovered tremendous amounts of Chinese ceramics and other types of trade ceramics helping to clarify the means of distribution and reception through archaeological methods. Unlike metallic or wooden products, ceramics remain relatively unchanged when interred. As a result of this durability, and thus the intrinsically high rate of survival of ceramics, analysis of unearthed trade ceramics reveals to us far more concrete patterns of usage and disposal than we are able to gain from the study of other major commodities imported from China such as textiles, written materials, and paintings. Third, in the Muromachi period we see the creation of a particular aesthetic, which became a distinct and valued element of traditional Japanese culture. This aesthetic was based on *karamono*, pottery was central to it, and it incorporated such elements as the tea ceremony, art objects, and a new class of items that we may call antiques.

This essay will first explore the methods by which the medieval Japanese imported and received trade pottery (also known as import pottery and shipborne pottery). Then we will look at information that we can glean from recovered pottery and the role of Hakata as a center for the pottery trade. Last, we will note some of the cultural impact of pottery. We shall finish with some concluding remarks.

Trade Ceramics and the Appreciation of *Karamono* by Medieval Japanese

The intense interest in acquiring *karamono* is well attested by edicts from 903 in which, concerned with the reckless buying of *karamono* by wealthy noble families with no regard to price, the Heian government outlawed smuggling and the violation of price regulations.[1] This passion of the Heian aristocracy for *karamono*, and the fact that *karamono* included the exotic and fabled, is also reflected in the items requested of her five suitors by the fairy-tale princess Kaguya-hime: the stone bowl used by the Buddha when achieving enlightenment; a branch of the tree with silver roots, a golden trunk, and fruits of white jewels that grew on the mythically fabled Mount Penglai across the Eastern Seas; a coat made from the Chinese fire-rat; five-colored sparkling jewels from the neck of a dragon; and a charm for easy birth made from the shell of a swallow's egg.[2]

As Japan's trade with Song China developed and prospered in the latter part of the Heian period,[3] the demand for *karamono* increased, showed no signs of slackening, and continued apace even as changes in China saw the Song replaced by the Yuan at the end of the thirteenth century. In the early fourteenth century the "fad" for *karamono* came to the attention of the noted essayist Yoshida Kenkō. Kenkō was critical of how current practices were devaluing standards of language and cultural appreciation. He appears not to have had much disposable income and, while well informed, was not otherwise known for being au courant. For Kenkō, the defined and inherited old was preferable to the fashionable new, as we see in a celebrated statement that he buttressed with allusions to classical Chinese texts that were for him familiar and not foreign.

> With the exception of medicines, an absence of Chinese goods (*karamono*) should not be mourned. As Chinese texts (*fumi, sho*) have spread throughout the land they are easily copied out by hand (*kaki utsushi*). Despite the dangerous crossing, Chinese (*Morokoshi*) vessels come ever more heavily laden with nothing but

useless things. This is the height of foolishness. Is it not written in the [Chinese] classics (*fumi, bun*) that "One does not make treasures of distant objects" and "One does not esteem expensive goods that are difficult to acquire"?[4]

Others, however, had a more positive perspective on the trend. One of the highest placed warriors of the same era, and one of the most enthusiastic afficianados and facilitators of *karamono* collecting, Kanezawa Sadaaki, noted that "*Karamono* and tea are growing more popular than ever before."[5] That assessment is supported by another contemporary, former emperor Hanazono (r. 1308–1318). Entries from Hanazono's diary from the 1320s and 1330s refer to such things as the hanging of *kara-e* Chinese paintings in rooms accompanied by the placement of vases and incense burners;[6] the drinking of tea after imbibing alcohol, which is possibly our earliest example of what a later Chinese observer noted was a customary Japanese practice;[7] and a tea identification competition between Hanazono and some companions.[8] We are left in no doubt that interest in tea and its associated paraphernalia was booming.

The appreciation of *karamono* unquestionably included Chinese ceramics. In fact, Kamei Meitoku's investigation into the vocabulary for glazed pottery that appears in Heian period texts has revealed that, as in other areas of cultural life, pottery was delineated in terms of indigenous or foreign: the term *tea bowl* indicated that an item was considered to be an imported ceramic from China, while an item referred to as being of "blue [white] glaze" indicated that it had been fired domestically in Japan.[9] Kamei's analysis also clearly demonstrates the high value placed on the use of imported ceramics in temples and monasteries and in the mansions of the imperial court and aristocracy in this era.

Trade statistics for the premodern era are lacking, making it difficult to know precisely the amount of goods imported during the Heian period. However, by the beginning of the fourteenth century it appears that—as with the case of Chinese coinage, millions and millions of units of which were imported during the thirteenth century—the quantities involved were immense. Some qualitative evidence offers clues.

Our single most useful material guide here comes from study of the goods raised from the Sinan shipwreck discovered off the coast of South Korea in 1976. According to the results of the survey of goods retrieved from the shipwreck, the vessel was a ship involved in the trade between Japan and Yuan China and sank off the southwestern coast of the Korean Peninsula in 1323. At the time it was being used as a joint venture ship in the China trade owned by a Chinese party and hired by a Japanese. It had been dispatched to acquire cargo in China, profits from the sale of which in Japan were to be put towards a fund to repair the Tōfukuji temple complex in Kyoto. The ship left Qingyuan (Ningbo) in China for Hakata in Japan heavily laden with copper coins, pottery, red sandalwood, metalwork, and other goods. The raised cargo includes no less than 20,661 pieces of pottery.[10] Aside from small amounts of Korean Koryŏ celadon and Japanese Koseto pots,[11] all of the pieces are Chinese ceramics. There are 12,359 pieces of Chinese celadon and 5,303 pieces of white ware. The celadon consists primarily of the Longquanyao type from southern Zhejiang Province, and the majority of the white ware came from Jingdezhen kilns in northern Jiangxi Province.[12] Typological analysis has revealed that by far most pieces are double-handled vases (approximately ten thousand pieces), followed by blue and white peony arabesque bottles (approximately thirty-five hundred pieces). The prevalence of vases, bottles, and other containers rather than bowls and plates is a distinguishing feature of this shipwreck and has given rise to the term *Sinan-type pottery*. This Sinan-type Chinese pottery has been unearthed at a number of sites throughout Japan.

One of the driving forces behind the acquisition of pottery appears to have been, as suggested by Kanezawa Sadaaki's comment cited earlier, the growing popularity of tea, more precisely that of the powdered green tea that is associated these days with the tea ceremony.[13] We might note that tea, while it originated in China, had been brought under cultivation in Japan and seems not to have been regarded as a *karamono*. However, one can easily imagine that specialty Chinese teas may have been a coveted luxury import and perhaps avidly used in the type of tea competitions that were engaged in by (as noted earlier) such people as Emperor Hanazono. Otherwise, almost everything else associated with tea was a *karamono*. The practice of drinking tea requires tea bowls, other implements, a place in which to drink the tea—which became, as the *chashitsu*, or "tea room," a new architectural addition—and decorations to adorn this place of tea. Japanese tea practitioners naturally replicated the "authentic tea environment" that had been introduced from China. As such it required *karamono* and naturally propelled the demand for them at the highest cultural levels. Various written sources, as well as an inventory of items stored at one of Kamakura's leading Zen temple complexes, Engakuji, suggest that warriors, aristocrats, monks, and others acquired large amounts of the *karamono* that entered Japan via trade with Yuan China.[14]

The Engakuji example is revealing, for it is thought that tea first took hold in Japan because of the close ties that Zen priests had with China. Zen monasteries were important sites for the reception of Chinese culture, and they sponsored the dispatching of many so-called "temple-shrine repair fund-raising China ships" (*jisha zōeiryō tōsen*). In addition, many Zen monks went to Yuan China to study and train. As a consequence of this direct contact with Chinese culture, Zen monks, as has been demonstrated by Murai Shōsuke, had a particular fondness for Chinese ceramics.[15] And tea was an important aesthetic experience for a Zen monk, as Betsugen Enshi (1295–1364), who spent the years 1320–1330 studying in China, conveys in his poem *Green Tea* (*Sencha*).

> Curling clouds of vapors jade green, into wisps of gossamer they breezily spool
> On the bowl's surface white blossoms to glean, in mind's eye refreshingly cool
> Mountain moonlight shines through window to me, plum's shadows wave and
>   slip
> Into the unglazed cup afresh I pour tea, the lingering fragrance I tranquilly sip.[16]

Still, we should reiterate that active interest in acquiring *karamono* extended beyond priestly circles. Private letters preserved in the Kanazawa Bunko library, which was established in the 1270s by the Kanezawa family, a branch of Kamakura's dominant Hōjō warrior family to which Kanezawa Sadaaki belonged, make this abundantly clear.[17] From these materials we learn that the arrival in Kamakura of ships laden with *karamono* was greeted with great delight not only by socially advantaged warriors and priests,[18] as we might expect, but by the population as a whole. On occasion disturbances broke out in the city as people tried to acquire items any way they could.[19] Not all the *karamono* were considered particularly valuable,[20] which reinforces the sense that they were ubiquitous. But the amount and value of some *karamono* made them, as noted with some concern even by Sadaaki himself, an attractive target for thieves.[21] No doubt Kenkō would have felt vindicated to know of this.

The *karamono* import phenomenon was regular enough that the ships bringing the cargo were referred to as "China Ships," an appellation denoting not only ships of Chinese origin but also trading vessels dispatched from Japan to China or ships that carried *karamono* from a Japanese entrepôt to the environs of Kamakura. Since we know that commercial networks were widespread throughout the Japanese archipelago by this time, it is not unreasonable to assume that, in addition to those residing in a center of political authority such as Kamakura, people residing elsewhere but connected to trade and information networks might have had the opportunity to acquire *karamono* either through dealers or through personnel networks. In fact, it appears that some people, at least, could commission (or order) people to get hold of desired objects on their behalf. As noted in one early-fourteenth-century letter:

> Regarding the tea bowls and pots you instructed me to procure, I searched in various places for those having a two-*shaku* diameter but did not find any. However, I did find some of one-*shaku* or even one-*shaku* two-*sun* diameter, though out here in the countryside they are very expensive. I await your instructions [to buy or not].[22]

In this excerpt from a letter dated the eighth month of 1310, one Tamenao, an estate manager for Shikanoshima in Kyushu's Chikuzen Province, has written to his proprietor in Kyoto. As noted, the Kyoto proprietor has instructed the manager to find a bowl or pot with a two-*shaku* diameter (one *shaku* = 30.3 cm, so 60.6 cm). Despite having searched in various places, Tamenao answered that he could not find a two-*shaku*-diameter vessel and that one-*shaku* or one-*shaku* two-*sun* diameter ones were very expensive. From the phrase, "searched in various places" it can be assumed that Tamenao boarded a ship and crossed over to Hakata on the opposite shore of Hakata Bay from Shikanoshima to search for the proper tea bowl, but even there he could not find the piece he had been sent to find. This tea bowl would, of course, have been *karamono*. Thus, another method of obtaining *karamono* would be for those residing in the capital but bearing absentee proprietorship posts in estates or other landholdings in northern Kyushu to ask someone resident on the holding to send it to them. We also see this in the following example.

> You did me the great favor of sending me one piece of Kensan ware that I desired and troubled you for. I am overjoyed with your efforts in this matter. As it is said that *karamono* are quite prevalent in your region, if you find a really nice piece and send it to me, I would be further gratified. The tea whisk is elegant and should be presented, but since it seems not possible to get it at this time, it can be sent up at a later date."[23]

This excerpt is from a letter written in the eighth month of 1362 by the Kyoto aristocrat Takatsuji Nagahira to one Kotorii Hōgen, the on-site monk administrator of Dazaifu's Anrakuji (Dazaifu Tenmangū) temple in Chikuzen, over which temple Nagahira held a proprietorship. We can track Nagahira and his contacts with various Kyushu administrators over a period of at least twenty-two years, so we are probably on safe ground in assuming that the request in this letter would not have been the only such instance.[24] In the letter, Nagahira asked Kotorii Hōgen to obtain for him a piece of Kensan pottery, and Kotorii fulfilled the request. Kensan is a type of Tenmoku tea bowl from the Jianyao kilns of modern-day Fujian Province, a place famous for its fine ceramics. Kotorii duly acquired the high-quality Tenmoku tea bowls Nagahira desired in the vicinity of Dazaifu and sent them to Nagahira in Kyoto.

Nagahira's further request to Kotorii Hōgen, asking him to acquire the bowls for him because "it is said that *karamono* are quite prevalent in your region," is made seemingly as a matter of course. In fact, it would have been common knowledge in the capital that Hakata was the major Japanese port involved in the Japan-Yuan trade and accordingly northern Kyushu was a place where *karamono* were prevalent.[25] It was certainly known to Takatsuji Nagahira, and he asked

Kotorii Hōgen to find *karamono* on yet other occasions. For example, in a letter dated the twenty-first day of the fourth month (year unrecorded) one of Nagahira's administrators, amid dealing with various aspects of estate management, informed Kotorii:

> We are delighted with the drinking vessel that you sent us. However, as to the *kara-e* Chinese paintings and other *karamono* that we have asked for more than once, these have not been sent. This is quite disappointing.[26]

Trade and the Ryukyu Connection

Nagahira and his administrators may have known that *karamono* was readily attainable in northern Kyushu. However, they may not have been aware of the actual trade routes by which the items arrived. Likewise, they may not have been cognizant of factors affecting the trade that might impact the fulfillment of orders that they seem to have placed as a routine matter.

The elements in Japan's overseas foreign relations in the medieval era have been well delineated in previous scholarship,[27] but let me note some of them before touching on a "nonstate" element that was crucial to maritime trade, the trade routes through the Ryukyu kingdom. Simply stated, a conjunction of political circumstances in Northeast Asia in the late fourteenth century led to a resumption of formal relations, based on the Chinese model of a Sinocentric tribute and vassalage diplomatic order, throughout the region. In Japan the resumption spurred lively debate over the question of whether the formal subordination required was too steep a price and over the propriety of the nomenclaturial legerdemain involved. Issues of frontier and border management were a key part of this, but so was licensed trade. Trade itself was an ongoing phenomenon, but official permission from the Chinese side to engage in this—or, permission to allow foreign elites to legally profit in the same manner as did "unlicensed parties"—was an attractive element. After the official tribute trade, operating under the mechanism of the "tally system," between Muromachi Japan and Ming China commenced in the late fourteenth century, *karamono* entered Japan in large quantities.

However, the trade was not unrestricted. Difficulties in obtaining the requisite credentials and raising sufficient funds prevented the easy outfitting and dispatch of ships to acquire *karamono*. The Ming government restricted Japanese commercial opportunities with China further by implementing the principle that "Chinese subjects are not to engage in foreign intercourse," making trade with the Chinese populace (at least officially) impossible. This was not a particular problem for the Muromachi bakufu, but it did present a problem for many of Japan's temples, shrines, daimyos, and others who wished to conduct trade with China, for they had no alternative but to travel on the tally trade ships of the "king of Japan." It is clear that over time the Muromachi bakufu licensed its prerogatives to allow others to trade under its aegis. And it is also clear that many parties simply resorted to the expedient of document forgery and misrepresentation, evidence for which appears in Korean and Chinese sources rather than Japanese ones. Moreover, "private parties" circumvented official restrictions, particularly after Ashikaga Yoshimochi (1368–1428) put official relations on hold early in the fifteenth century, through indirect trade. What facilitated this, and thus made it possible to meet the demand for *karamono,* was the fact that the Ryukyu kingdom functioned as a commercial intermediary between Ming China and Japan (and, via Japanese parties, Korea).

The fact that the trade in ceramics was an integral part of this trade and transshipment network emerges when we look briefly at Korean records. Let me use as an example information for just the years 1418–26 from the *Sejong sillok,* listing descriptions of ceramics presented to the Chosŏn court by people from Japan and Ryukyu (table 6.1).

Table 6.1: Ceramics Presented by Residents of Japan and Ryukyu, 1418–1426

Korean Date (year-month-day)	Western Calendar	Origin of Presenter	Goods Presented
0-8-14	1418	Second son of the king of Ryukyu, Katsuren	Ten pieces of celadon
0-10-29	1418	Hyūga no kami Genji Shimazu Motohisa	One pair of underglaze decorated bottles[a]
3-11-6	1421	Former Kyushu Deputy Minamoto Dôchin (Shibukawa Mitsuyori)	Five ceramic trays
5-1-28	1423	Former Kyushu Deputy Minamoto Dôchin (Shibukawa Mitsuyori)	Two suffused glaze wine goblets
5-1-28	1423	Bizen no kami Minamoto Masakiyo (Yoshimi Masakiyo)	Three hundred white ceramic Luo-style pots, ten small white ware bowls
5-5-19	1423	Sekijō [Hakata] Shikibu Shōyū Minamoto Shunshin (Younger brother of Shibukawa Mitsuyori)	Four tea bowls
5-6-21	1423	Taira Mitsukage (Itakura Mitsukage)	Five hundred plates
5-6-21	1423	Minamoto Toshinobu	Fifty single dishes

5-9–24	1423	Chikuzen no kami Minamoto [Shōni] Mitsusada	Seventy celadon trays, twenty white ware bowls, large and small
5-10-15	1423	Taira Mitsukage (Itakura Mitsukage)	Ten white ware tea bowls, thirty celadon tea bowls, thirty celadon dishes
8-6-1	1426	Governor of Tsushima Sōda Saemontarō	Fifty dishes
8-11-1	1426	Governor of Chikuzen Dazai Shōni Fujiwara Mitsusada	One hundred single dishes, one thousand ceramic tea bowls
8-12-14	1426	Former Kyushu Deputy Minamoto Dōchin (Shibukawa Mitsuyori)	One thousand ceramic tea bowls

Source: *Sejong sillok*, years 1418–1426.

ª Underglaze decorated pottery refers to the practice of applying blue, red, green, brown and other colored designs to white ware and then applying a clear glaze, also known as blue [white] ware. The cobalt Quinghua ware is perhaps the most famous variety. See He, *Chinese Ceramics: A New Comprehensive Survey*, p. 338.

As noted, the period under examination is confined to the nine years from 1418 to 1426, primarily because, due to a peculiarity in the compiling of the *Sejong sillok*, it is only for this period that detailed records of goods presented remain. This limited scope does not mean that ceramics were no longer presented after 1426, and it can be assumed that even after 1426 pottery continued to be presented to the king.

Not all of the goods listed in Table 1 can be definitively identified as Chinese ceramics, but descriptive prefixes such as *celadon, white ware, ceramic,* or *underglaze decoration* probably indicate pottery fired in China. The largest quantity recorded is the thousand ceramic tea bowls. In Japan, the period from 1418 to 1426 corresponds to the period during the shogunate of Yoshimochi when he interrupted the tally trade between Japan and Ming China. The only way to understand how the Japanese could possibly have presented such a large amount of Chinese ceramics to Chosŏn during this period of suspended tally trade would be to consider the role of Ryukyu as an intermediary in the relay trade along the alternate route of China-Ryukyu-Japan.[28] In fact, during this period the Chūzan court proceeded to unify Ryukyu, and Ryukyuan merchant ships actively sailed to and from Japan.

When we look at Table 6.1 we note that, with the exception of Katsuren of Ryukyu, Shimazu Motohisa of Satsuma, Sōda Saemontarō of Tsushima, and Shōni Mitsusada of Dazaifu, those sending goods to be presented at the Chosŏn court were family members and retainers of the Shibukawa, the Kyushu deputy resident in Hakata. Chinese ceramics were carried via Ryukyu to Hakata, where those individuals affiliated with the Kyushu deputy and others acquired them to present to the king of Chosŏn. In other words, the Ryukyu relay-trade routes bypassed the restrictions of the other two countries, since Ryukyu allowed trade between Japan and Ming China to continue indirectly.

Trade through Ryukyu was not the only indirect means by which ceramics might be circulated and acquired. Although the tally trade between Japan and Ming China ended in the mid-sixteenth century, the newly arisen Chinese maritime bandit-traders (the so-called latter *wakō*) continued to trade actively between Japan and Ming China. Chinese studies about Japan compiled in this period, such as the *Riben fengtuji* (Gazetteer of Japan) and the *Riben kao* (Thoughts on Japan), contain descriptions of silk and many other products the Japanese desired. In referring to ceramics, the *Riben kao* notes:

> [The Japanese] favor pieces with flower motifs. Censers with designs of small
> bamboo joints are preferred, as are bowls and plates with decorations of luxuriant
> chrysanthemum blossoms. Those with blooms of hollyhock are also favored. If
> it has no gloriously flowering design, even if it is a product of the official kilns,
> it does not please them.[29]

Obviously, the Japanese penchant for Chinese ceramics continued unabated through at least the sixteenth century.

Trade Ceramics Unearthed in Japan

To obtain a further sense of the extent and rhythms of trade ceramics, I shall now turn to consideration of the actual pottery items that have been unearthed in Japan. The majority of the ceramics that have been unearthed in Japan consists of Chinese wares, though pottery from Koryŏ and Chosŏn, Thailand, Vietnam, and other places have been found in smaller quantities. These finds indicate that in the medieval period trade with China and other lands of East Asia and Southeast Asia flourished and wide-ranging networks of distribution and exchange circulated these goods throughout Japan. The high survival rate of these trade ceramics has enabled scholars to determine the circumstances of use and amounts consumed. In addition, because textual sources about commerce and distribution are not extant in large numbers, unearthed ceramics supplement the written record. Archaeological discoveries also highlight close linkages between trade ceramics and Japanese ceramics production. For example, once white ware and celadon were brought to Japan, kilns in such places as Sanage and Seto began firing imitations.[30]

Our knowledge of trade ceramics has increased dramatically because archaeologists have focused significant attention on the topic. Most studies have focused on categorizing and dating the ceramics, and the typology and dating of the ceramics unearthed at Dazaifu, in particular, have become the standard for this. Excavations of trade ceramics have been catalogued, but, due to difficulties stemming from the sheer amounts of pottery unearthed, a comprehensive quantitative analysis of the entire country has yet to be undertaken. However, various trends in ceramic imports have emerged from the study of results of archaeological excavations. A consensus on how to understand the trends has yet to emerge, and debate remains vigorous. Let me present five of the major interpretations, which, as we will see, nonetheless share some points in common.

First, Yabe Yoshiaki argues that the nadir of Japanese importation of Chinese ceramics occurred in the latter half of the eleventh century. Then, from the twelfth century on, Longquanyao celadon imports gradually began to rise. Importation of trade ceramics drastically increased in the thirteenth century; by the end of the thirteenth and the beginning of the fourteenth century, import pottery flourished to the point that it was being trafficked all over Japan with the exception of Hokkaidō.[31]

Second, Narasaki Shōichi divides the importation of Chinese ceramics from the late eleventh century to the mid-fourteenth into three periods, summarized as follows.[32] White ware dominated the first period (from the late eleventh century to the late twelfth) until the mid–twelfth century, when imports of Longquanyao celadon bowls and plates began. Tonganyao ware from the coastal region of Fujian Province[33] arrived soon after. These ceramics have been found from Kyushu to Niigata Prefecture, but the majority of the finds are located in western Japan. In the second period (late twelfth century to the mid-thirteenth) Longquanyao and Tonganyao became the principal imported wares and various production centers and styles flourished. In the thirteenth century, the Longquanyao kilns added lotus petal motifs to their bowls. Pottery from this period was imported in enormous quantities and has been found from Tōhoku to the Okinawan islands. In the third period (late thirteenth century to the mid-fourteenth), imported celadon ware consisted mainly of Longquanyao pots and lotus petal decorated bowls. White ware consisted mostly of small plates of the so-called unglazed lip (J. *kuchihage*) style. Of urns and vases, four-handled urns and plum vases survive in the largest quantities. With Kamakura as an axis of trade in this period, tremendous amounts of *karamono* spread throughout the eastern lands.

Third, Kamei Meitoku divides the Japanese importation of ceramics from the Song and later dynasties into four periods, summarized as follows.[34] The first period (the ninth century through the early eleventh) is characterized by Yuezhouyao[35] celadon and represents the beginning of the first stage of import pottery. Most of this pottery has been unearthed in western Japan, indicating that the pottery had not yet acquired a far-flung demand. The second stage (the late eleventh century through the twelfth) witnessed vast improvements in quality and quantity as imported white ware production became concentrated in private kilns of Zhejiang, Fujian, and Guangdong. In the third period (from the thirteenth century to the mid-fourteenth), Longquanyao-type celadon bowls with lotus petal motifs rose to dominance. Hakata's preeminence as the major importation port ended, and the center of distribution shifted through the Seto Inland Sea to the Kinai and then to Kamakura. Excepting Hokkaido, ceramics from this period can be unearthed almost anywhere in Japan, although fewer trade ceramics have been found in eastern than in western Japan. The fourth period (the second half of the fourteenth century through the sixteenth) corresponds to the Ming dynasty, but satisfactory finds from the first hundred years of the early Ming period (the mid-fourteenth century through the mid-fifteenth) are extremely rare, so the period remains unclear.

Fourth, Sasaki Tatsuo has summarized the importation and reception of Chinese pottery in the ancient and medieval periods, as illustrated in Table 6.2.[36]

Table 6.2: The Importation and Reception of Chinese Ceramics

Period	Characteristic
Eighth century	Small amounts of pottery imported
Ninth–Tenth Centuries	Use of ceramics centered around people in the capital
Thirteenth Century	Large amounts of celadon used throughout Japan
Sixteenth Century	Underglaze-decorated pottery spread throughout Japan, everyday household usage
Seventeenth Century	Pottery made in Japan became the mainstream, and imports of Chinese ceramics dwindled

Source: Sasaki Tatsuo, "Hakusai ibutsu no kōkogaku."

In addition, though excavated in smaller quantities, Chosŏn pottery has been found from many eras, as have ceramics from Thailand and Vietnam from the fourteenth through the sixteenth centuries.

Fifth, and finally, Hasebe Gakuji and Imai Atsushi have summarized the circumstances of Chinese trade pottery importation outlined in Table 6.3.[37]

Table 6.3: Imports of Chinese Ceramics

Period	Characteristic
Late Eighth Century	Early period of trade pottery, imports of Yuezhouyao celadon, Tang-style white ware, Changsha yellow glazed ware, etc.
Late Tenth Century– mid-Eleventh Century	Nadir of imports of Chinese ceramics
Late Eleventh Century– early Twelfth Century	Large quantities of Chinese ceramics imported, age of superlative white ware, increase in archaeological finds, increased variation of types of vessels
Late Twelfth Century– early Fourteenth Century	One peak of imports of Chinese pottery, further increase in archaeological finds, regional distribution increases, widespread use as everyday objects, age of Longquanyao celadon
Late Fourteenth Century–mid-Fifteenth Century	Celadon, white ware, varied vessels all made in local, private kilns, few archaeological finds from this era
Late Fifteenth Century– Sixteenth Century	Rise in imports of celadon with flower motifs, mostly bowls and plates

Source: Hasebe Rakuji and Imai Atsushi, *Nihon shutsudo no Chūgoku tōji.*

Obviously these scholars offer differing periodizations and descriptions, but if we summarize the overall trends in medieval trade ceramics imports to Japan, we are able to divide the imports into three broad periods. The first period extends from the late eleventh century through the twelfth and is the age of white ware. The second period (from the late twelfth century or early thirteenth through the end of the thirteenth century or the early fourteenth) is characterized by Longquanyao celadon and represents the peak of imports, as finds from this period have been unearthed throughout Japan. The third period bridges a century of stagnation (the fourteenth and fifteenth centuries) and extends from the fifteenth through the sixteenth centuries and is known for underglaze-decorated ceramic ware.

All periods share one common factor, however, namely, the international port of Hakata was central to the circulation of trade ceramics. Accordingly, let us look at some of the information that derives from Hakata.

Hakata and the Ceramics Trade

Hakata in Kyushu was the center of commercial activities with East Asia in Japan from the ancient period onward.[38] In the ninth century, commercial exchange at the Foreign Dignitaries Hall, the Kōrokan, put Dazaifu at the center of the Chinese ceramics trade. Investigation of the goods unearthed from its ruins (located in Heiwa-dai, Chūō-ku, Fukuoka) revealed the largest amount of excavated Yuezhouyao celadon in the world outside of China. By the middle of the eleventh century, the preeminence of the Dazaifu Foreign Dignitaries Hall in overseas trade had ended and the center of exchange shifted 2.5 kilometers eastward to the city of Hakata. Chinese merchants resident in Hakata at this time conducted the majority of the trade between Japan and Song China trade that passed through Hakata.

Results of studies of trade ceramics unearthed at Hakata reveal large amounts of Song white ware from the latter half of the eleventh century through the late twelfth.[39] Large quantities of Longquanyao and Tonganyao celadon also have been unearthed from the mid–twelfth century. From the thirteenth century onward, celadon becomes much more prevalent than white ware. There are various special characteristics of the white ware and celadon unearthed at Hakata. For example, several pieces known as ink-inscribed pottery (*sumigaki tōjiki*) have Chinese characters written on their bases in black ink. Characters such as *Zhang* [張], *Wang* [王], *Ding* [丁], *Chen* [陳], and *Zhou* [周] are common. There is general consensus that these are the names of Song merchants engaged in the ceramics trade in Hakata or China. In addition, the unearthing of several hundred pieces of white ware and celadon bowls that had been discarded dating chiefly from the eleventh through the thirteenth centuries reveals the extent to which the trade in ceramics between Japan and Song China flourished.

From the fourteenth century on, Hakata continued to play an important role as a major entrepôt in the trade with Yuan and Ming China, and many Hakata merchants participated in that commerce. Yuan and Ming ceramics have been unearthed in Hakata, though in lesser quantities than Song wares. The great central temples and shrines, the Muromachi bakufu, and the provincial governors sponsored the majority of Japan's trade with Yuan and Ming China. Although they imported large amounts of pottery, it is thought that these participants had most of the ceramics from Hakata carried to the capital region.

Trade pottery from the fifteenth and sixteenth centuries unearthed at Hakata also contains significant amount of Chosŏn and Southeast Asian ceramics. Chosŏn wares notably accounts for about 10 percent of the total. With the exception of the islands of Tsushima and Iki, close to the Korean Peninsula, nowhere else has Chosŏn pottery been unearthed to such a degree in Japan, illustrating Hakata's busy trade with Chosŏn. Though in smaller amounts than pottery of China or Chosŏn, the presence of ceramics from Thailand and Vietnam in Hakata indicates the arrival of ships from Southeast Asia or at the very least trade with Southeast Asia through Ryukyu.

Comparison of the import trends for all of Japan and analyses of trade ceramics unearthed at Hakata reveals that the peak of Hakata's imports occurred during the first period for Japan as a whole, indicating a disparity in periodization. Japan as a whole reached its zenith of trade ceramics imports in its second period (the Kamakura era) when the development of commercial distribution networks allowed imports to be transported all over the country. This difference in periodization can be attributed to the fact that in the first period Chinese merchants based in Hakata conducted most of the trade while the infrastructure of internal trade networks characteristic of the second period had yet to fully mature.

The Standardization of the Reception of *Karamono* and Trade Pottery

I noted earlier that by the late Kamakura period *karamono* were in great demand. In the Muromachi period, the demand became a part of a new scene in the cultural landscape, namely, the development of trends in connoisseurship toward *karamono* and trade pottery. The connoisseurship encouraged greater stylization and ritualization, and it appears that the reception and appreciation of trade ceramics and *karamono* became increasingly standardized. *Karamono* were used as propitious decorations (*karamono sōgon*), and rules for their use began to be compiled in books of ritual.

Appreciation of *karamono* spread through the influence of Zen temples and warrior society, became part of aristocratic society, and in the Nanbokuchō and Muromachi periods came to constitute part of the medieval aesthetic consciousness.[40] The appreciation of *karamono* became highly stylized as the use of *karamono* as propitious decorations became an established cultural realm. One early Muromachi period text, *Kissa ōrai*, contains directions for room decoration that adorn a tea pavilion entirely in *karamono*. It lists such objects as Chinese paintings of Sakyamuni (Shaka) and Avalokiteshvara (Kannon), gold brocade and a bronze vase on a table, a small table for the censer covered in embroidered brocade, a chair covered in leopard skin, a bamboo chair covered in gold dust, Chinese paintings, a Chinese carved vermilion lacquer incense holder atop an incense censer base, and tea jars. Among ceramics, the text lists tea jars, Kensan ware, and pots for hot water, all of which are objects used in drinking tea.

Another work, the *Kundaikan sōchōki* (Record of Items to Be Viewed to the Left and Right of the Lord's Dais), a book of chamber decoration written by arbiters of taste for the Muromachi bakufu, contains descriptions that highlight the growing stylization of the use of *karamono*. There are two extant versions of the *Kundaikan sōchōki*, each produced by noted Japanese painters who served important roles as cultural advisers to Ashikaga shoguns. The first text is dated to 1476 and bears an earlier interlinear notation by Nōami (1397–1471), while the second is dated to 1511 and attributed to Sōami (d. 1525). Analysis of these two extant versions reveals that the content is divided largely between records of painters and directions on decorating. The section on painters is mostly evaluations of various Chinese artists. The section on decorative methods details rules of chamber adornment, and the entire latter half is devoted to interpretative commentaries on objects, among which are explanatory entries for tea bowls, celadon, white ware, Dingyao white ware, official ware, and others.[41]

In addition, the text contains pictures of all the jars used to hold powdered tea and detailed descriptions of the different varieties of Tenmoku tea bowls used for drinking tea. As we can see from Table 6.4, the *Kundaikan sōchōki* divides Tenmoku tea bowls into seven categories, from Yōhen to plain Tenmoku, and lists their characteristics and prices. As the highest class of Tenmoku, Yōhen tea bowls cost an exorbitant ten thousand *hiki* or one hundred *kanmon*.

Table 6.4: Tenmoku Tea Bowls as Recorded in the *Kundaikan sōchōki*

Variety	Description	Price
Yōhen	The highest quality of all *kensan*, none available in the world	10,000 *hiki*
Yuteki	Second most valuable, a little more available than Yōhen	5,000 *hiki*
Kensan	Not inferior to Yuteki	3,000 *hiki*
Usan	Tōsan-type *kensan*	Cheap
Bessan	Made from Tenmoku clay	1,000 *hiki*
Taisan	Made from Tenmoku clay	Cheap
Tenmoku	Everyday object, not used by the shogun	Price unknown

These high-class ceramics were favored for use at shogunal mansions, and a description of their actual use as propitious chamber decorations can be found in the *Muromachi dono gyōkō okazariki* (Record of Decorations for the Imperial Visit to the Muromachi Palace), a record of the chamber decorations used during the visit of Emperor Go-Hanazono to the shogun Ashikaga Yoshinori's mansion on the twenty-sixth day of the tenth month of 1437.[42] This text lists several pieces of Yuteki- and Kensan-style Tenmoku tea bowls. However, no use of the highest class Yōhen Tenmoku worth ten-thousand *hiki* is recorded, either because the Muromachi shogun did not possess any or because they were not used for chamber decoration on that occasion.

A final point is that the ceramics recorded in the *Kundaikan sōchōki* provide a sense of the types of ceramics preferred by Muromachi period connoisseurs. The ceramics noted in the *Kundaikan sōchōki* are mostly of Dingyao white ware, official ware, Yōhen Tenmoku, Yuteki Tenmoku, and the like. The most notable characteristic of these is that they are mostly pre-Ming styles of pottery fired primarily in the Song dynasty. From this we may conclude that in the Muromachi period those wielding political authority and cultural influence preferred antique ceramics. It follows, then, that the *karamono* carried to Japan in the trade with Ming China included not only those goods produced in Ming China but decorative pieces from previous eras. Analysis of pottery raised from the Sinan shipwreck further substantiates this trend since many of the pieces of pottery bear the marks of previous use.[43]

Concluding Remarks

This essay has explored aspects of *karamono* and the reception of trade ceramics in medieval Japan from written and archaeological sources. It is an early effort to understand more broadly the role of ceramics in medieval Japanese culture. A proper understanding of that, however, will require further wide-ranging exploration of written sources and the further accumulation and quantification of archaeological data. As the two types of sources have completely different characteristics, obtaining congruent conclusions is not easy. However, the fact that both the records of trade pottery in the *Kundaikan sōchōki* and the goods pulled from the Sinan shipwreck contain antique ceramics demonstrates a commonality between the two types of sources that must be recognized. We may anticipate that future research will lead to the establishment of new viewpoints and methods that utilize both sources comprehensively.

As a final note, at the end of the Higashiyama period, elite Japanese culture began to show signs of further domestication until eventually arriving at the early modern *wabi-sabi* aesthetic. In further studies, I hope to examine the effects these cultural transformations and their establishment within society had on the reception of ceramics.[44]

Notes

[1] Mori Katsumi, *Shintei Nissō bōeki no kenkyū*, pp. 96–97.

[2] See *Taketori monogatari*, p. 33; and Donald Keene, trans., *The Tale of the Bamboo Cutter.*

[3] For an overview of Japan's overseas trade through the sixteenth century, see Charlotte von Verschuer, *Across the Perilous Sea: Japanese Trade with China and Korea from the Seventh to the Sixteenth Centuries.*

[4] *Tsurezuregusa*, pp. 186–187. For a slightly different rendering, see Donald Keene, *Essays in Idleness*, no. 120, p. 101. The first quotation is from the *Shujing*, "Hounds of Lü" chapter: "If [the ruler] does not make treasures of distant objects, then distant people will come under [his] sway." The second quotation is from the *Daodejing*, chapter 3: "If one does not esteem expensive goods that are difficult to acquire, then the people will not resort to theft."

[5] (1330?).6.11 Kanezawa Sadaaki shojō (*KI*, 40:31063).

[6] *Hanazono tennō shinki*, entry for Gen'ō 1 (1319).7.29.

[7] Ibid., entry for Genkō 2 (1332).4.8. For the reference to Japanese drinking tea after consuming alcohol, see the *Riben kao* of Li Yangong, p. 41 text (p. 67 of the volume).

[8] *Hanazono tennō shinki*, entry for Genkō 2 (1332).6.5.

[9] Kamei Meitoku, *Nihon bōeki tōjishi no kenkyū*, part 1, chapter 5.

[10] Hanguk Munhwajae Kwalliguk, *Sinan haejo yumul chonghapp'yŏn*, p. 541.

[11] Koseto is pottery made in the Kamakura and Muromachi periods in the Seto region of Owari Province (modern-day Aichi Prefecture).

[12] Longquanyao ware consists largely of celadon and was produced from the Song dynasty onward in the Longquan area of southern Zhejiang Province. Jingdezhen ware comes from the Jingdezhen kilns of northern Jiangxi Province. See He Li, *Chinese Ceramics: A New Comprehensive Survey*, pp. 137, 208–11.

[13] For useful surveys of tea in medieval Japan, see Theodore M. Ludwig, "Before Rikyū: Religious and Aesthetic Influences in the Early History of the Tea Ceremony;" and H. Paul Varley and George Elison, "The Culture of Tea."

[14] Jōji 4 (1365).1.25 Butsunichian kōmotsu mokuroku (Kamakura Shishi Hensan Iinkai, *ed., Kamakura shishi, shiryō hen*, vol. 2, pp. 200–212; [*Engakuji monjo*, no. 167]).

[15] Murai Shōsuke, *Higashi Ajia ōkan*, pp. 82–104.

[16] *Gozan bungaku shū Edo kanshi shū*, p. 82; translation by Andrew Edmund Goble. For other translations, see Marian Ury, *Poems of the Five Mountains*, p. 36:

> Green clouds spiral and twine; are drawn into the wind in a long stream;
> On my cup's surface the faces of white foam flowers are cool;
> The mountain moon comes into my window; plum tree shadows move;
> Pouring again and again into my unglazed cup I sip the lingering fragrance.

and David Pollack, *Zen Poems of the Five Mountains*, p. 134:

> On clouds of jade green, drawn out on the breeze
> Stretch white blossoms over the bowl's surface, cooling to the touch;
> As the mountain moon stirs plum blossom shadows on the window,
> I fill the rough bowl again, sip the lingering fragrance.

[17] For an excellent sense of Sadaaki and *karamono* collecting in Kamakura, see Kanagawa Kenritsu Kanazawa Bunko, ed., *Cha to Kanezawa Sadaaki*.

[18] See, for example (year unknown).5.24 Kanezawa Sadaaki shojō (*KI*, 31:23504); and (year unknown).1.27 Kanezawa Sadaaki shojō (*KI*, 35:27127).

[19] (Year unknown).3.23 Kanezawa Sadaaki shojō (*KI*, 39:30734).

[20] (Year unknown).1.27 Kanezawa Sadaaki shojō (*KI*, 35:27127).

[21] See an undated Kanezawa Sadaaki shojō (*KI*, 31:23507) for the comment about the large numbers of *karamono* in Kamakura; see (year unknown).1.24 Kanezawa Sadaaki shojō (*KI*, 38:29321) for the concern about thieves.

[22] Enkyō 3 (1310).8.22 Shikashima Zasshō Tamenao shojō (*Shimada monjo*).

[23] Kōan 2 (1362).8.3 Takatsuji Nagahira shojō an (*NBI-Ky*, 4:4381); also in *Dazaifu, Dazaifu Tenmangu shiryō*, vol. 12, pp. 16–17, under the year Jōji 1 (Reading *chasen* 茶扇 [tea fan] as a miswriting of *chasen* 茶筅 [tea whisk]).

[24] Nagahira's last extant letter is from 1384. See Shitoku 1 (1384).9.2 Takatsuji Nagahira migyōsho (*NBI-Ky*, 5:5835).

[25] See Saeki Kōji, "Kyōgen Chikugo no oku kara mita chūsei no Kyūshū."

[26] (Year unknown).4.21 Takatsuji Nagahira ke migyōsho (*NBI-Ky*, 6:6449); also in *Dazaifu, Dazaifu Tenmangū shiryō*, vol. 12, pp. 410–411.

[27] For an overview, see Kawazoe Shōji, "Japan and East Asia."

[28] Saeki Kōji, "Hakata," p. 292.

[29] See *Riben kao*, by Li Yangong, p. 42 text, p. 68 of the volume.

[30] Yabe Yoshiaki, *Nihon tōji no ichiman nisen nen*, pp. 169–170, 213–230.

[31] Yabe Yoshiaki, "Nihon shutsudo no Tō Sō jidai no tōji," pp. 115–119.

[32] Narasaki Shōichi, "Nihon shutsudo no Sōgen tōji to Nihon tōji," pp. 37–44.

[33] Tonganyao ware comes from kilns on the coast of Fujian Province.

[34] Kamei, *Nihon bōeki tōjishi no kenkyū*, pp. 155–156, 243.

[35] Yuezhouyao wares originated in the northeastern area of modern-day Zhejiang Province. Large-scale production of celadons and underglaze decorated pottery dates from the Han dynasty. See He, *Chinese Ceramics*, p. 338.

[36] Sasaki Tatsuo, "Hakusai ibutsu no kōkogaku," pp. 190–196.

[37] Hasebe Gakuji and Imai Atsushi, *Nihon shutsudo no Chūgoku tōji*, pp. 98–126.

[38] For more on Hakata, see Bruce Batten's groundbreaking *Gateway to Japan: Hakata in War and Peace, 500–1300*.

[39] See Saeki, "Hakata."

[40] Murai Yasuhiko, *Buke bunka to dōbōshū*, pp. 51–52.

[41] Dingyao is primarily a white ware known for "mold-impressed, incised, and carved decoration" (He, *Chinese Ceramics*, p. 335). Official ware generally refers to pottery fired at state-sponsored kilns from the Tang through the Qing periods and also as another term for celadon ware (p. 336).

[42] For a survey of this record, see Carla M. Zainie, "The *Muromachi Dono Gyōkō Okazari ki*: A Research Note."

[43] Feng Xianming, "Shin'an kaitei chinbotsusen hikiage tōjiki ni kanrenshita mondai ni taisuru kentō," p. 31.

[44] The reader is also directed to Louise Allison Cort, "Shopping for Pots in Momoyama Japan;" and, for the Tokugawa period, Patricia A. Graham, "*Karamono* for *sencha*."

Part Three

Prescribing and Prescriptions

7

China as Classic Text: Chinese Books and Twelfth-Century Japanese Collectors

Ivo Smits

Even if we were deprived of Chinese goods, we should not miss them, except for medicines. Many Chinese books are available all over the country, and anyone who wishes can copy one. It is the height of foolishness that Chinese ships should make the dangerous journey over here, crammed with cargoes of useless things. I believe it is written in the classics somewhere, "He did not prize things from afar," and again, "He did not value treasures that were hard to obtain."[1]

The monk and poet Yoshida Kenkō (1283?–post-1352) wrote these words in the early fourteenth century at a time when many Japanese Zen monks went to China and brought back new Chinese texts and when Chinese Chan monks were likewise arriving in Japan with their own literary selections. The study and production of literature in Chinese (*kanbun*) in Japan surged to new heights of creativity. Traveling to China had almost become normal. By contrast, two centuries earlier there were but a few Japanese who would make the crossing from Japan to China. All in all, barely two dozen parties of Japanese travelers undertook the journey to the Asian continent during the whole of the twelfth century. If it had not been for Chinese and Korean merchants, Japan would have seen very little of Chinese products. In the hundred or so years of the late Heian (1086–1185) and the beginning of the Kamakura (1185–1333) periods, over a hundred groups of predominantly Chinese merchants came to Japan.[2] The products they brought with them were usually medicines, aromatic herbs, and brocade and other cloths. Kenkō would have approved. However, they sometimes also brought books.

The study of book imports from the Asian mainland to twelfth-century Japan is not only a study of intellectual history but also a study of objects. Contact between cultures is often of a very material nature, and it will become clear that late Heian court nobles valued Chinese books as much for their materiality, the technological innovations they presented (printed books, numbered pages), as for their content, the new insights they offered into a shared textual heritage (commentaries). As luxury import goods, Chinese books also had a dimension of power play to them. They granted their owners control over knowledge since they could control access to these books. The relationships between the collectors treated here and the scholars of their age implied that Heian nobles with vast libraries were brokers in knowledge of a "China" that was as much physical as it was intellectual. Ownership and usage of books hinged on social interaction that was very much of a patron-client nature. It should be noted that the book trade was a one-way street. Apart from a handful of Heian and early Kamakura texts that Japanese monks supposedly brought to China as gifts for their hosts,[3] books came from the continent to Japan and not the other way around. The study of this trade then is the study of Japanese uses of Chinese books as status symbols, guarded gateways to knowledge, and foreign objects.

This essay is an attempt to investigate which contemporary Chinese works were read and collected by twelfth-century Japanese courtiers. "Contemporary" here means Song China (960–1279). The question is asked how books from the Song were valued and appreciated by the Japanese nobility. The focus is on secular scholars in court circles, not on scholars in Buddhist communities. The two specific collectors treated here are Fujiwara no Yorinaga (1120–1156) and Fujiwara no Michinori (1106–1159).

In a sense Yorinaga and Michinori were politicians of a new type. They did not shrink from bloodshed and killing, and both met with violent ends because of their ruthless politics. Yet these unflinching politicians were also active literati. They mingled with scholars and poets of Chinese verse (*kanshi*) and had the money and political power to collect books on a large scale. It is obvious, too, that they were convinced of their dedication to intellectual pursuits. Yorinaga once recorded a meeting between himself and Michinori. Michinori, who had been thinking of taking the tonsure, complained that people were likely to think that all his studying had not paid off, that surely he was becoming a monk out of frustration over his career at court, and that consequently his action would lead to the decline of scholarship. He urged the younger Yorinaga not to give up on his studies, especially as he belonged to the Fujiwara Regent House, arguably the most powerful family in the classical Japanese polity. Yorinaga exclaimed, "'Oh, yes, I will never forget what you have just said to me,' I said as tears filled my eyes."[4]

Yorinaga and Michinori were kindred spirits. Compulsive in all things, they were bibliographically precocious and took no small pride in their efforts to accumulate libraries that would attest to their literati standing. For such gentlemen scholars, owning a library enabled personal cultivation and the ability to set an intellectual agenda in the salons through which knowledge was created and transmitted among the aristocracy. Accordingly, the book collections of these two dedicated scholar-politicians can tell us something of notions of China entertained by a larger circle of Japanese literati.

In twelfth-century Japan, books from Song China first of all meant Song editions of older texts. The Japanese interest was in reference works and commentaries, texts that helped clarify texts that were already known. By this time Japanese court culture had established an intellectual and literary tradition that was largely oriented toward its own past, in which Chinese classic texts were a part but did not involve an active interest in contemporary production of new primary texts.[5] In that sense, Kenkō's remark that Japan had no need for new Chinese books accurately describes the attitude of late Heian scholars toward the continent.

It is difficult to get a clear idea of which Chinese books made their way to late Heian Japan. Most books brought to Japan were of a religious nature. Japanese monks traveling through China collected, bought, and shipped home vast quantities of Buddhist scriptures and commentaries. The monk Jōjin (1011–1081), for instance, accumulated over six hundred volumes during the first years of his stay in China, but there is scarcely one literary text among them. These texts ended up in monastic libraries where they could be consulted by scholarly monks from various temples.[6] However, if one wishes to know which secular continental texts were read in late Heian Japan, historical sources often turn out to be a disappointment. "Today there was an imperial inspection of new goods from Song China" is a typical entry by an anonymous early medieval historian, who does not hint what those goods may have been let alone mention specific book titles.[7] Some answers are found in diaries kept by courtiers with an interest in Chinese studies, and a valuable source is the earliest extant catalogue of a private library. This catalogue will be treated below.

The pattern for the eleventh and twelfth centuries shows that, when it came to books from China, Japanese court scholars and poets were content with more of the same. After official relations between China and Japan were terminated in 894, while contacts between Japan and the Asian mainland were maintained by merchants and monks, Japanese court society constructed a self-contained image of China and consequently of the Chinese literary canon. The Japanese nobility felt little need to subject this image to new outside information.

Why this apparent indifference? One answer surely lies in the Japanese educational system. Since the late ninth century, the training of Chinese scholars had not changed noticeably in Japan. The corpus of texts and assumptions about Chinese culture that formed the core of long years of study focused on classic texts and did not stimulate an interest in more recent developments in Chinese literature. Ninth-century Chinese poetry was about as modern as twelfth-century Japanese reading habits would get. When in the late thirteenth and early fourteenth centuries Japanese interest in more recent literary texts from the mainland began to grow again, it was monks who kindled and developed this new curiosity. In a way, the twelfth century marks a breaking point at which court circles are very active in the composition of Chinese literature but have truly converted the study and practice of *kanbun* to an indigenous tradition. The composition of Chinese verse was no longer firmly linked to an explicit acknowledgment of the literature from China, and even reference works would list only Japanese poets.[8] Thereafter, scholarly interaction with the Chinese mainland would be the province of those in Buddhist monastic circles.

That is not to say that developments in contemporary China went completely unnoticed by the court scholars. Book printing, for one, was an innovation with a considerable impact on reading and study habits. The new book format was convenient for browsing and marking passages, as its paper was folded into numbered pages. More important, printed texts were nearly always new critical editions of classic texts, often with helpful commentaries. When they first noticed these new editions, the few Japanese who could afford them were eager to replace the contents of their libraries with updated versions of familiar texts. One high-ranking courtier who got into contact with a Chinese merchant in 1151 placed an order for 125 titles, practically all of them commentaries and annotated editions and mostly printed books.[9]

Fujiwara no Yorinaga

That contact between the merchant and the courtier was of sufficient note that over a century later it was included in a collection of anecdotes, the *Kokon chomonjū* (Collection of Stories Heard from Writers Old and New, 1254),[10] in the section "Literature Studies."

> *How the Song Traveler Liu Wenchong Presented the Uji Minister of the Left Yorinaga with Books*
>
> In the Ninpyō era (1151–1153) Liu Wenchong, a merchant from the Song court, presented the Minister of the Left with *Dongpo xiangsheng zhizhangtu* (Convenient Maps by Master Dongpo) (two volumes), *Wudai shiji* (History of the Five Dynasties) (ten volumes), *Tang shu* (History of the Tang) (nine volumes), and an official family register. The reply to this gift was drafted by Professor of Literature Shigeakira;[11] the former Master of the Imperial Household Sadanobu made the clean copy.[12] The Owari Governor Chikataka copied it out on high-grade paper.[13] The Chinese merchant was given twenty *ryō* of gold dust. Yorinaga also sent him a list of books that he wanted to purchase. In Manju 3 (1026) a man named Zhou Liangshi had presented the Uji Lord [Fujiwara no Yorimichi (992–1074)] with official family records. At that occasion, no books were presented.

This was a true story. In the ninth month of Ninpyō 1 (1151), Fujiwara no Yorinaga, then minister of the left, rewarded the Chinese merchant Liu Wenchong for the gift of a set of historical works that Liu had brought with him from China in the previous year. These books were valuable enough to be paid for with gold.[14] Since Yorinaga faithfully recorded them in his diary, we know exactly which books Liu brought along.[15] All three titles were books produced by writers from the Northern Song.

The first title that Yorinaga received was a work purportedly written by Su Shi (1036–1101).[16] Perhaps better known under his pen name, Dongpo, Su is arguably the most famous poet from Song China. This title very likely refers to a geographical work known as *Lidai dili zhizhang tu* (Convenient Maps in Historical Order), presumably compiled in the early twelfth century and quite possibly printed as late as 1150.[17] It is a collection of historical maps of China and a few of its neighboring countries, with commentary, roughly ranging from the Zhou (ca. 1100–256 BCE) through the Tang (618–907) dynasties. Its preface states that Su Shi was the original compiler of this collection, but his name may well have been added by a later, unknown compiler to increase its sales value, something that happened quite regularly. In China, Su's books had been banned, but after the 1130s his name regained popularity when the ban was lifted. In 1986, a Song edition of this historical atlas turned up in the Tōyō Bunko collection in Tokyo, and it appears to be the oldest known extant Chinese historical atlas. There are indications, such as taboo characters, that the work must have been compiled before 1160. Around 1150, after peace treaties were concluded with the Jurchen, China experienced something of a cultural restoration, and with it a surge in cartographic book production, and it seems plausible that this collection dates from those years. If this is one and the same book, then Yorinaga must have gotten his copy fresh from the printing presses. The Tōyō Bunko copy may even be the very one that Yorinaga held in his hands. This work, which until now has gone undetected by historians of Japan, shows two things. First, there were no logistical problems in getting books from China to Japan in a very short time span;[18] and second, reference books made good export articles for the Chinese.

Yorinaga was also given the *Xin wudai shiji* (New History of the Five Dynasties) by the statesman, poet, and historian Ouyang Xiu (1007–1072), which deals with the period 907–960, as well as Ouyang's *Xin Tang shu* (New History of the Tang).[19] The third book, an official family register (J. *meiseki*; C. *mingji*), also had a high utility factor. In China, inventories of family names such as *Bai xiajing* (Hundred Family Names) were used together with the *Mengqiu* (see below) as primers for writing lessons.[20] Perhaps such a use inspired their export to Japan. The three gifts from the Chinese merchant to the Japanese statesman already indicate what will become more apparent shortly, namely, that Yorinaga and his contemporaries craved recent Chinese reference works rather than new collections of literature.

Yorinaga had Shigeakira draft a thank-you note and placed another order with the merchant. Yorinaga's order list is still extant. It runs to 125 titles and gives the impression that Yorinaga immediately put Liu's gift of *Xin Tang shu* to good use. Most of Yorinaga's orders seem to come straight out of the first section of the *Yiwen zhi* (Monographs on Bibliography) of the *Xin Tang shu*. The *Yiwen zhi* comprises four categories: "Classics" (*jing*), "Histories" (*shi*), "Philosophers" (*zi*), and "Collections" (*ji*, that is, mainly poetry collections).[21] All books ordered by Yorinaga belong to the first category. Yorinaga also followed fairly closely the arrangement within this category, which makes it all the more likely that he had the "Classics" section beside him when he drew up his own list.

The most striking feature of Yorinaga's wish list is that it consists of commentaries of all sorts and shapes on age-old, classic texts such as the *Book of Odes*, *Book of Changes*, *Records of the Rites*, and *Spring and Autumn Annals*. Occasionally Yorinaga asked for more general reference works, one with the intriguing title *Shixue wuxing menlei zaomu yuchong shu* (Subcommentary on Grasses, Trees, Fish, and Insects Classified by the Nature of Things for Poetry Studies).[22]

Perhaps Yorinaga's reputation as a man who did not much care for poetry, which he reportedly regarded as a frivolous pastime unfit for serious scholars or statesmen, has some truth to it.[23] There is no indication that he composed any *waka* nor has he left any *kanshi*, and his order with the Chinese merchant is intriguingly devoid of curiosity about Chinese literary texts younger than a thousand years or so.

The Chinese merchant had brought Yorinaga texts by two authors who were quite famous in China and who, more important, were "contemporary" in the sense that they had been dead for only half a century. The story of Yorinaga's gift and its inclusion in *Kokon chomonjū* indicate that these books were a bit unusual. Few books from Song China were imported in twelfth-century Japan, and when they did arrive in Japan they usually turned out to be Song editions of older texts. Books attributed to Song poets or written by Song historians proved to be an extremely rare commodity in twelfth-century Japan. Liu's tribute of books to Yorinaga marks one of the rare occasions when Japanese courtiers got a glimpse of a China that was almost of the present. Even so, while these three titles may have been near-contemporary books, they did gaze into the past; they were histories and historical maps. As such they confirmed the rule that "China" was a construct based on texts that were, if not themselves centuries old, reflections of an age-old China.

Yorinaga's Reading Program

By all accounts, Yorinaga was an eager student of Chinese texts. In his youth things were different, he tells us himself. He did not listen to his father's admonitions; he loved riding horses and did not much care for books. Often he went out galloping in the mountains, but on a fateful day he fell from his horse, was seriously hurt, and was forced to give up outdoor sports. After that, he devoted himself to the study of Chinese texts. Some readers may be pleased to know that he was also extremely fond of his cat.[24] The story of his conversion to scholarship is almost too good to be true, but Yorinaga's subsequent fervor in his studies does suggest the zeal of the newly converted. As if to make up for lost time, Yorinaga sat down to an impressive reading program, using even time spent traveling onboard ships. In the span of eight years, from 1136 to 1143, he read, with the help of several tutors, some 70-odd Chinese classic texts totaling 1,030 volumes.[25] These he divided into three traditional categories: classics (*keika*), histories (*shika*), and miscellaneous (*zōka*). This last category features mainly literary texts. The reading list and its arrangement confirm a development, noted by several historians, that in the ninth century the study and exegesis of Confucian classics (*myōkyōdō*) as an academic discipline lost ground to the study of historical and literary texts (*kidendō, monjōdō*).[26]

The program Yorinaga set for himself gives us a fairly good idea of which texts were considered Chinese cultural icons in twelfth-century Japan. Most of these texts, officially or unofficially, were part of the curriculum of the court academy (Daigakuryō) and private academies such the Kangakuin.[27]

The only title Yorinaga read the first year, at age seventeen, was a well-thumbed textbook, *Mengqiu* (J. *Mōgyū*, Youth Inquires). Ever since it was introduced into Japan during the ninth century, this text had been an indispensable tool for any young man's first encounters with "China."[28] Precocious Japanese boys started their *Mengqiu* readings at the age of seven or even earlier, and at such educational institutions as the Fujiwara academy the book was such a well-used primer that a saying asserted, "At the Kangakuin even the sparrows chirp the *Mengqiu*."[29] Apparently compiled early in the eighth century by a minor Chinese official known as Li Han, the *Mengqiu* functioned as a who's who of Chinese cultural history. The text consists of nearly six hundred minibiographies arranged in pairs, all with headings of four characters so as to make their contents easy to remember. In simple but effective wording, Li Han describes the lives of famous and infamous men (and a few women) from Chinese legend and history, often citing his main source. Evidently, the book was quite successful as a textbook for young people starting their studies. Its influence on school exercises and literature in China lasted until the end of the Yuan dynasty (1279–1368).

In Japan, together with Xu Jian's *Chuxue ji* (Notes for First Studies, ca. 725), the *Mengqiu* acquired the status of an essential primer and served as a source of knowledge of Chinese history and thought. Japanese writers of the Heian period, in turn, drew on it to present their audiences with versions in Japanese in tale collections and poetic treatises.[30] In fact, together with *Qianzi wen* (Thousand Characters Text, ca. 500),[31] *Baiyong* (Hundred Compositions, early eighth century),[32] and *Wakan rōeishū* (Japanese and Chinese Poems to Sing, early eleventh century),[33] the *Mengqiu* was one of the four primers for young boys commencing their studies.[34] Yorinaga would, of course, also read *Baiyong* and *Qianzi wen* in annotated editions.[35]

Next on Yorinaga's reading list were *Lunyü* (The Analects) and the "three histories" (J. *sanshi*), that is, *Shiji* (Records of the Grand Historian), *Hanshu* (History of the Han), and *Hou Hanshu* (History of the Latter Han). Besides reading Confucian and Daoist classics, he read a substantial number of literary texts. Most prominent among these was the *Book of Odes*, technically a "classic" (*kei*) but an important tool in reading poetry, which as a literary genre would be classified as "miscellaneous." Another literary text was *Xijing zaji* (Miscellanies of the Western Capital), originally compiled by the Han imperial librarian Liu Xin (?–23 BCE), but in its form known to Yorinaga actually from ca. 520. Although *Xijing zaji* is loosely arranged as a standard dynastic history, it is more a potpourri containing entire *fu* (rhapsodies), catalogues of books and imperial processions, accounts of omens, and the like. Yorinaga also studied the *Yan Danzi* (Prince Dan of Yan, probably late fifth century), a fictional account of Jing Ke, the would-be murderer of the king of Qin. He also read the *Wenxuan* (Selections of Refined Literature), in the famous annotation by Li Shan (ca. 630–689),[36] the *Xinyuefu* (New Ballads) by Bai Juyi (772–846), Bai Juyi's biography, and the *Sanguozhi* (Records of the Three Kingdoms), a historical work by Chen Shou (233–297).

All the Chinese works that Yorinaga studied in this period were centuries old. His initial thorough training seems to have set the tone for his later tastes. In all his conservative preferences, Yorinaga nevertheless was representative of many of his contemporaries.

Yorinaga's reading program had political as well as intellectual dimensions. He was, after all, a powerful politician who was to act as de facto imperial regent in the period 1151–1155, prior to being killed in the Hōgen Incident of 1156, a bloody palace coup that he engineered. His role in that event was subsequently to provide much food for thought on the relationship between politics and the type of judgment that should emerge from an extensive reading program in Chinese classics.[37] In any event, the tutors he recruited were all tied to families of scholars. Yorinaga was to build a large network of personal advisers and household managers, many of whom he engaged through the state academy, of which he became the top administrator, superintendent (*daigaku bettō*), in 1147. While Yorinaga also built his network through extensive same-sex sexual relationships,[38] his choice to rely on the intellectuals of his age in setting up a dependable administrative organization of his own was in keeping with a newfound appreciation of people of "functional ability" (*shokunō*). What set Yorinaga's networking apart from others were his efforts to revive the state academy's waning eminence through the sponsoring of ceremonies held there. He was not content with employing scholars for his own sake but seems to have felt a need to make a gesture toward the institution that was so important in the scholars' lives.[39]

Printed Books

In 1145, Yorinaga finished the building of his Uji library (*fumigura*), which was located in the northeastern part of the capital. Until then he had stored his books in special wheeled chests (*fumiguruma*), which could easily be moved in the event that the house caught fire. It had taken him less than three months to build the storehouse for his books. The structure measured nearly seventy-eight square meters and was fenced off by a very thick earthen wall. The books were stored in numbered boxes, which were shelved on book racks, five shelves on the east, or *yang*, side of the storehouse (*yō no tana*) and six on the west, or *yin*, side (*on no tana*). The books were divided into four categories: study materials such as the Confucian classics; Chinese historical works; miscellaneous Chinese texts; and, finally, Japanese books.[40] The latter will have consisted of histories of Japan, *kanbun* diaries, and family records and probably did not contain works in Japanese. The book collection of Yorinaga's contemporary Michinori also contained only Chinese and *kanbun* titles. Given Yorinaga's penchant for male-oriented learning, he cannot be expected to have stored tales such as *The Tale of Genji*.

The three books given to Yorinaga by the Song merchant Liu Wenchong undoubtedly also found their way to a place in the Uji library, as did the ordered titles—if Yorinaga ever received them. These were not the first Song books to have found a niche in Yorinaga's book storehouse. Like several other Heian nobles, Yorinaga owned books that had been manufactured on the Asian mainland in the eleventh century. For an educated audience in early medieval Japan, books from Song China were interesting for a number of reasons. One was that very often these were printed books (*surihon* or *zanbon*).

Book printing was not exactly a novelty to the Japanese. In China printing had been known since the sixth or early seventh century,[41] but was not widely employed until the Song dynasty, when the technique was used mainly for the dissemination of the Confucian classics and Buddhist writings.[42] Song China also saw the printing of literature, if only of a few well-known texts. Printing was, after all, an expensive enterprise. As long as a large market justifying a printed edition was lacking, copying books by hand remained the cheapest way to have texts circulated. In late Heian and early Kamakura Japan, the literate public was small and in no way comparable to that of China; the need for book printing was equally limited.

Like writing, book printing came to Japan from the Asian mainland, but it took many centuries for it to be used on a large scale. The oldest extant text printed in Japan dates from the period 764–770. After Empress Kōken (718–770) put down the revolt of Fujiwara no Nakamaro (706–764) in 764, she ordered the manufacturing of a very large number of miniature pagodas which were to be spread among the Buddhist temples in and around Nara as an act of appeasement of the spirits of the warriors who had died during the revolt. In each of the pagodas a mystic formula, or *darani* (Sk. *dhâranî*), was hidden. These "mystical formulas in one million pagodas" (*hyakumantō darani*) are among the oldest extant printed texts in the world. In the course of the Heian period, and especially from the twelfth century onward, the monks of temples such as the Kōfukuji near Nara and the Hōryūji southwest of Nara started to print Buddhist texts. These "temple prints," such as the Kasuga-ban and Hōryūji-ban, were not meant for circulation, that is, they were not meant to be read. The printing of sutras, formulas, and commentaries, often ordered and paid for by courtiers, was a religious act; through the mechanical reproduction of religious texts one hoped to achieve merits that would influence one's karma favorably. Twelfth-century Japanese did not themselves print literary books.[43]

In Song China, on the other hand, competition between state printers and private printing houses ensured the commercial appeal of textual novelties and revised, annotated, collated, illustrated, or supplemented text editions. Although most of the activities of the printers focused on Confucian classics, examination materials, and encyclopedic works, there was also a market for printed editions of medical works and well-known literary texts. The efforts of Song printers notwithstanding, the majority of books in Song imperial and private libraries amounted to only a fraction, not even ten percent, of the total collections. Manuscript copies still were the standard.[44]

A good example of a printed literary text in Japan is the collected works of Japan's favorite Chinese poet, Bai Juyi. The first copies of Bai Juyi's poetry to reach Japan were Tang manuscripts. However, as Song text editions of the *Baishi wenji* (J. *Hakushi monjū*) grew more sophisticated, this edited and annotated Bai Juyi text also crossed over to Japan from the early eleventh century onward.[45] The statesman Fujiwara no Michinaga (966–1027), for instance, was an avid book collector with an impressive library. On a rainy day in 1010, he rearranged his books and counted over two thousand volumes.[46] Michinaga keenly collected printed editions of *Wenxuan* and Bai Juyi's poetry, which he obtained either through Chinese merchants or through Japanese monks abroad.[47] These were annotated Song editions, which differed from Tang manuscript copies at several points. It remains doubtful, however, whether these new editions really contributed in any major way to late-eleventh- and twelfth-century studies of Chinese poetry. For one thing, Michinaga may have owned a Song edition, but that does not necessarily imply that Chinese scholars also did. Occasionally, Fujiwara scholars from the Umakai Branch of the Ceremonial House and the Hino Branch of the Northern House were given Chinese books by Michinaga. These books found their way to the Kangakuin, a private institution operated by the Fujiwara. The older lineages of Chinese scholars such as the Sugawara and the Ōe, however, virtually had no access to these new editions. Moreover, the Sugawara and Ōe families based their authority in the field of Chinese literature on old Tang text variants that had been passed on within their clans. The idea of having to credit text editions that deviated from their classroom material probably did not appeal to them. Nevertheless, their conservative attitude does not mean that they were completely unfamiliar with this "new" Bai Juyi. The scholar and poet Ōe no Masafusa (1041–1111), for instance, pointed out more reliable variants in Song editions of Bai's popular lines.[48] The same held true for *Wenxuan*. Of course, by the mid-Heian period both Bai's poetry and *Wenxuan* had become part of the academic preparatory curriculum, and the demand for these texts grew correspondingly.

The appeal of printed editions, which often provided new collations and commentary, is easy to see. Also, since printed books were in book format with numbered pages, they were easier to use and more conveniently referred to than the long scrolls (*kansubon*) or the book formats (*sōshi*) for manuscripts. Speed-reading and browsing or marking passages by inserting scraps of paper were a novelty, too.[49]

Song commentaries on the classics generally differed from Tang commentaries in that they tended to be more concise. The new Song dynasty saw a surge in commentaries. Perceptions of the classics had in China always been linked to thoughts about state government, and the reform movement of the early Song went hand in hand with a new neo-Confucian orthodoxy that produced its own commentaries of a philological and exegetical nature (the so-called *zhangju*) as well as a wave of new historical works.[50]

Members of the Heian nobility went to great lengths to obtain copies of Chinese poetry and other texts and were eager to lay their hands on the new Chinese editions. Again Yorinaga may serve as an example. The copies of *Xin Tang shu* (New History of the Tang) and *Xin Wudai shiji* (New History of the Five Dynasties) that he received in 1151 may very well have been the printed editions, as the Imperial Directorate of the Song used printed books to disseminate authorized texts. Earlier, Yorinaga had tried hard to collect printed text editions from China. In 1143 he exchanged a printed edition of *Liji zhengyi* (Records of the Rites with Commentary) for a manuscript version in his own library. His own copy, handwritten as it was, must have been an older version from the Tang period or at least based on a Tang version. Three weeks later Yorinaga borrowed a printed edition of the *Zhouyi zhengyi* (Book of Changes with Commentary) from Fujiwara no Nobutoshi and had a calligrapher copy it out on high-quality paper. "I am happier than if I had been given a thousand *ryō* of gold," he noted on this occasion. He also asked whether he could borrow more printed books from Nobutoshi. Three years later he again asked to borrow printed books.[51] Yorinaga's collecting and bartering are indicative of the importance that Japanese attached to Song printed books as new editions of texts that they already knew.

Forbidden Books: *Taiping yulan*

The Song government, concerned that certain books should not be exported to foreign countries, had designated certain texts as "forbidden books" (C. *jinshu*) and outlawed the sale of them to non-Chinese. The ban was aimed mostly at Khitan (Liao dynasty), which threatened China from the north, but it was often extended to Korea and Japan as well. The Chinese fear that exporting knowledge to "barbarian" countries would in the end prove harmful to China was an old one. Under the Tang, Chinese court officials had often argued against granting foreigners access to China's cultural heritage. Embassies from Silla had experienced refusals to their requests for specific books. Since the Korean Peninsula bordered on the Khitan, the Song government feared that privileged information might reach Khitan through Korea. In the mid-eleventh century, Chinese merchant vessels were forbidden to operate on the route to Koryŏ.

However, the ban on the exportation of (printed) books was not strictly observed. The first printed books from China to arrive in Japan were the Kaibao era (968–975) imperial edition of the Buddhist *Tripitaka*, normally forbidden to foreigners. Nevertheless, after the Japanese monk Chōnen arrived in China in 983, he obtained permission to buy it. What may have helped is that Japanese monks such as Chōnen did not come empty-handed. They brought with them Chinese religious texts that were lost in China and even religious tracts by Japanese authors from which the Chinese might benefit.[52]

One forbidden book was the encyclopedic *Taiping yulan* (Imperial Digest of the Taiping Period), which had been ordered by the Song court in the year Taiping xingguo 2 (977) and compiled under the supervision of Li Fang (925–996), a fellow with the Hanlin Academy. Work on this massive and comprehensive encyclopedia, which ran to a total of a thousand volumes, was finished in 983, and it was printed under Emperor Renzong (r. 1023–1063). Very soon it was considered a "forbidden book." During the reign of Emperor Shenzong (r. 1068–1086), the king of Koryŏ sent an embassy asking for a copy of *Taiping yulan* but was refused access to the text. The Korean king was again refused the encyclopedia under the reign of the following emperor, Shezong (r. 1086–1101), in 1086.

It is possible, though not certain, that Yorinaga may have gotten hold of a copy. He notes in a diary entry in 1143 that he had recently been reading in his cart an "imperial digest" (*yulan*) in 138 volumes, though he regretted that he had only been able to get through ten of them and had given up on reading the rest.[53] His contemporary, Fujiwara no Michinori, also appears to have read such a work (see below). However, there is debate over whether the "imperial digest" to which Yorinaga refers is the Song period *Taiping Yulan* or else something like the early-sixth-century *Xiuwendian yulan* (Imperial Digest of the Hall for Cultivating Literary Skills), which is noted as having arrived in Japan in that era.[54] The first unequivocal evidence for the appearance of the *Taiping yulan* in Japan comes from 1179, by which time both Yorinaga and Michinori were long dead. A courtier notes that in that year a Song merchant managed to smuggle a printed edition of *Taiping yulan* to Japan, that "this marks the beginning of the circulation (*rufu*) of this book in our country," and that it had ended up in the hands of Taira no Kiyomori (1118–1181). This was a very incomplete edition and consisted of only 260 volumes. In the course of the thirteenth century, Japanese monks eventually managed to buy and import more complete versions of the *Taiping yulan*.[55] By the mid–thirteenth century, the *Taiping yulan* was used as a gift article among courtiers, and Fujiwara no Morotsugu was willing to pay thirty *kan* (i.e., 30,000 *monme*) for a complete set. As the equivalent of thirty *koku*, this price would have paid for a modest mansion on the edge of the capital.[56]

Michinori's Library

The image of Japanese hankering after more of the old but in updated editions is reinforced by the catalogue of a twelfth-century private library. *Tsūken nyūdō zōsho mokuroku* (Catalogue of the Library of the Lay Priest Michinori, ca. 1160) is the oldest extant record of a late Heian private library and yields valuable insights in the reading habits of the statesman and *kanshi* poet Fujiwara no Michinori.

After the untimely death of his father, Fujiwara no Sanekane (1085–1112), a talented student of literature (*monjōshō*), Michinori was adopted by Takashina no Tsunetoshi. Members of the Takashina clan had served as close retainers of the retired emperor ever since the reign of Shirakawa (1053–1129) and so Michinori was also appointed to various offices on the palace staff. Through the years he managed to work himself up to a position of great political influence. He became emperor Toba's (1103–1156) most trusted adviser and acted as counselor to the emperors Go-Shirakawa (1127–1192) and Nijō (1143–1165) as well as to Taira no Kiyomori. In 1144 he took the tonsure and adopted the name by which he is best known today, Shinzei. Politics brought him to prominence but also, as with Yorinaga, proved his undoing. After the Hōgen insurrection of 1156, in which Yorinaga lost his life, Michinori pressed for death penalties for the Minamoto warriors involved in this aborted coup d'état. His unprecedented desire for vengeance earned him the hate of the surviving Minamoto, and when they retaliated in the Heiji disturbance of 1159–1160 Michinori fled to Nara. His family was murdered, and when his pursuers were about to capture him he committed suicide. The Minamoto cut off his head and left it dangling from the Kyoto prison gate for several days.[57] These events ultimately ushered in an era of violence as yet unprecedented in the capital.

The story of Michinori's gruesome death bears on the history of the catalogue of his library. Besides being a ruthless politician, Michinori, whose father's family was raised in a tradition of Confucian scholarship, was a talented poet of Chinese verse, a musical expert, and one of the leading scholars and historians of his day. His *Honchō seiki* (Annals of Our Court, post-1153), for instance, is still extant and was compiled as the follow-up to the six national histories (*rikkokushi*), starting where *Nihon sandai jitsuroku* (Veritable Record of Three Reigns of Japan, commissioned 901) left off.

Michinori's talents did not stop there. According to an anecdote in the *Zoku kojidan* (Tales of Old Matters, Continued, 1219), Michinori knew how to speak Chinese and proved this in the presence of Retired Emperor Toba by talking to a Chinese (*karabito*) "without the aid of an interpreter." He claimed to have learned to speak the language thinking that he might be sent to China as an envoy. If the story is at all true, then Michinori obviously had acquired his conversational skills by conversing with Chinese who were visiting, or even living, in Japan. This is not entirely implausible since one could come across Chinese in Japan outside the Chinese settlement (*tōbō*) in Dazaifu, Kyushu. Yorinaga was told the story of a twenty-nine-year-old Chinese monk in Nachi, Kumano, who claimed to have come from China at the age of eleven. He was still able to read *Lunyü* (The Analects) and *Xiaojing* (The Classic of Filial Piety) "with Chinese pronunciation" (*tōsei*).[58]

The catalogue of Michinori's impressive personal library was compiled somewhere around the time of his death, either by himself or by someone else. There is some debate as to who actually compiled the catalogue and whether it was meant as an inventory of Michinori's books as part of his estate to be divided now that he was dead. In the library there once must have been a total of at least 158 consecutively numbered chests (*ki*), in which the books were kept. Nearly half of the original number of chests are missing from the list. The compiler of the list therefore probably did not know if the absent chests were actually missing and did not want to alter the existing consecutive numbering. That the old but incomplete numbering was retained strongly suggests that Michinori did not compile the catalogue but was already dead when someone else took stock of his books.[59]

In any case, Michinori's is the oldest extant Japanese record of a private library, and it contains a wealth of information concerning the collecting and reading habits of a late Heian scholar-poet and statesman. It gives a clear indication of what he actually read, and as such it is as near to a complete overview of a twelfth-century library as one can get. The question remains whether one can take Michinori's library and tastes as representative. In some ways, the answer must be no: Michinori disbursed funds in amounts that were out of reach for most other scholars, and we shall see that he owned some very rare books.

All the titles in the catalogue, including the Japanese ones, are of books written in Chinese. As one might expect from a statesman and scholar, Michinori owned several Japanese histories and legal codes, as well as books on medicine, music, and etiquette. He also had a large number of private *kanshi* collections of Japanese poets. Not surprisingly, he owned nearly all the Chinese classics and dynastic histories down to the *Taizong shilu* (Veritable Records of Taizong; Tang emperor, r. 627–649).[60] Michinori was also a poet, and he had several manuals for the composition of Chinese verse.[61]

Of concern here are the books that reached Michinori's library from Song China. Like Yorinaga, Michinori owned several Song annotated editions of the classics, some in the costly, deluxe "large character" format.[62] One title that stands out is a volume of Hanshan's poetry.[63] This is indeed a striking item because the recluse and poet Hanshan, or "[the Master from] Cold Mountain" (dates unknown, eighth-ninth century), seems to have been otherwise unknown in Heian Japan. When the Japanese monk Jōjin visited China in 1072, he was given a manuscript copy of Hanshan's poetry. This is itself remarkable because the oldest Chinese printed edition of Hanshan's poems dates from 1189.[64] Jōjin probably sent Hanshan's poems on to Japan, and one can imagine that Michinori somehow got his hands on this copy. There seem to be no other references to Hanshan in this period, however, and one should not attach too much importance to his poetry in connection with the development of late Heian *kanshi*. Jōjin himself seems to have been interested in Hanshan's poetry mainly out of religious motivations; it is the only literary title mentioned in his diary.

Michinori owned collections of seven more Tang poets. One of them is a famous early Tang poet, Wang Bo (650–677).[65] Bai Juyi's poetry is, of course, present in Michinori's library, as is that of Bai's friend Liu Yuxi (772–842).[66] The remaining four are all late Tang poets: Luo Yin (833–909),[67] Li Shangyin (812–858), Du Xunhe (846–907), and Zhang Xiaobiao (active in the early ninth century).[68] Except for Li Shangyin, these poets were known in Japan since the early tenth century, and Michinori's copies would have been based on Tang manuscripts. The presence of Li Shangyin in a Heian collection, on the other hand, is quite extraordinary. The poems of Li Shangyin, who is best known for his rather obscure love poetry, do not appear in such collections as *Wakan rōeishū* and quite likely reached Japan only during the Song dynasty.

The catalogue yields a few more surprises. Chest 41 not only contained Luo Yin's poetry but also the *Linchuan xianshengshi yibu* (One Portion of the Poetry of the Master from Linchuan) in five volumes.[69] This is the collection of none other than the famous Song reformer Wang Anshi (1021–1086). Wang was born in Linchuan, in Jiangxi Province, which is why his personal collection was called *Linchuan xiansheng wenji* (Collection of the Master from Linchuan). Since Wang wrote much Buddhist poetry, one can assume that Japanese monks visiting China were attracted by its religious qualities. This is, to my knowledge, the only evidence that late Heian poets actually read Song poetry except for the following item in Michinori's catalogue.

Another title that deserves attention is the no longer extant *Huang Song baijiashi* (Poems by a Hundred Poets from the Imperial Song) in three volumes. Given the "Imperial" in the title, this work must be a poetry collection but from the Northern Song and not the Six Dynasties Song (420–479).[70] We can only speculate on which poets were included in this anthology, but it must have given scholars and lovers of Chinese poetry in Japan a wonderful glimpse of wholly new generations of Chinese poets.

Like Fujiwara no Yorinaga, Michinori owned a copy of what may have been the *Taiping yulan*. In addition, he also had a *huiyao* ("Essentials," i.e. "Collected Documents on Administration") in his possession. The encyclopedic *huiyao* were compiled for every dynasty and were a more systematically classified version of the *shilu* (Veritable Records). Most *huiyao* were compiled by Song historians. Nagasawa Kikuya believes that the *huiyao* in Michinori's library cannot be the *huiyao* for the Tang or an earlier dynasty but must be *Song huiyao*, but why is not entirely clear; the *huiyao* from the Song as we have them were only recollected in the early nineteenth century by Xu Song (1781–1848).[71] If Nagasawa is right, which I find hard to believe, it would mean that Michinori had access to two formidable encyclopedias of the Song court. But even if the latter title is in fact *Tang huiyao*, it would still be a Song period encyclopedia since that work was compiled by Wang Pu (932–981) and others in 961. Finally, one would like to know what exactly was *Songren miyu chao* (Secret Tales by People from the Song), of which Michinori also had a copy.[72]

Surprisingly, few Chinese literary anthologies appear on the list except for the *Book of Odes* and *Wenxuan*. These formed official examination reading. An anthology such as *Yutai xinyong* (New Songs from a Jade Terrace, ca. 545), which was not part of the curriculum, is missing from this catalogue. In passing, one may note that many well-known Song compilations of Tang texts were probably not widely known in late Heian Japan. *Santi shi* (Poems in Three Forms), for instance, a Song collection of middle and late Tang poems compiled by Zhou Bi, was first introduced to Japan by Gozan Zen monks in the late Kamakura period.[73] It is possible that Michinori did have Chinese anthologies in his possession but kept them in the missing chests. He did own several Japanese anthologies of Chinese verse, but most of these contained Japanese *kanshi*. This makes one wonder whether Michinori relied on Chinese anthologies at all for comprehensive knowledge of matters poetical. The catalogue indicates that he did not but instead resorted to Japanese compilations.

All in all, where Chinese poetry is concerned, the emphasis in Michinori's library was on late Tang poetry. The Song books that did end up in Michinori's library, exceptional though they are in a twelfth-century collection, form but a minor part of the large number of texts in his possession. Michinori's tastes were more eclectic than Yorinaga's, but as a whole his library reflects the Japanese focus on texts already known.

Summary

By the twelfth century, Japanese court culture has established an intellectual and literary tradition that was largely oriented toward its own past. The implication of this development was that late Heian scholars and nobles made no effort to keep an eye on possible additions to Chinese literary traditions in the preceding two and a half centuries. Their image of China was self-contained, appropriated through a distant past, and they felt little need for improvements or changes. The fact that, apart from monks traveling to China, the Japanese hardly had an active policy of buying Chinese goods is a strong indication of this attitude. Trade was maintained by merchants from China and the Korean Peninsula. The books for which these traders found a market were mainly texts with a high utility factor: commentaries on the classics, new editions of known texts, and reference works. They also had value as status objects for they formed a tangible contact with the Asian mainland and its technological innovations. Within the libraries of twelfth-century Japanese collectors these books performed a role as keys to accessing other, namely, Song, traditions of analyzing shared classics and granted their owners additional power over those who sought to share in that knowledge. The story of this period's Japanese collecting of Chinese books is the story of books as tools of cultural contact, as markers of China's intellectual role as co-owner of the classics and as luxury import goods with the potential to strengthen their collectors' status as brokers of knowledge.

Notes

I wish to thank the Royal Netherlands Academy of Arts and Sciences and the Netherlands Organization for Scientific Research for enabling my research in Japan.

[1] *Tsurezuregusa*, 120, pp. 186–87; in Donald Keene, trans., *Essays in Idleness: The Tsurezuregusa of Kenko*, p. 101. Kenkō's quotations are from the *Shujing* and *Daodejing*.

[2] For an estimate of (groups of) Japanese traveling to China or Korea and (groups of) Chinese and Koreans traveling to Japan in the period circa 600–1600, see Charlotte von Verschuer, *Across the Perilous Seas: Japanese Trade with China and Korea from the Seventh to Sixteenth Centuries*, Appendix 4, p. 192.

[3] One of Fujiwara no Michinori's sons went to China and supposedly exported *Sangō shiiki* (Indications of the Goals of the Three Teachings, 797) by Kūkai; *Wakan rōeishū* (Japanese and Chinese Poems to Sing, early eleventh century); *Honchō monzui* (Literary Essence of Our Court, 1064); and *Heike monogatari* (Tale of the Heike, presumably a *kanbun* version). See Ivo Smits, "Song as Cultural History: Reading *Wakan rōeishū*," p. 400.

[4] *Taiki*, vol. 23, p. 94, Kōji 2 (1143).8.11. See also *Taiki*, vol. 23, p. 94, Kōji 2 (1143).8.5. The same story appears in *Zoku kojidan chūkai*, 2.56, pp. 248–250. Later Michinori visited Yorinaga when he was ill, and they discussed divination, taking copies of *Liji zhengyi* (a commentary on *Records of the Rites*, seventh century) and *Zuo zhuan Du Yu zhu* (a commentary on the *Spring and Autumn Annals*) off the shelves to prove their point. Yorinaga won the argument that tortoise shells are a better method than the *Book of Changes* (*Taiki*, vol. 23, p. 154, Ten'yō 2 (1145).3.8; *Zoku kojidan chūkai* 2.52, pp. 230–237. *Taiki* was obviously available to early-thirteenth-century writers; see notes 8 and 13.

[5] See Ivo Smits, "The Way of the Literati: Chinese Learning and Literary Practice in Mid-Heian Japan." Marian Ury, too, notes that Chinese learning in Heian Japan increasingly became a self-contained tradition, finding sufficient roots to craft a past of its own ("Chinese Learning and Intellectual Life," pp. 341, 389).

[6] For Jōjin, see the essay in this volume by Robert Borgen; and Fujiyoshi Masumi, "Jōjin no motarashita higa no tenseki: Nissō bunka kōryū no hitokusari." In 1094, the monk Eichō (1014–1095) compiled a catalogue of Buddhist texts available in Japan, *Tōiki dentō mokuroku*, which indicates that temple libraries were catalogued at certain intervals and could be consulted by visiting monks. See Inoue Mitsusada, "*Tōiki dentō mokuroku* yori mitaru Nara jidai sōryō no gakumon." In his history of the book in Japan, Peter Kornicki also deals with book imports from China

(*The Book in Japan: A Cultural History from the Beginnings to the Nineteenth Century*, esp. pp. 277–296).

[7] *Hyakurenshō*, p. 43, Enkyū 4 (1072).6.16.

[8] Two examples are *Sakumon daitai* (Basics of Composition, twelfth century) and *Tekkinshō* (Throwing Metal Notes, ca. 1206–1210). All the examples given in these two manuals are by Japanese poets, as they focus on the typical Japanese genre of topic verse poetry (*kudaishi*). See Ivo Smits, *The Pursuit of Loneliness: Chinese and Japanese Nature Poetry in Medieval Japan, ca. 1050–1150*, pp. 71–77; Ivo Smits, "The Way of the Literati," pp. 108ff; and Satō Michio in *Tekkinshō*, pp. 617–635.

[9] Abe Ryūichi believes that the books ordered by this courtier, Yorinaga, were mostly printed editions ("Kanseki," pp. 41–54). See below for details.

[10] *Kokon chomonjū*, 4.125, p. 131.

[11] Shigeakira (also read Shigeaki or Mochiakira, active early twelfth century) belonged to the Umakai Ceremonial House of the Fujiwara. His family had produced Chinese scholars for the state academy ever since his grandfather, Akihira (989?–1066), brought the family to prominence in academic circles.

[12] Fujiwara no Sadanobu (1087–1156?) belonged to the Northern House of the Fujiwara. Nagazumi Yasuaki and Shimada Isao point out that according to *Sonpi bunmyaku*, Sadanobu was dead by 1151 (*Kokon chomonjū*, p. 566, additional note 52). However, Yorinaga himself notes that Sadanobu was still alive in 1151 when he took the tonsure at the age of sixty-four (*Ukaikishō*, p. 203, Ninpyō 1 [1151].10.10). According to *Sesonji genkaroku*, Sadanobu died on Hōgen 1 (1156).1.18 at the age of sixty-nine (*Sonpi bunmyaku* 1, p. 384).

[13] Presumably this refers to Fujiwara no Chikataka (1099?–1165) (*Sonpi bunmyaku*, vol. 1, p. 117). Chikataka was appointed governor of Owari on Kyūan 3 (1147).12.21 (*Kokon chomonjū*, p. 131, note 34).

[14] Liu actually received thirty, not twenty, *ryō* of gold powder. In the Heian period, one *ryō* was the equivalent of five *monme* or 14.6 grams. It is rather difficult to estimate the worth of thirty *ryō* of gold powder, especially in an age when prices—for land, for instance—were calculated in amounts of rice or its equivalent (*koku*) or rolls of expensive cloth. However, we do know that the up to three hundred *ryō* gold powder given to Japanese monks traveling to China in the ninth century for their expenses was considered the equivalent of 1.5 *koku*. See Verschuer, *Across the Perilous Seas*, pp. 16–17, 65.

[15] *Ukaikishō*, pp. 200–201, Ninpyō 1 (1151).9.24. (*Ukaikishō* is a selection made

in 1517 from Yorinaga's diary by Sanjōnishi Kin'eda, 1487–1563.) *Hyakurenshō* also mentions the event but gives no specific titles (*Hyakurenshō*, p. 90, Ninpyō 1 (1151).9.24). The Chinese merchant Zhou Liangshi was rewarded on Manju 3 (1026).6.24; *Hyakurenshō* refers to the *Shibō [Sukefusa] ki*, that is, the *Shunki*. See also Verschuer, *Across the Perilous Seas*, pp. 62–63; and Komatsu Shigemi, *Heianchō denrai no* Hakushi monjū *to sanseki no kenkyū: Kenkyūhen*, p. 335. The anonymous *Hyakurenshō* historian also takes note of the precedent of Zhou Liangshi, who had presented Yorinaga's greatgrandfather, Yorimichi, with a Chinese register of family names and statuses, adding that Zhou was actually only half Chinese; his mother was Japanese.

[16] *Dongpo xiangsheng zhizhangtu* (Convenient Maps by Master Dongpo). For a long time I could not place this particular work, which I at first mistakenly assumed (*The Pursuit of Loneliness*, p. 36) to be a literary work by Su Shi, perhaps a lost collection. I would like to thank Dr. Achim Mittag for helping me to change my views.

[17] For a facsimile edition, with introduction, see *Songben lidai dili zhizhang tu*. Su Shi is mentioned as the compiler in the original preface (p. 5). See also the editor's introduction (pp. 1–4, 1–5); and Richard J. Smith, *Chinese Maps: Images of "All under Heaven,"* p. 28.

[18] This may be corroborated with a copy of *Xinding sanlitu* that Yorinaga read in 1143. This treatise on rites compiled by Nie Chongyi dates from the late tenth century, but it is likely that Yorinaga acquired a twelfth-century printed edition. See *Taiki*, vol. 23, p. 97, Kōji 2 (1143).9.15; and Ōba Osamu, *Kanseki yunyū no bunkashi: Shōtoku taishi kara Yoshimune e*, p. 62.

[19] [*Xin*] *Wudai shiji*, ten volumes; *Xin Tangshu*, nine volumes.

[20] Jan-Pierre Drège, "La lecture et l'écriture en Chine et la xylographie," p. 85.

[21] *Xin Tangshu*, vol. 5, pp. 1421–1626.

[22] *Shixue wuxing menlei zaomu yuchong shu*. Very likely, this is the ninth-century commentary on plants and animals in the *Book of Odes*, a work in twenty volumes ordered by Emperor Wenzong in the Kaicheng era (836–840).

[23] Yorinaga is supposed to have said, "Poetry is a frivolous pastime, and not at all necessary at our court. Calligraphy is only a hobby and should not be prized by wise counselors." In this passage Yorinaga is maligning his elder brother and nemesis Tadamichi (1097–1164), who was an active *kanshi* and *waka* poet and a widely admired calligrapher (*Hōgen monogatari*, p. 348). Wilson, *Hōgen Monogatari*, p. 8, has a slightly different rendering. See also Hashimoto Yoshihiko, *Fujiwara no Yorinaga*, pp. 60–61.

[24] When his cat fell ill, Yorinaga offered prayers to the Thousand-Armed Kannon. The cat did indeed recover and lived on until it was ten. After the cat died, Yorinaga conducted elaborate funeral rites (*Taiki*, vol. 23, p. 71, Kōji 1 [1142].8.6). See also Hashimoto Yoshihiko, *Fujiwara no Yorinaga*, pp. 14, 16; and Yokoi Kiyoshi, *Chūsei o ikita hitobito*, pp. 15–16.

[25] *Taiki*, vol. 23, pp. 98–100, 110, Kōji 2 (1143).9.29; Kōji 2.12.30. See also Kawaguchi Hisao, *Heianchō Nihon kanbungakushi no kenkyū*, vol. 3, pp. 919–929; Hashimoto Yoshihiko, *Fujiwara no Yorinaga*, pp. 32–50; Ōba Osamu, *Kanseki yu'nyū no bunkashi*, pp. 54–56; and Peter Kornicki, *The Book in Japan*, pp. 254–255.

[26] Robert Borgen, *Sugawara no Michizane and the Early Heian Court*, pp. 80–88; Momo Hiroyuki, *Jōdai gakusei no kenkyū*, pp. 63–67, 81–86; Hashimoto Yoshihiko, *Fujiwara no Yorinaga*, pp. 36–37.

[27] For a good English introduction to the court university, see Borgen, *Sugawara no Michizane and the Early Heian Court*, pp. 71–88, and Marian Ury, "Chinese Learning and Intellectual Life," pp. 367–375.

[28] *Mengqiu* was definitely known and used as textbook in Japan by 878 (*Nihon Sandai jitsuroku* 34, p. 499, Genkei 2 [878].8.25). See also Hayakawa Mitsusaburō, "*Mōgyū* kaisetsu," pp. 95–130. For a partial English translation of *Mengqiu*, see Burton Watson, trans., *Meng ch'iu: Famous Episodes from Chinese History and Legend*.

[29] "*Kangaku-in no suzume wa* Mōgyū *o saezuri*": *Gikeiki* 6.6, p. 277; Helen Craig McCullough, *Yoshitsune: A Fifteenth Century Japanese Chronicle*, p. 221. See also Ōta Shōjirō, vol. 1 of *Ōta Shōjirō chosakushū*, pp. 218–235.

[30] Examples are *Genji monogatari* (Tale of Genji,), *Konjaku monogatari shū* (Tales of Times Now Past, late eleventh century), *Toshiyori zuinō* (Toshiyori's Poetic Treatise, ca. 1115), and *Kara monogatari* (Tales of China, twelfth century). See Hayakawa Mitsusaburō, "*Mōgyū* kaisetsu," pp. 98, 99, 107; Tochio Takeshi, "Nihon ni denrai shita ruisho to sono kōyō," pp. 65–67; and Ward Geddes, *Kara Monogatari: Tales of China*, pp. 5, 45–46, 52–54.

[31] *Qianzi wen* supposedly was brought to Japan by Wani from Paekche during the reign of emperor Ōjin (r. 270–309). Since *Qianzi wen* was composed by Zhou Xingsi (470?–521) two centuries after Wani's somewhat mythical visit to Japan, the report in the *Kojiki* is one instance of rewriting history. See Wang Zhenping, "Manuscript Copies of Chinese Books in Ancient Japan," p. 36. For *Qianzi wen* in general see Paul Pelliot, "Le Ts'ien tseu wen ou Livre des Mille Mots."

[32] *Baiyong*, which actually contains 120 poems, is also known as *Li Jiao zayong* (Li Jiao's Miscellaneous Compositions). It is an anthology of poems on simple (i.e., noncompound) topics by Li Jiao (644–713), a poet who excelled at the genre of *yongwu shi*, "poems about things." *Baiyong* was lost in China but preserved in Japan. For an introduction to the history of the reception of *Baiyong* in Heian Japan, see Takashima Motomu, "Nihon koten ni okeru Ri Kō hyakuei o megutte."

[33] For *Wakan rōeishū*, see Ivo Smits "Song as Cultural History: Reading *Wakan rōeishū*."

[34] These are so-called *shibu no dokusho* or *shibu no shomotsu* (Ōta Shōjirō, vol. 1 of *Ōta Shōjirō chosakushū*, pp. 236–246). See also Minobe Shigekatsu, "Bunkaken to shite no sōbō," p. 268; and Hayakawa Mitsusaburō, "*Mōgyū* kaisetsu," p. 69.

[35] *Taiki*, vol. 23, p. 100, Kōji 2 (1143).9.29. Yorinaga read these in Hōen 6 (1140).

[36] *Lishi zhu Wenxuan*. Li's commentary was partly prompted by the inclusion of the *Wenxuan* in the Tang examination syllabus as a preparatory text. Although it was followed by later commentaries, Li's was considered the best. See David R. Knechtges, *Wen Xuan or Selections of Refined Literature*, vol. 1, pp. 53–63. It took Yorinaga nine months to work his way through *Wenxuan*. He copied out the text while reading; this was a normal way of acquainting oneself thoroughly with a text (Susan Cherniack, "Book Culture and Textual Transmission in Sung China," p. 33, note 64). His tutor was Fujiwara no Yoshiakira (?–1143), a brother of Shigeakira (*Taiki*, vol. 23, p. 99, Kōji 2 [1143].9.29; Hashimoto Yoshihiko, *Fujiwara no Yorinaga*, p. 35). Yorinaga's great-great-grandfather, Michinaga, on the other hand, relied on later commentaries collectively known as the *Wucheng zhu* (Commentaries by the Five Officials, eighth century). See *Midō kanpakuki*, vol. 1, p. 196, Kankō 3 (1006).10.20.

[37] See Andrew Edmund Goble, "Social Change, Knowledge, and History: Hanazono's *Admonitions to the Crown Prince*," pp. 91–92, 113–116.

[38] See Gomi Fumihiko, "Inseiki no sei to seiji, buryoku"; and Tōno Haruyuki, "Nikki ni miru Fujiwara Yorinaga no nanshoku kankei."

[39] Togawa Tomoru, "Inseiki no daigakuryō to gakumon jōkyō: Fujiwara no Yorinaga no jiseki o chūshin ni," pp. 79–83.

[40] *Taiki*, vol. 23, p. 149, Kyūan 1 (1145).4.2 and 14. See also Hashimoto Yoshihiko, *Fujiwara no Yorinaga*, pp. 55–58, who provides a reconstructed plan of the library building. Yorinaga gives the storehouse's measurements as 2 *jō*, 3 *shaku* (i.e., 23 *shaku*, ca. 7 meters) by 1 *jō*, 1 *shaku* (i.e. 11 *shaku*, ca. 3.3 meters) with a height of 1 *jō*, 2 *shaku*, including a foundation of 1 *shaku*. The building was located at

the northwest corner of Yorinaga's villa on the Ōimikado and Takakura crossing, just above eastern Nijō. For the existence of other private libraries in Heian Japan, see Peter Kornicki, *The Book in Japan*, pp. 369–370.

[41] The oldest extant printed text in China is Kumârajîva's translation of the *Diamond Sutra* (Sk. *Vajra prajñâ pâramitâ sutra;* C. *Jingang banruo boluomi jing;* J. *Kongō hannya haramitta kyō*) of 868, which was discovered by Aurel Stein (1862–1943) in Dunhuang. Korea can boast of the world's oldest extant printed text, a *dhâranî* discovered at Pulguksa temple in 1966 dating from the early eighth century, (Cherniack, "Book Culture and Textual Transmission in Sung China," p. 32, note 62). Another early example is a prayer (J. *darani*) from 764 held in the Hyakumantō pagoda at Hōryūji temple in Japan.

[42] Prior to the Song dynasty, one of the most important methods of circulating the Confucian canon was via stone tablets onto which the authorized standard texts had been carved. These tablets were erected in public places by government decree. People could make a rubbing on paper and take the text home with them. The first record of this reproduction technique comes from 175 BCE. This was done on at least another six occasions thereafter, but the best known are those erected during the Tang dynasty (618–907) in the capital, Changan. See Cherniack, "Book Culture and Textual Transmission in Sung China," pp. 19, 61.

[43] Kornicki, *The Book in Japan*, pp. 114–125; Kawase Kazuma, *Zoku Nihon shoshigaku no kenkyū*, pp. 691–696; David Chibbett, *The History of Japanese Printing and Book Illustration*, pp. 29–32. On a note of interest, given the rough but constant quality of the 770 *dhâranî*, some scholars have supposed that bronze, rather than standard wooden, plates were used. The advantage of bronze is that it does not wear as quickly as wood, which is convenient when printing large quantities. However, some of the *dhârâni* show evidence of contact with wood.

[44] Cherniack, "Book Culture and Textual Transmission in Sung China," pp. 33, 78–82.

[45] See Hanabusa Hideki, "Sōhon *Hakushi monjū* ni tsuite," p. 489; Komatsu Shigemi, *Heianchō denrai no* Hakushi monjū *to sanseki no kenkyū: Kenkyūhen*, pp. 334–338; and Satō Michio, "Shitai to shisō: Heian kōki no tenkai," p. 231. See also Chen Jie, "*Hakushi monjū* no Sōhan shohon ni tsuite." Incidentally, there are strong indications that the Heian and Kamakura reading of the characters for "Collected Works" was *bunshū* or *bunsu* rather than *monjū*.

[46] *Midō kanpakuki*, vol. 2, p. 74, Kankō 7 (1010).8.29.

[47] Examples include ibid., vol. 1, p. 196, Kankō 3 (1006).10.20; vol, 2, pp. 82, 243, Kankō 7 (1010).11.28 and Chōwa 2 (1013) 9.14; and vol. 3, p. 20, Chōwa

4 (1015).7.15. Most often, Michinaga received these books together with similar editions of the *Wenxuan*. Minamoto no Tsuneyori saw printed editions of the *Wenxuan* in 1025 (*Sakeiki*, p. 149, Manju 2 [1025].7.3).

[48] *Gōdanshō chū* 6.420, pp. 1297–1300. Masafusa comments on a faulty phrasing in *Wakan rōeishū* 780, a quotation from the *Changhen ke* (Song of Everlasting Sorrow).

[49] For insights into changes in book formats and their impact on reading habits see Cherniack, "Book Culture and Textual Transmission in Sung China," pp. 36–40; and Jan-Pierre Drège, "La lecture et l'écriture en Chine et la xylographie," pp. 101–103.

[50] See Peter K. Bol, *"This Culture of Ours": Intellectual Transitions in T'ang and Sung China*, pp. 148–60.

[51] *Taiki*, vol. 23, pp. 103, 104–105, 175–176, Kōji 2 (1143).11.3, Kōji 2 (1143).11.24, and Kyūan 2 (1146).3.11. Yorinaga mentions Kong Yingda's (574–648) *Liji zhengyi* and the *Zhouyi zhengyi*. These commentaries date from the early Tang, but here Song prints are meant. Ōta Shōjirō points to several examples of Song editions of the *Book of Changes* and the *Book of Odes* in twelfth-century Japanese collections (Ōta Shōjirō, vol. 1 of *Ōta Shōjirō chosakushū*, pp. 319–321). See also *Xin Tangshu*, vol. 5, p. 1426.

[52] See Mori Katsumi, "Sōdai zanbon no kin'yu to Nihon e no ryūden;" Mori Katsumi, *Nissō bunka kōryū no shomondai*, pp. 183–186; Verschuer, *Across the Perilous Seas*, pp. 62–63; and Wang Zhenping, "Manuscript Copies of Chinese Books in Ancient Japan," pp. 44–45.

[53] *Taiki*, vol. 23, pp. 98, 100, Kōji 2 (1143).9.29.

[54] On the issue of which *yulan* Yorinaga perused, Kawaguchi Hisao (*Heianchō Nihon kanbungakushi no kenkyū*, vol. 3, pp. 922–923, 924) believes that it was the Song period edition. Tochio Takeshi and Ōba Osamu make the case for it being the *Xiuwendian yulan* (Imperial Digest of the Hall for Cultivating Literary Skills), which had already reached Japan before the reign of Empress Suiko (r. 593–628).

[55] *Sankaiki*, vol. 27, p. 225, Jishō 3 (1179).2.13. See also *Hyakurenshō*, p. 132, Jishō 3 (1179).12.16. Both texts explicitly mention the *Taiping yulan* and make remark on the "beginning of the circulation (*rufu*) of this book in our country." The *Sankaiki* entry provides the main evidence for believing that Yorinaga did not read the *Taiping yulan* in 1142. See Tochio Takeshi, "Nihon ni denrai shita ruisho to sono kōyō," p. 79, note 12; Ōba Osamu, *Kanseki yu'nyū no bunkashi*, pp. 50–51, 54, 60–62; Mori Katsumi, *Nissō bunka kōryū no shomondai*, p. 186; and Verschuer, *Across the Perilous Seas*, pp. 62–63.

56 *Myōkaiki*, p. 196, Bun'ō 1 (1260).4.22. For estimates of land prices in the capital throughout the Heian period, see Murai Yasuhiko, *Heian kizoku no sekai*, pp. 397–403. In 1176, 450 square meters (one *henushi*) on Hachijō sold for eleven rolls of twenty-four yards each of silk and fifteen *koku*.

57 The *Heiji monogatari* tells the story of Michinori's flight and subsequent death (*Heiji monogatari*, pp. 198–202). There is a famous scene in the *Heiji monogatari emaki* showing courtiers who stare in horror at Shinzei's severed head.

58 *Zoku kojidan chūkai* 2.56, pp. 248–250; *Taiki*, vol. 23, p. 86, Kōji 2 (1143).3.8. The Chinese may have been a merchant. The same story about Michinori's talent for speaking this foreign language appears in *Heiji monogatari*, which claims that the event took place in 1155 and that the Chinese conversation partner was the Chinese acolyte Danhai (J. Tankai) from Nachi, presumably the very same person that Yorinaga had heard about (*Heiji monogatari*, pp. 202–204).

59 Yoshimura, "Tsūken nyūdō zōsho mokuroku ni tsuite no gimon," pp. 100–103. See also Kornicki, *The Book in Japan*, p. 424. Another curious thing about the catalogue is that it does not list as many books on music as one might have expected because Michinori was very much involved in this art and titles that he was known to have possessed are lacking from the list.

60 Michinori also owned a copy of *Tangshu mulu* (Contents of the Book of the Tang) (*Tsūken nyūdō zōsho mokuroku*, pp. 940, 949).

61 Among them were Sugawara no Koreyoshi's (812–880) *Tōgū setsuin* (First Rhyme Rhyming Dictionary), ibid., p. 950). The title probably derives from the fact that the character *tō* is the first rhyme and *gū* is the first sound in the traditional system of arranging characters phonetically (Robert Borgen, *Sugawara no Michizane and the Early Heian Court*, p. 348, n. 47).

62 An example is *Dazi zhu Liezi* (Annotated *Liezi* in Large Character Format). See *Tsūken nyūdō zōsho mokuroku*, p. 940. For the *dazi* editions, see Cherniack, "Book Culture and Textual Transmission in Sung China," pp. 41–42.

63 *Tsūken nyūdō zōsho mokuroku*, p. 939.

64 Jōjin writes, "In the early afternoon Yu Gui presented me with one book of Master Hanshan's poetry. My heart is filled with joy" (*San Tendai godaisanki*, p. 18, Enkyū [1072].5.22; Fujiyoshi Masumi, "Jōjin no motarashita higa no tenseki: Nissō bunka kōryū no hitokusari," p. 56). The printed edition of Jōjin's diary reads Saishan, but that must be a misprint for Hanshan. For more details of Jōjin's knowledge of Hanshan, see Robert Borgen, "The Legend of Hanshan: A Neglected Source." The first printed edition of Hanshan's poetry in Japan dates from Shōchū 2 (1325) and was an initiative of a Gozan nun by the name of Sōtaku. This 1325 edition is based

on Song printed editions of Hanshan's poetry, the first of which appeared in 1189 and was the work of a monk, Zhinan. Copies are extant in Japanese collections (Abe Ryūichi, "Kanseki," pp. 66–67; Iriya Sensuke and Matsumura Takashi, "Kaisetsu," pp. 503–504; Hiroyama Hidenori, "Shōchū-ban Kanzan shishū ni tsuite").

[65] *Collected Poems of Wang Bo*, 1 vol. (*Tsūken nyūdō zōsho mokuroku*, p. 948).

[66] *Baishi wenji* (Bai Juyi's Collected Works), eight volumes bound together, two covers (*Tsūken nyūdō zōsho mokuroku*, p. 947). This item is a bit unclear. I am unsure whether all the unspecified volumes (*chō*) in this group (chest 105) belong together. If so, then this edition of Bai's collected works runs to a total of fifty-nine volumes. Chest 109 contains the *[Liu Bai] Changhe ji* ([Liu Yuxi's and Bai Juyi's] Chanting in Harmony Collection) (*Tsūken nyūdō zōsho mokuroku*, p. 947).

[67] *Luo Yin shi* (Luo Yin's Poetry), 2 vols. (*Tsūken nyūdō zōsho mokuroku*, p. 943).

[68] *Li Shangyin ji* (Collected Poems of Li Shangyin), 3 vols.; *Du Xunhe ji* (Collected Poems of Du Xunhe), 1 vol.; *Zhang Xiaobiao ji* (Collected Poems of Zhang Xiaobiao), vol. 1 (*Tsūken nyūdō zōsho mokuroku*, p. 948). For more information on these poets, see Ivo Smits, *The Pursuit of Loneliness*, pp. 61–65. Incidentally, the *Gunsho ruijū* text incorrectly gives the character *kyoku* (office) for what in the manuscripts is a variant character (*itaiji*) for *kan* (scroll).

[69] *Tsūken nyūdō zōsho mokuroku*, p. 943. This little gem has generally been overlooked by scholars with the exception of a mention in an article by Nagasawa Kikuya, originally published in 1935, and a reference in Okada Masayuki's 1929 history of Chinese literature in Japan. See Nagasawa Kikuya, *Shina gikyoku shōsetsu no kenkyū*, vol. 5 of *Nagasawa Kikuya chosakushū*, pp. 267–268; and Okada Masayuki, *Nihon kanbungakushi*, p. 429.

[70] *Tsūken nyūdō zōsho mokuroku*, p. 950. See also Nagasawa Kikuya, *Shina gikyoku shōsetsu no kenkyū*, vol. 5 of *Nagasawa Kikuya chosakushū*, p. 267.

[71] *Yulan*, totaling 127 volumes, numbered "book 121;" *Huiyao*, for a total of 43 volumes (*Tsūken nyūdō zōsho mokuroku*, p. 941). See Nagasawa Kikuya, *Shina gikyoku shōsetsu no kenkyū*, vol. 5 of *Nagasawa Kikuya chosakushū*, p. 267.

[72] *Tsūken nyūdō zōsho mokuroku*, p. 941.

[73] Kōjirō Yoshikawa, *An Introduction to Sung Poetry*, pp. 182–183.

8

Volumes of Knowledge: Observations on Song-Period Printed Medical Texts

Kosoto Hiroshi

Translated and adapted by Andrew Edmund Goble

The development and dissemination of printing technology in the Song era fueled an information revolution.[1] Printing moved the production and reproduction of written material from the handwritten manuscript to the woodblock-printed text, from the scroll format to the book format, from the uniquely compiled to the mass produced. The new technology created portable items ("books") that could be readily acquired and transported, facilitated the emergence of official bookstores and private commercial outlets, and made it possible for individuals to have items printed more or less on demand. It also meant that earlier knowledge could now be readily preserved. Amid an intellectual climate that encouraged the retrieval and renewal of Chinese culture,[2] printing made possible the creation of authoritative texts that could be defined as the "the classics," as with the well-known example of what came to be the Confucian classics. But it also became possible, as Ivo Smits's essay has pointed out (Chap. 7), for classical bodies of knowledge to be defined in more than one way and in more than one place. And knowledge that might previously have been preserved only orally, or considered ephemeral, might now be preserved and could cater to an audience that was focused more on the present than on the past.

These printed Chinese materials were in great demand throughout East Asia. We know that they played a significant role in providing new tastes and new influences and were used to prescribe new forms or areas of intellectual and cultural legitimacy. And, as we shall see in Chapter 9, printed Song medical works provided the foundation for significant developments in medieval Japanese medicine. What I would like to do in this essay is to elucidate an "appropriating context," that is, the potential range of material from which a selection might have been made. I shall focus on the area of printed medical texts and the rhythms of publishing in the Northern (960–1127) and Southern (1127–1279) Song dynasties (with some mention of Jin [1115–1234] and Yuan [1271–1368] works).

The roughly three-hundred-year Song period divides neatly into a century and a half each of the Northern and Southern Song. As we shall see, there was a notable difference in the nature of, and motivations for, medical printing in the two eras. In the Northern Song printing was sponsored by the imperial state, which, out of a sense of responsibility for the health and well-being of its subjects, wished to make authoritative knowledge and definitive editions of texts as widely available as possible. In the Southern Song, by contrast, there was little official sponsorship. Rather, printing occurred at the behest of individuals who wrote up their own clinical experiences or wished to see disseminated relatively unknown works whose information they and their families had found efficacious. Some of this printing was motivated by a desire for "self-marketing," and some derived from a sense of compassion. The broader rhythms of Northern and Southern Song produced different types of medical literature, which suggests that for those engaging it there was perhaps little sense that either was a better embodiment of "Chinese medicine."

Northern Song Medical Publishing

Any effort to comprehend Northern Song medical publishing, or at least to give it some definition, needs to deal with two basic limitations. First, while medical publishing in the Song preserved some older texts and added some new ones to the record, the advent of printing does not mean that we have a full record of everything that was printed. Some works undoubtedly passed without trace. Some are known to have been well received, even influential, but were lost, such as Chu Yushi's *Yangsheng biyong fang* (Essential Prescriptions for Nurturing Life, 1097).[3] Second, while we may suggest that there were some "phases" in publishing, this does not necessarily mean that we have incontrovertible proof that these phases reflect a consciously articulated contemporary program of publishing. Nonetheless, and while I will not mention here all works known to have been published, let us proceed.

The Northern Song emperors believed that it was incumbent on the state to look to the physical well-being of its subjects. As part of that they were very interested in issues of medicine and seem to have believed that knowledge of treatments, theories, and of materia medica, should be as readily available as possible. To this end official support was given to medical publishing.

The first phase of Northern Song publication focused on providing information on crude drugs and prescriptions. Leading off the "program" were two pharmaceutical works published in 973 and 974. The actual blocks were carved in the Guozizian, the functional equivalent of a national university. These works were the twenty-volume *Kaibao xinxiang ding bencao* (Kaibao Era Newly Edited and Revised Pharmacopeia) and the *Kaibao chongding bencao* (Kaibao Era Second Revised Edition of the Pharmacopeia) in twenty volumes with a one-volume table of contents. As was common, the titles incorporated the era name in which they were produced. There has been some speculation about why a work would need to be revised within a year of its first appearance. However, we might assume either that the first edition was found in need of something as elementary as a table of contents or that sufficient mistakes were found in it that the emperor—who formally authorized the commencement of any printing project, formally sanctioned publication of a work once the project was complete, and sometimes selected the title by which it was to be known—deemed it necessary. Expense was not an object.

But we might also, in noting the rapidity with which a revised edition appeared, take cognizance of the fact that the works dealt with pharmaceutical knowledge. Knowledge of materia medica is fundamental to the medical enterprise, and fundamental to that was the provision and correct identification of the crude drugs themselves. Any number of formulas might be in circulation, but their effectiveness depended on authentication of the ingredients. We might not be far wrong in suggesting that the selection of this type of work as the first effort in bringing medical knowledge to the people derived from a desire to address the need for accurate and clinically useful information and information that could be held to a common standard of assessment. These works were also a legitimating statement of a new dynasty for they represented an authoritative update of the Tang dynasty's benchmark compilation, the *Zhenglei bencao* (Classified Pharmacopeia).

Two decades later, in 992, the concern with providing clinically applicable knowledge was further advanced with the appearance of the original compilation of the *Taiping shenghui fang* (Prescriptions of Great Peace and Sagely Benevolence).[4] It is a massive work in 100 volumes, with 1,670 sections, and contains 16,834 formulas collected from throughout the country. These latter included both well-known prescriptions and, perhaps more crucially, as many "private" or "family" prescriptions as possible. This large-scale project took ten years to complete and occurred in a period marked by other major printing projects that were designed to preserve the heritage of the Tang era, such as the 1,000-volume encyclopedia the *Taiping yulan* (Imperial Digest of the Taiping Era), completed in 977; the printing of the Buddhist canon (the *Tripitaka*) in 5,048 volumes carried out in 972–983 by Buddhist clergy, one copy of which was taken back to Japan by the priest Chōnen; and the 100-volume *Wenyuan yinghua*, completed in 982. The second Song emperor, Taizong (r. 976–997), appears to have had a personal interest in medicine, and ensured that the project received all the resources required for completion. Taizong also ordered that the work was to be as widely distributed as possible, most likely in the first instance to government offices throughout the country.

However, while this work seems to have been widely available, getting medical information to the general population was not automatic, a problem recognized both by officials and by emperors. For example, in the case of the

Qingli Shanjiu fang (Qingli Era Prescriptions for Wonderful Relief), completed in 1048, the motivation of the compiler was very clear.

> Since those suffering from afflictions in the southern regions were lacking in both medicines and prescriptions, I made available [a work known as] the *Shanjiu fang*, and I also distributed the formula Tongtianxi; furthermore, I ordered that a great number of medicinals were to be distributed to the needy.

However, this *Shanjiu fang* seems not to have been actually printed, but, in a telling commentary on the difficulties of dealing with local officials, in at least one location it was carved onto a stele.

> Humbly I took the stone inscription and had it placed to the left of the gate near a tree, and all those who came to read it were encouraged to copy it for themselves and did not need to request any formal permission to do so.

The distribution problems of the era are also highlighted in comments from the 1051 *Huangyou jianyao jizhong fang* (Huangyou Era Collection of Simple and Basic Prescriptions). Compiled under imperial order, this "how-to" work in three volumes and five books "focuses on pulse diagnosis; it excepts disease origins, and leaves out the comments on the various schools." It was published by being written in ink on wooden tablets, copied, and then distributed. The decision to not have it carved on blocks and then printed reflected the difficulties of distribution and transportation that are sometimes noted for the era,[5] as well as the sloth of local officials. As a later commentary notes:

> [This work] was written with the intention that it be copied and disseminated, be widely employed in giving medical treatment, give the populace the enjoyments of good health, and enable them to enjoy long lives; yet in the official offices in the many prefectures it has been treated in no way different than if it were just another official rule or regulation, and, even though a good twelve years have passed, the straitened and impoverished commoners have not been made aware of it. That the affection and solicitude of the emperor has not been thus transmitted to the commoners is a crime of the officials. That this book is to be written on boards, set up by the roadsides, and transmitted widely to the population, that their illnesses and sufferings may thereby be relieved, is so the population will be aware of the benevolence of the emperor. Sages of ages to come are not only to multiply these but every year are to examine them anew, and the officials are to ensure that they are not in disrepair.

Perhaps as a result of problems like this, and a perceived need to put medical publishing on a firmer footing, in 1057 a Bureau for Emending Medical Texts, devoted exclusively to medical writings, was established within the Editorial Office, thus taking over the responsibility for emendation and publication of medical texts that until this time had been carried out by the educational administrative office that was the Guozizian. This initiated a burst of medical publication designed to produce a new series of standard, definitive texts.

However, the interest in standardizing texts was not new. In 1027 two major projects were completed. The first, following an imperial order of the preceding year, was the editing, by the officials Cao Zongque and Wang Juzheng, of three works fundamental to the Chinese medical tradition, namely, the *Huangdi neijing suwen* (Huangdi Internal Classic Plain Questions), *Nanjing* (Classic of Difficult Cases), and *Chaoshi bingyuan houlun* (Mr. Chao's [Chao Yuanfang's] Treatise on the Etiology and Symptomology of Disease). The second project, dealing with acupuncture, brought the study and practice of the art to a new level of sophistication. Concern had been expressed that over time the River Point acupoints (acupoints in general) and the channels and collaterals (conduits through which vital energy and blood circulate) had become disordered and nonstandard, and so by imperial order the medical official Wang Weiyi was ordered to effect standardization. The result was the *Tongren shuxue zhenjiutujing* (Illustrated Manual on the Points for Acupuncture and Moxibustion as Found on the Bronze Figure) in three volumes, completed and distributed to the provinces in 1029. Wang's achievement was to combine text with visual references, namely, the anatomical drawings included in the work and the metal-cast standard human body models on which the meridians were drawn and the acupoints indicated by small holes. It is fair to say that this project effectively defined the future understanding of acupuncture.

As important as these efforts were, and the use of visual referents in acupuncture is a major development for acupuncture treatment,[6] they were overshadowed by a major project in the 1060s that combined the two goals of bringing information on materia medica up to date and publishing definitive editions of earlier (and now classic) medical works. The pharmaceutical project was completed first and involved the revision, in 1062, of the earlier *Kaibao bencao* under a new title, *Jiayou buzhu bencao* (Jiayou Era Annotated Pharmacopeia). And in the same year a second work was completed, the twenty-volume illustrated, and aptly titled, *Tujing bencao* (Illustrated Materia Medica). The second project was to be of fundamental importance to the tradition of Chinese medical literature.

Between 1056 and 1069, three officials—Gao Baoheng, Sun Qi, and Lin Yi—supervised the revising and editing of nine medical texts, which, when published, came to a total of 167 volumes. We do not know whether other works were available for publication but were deemed not sufficiently important to the medical tradition to merit the allocation of resources for their official preservation. But, in any event, publication of these works established them as central to the

Chinese medical tradition, and, indeed, it would not be going too far to suggest that the simple fact of publication effectively delineated the future shape of the Chinese medical canon. By this I am making a point beyond that of noting that the act of selection naturally defines any canon. That is, had this publication project not been carried out the medical canon would not only look very different, but it would be a significantly diminished canon. Although archaeological discoveries in the future may alter the picture, to date not one fragment of the original scroll copies of these works has survived. All of the common extant editions in circulation are based solely on these Northern Song revised printed editions.

The project may be divided into four phases. The first phase, involving three separate works, focused on the original or revised writings of the Han dynasty figure Zhang Zhongjing. Between 1065 and 1066 the editors revised the ten-volume *Shanghanlun* (Treatise on Febrile and Miscellaneous Diseases);[7] the eight-volume *Jingui yuhanjing* (The Jade Box of the Golden Chamber Classic), something of a variant version of the *Shanghanlun*;[8] and, finally, the three-volume *Jingui yaolue fanglun* (Synopsis of Prescriptions of the Golden Chamber), an abbreviated version of Zhang's works, which reedited product excised sections on cold damage that appeared in the other two works.[9]

The second phase, in 1067 and 1068, concentrated on editing two works produced by the Tang figure Sun Simiao,[10] his thirty-volume *Beiji qianjin yao fang* (Prescriptions Worth a Thousand in Gold for Emergencies, originally titled *Qianjin fang*) and the likewise thirty-volume supplementary *Qianjin yi fang* (A Supplement to the Prescriptions Worth a Thousand in Gold).[11] The *Beiji qianjin yao fang* required only three months from the commencement of carving to its initial printing, which gives us an opportunity to comment on some technical aspects of printing. With 1,084 leaves produced in ninety days, this gives us an average of twelve leaves per day. If we assume that one person could carve one leaf per day, then at the very least this means that twelve carvers would have had to have been employed continuously on this. If we take account of breaks and the like, there were probably fifteen carvers on hand. Since we know that thirty-eight carvers were employed on the Gu Congde edition of the *Suwen* (Plain Questions), dating from the early Southern Song, this is not a particularly large number (by way of comparison, 150 carvers were employed on the *Taiping Yulan*). What this also means is that, at a rough estimate of one volume every three days, the contemporary carving work was quite advanced. Of course, for the printing and bookbinding quite separate artisans would have been employed at the same time. Bearing this in mind and estimating from the number of leaves in the *Shanghanlun*, the process from presentation to printing was probably completed in under a month, probably around twenty days. This was somewhat faster than the publishing of medical texts in Japan some six hundred years later during the

Edo period. So we can well imagine the scale of the Song government's printing facilities.

The third stage of the project involved publication of works on acupuncture and pulse diagnosis written in the Jin period (western Jin, 265–316; eastern Jin, 316–419), and it appears that some need was felt to standardize but also simplify the information that had accumulated. The first to be completed was the ten-volume *Maijing* (Pulse Classic), a diagnosis manual centered on the pulse that was compiled by Wang Shuhe (alt. Wang Xi, ca. 210–285). There is considerable overlap with the information appearing in such works as *Suwen, Lingshu* (Miraculous Pivot), *Nanjing, Shanghanlun, Jingui yuhanjing,* and *Jingui yaolue [fanglun]*. But, while there is overlap, it is the only work dedicated to pulse diagnosis, which was one of the central—indeed, perhaps the most important—elements in overall diagnosis. A similar consideration, that it was important to preserve a work that was dedicated to a specific topic, seems to have underlain the editing of the second text in phase three, the twelve-volume *Huangdi sanbu zhenjiu jiayijing* (Huangdi Three-Part Classic of Acupuncture and Moxibustion). This work, an instructional manual for acupuncture and moxibustion, was compiled by Huangfu Mi (215–282) and is a recompilation of material appearing in *Suwen, Lingshu,* and *Mingtang* (*Huangdi Neijing Mingtang,* Huangdi Internal Classic Bright Hall).[12]

The fourth stage of the 1060s editing and printing project involved two Tang period works. The first was the forty-volume pharmaceutical compilation *Waitai miyao fang* (Medical Secrets of an Official); the second was the Tang emendation of a previously emended text of the *Huangdi neijing suwen* (Plain Questions of the Huangdi Classic of Internal Medicine). The *Waitai miyao fang* was compiled by Wang Tao of the Tang.[13] It is the largest in length of the works in the 1060s project, and, with the editing of the works in phase three proceeding concurrently, took two years to be completed. The last work was the twenty-four-volume *Chongguang buzhu Huangdi neijing suwen* (Revised and Expanded Annotated Huangdi Plain Questions). This had been transmitted to the Northern Song via the process whereby the original text of the nine volumes of the *Huangdi neijing Suwen* had been augmented by the Song Cai period emendations of Jin Yuanqi, and the Tang period collations of Wang Bing. As noted earlier, this was previously published in 1027; however, that publication was now revised and republished by the Bureau for Emendation and Publishing of Medical Books. This text is the ancestral text for all currently extant editions. The product quality of the overall project no doubt immensely raised the prestige of the Bureau for Emendation and Publishing of Medical Books.

The next notable project, or at least a major project for which we have evidence, was carried out in the 1090s and was another step in the broader mission of identifying and preserving noteworthy medical writings of the past. In this instance the Northern Song government became aware that a surprisingly large number of medical works that were lost in China had been preserved in Korea and so requested that its vassal Koryŏ "present" these lost works. One work that was requested was the *Huangdi zhenjing* (Huangdi Canon of Acupuncture), the ancestral text of the extant *Huangdi neijing lingshu* (Huangdi Internal Classic Miraculous Pivot). The Northern Song Privy Library probably contained an incomplete version of this, which was probably utilized during the 1060s project but was not given prominence because the accepted wisdom from the time of Huangfu Mi was that the *Huangdi neijing* was composed of the *Suwen* and the *Zhenjing* (Canon of Acupuncture). However, once it was discovered that among the works preserved in Korea was the *Huangdi zhenjing* (Huangdi Canon of Acupuncture), which was a separate and independent work in nine volumes, acquisition was given priority. The request was made to Koryŏ in 1091, the work was received in 1092, and it was published in 1093. This 1093 publication was the copy on which was based the 1155 Shi Song revised printing of the *Huangdi neijing lingshu*, and it is this work that has been transmitted to the present and constitutes the extant edition of this acupuncture classic.

The next and final burst of activity in Northern Song medical publishing occurred in the first two decades of the twelfth century. The works printed in this period included the first printing in 1107–1110, of the *Taiping huimin hejiju fang* (Prescriptions of the Pharmacy Service for Great Peace and for the Benefit of People) in five volumes; the thirty-one-volume *Daguan jingshi zhenglei beiji bencao* (Daguan Classic Classified Materia Medica for Emergencies) in 1108; the thirty-volume *Zhenghe jingshi zhenglei beiji bencao* (Zhenghe Classic Classified Materia Medica for Emergencies) in 1116; the ten-volume *Shengjijing* (Classic of Holy Relief Imperial Encyclopedia) between 1111 and 1118; and, finally, the two-hundred-volume *Shengji zonglu* (Comprehensive Record of Sagely Beneficence), also compiled sometime during the period 1111–1118. We gain a sense of the motivations behind this medical publishing, and the factors that might influence how that collected information might be disseminated, by briefly noting two of these works, the *Taiping huimin hejiju fang* and the *Shengji zonglu*.

The *Taiping huimin hejiju fang*, compiled between 1107 and 1110, is a collection of the formulas used in the Pharmacy Service, which had been established in the years 1102–1106. These two endeavors are, of course, closely linked and sprang from a concern at the highest imperial level that effective medicines be provided to the general population. The preface to the work lays out the overall background. In the period 1102–1106, a pharmaceutical bureau known as the Pharmacy Service was set up and established in seven locations and engaged in the preparation and sale of medicines. Offices for the purchase of materia medica were also set up in order to deal with an apparent problem in the marketing of counterfeit items. After the establishment of the Service a large number of formulas were collected but apparently in some haste and without a proper evaluation process. Unfortunately the information was printed and put into circulation, and it was realized before long that there were deficiencies in the information regarding freshness of ingredients, measurements, and the effectiveness of the formulas themselves. This was brought to imperial attention, with the result that the Service was granted immediate authority to examine all confidential official materials, to consult the records of the eminent, and to examine all materials, public and private, without exception; in the course of a year the errors were corrected and the present work published.

The resulting work was, in fact, the world's first official pharmacopoeia. It was reprinted and augmented continuously, starting with the original edition of 1107–1110 and going through to a fifth one in 1241–1252 (from which all currently extant copies descend). In other words, while the work is commonly referred to by one title, there is in fact no single work (which presents its own challenges to the study of medical, pharmaceutical, and bibliographic history, as a work might simply cite the title and not note the edition). While the overall order of ten volumes and the more precise divisions within them remained the same, the original 301 formulas were progressively expanded to 796 by the fifth edition, thus more than doubling the size of the original.

The *Shengji zonglu* had a very different history. This imperially commissioned work appears to have been completed sometime during the period 1111–1118, although the carving of the blocks for the two-hundred-volume work was not completed until immediately prior to the fall of the Northern Song capital of Kaifeng in 1126. The blocks (along with everything else in the Guozizian) were confiscated as a war prize by the Jin, and it remained in effect an unknown work until it was printed by the Jin sometime between 1161 and 1189. It was employed in Jin medical circles thereafter, but it only became widely known after it was reprinted by the Yuan in 1300. Indeed, its very existence seems to have been unknown in the Southern Song; it is not mentioned or cited in any Southern Song medical works, and the title does not appear in any general reference works. It gives one pause to consider that political and social circumstances were such that a massive, two-hundred-volume work comprised of some sixty-six topic areas and twenty thousand formulas, the most comprehensive medical publishing project undertaken in China until a Ming era project in the early 1400s, was virtually invisible for a period of nearly two hundred years.

The fate of the *Shengji zonglu*, and, indeed, of all the printing blocks for the medical literature produced by the Northern Song regime, provide an important context when we come to examine the range of works produced, and under what auspices, during the Southern Song (1126–1279).

Southern Song Medical Publishing

Although the Northern Song's official medical publishing enterprise (symbolized by the activities and productions of the Bureau for Emendation and Publishing of Medical Books) was designed to preserve and define the medical canon and make information available as widely as possible, these aims were continued less enthusiastically by the Southern Song regime. However, "nonofficial" Southern Song medical publishing was an extensive enterprise. The revolution in print publishing continued to shape the production and dissemination of medical knowledge. Indeed (and taking note of medical publishing under the Jin and the Yuan), we may fairly note that there was an explosion in medical knowledge from the middle of the twelfth century.[14]

While the Southern Song government may not have lent much support to medical publishing, many of its officials did, and on their own initiative they saw to the publication of works they deemed useful for the population. Some of these works were compiled from information in their own lineages (lineage-based and family-based interests in matters of healing are well attested). Others were originally the work of local physicians who the official felt deserved a wider audience. This might involve having clinical information and prescriptions gathered and published for the first time or it might involve republishing in a different region a work produced for and known in only one area in order to give that information wider dissemination. And, of course, we have all of the private publishing by physicians whose qualifications were of varied type (formally trained, continuing a family interest, or self-taught, perhaps using other available medical works) and who convey the sense of a segment of the medical "profession" closely involved in clinical experience, testing of medicines, and "local" medical practice.

Southern Song medical publishing is distinguished by four characteristics. First, it was decentralized. Second, there was no unified editorial thrust. Third, it represented an enormous range of medical knowledge from a broad spectrum of practitioners and people of diverse educational and social backgrounds.[15] Fourth, the self-publishing impulse produced not so much venerable canons as a large number of ephemeral handbooks that represented the most current knowledge of approaches to medicine and of materia medica. Thus, medicine and medical publishing were areas "in process" and were more vibrant than one might imagine from later efforts to define mainstream "Chinese medicine" based on works that were later canonized or privileged or simply survived through time. Indeed, this sense is strengthened by the fact that many items lost in China were acquired by overseas visitors because they were available and well regarded, and these works served to shape a different sense of the Chinese medical heritage than what might have occurred within China. As with the survey of the Northern Song, I will not pursue a full listing of known and extant works but will focus on some authors and works that can help illustrate some of the above points.[16]

Perhaps it will be useful at this juncture to make a broader observation, namely, that, even though we use terms such as *Southern Song* and *China* as convenient shorthand references, there really was no such thing as a unified or monolithic Southern Song or Chinese medicine. Knowledge was available, but it was not channeled, and it represented an extraordinary marketplace of information. People in China or visiting China would encounter only a portion of that vast body of information. This was not a "deficiency," however, but a reflection of the riches of a highly democratized information revolution. The dissemination of medical works reflected the randomness of marketing networks and the serendipity of coming to know of the existence of works, of knowing whether a work was privately or commercially published, and of knowing whether it was intended for a limited area or a wider region. The long-term survival of any medical work reflected these factors, as did the acquirer's sense of whether a work was ephemeral or worthy of preserving for posterity. Indeed, when we examine medical publications from these perspectives, our overall picture is a richer one than were we to focus on elite traditions.

Some works were widely known and well preserved and had an identifiable impact on the development of the healing arts across the East Asian macroculture. One such work was the 1150 *Youyou xinshu* (New Pediatrics). The impetus for the compilation of the work came from a perceived need, but a need perceived by an individual rather than any formal body. The Song official Liu Fang was concerned that there was no widely available work on pediatrics, and so he had two other people (Wang Li, and Wang Shi) seek out information. It was a landmark effort, that drew not only from a large number of existing works but from a number of private medical traditions. Not only did the work provide a highly pertinent body of knowledge in one of the most important areas of social and medical concern, but the collated listing of sources (most no longer extant) provides a guide to the "development" of the field of pediatrics over a couple of centuries.

A related concern with matters of reproduction appears in the 1237 *Furen daquan liang fang* (Complete Effective Prescriptions for the Diseases of Women) of Chen Ziming, which addressed an area not well served in medical literature heretofore.[17] But, while not the very first specialized treatment (that was the poorly organized Tang period work on women's medicine *Jingxiao chanbao* ([Tested Treasuries in Obstetrics] of Zan Yin), it is generally considered the first useful engagement of obstetrics and gynecology. Ziming, like others, was of the opinion that the most difficult area in the medical arts was that of women's medicine and that in general women's symptoms are difficult to treat (especially during pregnancy). In his preface he gives us a good sense of the mechanics involved in compiling his knowledge. He notes that his family had been interested in learning about medicine for three generations and had collected a number of works. He had also studied various formulas that he had sought out and examined while traveling, and he selected the best books and augmented these with formulas that had been used in [his?] family and compiled these in one book. He divided the work into eight sections, starting with menstruation and ending with birth. Each section records several tens of symptoms, and he included around 260 of his own disquisitions regarding them. After each disquisition he arranged the appropriate formula. It is evident that the work reflected direct personal experience with prescriptions and patient responses, irrespective of how the medicines might be regarded more generally. Finally, he tells us that all has been organized into an easily understandable form, edited, and then indexed. The work had a substantial impact on the development of women's medicine, and there is little doubt that the ready availability of published texts—the ones used by Ziming and, of course, his own—played a large part in this.

A third example of a well-circulated work was the mid-twelfth-century compilation of Xu Shuwei, the *Puji benshi fang* (Effective Prescriptions for Universal Relief), which was a portable guide to ailments and treatments that inter alia provides a close look at aspects of contemporary clinical medicine. The ten volumes and the twenty-six sections (or illness categories) include discussions of acupuncture and moxibustion and a guide to three hundred handy prescriptions. In general the prescriptions are ones employed in treating a specific problem and reflect the details of actual case records rather than a more generalized "one size fits all" formula. Thus, for itchiness, we encounter separate prescriptions for a young boy with pain in both armpits and for another patient with itchiness and pain in the stomach and armpits. The same approach is encountered in areas such as an aching head and dizziness; there are many prescriptions for women's and children's ailments. More complex cases merit several lines of description of the symptoms and provide great detail regarding a patient's prior condition, after which the formula is given. There is thus a very clear sense that what is being written down is a description somewhat equivalent to "this is what I used in this case, and it was successful, thus it is here recorded." That is, we have the sense that what we are reading is the product of clinical testing and experience rather than abstractly applied formulas. This, no doubt, was a major reason for its popularity.[18]

However, while works like those of Xu Shuwei achieved recognition on the basis of content alone (there may also have been some deft marketing involved, of course), other works might become widely known because of their provenance. A good example of this is the 1267 *Yuyaoyuan fang* (Prescriptions of the Imperial

Dispensary) of Xu Guozhen, offspring of a family of doctors from Shanxi that had served the Jin in northern China. The work is in twenty volumes, fourteen sections, and contains some 1,059 formulas. What gave it particular distinction, particularly after the final fall of the Southern Song in 1279, were two factors. First, it was compiled by Xu Guozhen, who was the personal physician to Khubilai Khan and his wife even before Khubilai came to the throne. Second, it is an authoritative selection of the formulas used by the Yuyaoyuan (Imperial Dispensary), the office responsible under the Song, Jin, and Yuan dynasties for the management and provision of medicines at the imperial court. The work does not suggest any obvious breakthroughs in treatment, and may not cover everything that it is possible to cover, but it is a good guide to the medicine used for the elite of the Mongol empire and is a good guide to the range of medicines available more broadly throughout that entity.[19]

Beyond these works, which became almost universally known and acquired a reputation through time, we have a broad range of works that did not enjoy such currency. However, they all attest to the vibrancy of medical publishing and to the range of literature potentially "available." Perhaps the rarest work is the 1154 *Beiji zongxiao fang* (Emergency Effective Prescriptions) of Li Zhaozheng, known only in one copy and in an original Song printing.[20] The author was inspired to compile the work after he had provided successful emergency treatment (based on the prescriptions in the *Zhenglei bencao*) to a daughter who was suffering from smallpox; she survived while others in the vicinity died. He was guided by the notion that emergency information should be readily available, so accordingly the work lists easy to acquire materia medica and simple prescriptions (thus constituting an excellent guide to popular healing practices and concerns of the era). The author was not a medical practitioner but was able to draw on a variety of works that are no longer extant and themselves would have been available because they had been printed. It is entirely possible that Li's work enjoyed quite limited circulation and was preserved by those who acquired control of his estate after his death the following year in 1155. This may have been an unusual case, but it was by no means the only instance in which a work did not enjoy wide circulation.

Zhang Rui's 1133 *Jipeng puji fang* (Jipeng's Prescriptions for Universal Relief), extant in only four of the original thirty volumes, is not cited in any Song or Ming period medical work. Another work is Zhu Ruizhang's 1184 *Weisheng jiabao chanke beiyao* (A Precious Medical Book on Obstetrics for Home Use), an eight-volume collection of prescriptions dealing with women's medicine that was published by a local government office. In circulation only through the Ming period (and not noted again until 1801 in Beijing), the work drew on the *Youyou xinshu* and a number of other works (including at least three no longer extant

Song works on obstetrics). Whoever used the book would have had a good sense of the state of the field of obstetrics and pediatrics at that time. A third example is Fang Dao's 1197 *Fangshi jiyong fang* (Mr. Fang's Collected Useful Prescriptions), which the author literally compiled from a collection of noted formulas that were to be found in his family's storehouse. While its existence is noted in the Song dynastic history, it appears to have disappeared in China before reappearing when an incomplete Song edition was reprinted in Japan. A final example is Yan Yonghe's 1253 *Yanshi jisheng fang* (Mr. Yan's Prescriptions for Benefiting Life), in ten volumes with eighty discussions and around four hundred prescriptions. This work was received sufficiently well that a second work, *Yangshi jisheng xu fang* (Mr. Yan's Additional Prescriptions for Benefiting Life) appeared in 1267. Yan's work, the first of which was written some thirty years after he had begun practicing medicine, appears to have achieved a wider reputation than other prescription handbooks. It was cited in a number of major late Yuan and Ming works, as well as identified as a basic text in Sun Yunxian's early-fourteenth-century (ca. 1314–1320) *Yifang jicheng* (Collection of Medical Prescriptions). While it disappeared in China by the early Qing (which nonetheless meant that it was around for approximately three hundred years), it had a substantial influence on Japanese medicine, having been copied as early as the mid–fourteenth century, and it is cited in all of the most important works published through the end of the sixteenth century (indeed, some of its prescriptions are still in contemporary use).[21]

The serendipity that might account for publication and the motives for publication is highlighted in the example of the anonymous *Xiaoer weisheng zongwei lunfang* (Prescriptions and Detailed Essays on Infant Health), which dates from perhaps the 1150s and was first published around 1216. As in other cases, it owed its visibility to the intervention of a Southern Song official, in this instance the well-connected bibliophile He Daren, who supervised the publication, at official expense and under official auspices, of works in a number of fields that he felt deserved wider audiences. The work, which seems to have been compiled around the same time as the *Youyou xinshu*, is an exceptionally detailed one. It is particularly distinguished by the fact that, whereas the *Youyou xinshu* is essentially a collection of citations chosen by a nonphysician, the *Xiaoer weisheng zongwei lunfang* is a compilation by a clinical practitioner and reflects working rather than book knowledge. This is not to question the importance of the *Youyou xinshu*, but it may well be that the *Xiaoer weisheng zongwei lunfang* provides a superior sense of Song medicine than its better remembered contemporary. In any event, He Daren's preface is of interest.

The twenty-volume *Xiaoer weisheng zongwei lunfang* has been in our family from my father's time, for over sixty years. The author's name is unknown. I have inquired widely, but I have heard nothing about the transmission of this book. It covers [pediatrics] from the infant's very first until its development into a child, and is minutely detailed, and it has dug deeply and in great detail into prescription handbooks old and new. Every time children of relatives or friends get ill we have recourse to this work, and it is effective. And if we increase the dosages and use it for adults it is marvelously effective. How is it possible that this book is so unknown? So, working with two or three people of like mind, we corrected the mistakes that had been made at the time of the original transcribing, had it published by the Medical Office *Dayiju*, and made it widely known in the world.

We obtain an additional perspective on the range of publishing and dissemination in this era when we turn to works that did not circulate much, or became lost in China, but were preserved overseas, primarily in Japan, but also in Korea, and sometimes in both.[22] Perhaps the most successful of such "diasporic texts" was Yang Shiying's 1264 *Renzhai zhizhi fanglun* (Renzhai's Discussions on Prescriptions for Direct Diagnosis). Not only was it referred to in Japan, but it was reprinted in Chosŏn Korea in 1431 and used as the basis for official medical lectures for several centuries thereafter. Let us note further examples relevant to Japan.

A wide variety of medical publications found their way to Japan. Of particular note are the prescription handbooks produced in local areas for local consumption or works that addressed particular regional medical challenges. Most appear to have been highly valued and found their way into very prestigious collections in Japan, where they have been preserved.

Yang Dan's 1178 (second printing 1185) *Yangshi jiacang fang* (Mr. Yang's Prescriptions from the Family Treasury) was printed by the author himself at the county office. Contemporary references imply that it was widely used in the immediate locality, suggesting that its 1,311 prescriptions (contained in fifty-nine topics distributed throughout twenty volumes) met a direct need for such information and even, perhaps, that other medical works were not readily available in the area. It went through both Song and Yuan printings but was lost soon thereafter. Both printings, however, circulated in Japan and found their way into the renowned Kanazawa Bunko library of the nation's leading warrior family, the Hōjō.[23]

Another prescription handbook that was lost in China (by the end of the Yuan) but found its way to Japan was the *Yeshi luyan fang* (Mr. Ye's Effective Prescriptions) by Ye Dalian, which was first published by the author in 1186 and then "recarved" by an admiring reader (Li Jinghe) in 1204. The book, which lists the names of the original inventors of a large number of prescriptions, is a useful window into popular medicine. We also have further confirmation of the process by which information would eventually come to a wider audience. Let us note the preface by Ye Dalian and the additional note by Li Jinghe.

> [Ye Dalian:] A lot of what is contained in this book are formulas transmitted in my family and used on a daily basis. From when I was young I was fond of books, and I gave particular attention to medical works. As an official I have traveled to many places and collected much material, but I have not passed on to people those things of which I have had no experience, which I have tested and found to have no efficacy, or which seemed dubious. I have met many physicians who have treated people, but they do not want to pass on their prescriptions to people. So I thought that I would like to make widely known in the world those items that I have tried myself, and I have classified and organized them in three volumes. I have had them checked by (two named physicians, both from Anhui).

> [Li Jinghe:] I acquired a copy of the work from the author, returned home and tried the prescriptions, and found them to be wonderfully efficacious. Currently large numbers of people in the Jianghuai region have great faith in this, and it is widely employed, but in other regions people do not even know of its existence. So I carved it in the Dongyang county office in Jiangsu.

Another highly regarded work (it is cited in Sun Yunxian's influential *Yifang jicheng*, Collection of Medical Formulas, of 1321) that became lost in China is Wei Xian's 1227 *Weishi jiacang fang* (Mr. Wei's Prescriptions from the Family Treasury). This work is a selection of long-tested family formulas, including those handed down from his grandfather and ones that Wei had used himself. Organized into ten volumes and forty-one sections, and containing 1,051 prescriptions, the work is directed to the practicing healer. While it contains few reflections on medical theory, the work is, among other things, an absorbing guide to the newer prescriptions and materia medica of non-Chinese (Southeast Asian, Middle Eastern) origin that was one of the major developments in Song medicine. These crude drugs are readily seen, too, in better-known medical texts (such as the *Hejiju fang*), but their appearance in Wei Xian's work is strong confirmation that they were not rare or exotic items but ones that were readily available and in widespread use. The high regard in which the work was held is confirmed by the fact that it was among the works brought back from China by one of the leading Japanese religious figures of the thirteenth century, Enni Ben'en (1202–1280, also known as Shōichi Kokushi). Enni wanted to establish the core collection for a new Zen intellectual enterprise at Tōfukuji and so returned with a carefully selected collection of key classical works, histories, and a range of the latest and highly regarded works of the time.[24] Thus, *Weishi jiacang fang*, which appeared in Japan only nine years after its publication, appears to have had an impact in the medical world well beyond what the author might have anticipated.

This example reminds us that people involved in the Buddhist enterprise were often central to the dissemination of both Chinese culture and the printed word. That Buddhist connection is highlighted in two final examples. One is the 1241 *Chabing zhinan* (Surmises on Illness Diagnosis) of Shi Fa (an unsuccessfiul examination candidate who turned to medicine at the age of fifty). A brief three-volume work that concentrated on the method of pulse diagnosis, it was lost in China by the end of the Yuan period and preserved only in Japan. No originals remain, but it was hand copied frequently in Japan (the oldest dates to the fourteenth century). It was issued in a Zen woodblock printed edition sometime in the fifteenth century, which most likely makes it the first medical work printed and published in Japan. The second example is a work (ca. 1283) by the Buddhist priest Jihong, the *Lingnan weisheng fang* (Prescriptions for Safeguarding Life in Lingnan). The work represents that genre of medical writing that specializes in the medical challenges to be found in a specific region. Jihong's work addresses issues of medicine in Lingnan (modern Guangdong and Guangxi) and it may be regarded as one of the earliest works devoted to tropical medicine. The author had traveled around the near-frontier region (as a missionary?) and noted that the maladies prevalent in the area were somewhat different from the ailments normally found in medical works; accordingly, he wished to bring to wider attention the medical knowledge that had been developed in the region to deal with those special conditions. The work, lost in China but preserved in Japan via a Ming edition, covers such problems as malaria, miasmic afflictions, and various lesions and infections such as those caused by a destructive rice worm or a certain type of grass. Of note is the reference to a sore or ulcer known (due to its coloration and similarity to a plum blossom?) as a "plum sore," which was one of the terms later applied to syphilitic lesions.

Concluding Comments

This brief survey of medical publishing in the Song (and Yuan) has suggested at least three points that are directly related to both the general topic of the dissemination of Chinese knowledge in East Asia and the more specific topic of the dissemination of medical knowledge throughout that macroculture.

First, the development of printing, initially under state sponsorship and then substantially expanded by commercial and private publications, ushered in a veritable revolution in the preservation, creation, and dissemination of medical knowledge. The laborious process of hand copying texts was replaced by the carving of woodblocks and thus the possibility that any text might be easily reproduced in multiple copies and numerous editions and in more than one location. Knowledge was literally more accessible than it had ever been before, and it was preserved more securely in print than it had been in memory (oral traditions) and rare handwritten scrolls.

Second, printing technology simultaneously preserved a defined, and thus prescriptive, cultural legacy and initiated a decentralization of medical writing and a steady "democratization" of medical knowledge. On the one hand, the printing programs of the Northern Song government were crucial to the survival of any semblance of the written Chinese medical heritage and created the basis for what has come to be considered the canon of traditional medicine. On the other hand, the range of printing carried out during the Southern Song and the Yuan—official, sponsored by officials, commercially published, and "privately printed"—attests to an eclectic culture of medical writing and thus of medicine itself. There was no standard "medical tradition," and the publishing of medical works written (as a general rule) in the Southern Song and Yuan attest to the vibrancy of medical culture.

Third, the dispersed nature of Song medical knowledge, in an environment where it seems that venerable classics coexisted with commercial or private productions not intended to be regarded as "classics," meant that almost any acquisition of a printed medical work could be regarded as inherently representative of up-to-date Chinese medicine (if not the "tradition," which was not contemporarily formed). This may in part account for the survival outside of China of works otherwise lost in China. Works thus preserved may not have attained any status as a classic text, and some may have been intended as ephemera, but they are good examples of contemporary, and changing, medical knowledge.

Notes

[1] For an introduction to this topic, see Lucille Chia, "Mashaben: Commercial Publishing in Jianyang from the Song to the Ming;" and *Printing for Profit: The Commercial Publishers of Jianyang, Fujian (Eleventh–Seventeenth Centuries)*.

[2] For a broader background, see Peter K. Bol, *"This Culture of Ours": Intellectual Transitions in T'ang and Sung China*.

[3] For a description of this work, see Kosoto Hiroshi, "Hokusō jidai no iyakusho (Sono 1)," pp. 87–88. Unless otherwise specified, details regarding Northern Song works may be found in that article; in Kosoto, "Hokusō jidai no iyakusho (2);" and in Kosoto, "Kansu bon kara Sōgenban e: Chūsei Nihon ni okeru Chūgoku isho juyō no yōsō." In addition, for detailed information regarding authors, publication, and printing up through the Song, the reader is referred to the definitive bibliographical work on early Chinese medical literature, Okanishi Tamendo's four-volume *Song yiqian yiji kao*.

[4] The edition consulted was the copy of the work reproduced in the *Tōyō igaku zenpon sōsho* series, which includes a helpful commentary by Miyashita Saburō.

[5] Chen Jie and Kosoto Hiroshi, "Hokusō kankoku isho no minkan e no ryūtsū."

[6] See Asaf Moshe Goldschmidt, "The Transformation of Chinese Medicine during the Northern Song Dynasty (AD 960–1127)," chap. 4, for a discussion of acupuncture and moxibustion treatment in the Northern Song.

[7] For further details, see Kosoto Hiroshi, *Chūgoku igaku koten to Nihon*, chap. 3, sec. 1.

[8] See ibid., chap. 3, sec. 1.

[9] See ibid., chap. 3, sec. 2.

[10] See ibid., chap. 4, sec. 5.

[11] See ibid., chap. 4, sec. 6.

[12] For a reproduction, transcription, and study of the surviving first scroll of this work, which was lost in China and transmitted only in Japan, see Kitasato Kenkyūjo Fuzoku Tōyō Igaku Sōgō Kenkyūjo, *Shōhinhō, Kōtai daikei meidō koshōhon zankan*.

[13] See Kosoto, *Chūgoku igaku koten to Nihon*, chap. 4 sec. 7.

[14] See Angela Ki-che Leung, "Medical Learning from the Song to the Ming."

[15] On the general question of the social status of doctors in this era, see Robert P. Hymes, "Not Quite Gentlemen? Doctors in Sung and Yuan."

[16] For detailed information, readers are referred to Kosoto Hiroshi, "Nansō jidai no iyakusho;" "Kindai no iyakusho;" and "Gendai no iyakusho."

[17] For a broader study of women's medicine, see Charlotte Furth, *A Flourishing Yin: Gender in China's Medical History, 960–1665.*

[18] This text is also referred to as the *Leizheng puji benshi fang* and the *Benshi fang*. The demand for this type of work is underlined by the fact that Xu produced a second, similar work, the *Leijeng puji benshi fang hou fang,* shortly thereafter, which contained a further three hundred prescriptions. Xu was a prolific author, producing at least another five works, but these have not survived. It is rarely clear exactly why one work might survive and another not, but we might speculate that even in the author's lifetime products were subject to some measure of consumer evaluation.

[19] For a recent study of Yuan medical systems and support for medicine, see Reiko Shinno, "Medical Schools and the Temples of the Three Progenitors in Yuan China: A Case of Cross-Cultural Connections."

[20] See *Beiji zongxiao fang.* For an introduction to this work and its transmission, see the preface by Kosoto Hiroshi in that volume and see also Kosoto Hiroshi, "Sōban *Bikyū sōkōhō* (*Bizen sōkōhō*) no shoshi kenkyū." The *Beiji zongxiao fang* has also enjoyed its own history as a rare antiquarian work.

[21] It is cited in the fourteenth-century works *Ton'ishō* and *Man'anpō* of Kajiwara Shōzen and the *Fukudenpō* of the priest Yūrin, the printed *Isho daizen* of 1528, and Manase Dōsan's late-sixteenth-century *Keitekishū.*

[22] As examples we may note the following, all from the 1260s. Li Minshou's *Yijian fang lun* (Discourse on Simple Prescriptions, 1260?), compiled by an unsuccessful examination candidate who transferred his interests to medicine, seems not to have been circulated in China following its publication and seems to have been lost (like all his other works) by the time of the Ming dynasty. It was transmitted separately very early to both Japan (cited extensively in *Man'anpō* and *Fukudenpō*) and Korea. Another work, Zhu Zuo's *Leibian Zhushi jiyan fang* (The Categorized Mr. Zhu's Collected Effective Prescriptions, 1266?) did not make it to Japan, but it is cited extensively in the 1443 Korean work *Ŭibang yuch'wi* (Classified Collection of Medical Prescriptions).

[23] For a useful introduction to this library and family, see Fukushima Kaneharu, *Kanesawa Hōjōshi to Shōmyōji.* The classic study remains Seki Yasushi, *Kanazawa bunko no kenkyū.*

[24] See Kosoto, "Kansu bon kara Sōgen ban e," pp. 468–470; and Shiraishi Kogetsu, *Tōfukujishi,* pp. 381–395 (medical texts noted pp. 392–393).

9

Kajiwara Shōzen (1265-1337) and the Medical Silk Road: Chinese and Arabic Influences on Early Medieval Japanese Medicine

Andrew Edmund Goble

From the late twelfth century on, interactions involving Japan and, successively, the Southern Song and the Yuan expanded dramatically. Monks, members of a Buddhist macroculture, played a key role in that engagement. All were literate in written Chinese, and many were bilingual. Japanese monks traveled to China for training or on quests for materials, and Chinese monks traveled to Japan in order to spread both teachings and the material and cultural environments of those teachings.

Many of the transmitted and appropriated elements that added significantly to the Japanese cultural tradition as a result of this interaction are well known, for example, models of institutional organization, new forms of architecture, new styles of painting and portraiture, and new forms of aesthetic appreciation that we may broadly associate with the culture of green tea. The written word, enhanced by the information revolution that sprang from the development of printing under the Song, was also integral to interaction. We see the development of a printing industry in Zen monasteries, new forms of literary expression, study of "non-Buddhist" Chinese classics and texts, and efforts to acquire books on an eclectic range of topics. And, as we are aware, there was great demand for printed sets of the Buddhist *Tripitika*, as well as for printed editions of specific sutras that were important in individual teaching traditions.

Less well known is the fact that interactions exercised a great influence on medieval Japanese medicine. Now, since there were multiple medical systems in Japan, we would be unwise to claim that interaction had a uniform or complete impact. However, it is clear that new information, from both oral sources and printed medical texts, produced three major results. First, there was a significant improvement in the understanding of the field of medicine and of medical knowledge in general. Second, medical formulas became more complex, and the forms in which they were delivered evolved markedly. Third, there was a major expansion in the range (geographical and pharmaceutical) and quantity of crude drugs employed in Japanese medicine. We may also note, though it is not taken up here, that the medical interactions produced an epochal shift in the locus of medical authority from the court aristocracy to Buddhist priests. Moreover, while the immediate site of interaction was East Asia, and thus naturally we suggest that "Chinese" influences were most prominent, the information available in East Asia was the result of broader interactions that reached geographically as far as the "western regions" (extending as far as the Middle East) and included information gained from Arab and Islamic medicine. In short, we can identify a Medical Silk Road that incorporated the Japanese archipelago.

To illustrate the influence of this Medical Silk Road in medieval Japan, we shall examine the writings of the Buddhist priest and physician Kajiwara Shōzen (1265–1337). Shōzen was based in Kamakura at Gokurakuji temple, one of the main centers of the Shingon Ritsu sect revival movement, which was motivated by the teachings of the Healing Mañjuśrī Buddha.[1] Under the priest Ninshō (1217–1303), from the mid–thirteenth century on the Gokurakuji community engaged in extensive charitable and hospice activity, and the precincts of Gokurakuji were home to what appears to have been the most extensive medical facilities in existence in Japan at that time (if not for the entire premodern era). Those facilities included a treatment clinic, a hospice facility for "leprosy" (*rai*) sufferers, a bathhouse for medicinal baths, a medicine dispensary, lodging for the ill, and an equine veterinary facility.[2] For over three decades, Shōzen was professionally involved in clinical hospice treatment for the socially disadvantaged, and in catering to the medical requirements of the monk population, as well as providing medical services to Kamakura's warrior elite.

Shōzen was dedicated to his healing profession. And he was acutely aware of the shortcomings of Japanese medicine. He felt that the level of knowledge among average physicians left much to be desired,[3] and that they used their own "judgment" rather than consulting medical handbooks to prescribe treatment, with deleterious effects upon patients.[4] As part of his efforts to provide the best medical treatment available, he spent decades compiling two works, the *Ton'ishō* (Book of the Simple Physician) of 1304 and the monumental *Man'anpō* (Myriad Relief Prescriptions) of 1327, which is the most substantial Japanese medical compilation prior to the seventeenth century. While in compiling these works Shōzen drew on his clinical experience and interactions with other healers, the major source of information came from printed Chinese medical texts. In order to see how access to this information benefited his healing enterprise, we will look first at the influence of new Chinese medical texts, noting their availability, and then at the clinical use of the knowledge they contained. We will then next examine the impact of materia medica, noting the background to the importation of crude drugs, and then examine the influence of Arabic medicine in China and how that influence extended to Japan. I will conclude with some general remarks.

The Influence of Medical Texts

Prior to the late thirteenth century, few medical works circulated in Japan, and medical writing was sporadic. Apart from some works on aromatics and materia medica, little was written anew after Tanba Yasuyori's *Ishinpō* (Prescriptions from the Heart of Medicine) in 984.[5] The Tanba family jealously guarded this important repository of Tang era medical knowledge. Few copies of the scrolls were made. Although outsiders were rarely allowed to consult more than extracts or limited portions, it provided information for occasional works penned by hereditary court physicians such as Tanba Yukinaga's health and longevity treatise *Eisei hiyōshō* (Secret Essentials for Safeguarding Life, 1288).[6]

But the aristocracy was not completely bereft of post-Tang medical information. For example, in an effort to rationalize the knowledge of materia medica available to court physicians, in 1284 Koremune Tomotoshi (fl. late thirteenth century) produced the *Honzō iroha shō* (Materia Medica in Japanese Alphabetical Order), a systematized guide to variant nomenclature based on the *Daguan bencao* (Daguan Era Pharmacopoeia, compiled 1108, revised 1116 and later). In this effort he used at least sixteen Song printed medical works that were either compiled after the date of compilation of the *Daguan bencao* or, if compiled earlier, whose citations cannot have been taken from it.[7] Still, the fact remains that physicians in the aristocracy were passive and sedentary consumers. Like aristocrats in other fields of endeavor, their interests appear to have lain in confirming or systematizing existing knowledge rather than testing or expanding it.

By contrast, Buddhist priests drew eagerly from the well of Song medical knowledge, as the following examples suggest. Myōan Eisai (1141–1215), who twice traveled to China (1168, 1187–1191), produced a groundbreaking text, *Kissa yōjōki* (On Drinking Tea and Nurturing Life), devoted to the topic of health and illness, which drew on both written sources and living informants.[8] Enni Ben'en (1202–1280), who was resident in China in 1235–1241, brought back with him to Japan quantities of medical texts that would form part of a new library collection and would also make that knowledge available in a monastic environment. The esteemed Chinese Zen prelate Mingji Chujun (Minki Soshun, 1262–1336) brought with him, as tangible contributions to the good health of his enterprise in Japan, no fewer than eleven different medicines (including the subsequently famous "secret tradition," *Tsūritsu-san*).[9] Dōsei (fl. mid–thirteenth century) spent nine years in China receiving instruction in formula preparation and special "oral transmissions" for pulse analysis, acupuncture, and moxibustion. As proof of his "medical lineage succession," he received the prescription for a "secret" patent medicine (the miraculous and efficacious purgative *Yūkegusentan*), which information later passed, via intermediaries, to Kajiwara Shōzen.[10]

Finally, Chinese monk physicians came to Japan, two such being Lianyuanfang and Hanzhang, who attended Hōjō Tokimune, the leader of the Kamakura bakufu at the time of the Mongol Invasions.[11]

We may assume from this that there was an ongoing flow of information and items into the Buddhist world. Yet, while these examples suggest a rhythm of engagement, they do not provide great detail. Fortunately, we are able to get a concrete sense of the fruits of engagement and interaction from Kajiwara Shōzen.

Shōzen's Access to Medical Information

The most direct way to gauge Shōzen's access to medical information is to survey the number and types of titles utilized by him in his writings. In the *Ton'ishō* Shōzen cites at least forty-eight medical works by name, and in the *Man'anpō* he cites at least eighty-eight. While he did not have access to every work cited,[12] the significant difference in these numbers suggests a process of ongoing access and acquisition. A comparison of the sources of prescriptions contained in the two works provides one guide. The largest source of formulas in the *Ton'ishō* was the *Taiping Shenghui fang* (Prescriptions of Great Peace and Sagely Benevolence, first published in 992; the edition used by Shōzen was a printed one of 1147).[13] The largest sources of formulas in the *Man'anpō* were the *Shengji zonglu* (Comprehensive Record of Sagely Beneficence, compiled in 1111–17; Shōzen used a printed edition of 1300) and the *Youyou xinshu* (New Pediatrics, printed in 1150).[14] The *Shengji zonglu*, containing some twenty-thousand prescriptions, provided some sixty percent of the 3,100 formulas noted in the *Man'anpō* (relegating the *Taiping Shenghui fang* to second place), while the *Youyou xinshu* was the dominant source of information for the eleven pediatrics chapters (which constitute about twenty percent of the *Man'anpō*).

Shōzen consulted other works besides these three. Some became highly regarded within the Chinese medical tradition, such as the Northern Song *Hejiju fang* (1107–1110) and the Southern Song *Sanyin fang* (1174). Many others, mainly Southern Song clinical works, were more ephemeral. Compiled and printed under private or commercial rather than official auspices, they disseminated the "up-to-date" knowledge of both professional and "amateur" practitioners. They were rarely, if ever, cited in other contemporary texts. A few were reprinted, many became "lost works," some were preserved, and some enjoyed long-term reputations. However, the appearance of such titles in the *Man'anpō* attests to Shōzen's familiarity with contemporary clinical medicine in China. His knowledge did not derive from antiquarian study.

Among Shōzen's listings we find the late-twelfth-century *Puji benshi fang* (Effective Prescriptions for Universal Relief), the 1186 *Yeshi luyan fang* (Mr.

Ye's Effective Prescriptions), the 1189 *Yishuo* (Conversations on Medicine), the 1226 *Huoren shizheng fang* (Proven Prescriptions for the Living), and the 1253 *Yanshi jisheng fang* (Mr. Yan's Prescriptions for Benefiting Life), as well as Chen Zhiming's important treatises on gynecology and obstetrics (*Furen daquan liang fang*, Complete Effective Prescriptions for the Diseases of Women, 1237) and external medicine (*Waike jingyao*, Essentials of External Medicine, 1263). Among the "lost" works we find the late-twelfth-century *Yijian fang* (Easy Prescriptions), the 1178 *Yangshi jiacang fang* (Mr. Yang's Prescriptions from the Family Treasury), the 1197 *Shizhai baiyi xuan fang* (Shizhai's 101 Selected Prescriptions), the 1226 *Beiji jiu fang* (Emergency Moxibustion Prescriptions), the 1227 *Weishi jiacang fang* (Mr. Wei's Prescriptions from the Family Treasury), the 1243 *Xu yijian fang* (Easy Prescriptions, Continued), and the 1260 *Jianyi fang* (Simple Prescriptions). One work, the undated and unattributed *Keyong fang* (Indispensable Prescriptions), is otherwise unattested. Rounding out our picture we find such Yuan titles as the circa 1242 *Yuyaoyuan fang* (Prescriptions for the Imperial Dispensary) and the 1306 *Fengke jiyan ming fang* (Famous Effective Prescriptions for Wind Disorders).

Shōzen sometimes had access to more than one edition of a work. Let us take the example of the *Hejiju fang*. Between its first appearance, in 1107–1110, and 1252, the *Hejiju fang* went through at least four revisions and expansions, which means that a simple reference to it may or may not give us a sense of what precise content was being accessed.[15] A study of Koremune Tomotoshi's *Honzō iroha shō* reveals that he used at least three different editions (1108, 1185, and 1195) of the *Hejiju fang*.[16] In the *Man'anpō* Shōzen also refers to different editions of the work. In one place he notes that in one *Hejiju fang* formula (for *Gokō-san*) the "different edition" (*betsuhon*) leaves out the agastache and adds musk.[17] In another he notes that a different edition has a formula, Mr. Guang's Divine Response Pill (*Kōshi kannō-en*), which adds a number of ingredients, and, since Shōzen hasn't written down the full formula here, the reader wishing to use it should consult the *Hejiju fang* itself.[18] And, in a different vein, having the work to hand enabled Shōzen to note that a work cited in the *Youyou xinshu* as the *Dayiju fang* (Prescriptions from the Great Medicine Bureau) was actually the *Hejiju fang*.[19]

Additionally, simply becoming aware of a plethora of titles and the range of works would itself have been a revelation, especially as Shōzen mentions only three Japanese works, the *Ishinpō*, Fukane Sukebito's *Wamyō honzō* (Japanese Handbook of Materia Medica, early tenth century), and Renki's *Chōsei ryōyōhō* (Prescriptions for Fostering Long Life, 1184). Access to so many Chinese works provided Shōzen with a sense of the development of particular branches of medicine. For example, the *Youyou xinshu* has a listing of those works deemed most significant for that compilation and thus for the field of pediatrics. The listing of eight "former age" and forty "recent age" works and twenty-five private works provides a sense of "old" and "new" in medicine that was unknown in Japan, and it established a sense of "the field." That this information was copied verbatim by Shōzen only emphasizes its importance.[20]

The importance of new works is revealed in yet another way. For example, while we are not certain whether Shōzen actually consulted a copy of the priest-physician Chu Yushi's famous but now lost *Yangsheng biyong fang* (Essential Prescriptions for Nurturing Life, 1098) or only knew of it secondhand, he clearly understood its value. While in the *Man'anpō* he cites only sixteen formulas from it, Chu's name appears at least forty times and the work is mentioned seventy-seven times. When it is cited the purpose is to make very important points about new approaches to medicine.

In sum, while Shōzen did not have access to all the titles he cites, he had access to many printed works that were broadly representative of contemporary Chinese clinical medicine. He gained knowledge of pharmaceuticals, prescriptions, and views on disease. Additionally, he would have understood that medical knowledge was not static but was being continuously tested and updated. Shōzen would also have realized that any practitioner might, based on clinical experience, be a participant in a broader "medical conversation" rather than a passive recipient content to accept and pass on prior knowledge (a hallmark of the *Ishinpō*).

The Clinical Impact of New Medical Information
In order to obtain a sense of how Shōzen used the new knowledge available from Chinese texts, we shall look at three areas. First, we shall note Shōzen's comments on the information he was encountering. Second, we shall note Shōzen's observations on medicine in Japan. Third, we shall provide examples relating to Shōzen's clinical experience with and use of new information.

First, in commenting on information, sometimes Shōzen directly compares older and newer methods. For example, in a prescription for dealing with fetal movement and pelvic pain between the second and third to eighth and ninth months of pregnancy, he notes the old method for preparing the medicine; then, noting that he is patterning himself on the new prescription, he elucidates the new method.[21] In another prescription, for *Sogōkō-gan*, he notes that the old method employs one pill whereas the newly arrived *Daquan liang fang* suggests four pills.[22] On other occasions he comments on newly-arrived medicines: a secret and miraculous stomachic formula that has recently been transmitted from Song China;[23] and a newly arrived purgative medicine to be given for many illnesses, with the application to be altered according to the illness.[24]

Shōzen also refers to broader changes in practice. For example, with respect to vomiting, he notes that, whereas old medical works sought to treat the problem with warmth medicines, newly arrived works take the position that vomiting arises from heat and so warmth medicines should not be prescribed.[25] Another observation was that a newly arrived work provided better information for treating infant and child depression, that the ingredients listed are slightly different from those for the same medicine listed in the *Hejiju fang*, and that, apart from karmic illnesses (*jōgō no yamai*), the new formula is effective in treating ninety-nine out of one hundred people.[26] In another case, a newly arrived book enables him to finally identify, and gain new information regarding treatment for, the condition known as *hiki* or infant malnutrition.[27] As a final example, after listing a prescription from the *Shenghui fang* for treating depressed spirits and lack of sleep due to macule sores and smallpox sores, he observes that in the case of epidemic or exogenous febrile diseases the heat in the chest does not disperse and so patients want to drink cold water. However, based on a newly arrived work, administering a small amount of ice is effective in dispersing dryness-heat syndrome in the chest and stomach.[28]

The second area of impact may be seen in Shōzen's observations on medicine in Japan. Since Shōzen was primarily a clinical physician rather than a medical theorist, his comments provide a good window into what he was learning and applying. Let us note some comments related to pregnancy and on prescribing medicines.[29]

Nineteen chapters of the *Man'anpō* are devoted to obstetrics and pediatrics, a reflection of Shōzen's concern over such perennial issues as successful nurturing of the fetus, the health of the mother, miscarriages, death in childbirth, and infant mortality. Indeed, Shōzen noted in his introduction to the obstetrics section of the *Ton'ishō* that it was ten times more difficult to treat female ailments than male, since they sprang from more complex causes, and that pregnancy was of the greatest importance to women.[30] In the *Man'anpō* he expressed frustration that, even though he had devoted a chapter to morning sickness (the "child illness"),[31] what he had covered amounted to "no more than one drop in the vast ocean or one hair of all those on nine oxen."[32] He questioned conventional wisdom when it was at variance with his own clinical experience, for example, as to when conception might occur.

> I say [it is the standard view that] after menstruation every month, the days when one can [conceive] a child are akin to the fertility of the earth itself. However, it is also the case that there are women who become pregnant as a result of intercourse before menstruation. Knowing this, is it true that one can become pregnant within six days before menstruation? Before menstruation, on days one, three, and five, it will be a male fetus. On days two, four, and six, it will be a female child. The day of menstruation each month is determined by the woman. Prior to the monthly event, know the *yin* and *yang* days [prior days]: one, three, and five are *yang*; and two, four, and six are *yin*.[33]

Regarding the apparent tendency to withhold medicines from pregnant women, Shōzen's stance was that not prescribing did greater harm than prescribing. This did not mean that Shōzen ignored the condition of pregnancy when prescribing medicines; *Ton'ishō* notes that one medicine must not be administered to pregnant women.[34] Rather, he disagreed with a blanket prohibition. He buttressed that view with an appeal to the authority of both Chinese medicine and Chinese literature.

> I say that in treating the ailments of pregnant women there are no proscribed medicines. Illnesses kill people. Poisons are themselves serious. Neither the old texts nor the new texts are concerned about proscribed medicines. Now, in pregnant women there are cold damage [disorders], diarrheas, cramps and stiff shoulders, coughing, apoplexy, beri-beri, and other assorted illnesses that compete to arise. Therefore the various texts have set down "multiple medicines" (*shūyaku*) in order to treat them. Sometimes the fetus is dead but the mother is still alive; sometimes two lives are joined as one; how can one take just one view [that medicines ought not be prescribed] and get rid of the wonderful techniques of the old methods? . . . One should not guard the tree stump or carve the boat [i.e., operate on the basis of wrong assumptions]![35]

And, since Shōzen felt that "physicians" did not read prescription handbooks and tended to administer medicines based on little more than guesswork about the patient's condition,[36] it was important to make a strong case for new approaches. It is perhaps no surprise, then, that he would cite the views of the famous Song priest-physician Chu Yushi,[37] author of the *Yangsheng biyong fang*, in arguing for an aggressive use of medicines.

> I, Shōzen, state that for people who are weak and debilitated one must give a four-type cluster mix of medicine. Five to six times day and night give medications and meet with them. Even though the person is weak and the medicines strong, one cannot do damage. In recent times patients have been afraid of medicines that are aggressively effective and avoid multiple medicines; simply, this strengthens the illness, and, conversely, if one increases the strength of the medicines this only reduces [their effectiveness?]. This is what Yu Shinan [Chu Yushi] calls nurturing illness and avoiding treatment. If a person, however, experiences one illness, then numerous illnesses will break out in contention, and then one must hurl all kinds of medicines throughout the body. If one comprehends this import, then one should not be afraid of medicines that are aggressively effective and one should not regard them as the source of weakening of *qi/ki* vital energy. With dispatch, pursue ailments as a soldier pursues an enemy; if one's military might is not continuously applied then one cannot achieve conquest over the enemy. From the outset employ Yu Shi[nan]'s [Chu Yushi's] import.[38]

And, since one of the general advances from Tang to Song was the greater use of multiple-ingredient medicines, it was important to assert the desirability of "the new."

> I, Shōzen, say that doctors in recent times (*kinsei*) either fear administering and mixing many medicines or are afraid of giving many administrations day and night. This is just like fearing medicines and nurturing illnesses. Now the prescriptions of Yu Shinan [Chu Yushi] treat weak people and employ four cluster medicines and advocate six administrations day and night. I think, how can this not be a marvelous injunction?[39]

The third area of impact was clinical experience and use, and Shōzen supplies a range of information. We see evidence that he has compared at least two versions of a named prescription that appears in different works and has concluded that one of them works better, for example, when he notes that the *Hejiju fang*'s version of the *Akasekishi-san* formula or the *Hanryū-en* formula is the best.[40] Other times he notes that different works list different ingredients. For example, having listed a prescription from the *Hejiju fang*, he notes that the *Yuyaoyuan fang* version adds one-half *ryō* of prepared aconite root,[41] and having given the *Hejiju fang* prescription for *Shōshoku-en*, he notes that the *Yuyaoyuan fang* builds on this, adding one-half *ryō* each of ginseng, poria, and cassia, substituting large barley sprouts for small barley sprouts, and calls that formula *Shishoku-en*, which is "marvelous".[42] In other cases he recommends that the formula be adjusted in some fashion. Commenting on the formula for *Sanwa-san* (prescribed for a number of symptoms) from the *Hejiju fang*, he notes that should there be no large bowel movement, one should add three *ryō* of rhubarb.[43] For the eucommia-*sake* prescription from the *Sanyin fang* for colds and such, he suggests that the dose be increased from one to two *seni* to three to five *seni*.[44] For the *Jiō-gan* prescribed for "bone-steaming syndrome" (which includes fever, night sweats, dyspnea, irritability, sleeplessness, and yellowish urine), he recommends doubling the dose and administering it every two to three days.[45] Respecting advice given in the *Qianjin fang* (Prescriptions Worth a Thousand Gold) for bed-wetting by infants, he notes some medicines that should be administered in addition to moxibustion treatment.[46] For a *Hejiju fang* prescription designed to inhibit illness-related sweating, he notes that when sweat breaks out from below the armpit and the neck and bathes the body the medicine is to be administered every night.[47]

Further examples demonstrate his clinical engagement. He notes that in Japan, unlike China, not everyone responds well to *Goshaku-san*, so instead one should use Rectify *Qi/Ki* Vital Energy Powder (*Shōki-san*) since it is superior for producing sweat and dispelling heat.[48] Commenting on a "very secret" medicine that treats a regurgitating stomach, as well as food not going down, and has the effect of opening the stomach and harmonizing the spirits, he notes that, if it is used in cases of difficult to treat vomiting ailments and *kakuran* vomiting and diarrhea, one never loses out even once in a hundred occasions. With one or two administrations the vomiting and diarrhea are settled and the vomiting is treated; he considered it "marvelously efficacious".[49] With respect to postpartum pudendal and labial swelling, and the vaginal opening not closing, he remarks that the *Chanbao fang* (Treasured Prescriptions for Obstetrics) notes without discussion a formula using lime (*sekkai*, calcium oxide), but in his view a lime decoction (*sekkaitō*) is effective in treating vaginal weepy discharge (*rinshin inmon*).[50] In commenting on formulas that help women to conceive, he notes that *Shichiko-san*, *Tōhō-san*, and the like are wonderful medicines and are to be found in volume 9 of the *Furen daquan liang fang* in the section on wanting an heir.[51]

As noted earlier, issues related to birth were of great concern, so let us end this section with an observation in this area. One of Shōzen's comments was on a formula from the *Hejiju fang*, for *Yūhakuhi-san*, which was designed to promote a slippery fetus and an easy birth. It was to be administered in all cases when the pregnant woman is losing blood because of a leaky placenta; when parturition is approaching, the pregnant mother is frightened, and so the fetus comes faster; when, even though the time of parturition has not arrived, one sees the prior emission of unclean excretions; and when the fetus is dehydrated (rather than moist) and thus at the time of approaching birth there are complications. (In a headnote, Shōzen also directs the reader to the *Daquan liang fang*'s section on birth difficulties for further information, noting that where the birth channel is ripped and dry the placental fluid is astringent.) Shōzen addresses both how the formula may be adjusted when not all ingredients are available and having the appropriate clinical knowledge of the problems that are being treated.

> I say that if there is no Abutilon, then you should use Yellow Hollyhock; if there is no white bark of Elm, then you should use instead the root of Abutilon. Now, if first unclean excretions come out, this is the placental fluid. The *Qianqin fang* notes that "leaky placenta" is [a condition in which] blood that resembles menstrual blood comes out prior to the birth and [indicates that] the fetus is dehydrated, which at the time of birth will cause difficulties. Also, if the placental fluid itself is not bloody, the placenta and the fetus are dehydrated. This is a bad sign, and [the condition] is to be restored [to normal]. For this reason I have recorded below the *Hejiju fang*'s *Yūhakuhi-san*. For leaky placenta, one administers the same way. Now fresh fluids of the placenta and fetus are to be regarded as most welcome.[52]

Crude Drugs and Pharmaceuticals

Trade in Overseas Drugs

Japanese interest in overseas materia medica is attested from an early date. However, our general knowledge of the trade in materia medica is hampered by two factors. The first is lack of detailed statistics. Even though we have some Heian era records, and during the Muromachi period some overseas trade ventures were actively sponsored by the bakufu, these offer only fragmentary clues and provide nothing like the detail that is available for the post-1600 Edo era.[53] Nonetheless, we do have a general picture. Goods carried from Korea generally came from Korea. Ryukyu served as transshipment points for items from China or from the "southern regions" (*nanban*), the goods either having been shipped directly to Ryukyu or via China.[54] Southern Chinese ports might ship items directly, and those items might originate from as far away as Africa. However, apart from occasional references—such as a pharmacist noted as returning from a drug-purchasing trip to China—a clear sense of the acquisition process is elusive.[55] Most likely there was a combination of shipping goods as a result of an order and of goods shipped on spec. But incompleteness of information is not something limited only to historians, for even some contemporaries did not have a full picture. For example, so much pepper was shipped through Japan that in Korea it was thought to be a Japanese product,[56] and, as the Chinese priest Jin Zixi pointed out in 1486, Japanese believe *kansho*, or sugarcane, to be *satō*, or sugar, when in fact sugar is the liquid product of decocted sugarcane.[57] But, if we cannot be certain of every detail, we are probably on safe ground in assuming that there was a continuous and active trade.

The second factor hampering our knowledge of overseas trade is that imported materia medica have left few physical traces. But we do have some records such as those for the use and storage of the "museum pieces" preserved in the Shōsōin from the mid–eighth century.[58] These were carefully weighed and packed,[59] and access to them was restricted.[60] Wake and Tanba family court physicians also seem to have kept hoards. A mid-fourteenth-century pharmacist received a special order of some poppy capsules, wild Siamese cardamom, and ginseng from Wake Tadakage.[61] And a fifteenth-century author notes that the Wake and Tanba families had, in addition to quantities of Japanese medicinals (*wayaku*), stores of such imported (*shinto*) materia medica as ginseng, Borneo camphor, dragon's blood, birthwoot root, black pepper, wild Siamese cardamom, lesser galangal, cassia, licorice, Sichuan lovage, Chinese angelica, croton, rhubarb, realgar, dried tiger's gallbladder, cinnabar, and "honey-ball."[62] Temples, with their ceremonial and internal medical needs, may have kept their own supplies, but inventories of such items seem not to have survived. We are otherwise left with fragments of information connected to named individuals. Hōryūji temple preserves a box originally containing such aromatics as aloes and white sandalwood, on which is branded in Pahlavi script the name of the merchant who had originally supplied them.[63] And we might suspect that the Chinese physician of Persian origin "Li the Secret Healer," who went to Japan with a returning Japanese mission in 734, brought some crude drugs with him.[64]

It is possible that some materia medica may have been valued for other than its pharmaceutical properties. Indeed, we might make the broader point that at this earlier time there may not have been a clear distinction between the "aromatic" and "medicinal" uses of what I refer to as materia medica. Descriptions of life at the imperial court make it clear that incense and fragrances such as musk and sandalwood were highly valued for creating ambience and scenting garments.[65] The correct performance of Buddhist ritual and ceremony, particularly in the esoteric sects of Tendai and Shingon, required access to and accurate knowledge of (broadly defined) materia medica. That concern is reflected in the compilation of a series of works—*Kōjishō* (Dictionary of Fragrances), *Kōyōshō* (Essentials of Fragrances), *Kōyakushō* (Book of Fragrances and Medicines), and *Yakushushō* (Treatise on Materia Medica)—by the priest Ken'i that note the properties, origins, and some medical uses of aromatica and materia medica that are listed in Buddhist sutras.[66] The information about the items is drawn from Chinese pharmaceutical works. While the use of these items in Buddhist circles might suggest a strong demand, in all likelihood they did not circulate more broadly. Similarly, the major Japanese reference work on materia medica, the *Honzō wamyō* (alt. *Wamyō honzō*), provides an excellent survey of which materia medica noted in Chinese pharmacopoeia exist in Japan, equivalent Japanese names, items for which there was no indigenous Japanese name, and sometimes a remark on a specific foreign origin, but it does not (nor was it intended to) provide a sense of the frequency with which the 1,025 items noted were used. We may make similar observations about Renki's *Chōsei ryōyōhō*.

Nonetheless, there seems to have been a steady demand for imported items (*karamono*). For example, the *Shinsarugaku ki* (Account of the New Monkey Music) of 1045 lists, among the goods traded by a merchant, twenty-three aromatic and medicinal items: aloes, musk, cloves, Chinese spikenard, frankincense, birthwoot root, Borneo camphor, white sandalwood, the prepared compound "violet snow," croton, realgar (red arsenic sulphide), chebulic myrobalan, betel nut, copper rust, cinnabar, pepper powder, rhinoceros horn, ox bezoar, "chicken-tongue" cloves, cnidium, Burmese rosewood, sappan wood, and safflower rouge.[67] This is a valuable source of information for trade items, even if we do not know if it is a full list.

From the late thirteenth century on, we are on firmer ground in assessing the availability, and relatively common use, of imported materia medica. Sources enable us to observe that crude drugs came to be used in greater numbers and that there was a clear shift in emphasis on their use from "incense and ceremonial" toward the unequivocally medical. That is, for example, even though musk and sandalwood had long been "known" in Japan, they became "newly known" in their pharmaceutical role. They were joined in this by a wider range of materia medica that had come into the Chinese pharmacopoeia from around the tenth century on. We will examine the evidence of the *Ton'ishō* and *Man'anpō* presently, but here let us note two other sources from later in the fourteenth century.

Our clearest sense of the overseas materia medica in use comes from a previously unconsidered source, the field of wound medicine. As is attested by the first works on the topic, the *Kinsō ryōjishō* (On Treating Incised Wounds, 1357) and the *Kihō* (Demon Formulas, 1391), wound medicine only emerged as a specialty in the fourteenth century. The demands of a new style of warfare required physicians to seek effective treatment for large numbers of casualties and for such problems as bleeding, vomiting,[68] killing maggots, drying wounds to prevent infections,[69] and masking the smell of blood and rotting flesh. The materia medica record is thus a guide to what was in active use and what was assumed to be readily available (if not equally available to all physicians).

The *Kinsō ryōjishō* and *Kihō* note at least twenty-one overseas materia medica: wild Siamese cardamom, dragon's blood, musk, cloves, cassia, Burmese rosewood, white sandalwood, aloes, Chinese licorice, turmeric, ginseng, Borneo camphor tree, fennel, frankincense, costus, fossil bones, tiger bones, chebulic myrobalan, ginger, and croton.[70] Of these, ten (fennel, cassia, ginger, Chinese licorice, dragon's blood, cardamom, turmeric, ginseng, fossil bones, and tiger bones) are not noted in the *Shinsarugaku ki* list and thus can be regarded as new additions to both trade and the repertoire of materia medica. This information also places the use of both cardamom and dragon's blood in Japan as much as a century earlier than previously thought.[71] And, of the others, ten items that were listed in the *Shinsarugaku ki*, particularly aromatics, were now being employed for demonstrably medical purposes: white sandalwood, cloves, Borneo camphor, frankincense, birthwort, Burmese rosewood, croton, chebulic myrobalan, musk, and aloes. Given the scope and intensity of the warfare of the fourteenth century, and the production of large numbers of casualties on a continuing basis, it is entirely reasonable to suggest that wound medicine created a new demand for overseas materia medica.

Another fourteenth-century clinical text, the *Fukudenpō* (Prescriptions from the Fields of Merit),[72] written, as are the wound medicine texts, in mixed script Japanese and directed to a general rather than scholarly audience, provides a gauge of the materia medica regime. It also contains more comprehensive information than we note in general reference works from the era.[73] Of the 114 materia medica noted, twenty-eight are items reflecting Song and later additions to the Chinese pharmacopoeia.[74] These "new" items are Chinese clematis, corydalis, poppy capsule, pagoda tree, chianghuo, greater galangal, rice sprout, black pepper, fenugreek, Siberian moonseed, persimmon, immature orange, pokeroot, tsaoko, Chinese honey locust, mulberry, Katsumada's galangal (round cardamom), betel seed, bamboo juice, bamboo shavings, matrimony vine, cardamom, rice paper, barley sprouts, arsenic, fushen, borax, and Chinese myrica.

Some *Fukudenpō* formulas contain aromatics and spices from "southern regions" that were used for treating colds (aloeswood, cloves, agastache, costus, mandarin orange, immature orange, lesser galangal, ginger, tsaoko, Katsumada's galangal, cardamom, grains of paradise, ichihjen, zedoary, black pepper, nutmeg, greater galangal, and cassia). Some other crude drugs originated from Asia Minor, India, and the area around Malaya (such as asafetida, Sumatra benzoin, frankincense [*kunrokukō*], frankincense [*nyūkō*], betel nut [*binrōshi*], another betel nut [*daifukushi*], chebulic myrobalan, cloves, and dragon's blood).[75]

This information is inherently interesting. But, more crucially, it enables a new discovery, namely, that medieval Japanese medicine, via a chain of transmission through China, was influenced by Arabic (or Islamic) medicine.

The Influence of Arabic (Islamic) Medicine

Research into changes in China's pharmaceutical regime from late Tang to mid-Song has shown that Arabic (Islamic) medicine contributed to those changes. Recent study of the *Hejiju fang* has provided more specific information and suggests that items common in Arabic medicine underwent substantial clinical testing in the Chinese medical world, with varied results. For example, in the area of treatments for cold damage disorders (exogenous febrile diseases), Arabic medicine had a visible but relatively small impact.[76] However, in the new category of "all forms of [disorders of] vital energy" (C. *qi*, J. *ki*), Arabic medicine had a substantial influence, notably in the area of aromatic stomachics.[77]

Pre-Tang Chinese medical literature contains very few prescriptions for aromatic stomachics. In contrast, such works as the *Hejiju fang* contain many such prescriptions. Moreover, in those prescriptions many "western-origin" (in general, Middle Eastern and Indian) crude drugs are employed. It is difficult to attribute this to developments "internal" to Chinese medicine. However, the use of aromatic stomachics (known as Jawarish) is highly developed in Arabic medicine. Using Ibn-Sīnā's classic *Canon of Medicine* as a guide, we may note several characteristics of aromatic stomachics. There are large numbers of crude drugs compounded in any one prescription (one contains sixty-four drugs, and over half contain over fifteen). While many crude drugs may be included, many have similar qualities. The most frequently used crude drugs are of a refined-oil nature, with great use of such items as ginger, cardamom, pepper, fruits in the parsley family, items in the camphor family such as cinnamon bark, and tannin crude drugs of the myrobalan variety (such as chebulic myrobalan). Occasionally we find drugs of a resinous nature from the Convolvulus and Anacardiaceae families.

A comparison of the Tang *Waitai miyao* (Medical Secrets of an Official, 752), the early Northern Song *Taiping shenghui fang*, and the late Northern Song *Hejiju fang* demonstrates the influence. An examination of 108 prescriptions in the "all forms of [disorders of] *qi/ki* vital energy" section of the *Hejiju fang*, focusing on the number of crude drugs in the aromatic and the salty categories, and ascertaining which ones are of traditional Chinese and which are of "western" origin, provides the specifics. Three main points may be noted. First, over half (twenty-nine compared to twenty-one) of the aromatic or salty items in the *Hejiju fang* are of western origin; only four of these twenty-nine are noted in the *Waitai miyao* (lesser galangal, birthwoot root, cardamom, and black pepper), although nineteen are cited in the *Taiping shenghui fang*. Second, there is little difference in the listing of traditional Chinese aromatics and spices between the *Waitai miyao* and the *Hejiju fang*, suggesting that the drugs of western origin augmented rather than supplanted Chinese ones.[78] Third, in traditional Chinese medicine few aromatics and spicy types of aromatics were employed, but they enjoyed a high *rate* of usage because one or two were generally mixed into a prescription. By contrast, the prescriptions in the *Hejiju fang* reflect the characteristics of formulas in Ibn-Sīnā's *Canon of Medicine*. A large number of aromatics and spicy medicinals are employed, though the rate of usage of any one is comparatively low since many were compounded in any one prescription.

That there was a substantial change in the usage of crude drugs of western origin in the 350 years between the compilation of the *Waitai miyao* and that of the *Hejiju fang* might not occasion surprise. But there was also a significant change in usage in the period between the compilation of the *Taiping shenghui fang* and the *Hejiju fang*. Comparing these latter two texts, we note the following.[79] Ten crude drugs are new: nut grass, clove peel, spikenard, sandalwood, turmeric, Sumatra benzoin, storax, frankincense, birthwort root,[80] and myrrh. There is a dramatic increase in the use of six items previously known: grains of paradise, zedoary, aloeswood, agastache, fennel, and black pepper. There is a notable rise in the use of another six previously known items: musk, ichihjen, cardamom, nutmeg, lesser galangal, and cloves. And there is a slight drop in the use of costus root, although it still figures prominently. The remaining six crude drugs that round out our list, none of which appear in the *Waitai miyao*, are tsaoko, cubebs, another reference to frankincense, asafetida, long pepper, and Borneo camphor. The reader may observe that there is considerable overlap between these crude drugs and those noted earlier from the *Fukudenpō*, which reflects the fact that it uses the *Hejiju fang* extensively.

Let us return to Kajiwara Shōzen for a sense of the clinical use of Arabic medicine. Shōzen cited formulas from the *Hejiju fang* in both the *Ton'ishō* and the *Man'anpō*. In the former, 220 formulas were cited (the second-largest source after the *Taiping Shenghui fang* with 258), and in the latter 156 were cited (third largest after the *Shengji zonglu*, with 1,797, and the *Taiping shenghui fang* with 217). However, these figures do not fully convey the importance of the *Hejiju fang* citations, a large proportion of which are concentrated in sections of the works dealing with the category "all forms of [disorders of] *qi/ki* vital energy." Many prescriptions in that category are designed to deal with enteric ailments, which are manifested in vomiting, diarrhea, and nausea, either singly or multiply, as in the case of *kakuran* (*Cholera morbus*), a feared, debilitating, and potentially fatal combination of vomiting and diarrhea. (Indeed, it is probably not coincidental that the formulas found in a fragmentary and rare late-twelfth-century prescription manual all deal with acute diarrhea.)[81]

The "all forms of [disorders of] *qi/ki* vital energy" category first appeared in Chinese medical writing in the *Hejiju fang*. It seems to have been readily adopted, along with the western-origin materia medica that are in the formulas, from that point. For example, chapter 2 of the privately printed *Weishi jiacang fang* is devoted to those ailments and lists a considerable number of crude drugs of western origin.[82] Thus, Shōzen's appropriation of the category is an indication of his familiarity with currents in Chinese clinical medicine. We also have a sense that he had direct experience with prescriptions in this category since he did not rely just on the *Hejiju fang* for formulas but selected them also from other works. Of the 155 or so formulas included in the *Ton'ishō* and *Man'anpō* that apply to "all forms of [disorders of] *qi/ki* vital energy," only thirty-two are drawn from the *Hejiju fang* itself. The remaining 123, that is, eighty percent of the total, are drawn from a dozen or so other works. The *Shengji zonglu*, which does not even have the ailment category "all forms of [disorders of] *qi/ki* vital energy," is the source of seventy-seven formulas, the *Keyong fang* provides twelve, and the *Yuyaoyuan fang* provides ten.

Let us look now at some examples of Shōzen's clinical engagement of Arabic medicine and thus obtain a sense of where it had an impact in medieval Japan. The formulas that we encounter, notably those in the "all forms of [disorders of] vital energy" section of the *Man'anpō*, are varied. They could contain different numbers of crude drugs, for example, three, five, eight, twelve, sixteen, twenty-three, and twenty-four.[83] And they could range from formulas with mainly drugs of western origin to ones with mainly crude drugs of Chinese origin. Nonetheless, the significant use of western crude drugs, in both simple and complex formulas, implicitly indicates the influence of Arabic medicine.

We will start with a formula that counts as one of its ingredients storax, or Storax (*Sogōkō*), which name appears in the title of the formula Storax Pill (*Sogōkō-en*). The existence of this formula, an aromatic stomachic, appears to have been well known in the warrior city of Kamakura in Shōzen's day. One early-fourteenth-century resident, a Chinese physician by the name of Zhiguang (Chikō), enjoyed a reputation as a compounder of medicines and a particularly good provider of *Sogō[kō]-en*.[84] Storax Pill was comprised of fifteen crude drugs (in total seventeen crude drugs appear in the formulas; see below), which are ordered differently in formulas appearing in different works. Of the five versions of the formula that I examined,[85] only two were exactly the same, although the variations were minor (not a comment on the pharmaceutical efficacy). Thirteen of the fifteen crude drugs were common to all formulas: storax, frankincense, Borneo camphor, white atractylodes, white sandalwood, cloves, cinnabar, nut grass, rhinoceros horn, musk, Sumatra benzoin, long pepper, and chebulic myrobalan. Otherwise, for the remaining two crude drugs that make up the fifteen, four used aloeswood while one other used gypsum, and three used costus while two used birthwort root. Other slight variations were that four wrote frankincense as *kunrokukō* and the other as *nyūkō*, four referred to nut grass as *kōbushi* while one used the term *shasōkon*, and one specified that the rhinoceros horn was to be black. Of the total of seventeen crude drugs employed, only one (white atractylodes) is of Chinese origin. Gypsum is a mineral. Only three of the fifteen crude drugs of western origin are found in the *Waitai miyao*, another seven are employed in the *Shengji zonglu*, and another five are employed for the first time in this *Hejiju fang* preparation.

Shōzen held the Storax Pill formula in the highest regard and had great clinical familiarity with it. For example, in commenting on the formula Shiso-in, from the *Keyong fang*, for treating postdiabetes bodily changes and bloated feelings, he noted that for the condition one should administer Storax Pill or Rectify *Qi/Ki* Vital Energy Powder (*Shōki-san*), it being very good to add burpleurum or ginger.[86] In another instance, he compared a formula from the *Hejiju fang* with one from the *Daquan liang fang*, noting that the old method was to give one pill but the latter suggests four pills.[87] In another case, he made two observations. First, reflecting this habit of comparing formulas in different works,[88] he wondered whether the formula Atractylodes Pill (*Byakujutsu-gan*), which appeared in the *Shengji zonglu*, was not in fact a formula for Storax Pill. Second, after noting that the *Shengji zonglu* directed that the dose should be ten pills (three pills for old people and children), on an empty stomach and washed down with well water, he remarked that the dose should be thirty to fifty pills.[89] On another occasion, he felt that he had come up with his own improvement on the original. Not only was it "marvelously efficacious" to double the amounts of Borneo camphor, musk, and cinnabar, but one could omit Borneo camphor and increase the amount of musk and rename the formula *Jakōsō*, which was marvelous for treating people suffering from cold of the deficiency type and from intestinal worms.[90] Shōzen felt that Storax Pill was a "wonder medicine."[91]

> I say that this medicine is the absolute best for suffering associated with all kinds of rising of lung energy [shortness of breath, dyspnea] and irritability. Therefore it is explained clearly at the beginning of this chapter. For infant measles, exogenous febrile diseases and diseases due to summer heat, and those of internal heat and dryness heat syndrome, in all cases one should administer cold water. If the body is cold and fatigued, one should warm up the medicine with heat and have it prepared as a warm decoction. Or else administer it along with warm rice wine. This is the lore of Storax Pill. One must be extremely grateful for this.[92]

Shōzen was impressed by other formulas, too. One from the *Hejiju fang*, Leek Powder (*Hansō-san*), was prescribed for a variety of ailments that affected males, females, and pregnant women and resulted in such things as lack of appetite; regurgitation; *Cholera morbus*; leukorrheal discharges; and prepartum and postpartum chills, fevers, and abdominal pains. Its combination of Chinese crude drugs (Chinese atractylodes, licorice, bur reed, immature orange, poria, and corydalis [a "new" materia medica]) with western drugs (zedoary, cardomom, cloves, betel palm, cinnamon, and dried ginger) apparently had great efficacy.

> This is a wonderful medicine for treating "all forms of [disorders of] *qi/ki* vital energy," and one cannot write enough about it; it is explained and discussed in various works. The hundred ailments arise from the *qi/ki* vital energy. But medicines that readjust the vital energy thereby treat the myriad illnesses, and, [one] can't go wrong. Further, the *Sanyin fang* takes the seven *qi/ki* vital energy illnesses and considers them to be illnesses from internal causes [endogenous pathogenic factors]. It takes summer heat wetness syndrome caused by wind evil, relapse of illness caused by overconsumption, and considers them illnesses from external causes [exogenous pathogenic factors]. It takes hot water, fire, arrow, and blade injuries and considers them illnesses from neither internal nor external causes [pathogenic factors neither endogenous nor exogenous]. Consequently, those arising from within and the heart are considered internal causes [endogenous pathogenic factors]. Most certainly [this formula] accords with this reasoning. One must certainly be grateful for the various works and formulas.[93]

Another formula, Ox Gallstone Agada Pill (*Goō Agada-en*) (which might well be originally an Indian Buddhist formula), prescribed for diarrhea, likewise combined Chinese and western drugs among its fifteen ingredients. The seven in the Chinese category included achyranthes, Baikal skullcap, golden thread, ginseng, madder, big-head atractylodes, and Amur cork tree; the eight in the western category included white sandalwood, Burmese rosewood, safflower, turmeric, black pepper, nut grass, musk, and Sumatra benzoin. Shōzen's comments on its importance suggest its effectiveness: "As to the method of compounding, one must receive the oral transmission. This is not to be transmitted casually. The oral transmission is written down separately; it is the most secret of the secret."[94]

Diarrhea was a major concern, and Shōzen recommended various formulas. In the *Ton'ishō* we find the "nutmeg formula," Nutmeg Powder (*Nikuzuku-san*), which employs the western items nutmeg, poppy capsules, and ginger, and Chinese licorice. Shōzen remarks that it is used to treat all types of red and white diarrhea when other medicines have no efficacy and there is no end to the shitting (*kudasu koto kiwamari naki*).[95] In the *Man'anpō* section on diarrhea, he recommends that three *ryō* of nutmeg be added to the formula Ginseng China-root Atractylodes Powder (*Jinbuku byakujutsu-gan*) (comprised mainly of the Chinese crude drugs ginseng, porea, atractylodes, Chinese yam, Chinese licorice, hyacinth bean, cardomom, lotus shoot, balloon flower, and Job's tears), which appears in the "all forms of [disorders of] vital energy" section of the *Hejiju fang*.[96]

But most revealing of the need for effective diarrhea medicines is that Shōzen developed his own formula (he notes another as an "oral tradition").[97] It is the only example of such invention that I have encountered, and the constituent drugs (nutmeg, cardomom, and cloves) are all of western origin. Claiming that his Hundred Centered Powder (*Hyakuchū-san*) is 100 percent effective for all diarrheas, he notes:[98]

> Grind the ingredients, each dose to be five to seven *seni* or six to seven *seni*. It is to be administered on an empty stomach before meals, either with rice gruel or chestnut gruel; three to four doses per day, or at the very least two to three doses; this is guaranteed to work. If the diarrhea has stopped, you can administer [either ?] Grain Fragrance Powder (*Kakō-san*) [Kōka-san?] or Six-Flavor Eight-Flavor Calming Stomach Powder (*Rokumi Hachimi Heii-san*).[99] If there is still a little diarrhea, then to [either?] Grain Fragrance Powder (*Kakō-san*) [Kōka-san] or Calming Stomach Powder (*Heii-san*) add two to three *seni* of nutmeg and administer that; then the person will be cured. This is to be used for high and low, old and young, adults and children.

In sum, Arabic medicine provided medieval Japan with new crude drugs and prescriptions that provided a means of treatment for stomach and enteric ailments that were superior to what had been available previously.

Concluding Comments

In the preceding discussion I have made a number of points regarding Chinese printed texts, their availability and use, particular materia medica, Shōzen's clinical observations, and the influence of Arabic formulas. Rather than repeat them here, let me make three more general observations.

First, the development of Chinese printing in the early Song opened up a new world of medical knowledge for medieval Japanese. The ready availability of "recent" printed texts made possible a qualitative leap in the understanding of the field of medicine itself, enabling practitioners to better deal with known medical challenges, and to become familiar with both the shortcomings of existing knowledge and advances made in medicine in China. Concomitantly, the access to new information demolished the old structure of proprietary cultural capital that had previously dominated—we might even say stunted—access to medical knowledge. Since access to new medical knowledge was integral to the activities of the Zen religious world, and matters medical were of great concern in monastic communities, it is no surprise that—as represented by Kajiwara Shōzen and embodied in his *Man'anpō* and *Ton'ishō*—Buddhist priests emerged as leaders in the medical field.

Second, while I have focused on the important role of Buddhist priests in the acquisition and dissemination of new knowledge, it is not unlikely that there were numerous additional channels: maritime traders, Chinese physicians, non-monastic Japanese sojourning in China, and the interaction between residents and travelers in any number of port communities. Thus, while we have sporadic references to the dates when crude drugs were acquired in Japan, it seems reasonable to assume that there was an ongoing trade propelled both by the random activities of individuals or small groups and by traders dealing in larger quantities. It is also clear that the influx of crude drugs into Japan increased in both quantity and variety over time and that they were acquired over an increasingly broader geographical range.

A final point goes beyond the topics addressed above. We may recognize that theories regarding disease, illness, the relationships of medicines to bodily systems, and the correspondence of the body to the cosmos were different in, for example, Chinese and Arabic medical epistemologies. Thus, there is a possible question of whether a prescription created for an "Arabic medical body" would work on a "Chinese medical body." However, it seems that the transmission of knowledge about drugs and prescriptions owed less to theoretical contemplation than it did to practical necessity. Indeed, while ingredients might be known to be of western origin, they were not known as a product of Arabic medicine, so the theoretical issue probably never arose.

Notes

[1] For a recent study of the Ritsu school, and translations of many key documents related to the inspiration for healing and hospice, see David Ralph Quinter, "The Shingon Ritsu School and the Mañjuśrī Cult in the Kamakura Period: From Eison to Monkan."

[2] On Ninshō, see Matsuo Kenji, *Ninshō*. For some hospice and medical matters, see esp. p. 94ff and p. 143ff.

[3] *Ton'ishō*, chap. 8 (Kagaku Shoin edition, 1986, p. 177, sec. V, leaves 71, 72); hereafter cited as *Ton'ishō*, chap. 8 (*KS*, p. 177, V–71, 72). Page references are to the Kagaku Shoin edition. Chapter references are to an unpaginated but more legible text also from the Naikaku Bunko (see "Bibliography of Primary Sources").

[4] *Man'anpō*, chap. 23 (Kagaku Shoin edition, 1986, p. 661, sec. XXIII, leaf 51); hereafter cited as *Man'anpō*, chap. 23 (*KS*, p. 661, XXIII–51). The full passage is translated in Andrew Edmund Goble, "Medicine and New Knowledge in Medieval Japan: Kajiwara Shōzen (1266–1337) and the *Man'anpō*," (pt. 2) p. 442.

[5] For a translation of chapters 1, 2, 28, see Emil Hsia, Ilza Veith, and Robert Geertsma, *Tanba Yasuyori: The Essentials of Medicine in Early Japan*. For an introduction to the text and its transmission, see Sugitatsu Yoshikazu, ed., *Ishinpō no denrai*.

[6] It is worth noting that the *eisei* (safeguarding life) was a Song term and here replaces the more common *yōjō* (nurturing life). See Ishihara Akira, "*Eisei hiyōshō*," p. 288.

[7] See Ishihara Akira, "*Honzō iroha shō* kaidai," pp. 622–28. For the Chinese medical works cited, see Mayanagi Makoto, "*Honzō iroha shō* shoin no igaku bunken." Among them we note such titles as *Baiyi xuan fang* (One Hundred and One Selected Prescriptions), *Sanyin fang* (Treatise on the Three Categories of Pathogenic Factors of Disease), *Benshi fang* (Effective Prescriptions for Universal Relief), *Hejiju fang* (Prescriptions of the Pharmacy Service for Great Peace and for the Benefit of the People), *Yishuo* (Conversations on Medicine, 1189, first printed in 1228), and the *Waike jingyao* (Essentials of External Medicine, 1263).

[8] See *Kissa yōjōki*. See, too, the study of Eisai's life by Miyawaki Takahira, *Eisai monogatari*; and Theodore M. Ludwig, "Before Rikyū," pp. 376–380.

[9] Kyōtofu Ishikai, comp., *Kyōto no igakushi*, p. 149.

[10] *Man'anpō*, chap. 52 (*KS*, p. 1398, LII–134, 135). For a translation of the relevant passage, see Goble, "Medicine and New Knowledge in Medieval Japan," (pt. 1), p. 223.

[11] Shinmura, *Nihon iryō shakai shi no kenkyū*, p. 331. Note especially an entry from the record of Wuxue Zuyuan (Mugaku Sogen, 1226–1286), the *Bukkō kokushi goroku, kan 7, Seieki mondō hiyō*.

[12] For example, the *Youyou xinshu* citations are verbatim ones from other named medical works, and it does not contain any of its "own" prescriptions. Accordingly, going just by this one example, we know that the number of titles appearing in the *Man'anpō* is greater than the number that Shōzen would have read. For a guide to the titles cited in *Youyou xinshu*, see Liu Shukui, "*Youyou xinshu* yinyong yixue wenxian kao."

[13] Hattori Toshirō, *Kamakura jidai igakushi no kenkyū*, p. 121.

[14] For a guide to the works cited in the *Man'anpō*, see ibid., pp. 148–151; and Guo Xiumei, Kosoto Hiroshi, and Okada Kenkichi, "*Wan'an fang* yin zhongguo yishu guankai."

[15] See Kosoto Hiroshi, "*Taihei keimin wazai kyokuhō* kaidai 2," p. 2.

[16] Ishihara Akira, "*Honzō iroha shō* kaidai," p. 627.

[17] *Man'anpō*, chap. 13 (*KS*, p. 327, XIII–120).

[18] Ibid., chap. 13 (*KS*, p. 309, XIII–48), headnote, refers to both a "separate edition" (*betsuhon*) *Ju fang* (Formularies of the Bureau) and an annotated and expanded *Daquanju fang* (Great Complete Formularies of the Bureau).

[19] Ibid., chap. 49 (*KS*, p.1295, XLIX–104). However, on at least one occasion Shōzen lists a formula from the *Dayi fang*: *Man'anpō*, chap. 46 (*KS*, p. 1186, XLVI–9).

[20] *Youyou xinshu*, chap. 40, sec. 13~15; *Man'anpō*, chap. 49 (*KS*, pp. 1295–1299, XLIX–101~118).

[21] *Man'anpō*, chap. 36 (*KS*, p. 933, XXXVI–7).

[22] Ibid., chap. 15 (*KS*, p. 449, XV–134, 135).

[23] Ibid., chap. 12 (*KS*, p. 317, XII–79, 80).

[24] Ibid., chap. 52 (*KS*, p. 1424, LII–240).

[25] *Ton'ishō*, chap. 13 (*KS*, p. 239, VII–73).

[26] Ibid., chap. 18 (*KS*, p. 329, IX–168).

[27] Ibid., chap. 35 (*KS*, p. 541, XVI–103, 104). See also *Man'anpō*, chap. 40 (*KS*, pp. 1022–23, XL–31~34). Shōzen notes that *hiki* was referred to in one materia medica work as *keibyō* and was known popularly as *otomi tsuwari*.

[28] *Man'anpō*, chap. 42 (*KS*, p. 1075, XLII–33).

[29] For other observations, on mistaken applications of cold treatments, mistaken understandings of the use of ointment to foster an easy birth, and postpartum customs and practices inimical to the health of the mother, see Goble, "Medicine and New Knowledge in Medieval Japan," (pt. 2), pp. 443–442, 441, 441–440, respectively. For comments on the indiscriminate application of needling and moxibustion, see *Man'anpō*, chap. 22 (*KS*, p. 643, XXII–167).

[30] *Ton'ishō*, chap. 27 (*KS*, p. 422, XIII–10).

[31] *Man'anpō*, chap. 32 (*KS*, p. 876, XXXII–35). One of his observations was that morning sickness was not limited to the first months of pregnancy: *Man'anpō*, chap. 32 (*KS*, p. 881, XXXII–57, headnote).

[32] Ibid., chap. 32 (*KS*, pp. 884–885, XXXII–70, 71).

[33] Ibid., chap. 32 (*KS*, p. 869, XXXII–9, 10).

[34] *Ton'ishō*, chap. 12 (*KS*, p. 237, VII–67).

[35] *Man'anpō*, chap. 32 (*KS*, pp. 875–76, XXXII–34, 35). The phrases in the final sentence are taken from two classical Chinese stories. In the former, after a hare ran into a tree stump and killed itself, a farmer gave up farming, with its predictable yield, in favor of waiting for another hare to appear, run into the stump, and thus provide food. The second refers to a story about carving a notch into the side of a boat from which a sword has fallen into the sea and assuming that the mark on the boat will indicate the sword's location, quite oblivious of the fact that the boat floats around and never keeps to the same position.

[36] Ibid., chap. 23 (*KS*, p. 661, XXIII–51). The full passage is translated in Goble, "Medicine and New Knowledge in Medieval Japan," (pt. 2), p. 442.

[37] Shōzen has here jumbled the names of two people, the Song priest-physician Chu Yushi (初虞世) and the Tang bureaucrat Yu Shinan (虞世南). The latter is listed instead of the former at least six times in the *Man'anpō*. See for example, *Man'anpō*, chap. 1 (*KS*, p. 40, I–42) headnote; and the citations noted in the main text. However, Chu is correctly referred to at least forty times, for example in *Man'anpō*, chap. 13 (*KS*, p. 304, XIII–27), and chap. 14 (*KS*, p. 391, XIV–138).

[38] Ibid., chap. 14 (*KS*, pp. 393–394, XIV–146~148).

[39] Ibid., chap. 52 (*KS*, p. 1446, LII–83).

[40] See, respectively (at the same page), ibid., chap. 45 (*KS*, p. 1178, XLV–106); and chap. 45 (*KS*, p. 1178, XLV–106).

[41] Ibid., chap. 13 (*KS*, p. 321, XIII–95).

[42] Ibid., chap. 13 (*KS*, p. 312, XIII–58).

[43] Ibid., chap. 13 (*KS*, p. 311, XIII–55).

[44] Ibid., chap. 51 (*KS*, p. 1352, LI–135).

[45] Ibid., chap. 15 (*KS*, p. 444, XV–116).

[46] Ibid., chap. 49 (*KS*, p. 1292, XLIX–89, 90).

[47] Ibid., chap. 14 (*KS*, p. 383, XIV–106).

[48] Ibid., chap. 6 (*KS*, p. 137, VI–74).

[49] Ibid., chap. 11 (*KS*, p. 272, XI–14).

[50] Ibid., chap. 38 (*KS*, p. 985, XXXVIII–36).

[51] Ibid., chap. 32 (*KS*, p. 870, XXXII–13, 14).

[52] Ibid., chap. 36 (*KS*, p. 934, XXXVI–11).

[53] For thoughtful treatments of issues in premodern trade, see Bruce Batten, *Gateway to Japan: Hakata in War and Peace, 500–1300*; and Charlotte von Verschuer, *Across the Perilous Seas: Japanese Trade with China and Korea from the Seventh to the Seventeenth Centuries*. For an example of the detailed information available for the Tokugawa era, see the studies of the Japan-Korea pharmaceutical trade by Tashiro Kazui, "Kinsei zenki Chōsen iyaku no juyō to Tsushima han-igakusho, yakuju, ishi ni tsuite," pp. 265–299; and *Edo jidai Chōsen yakuzai chōsa no kenkyū*.

[54] Seki Shūichi, "Kōryō no michi to Nihon, Chōsen," pp. 267–268, notes the knowledge in Kyoto that musk and cloves came from southern barbarian regions (*nanban*) and were brought to Japan via Ryukyu.

[55] *Shaken nichiroku* Bunmei 18 (1486).7.15.

[56] Ts'ao Yung-ho, "Pepper Trade in East Asia," p. 242.

[57] *Shaken nichiroku* Bunmei 18 (1486).3.14.

[58] See Asahina Yasuhiko, *Shōsōin no yakubutsu*.

[59] Regarding a stock of cinnabar (used for dyeing) that was wrapped in individual parcels made of recycled documents and upon which precise notations of weight were recorded, see Nojiri Tadashi, "Kinryō kisai kara mita Shōsōin tan uramonjo no kenkyū."

[60] For a table of the depletion of the original stores between 756 and 856, see Mori Shikazō, *Honzōgaku kenkyū*, pp. 152–155. For an example of a requisition request, see the 764.7.25 petition from the Imperial Pharmacy (Seyakuin) requesting further supplies of cassia, since current supplies had been exhausted and compounding of medicine has thereby had to cease, in Hayakawa Shōhachi, *Shoku Nihongi*, pp. 65–67.

61 Shibata Shōji, *Hōryūji shozō iyaku chōzai koshō*, pp. 35, 50.

62 *Sekiso ōrai*, p. 609. The Japanese crude drugs are Chinese yam, bidentate achyranthes, pharbitis (morning glory), nutgrass, perilla (shiso), schizonepeta, dried ginger, magnolia, sophora, tuckahoe, tangerine peel, white atractylodes, rehmannia, deer antler, calcite (lime), sulphur, and ivy.

63 Tōno Haruyuki, *Kentōshi to Shōsōin*, pp. 184–185, notes that the Pahlavi is written in what is known as late Sassanian cursive script.

64 Edward H. Schafer, *The Golden Peaches of Samarkand*, p. 178.

65 Such usage continued. *Sekiso ōrai* notes (p. 604) that for compounding incense there were six main ingredients—aloes, cloves, mussel shells, frankincense, white sandalwood, and musk—that formed the main base, to which were then added one or another of various items to produce a specific named incense.

66 For a discussion of these works, see Mori Shikazō, *Honzōgaku kenkyū*, pp. 244–339.

67 See *Shinsarugaku ki*, pp. 150–51.

68 See, for example, *Kinsō ryōjishō*, sec. 29.

69 See, for example, ibid., sec. 12.

70 See Andrew Edmund Goble, "War and Injury: The Emergence of Wound Medicine in Medieval Japan," pp. 318–319. For a list of some 120 materia medica items that were employed in the treatment of wounds, see appendix 2, pp. 328–332.

71 Okazaki Kanzō, *Kusuri no rekishi*, p. 90, notes these as two of the five items in Ichijō Kaneyoshi's *Sekiso ōrai* that had not been noted previously in a Japanese source. Okazaki seems not to have had the opportunity to consult *Ton'ishō* or *Man'anpō*.

72 *Fukudenpō* is generally regarded as a work from the 1360s, but it may have been compiled as late as the mid-fifteenth century. See Sasaki Toshikazu, "Hakubutsukan shomoku shikō Teishitsu bon no bu Igakukan hon hen, *Yūrin Fukudenpō* ni tsuite."

73 For a comparison of items appearing in the *Fukudenpō* and in the fifteenth-century reference works *Satsujōshū* and *Ruijū mojishō*, see Okanishi Tamendo, "Chūgoku honzō no torai to sono eikyō," pp. 150–153.

74 For a convenient tabulation see Takahashi Shintarō, "Chūgoku no yakubutsu ryōhō to sono eikyō," pp. 414–415.

75 Ibid., pp. 419–420.

[76] Nakamura Teruko, Kawaguchi Naomi, and Endō Jirō, "*Wazaikyoku hō shōkanhen no kentō.*"

[77] Nakamura Teruko, Matsuzaki Aiko, and Endō Jirō, "*Wazaikyoku hō* ni okeru hōkōsei ken'i yaku no kentō: Seiiki no igaku no eikyō ni tsuite;" Nakamura Teruko, Matsuzaki Aiko, and Endō Jirō, "*Wazaikyoku hō issaiki* hen no kentō;" Nakamura Teruko, Miyamoto Hirokazu, and Endō Jirō, "*Wazaikyoku hō* ni mirareru seizai no tokuchō."

[78] There were also changes in the usage of Chinese crude drugs. From the *Waitai miyao* to the *Hejiju fang*, we can note a substantial increase in the use of spicebush, Dahurian angelica, perilla, immature orange peel, and Chinese atractylodes; roughly the same use of ginger and cinnamon bark; and a decrease in the use of magnolia, big-head atractylodes, wild ginger, and Chinese angelica.

[79] The following is based on Nakamura Teruko, Matsuzaki Aiko, and Endō Jirō, "*Wazaikyoku hō* ni okeru hōkōsei ken'i yaku no kentō," Table 5, p. 156.

[80] Birthwort root is, however, one of the four drugs of western origin listed in the *Waitai miyao.*

[81] Kosoto Hiroshi, "Koisho dankan *Shinpukuji shozō reihon Kanzō-gan* tō hō kō."

[82] *Weishi jiacang fang*, chap. 2. Among the items of western origin we find costus root, black pepper, fennel, asafetida, long pepper, lesser galangal, dry ginger, zedoary, spikenard, cardamom, nutmeg, clove, and sandalwood. Chapter 1 additionally notes such items as frankincense, myrrh, agastache, and dragon's blood.

[83] One of the largest numbers of crude drugs in one formula is thirty-three, contained in *Ki'myaku-en*, a secret medicine for treating colds and ghost diseases: *Ton'ishō*, chap. 14 (*KS*, p. 265, VIII–55–56). The crude drugs are magnetic oxide of iron, Sumatra benzoin, Japanese arisaena, tiger bones, actinolite, ox gallstone, costus, aloeswood, yams, fungus-infested bamboo, *basōfu* (unidentified), extract of blumea, mimosa, bletilla (?), musk, frankincense, giant typhonium, ledebouriella, black rhinoceros horn, antelope horn, Borneo camphor, ginseng, gastrodia, cloves, white-banded krait, safflower, sandalwood, turmeric, atractylodes, loranthus, gold flakes, amber, and "honey-ball."

[84] The initial reference is from Shinmura, *Nihon iryō shakai shi no kenkyū*, p. 132, n. 7, noting the *Muchū mondō* of Musō Kokushi (1275–1351). See *Muchū mondō shū*, "Yūryoku no danna no kitō, tsuketari Tōjin'i Chikō," pp. 59–60.

[85] *Ton'ishō*, chap. 9 (*KS*, p. 181, V–87, 88); *Ton'ishō*, chap. 10 (*KS*, p. 193, VI–14~16); *Man'anpō*, chap. 10 (*KS*, pp. 261–262, X–102, 103); *Man'anpō*, chap. 13 (*KS*, p. 302, XIII–17); *Man'anpō*, chap. 15 (*KS*, pp. 448–449, XV–131~35).

⁸⁶ *Man'anpō*, chapter 14 (*KS*, p. 396, XIV–156).

⁸⁷ Ibid., chap. 15 (*KS*, p. 449, XV–134, 135).

⁸⁸ For other examples see ibid., chap. 13 (*KS*, p. 307, XIII–40), which notes that the *Sanyin fang* formula *Shichiki-tō* is called *Yonshichi-tō* in the *Keyong fang*. *Man'anpō*, chap. 13 (*KS*, p. 338, XIII–161) notes that the phrasing of a formula in the *Sanyin fang* is slightly different from that in the *Hejiju fang*.

⁸⁹ *Man'anpō*, chap. 10 (*KS*, pp. 261–262, X–102, 103).

⁹⁰ Ibid., chap. 13 (*KS*, p. 302, XIII–17).

⁹¹ Ibid., chap. 14 (*KS*, p. 389, XIV–129).

⁹² *Ton'ishō*, chap. 10 (*KS*, p. 193, VI–14~16).

⁹³ *Mananpō*, chap. 13 (*KS*, pp. 331–332, XIII–135~137).

⁹⁴ *Ton'ishō*, chap. 7 (*KS*, p. 159, IV–191, 192).

⁹⁵ Ibid., chap. 8 (*KS*, p. 176, V–67).

⁹⁶ *Man'anpō*, chap. 19 (*KS*, p. 523, XIX–23).

⁹⁷ Ibid., chap. 19 (*KS*, p. 525–526, XIX–32, 33).

⁹⁸ Ibid., chap.19 (*KS*, p. 525, XIX–31, 32).

⁹⁹ I have not found a *Kōka-san*. However, a Grain Fragrance Powder (*Kakō-san*) and also the Calming Stomach Powder (*Heii-san*) noted here, is included in the "all forms of [disorders of] vital energy" sections of the *Hejiju fang* and in *Man'anpō*, chap. 13 (*KS*, p. 304, XIII–27, 28). *Kakō-san* is also noted, with virtually identical ingredients, in another work used by Shōzen, the 1283 *Lingnan weisheng fang* (Prescriptions for Safeguarding Life in Lingnan), pp. 72–73.

Bibliography

Bibliography of Primary Sources

For a list of abbreviations, see p. ix.

Unless otherwise specified, place of publication for Chinese titles is Beijing, for Japanese titles is Tokyo, and for Korean titles is Seoul.

Azuma kagami 吾妻鏡. In *SZKT*, vols. 32–33.

Banreki kanai nenkan 萬歴家内年鑑. In *Kin'in monogatari* 金印ものがたり, pp. 125–148. Ed. Ōtani Mitsuo 大谷光男. Fukuoka 福岡: Nishi Nihon Toshokan Konsarutanto Kyōkai 西日本図書館コンサルタント協会, 1979.

Beiji zongxiao fang 備急総効方. By Li Zhaozheng 李朝正. In *Kyōu shooku zō Sōban Bikyū sōkōhō* 杏雨書屋蔵宋版備急総効方. Osaka 大阪: Takeda Kagaku Shinkō Zaidan 武田科学振興財団, 2005.

Bingashū 岷峨集. By Sesson Yūbai 雪村友梅. In *GBSS*, vol. 3, pp. 863–904; *GBZS*, vol. 1, pp. 519–566.

Bunrui kiji taikō furoku 4 分類記事大綱附録 4. Held at Kokuritsu Kokkai Toshokan 国立国会図書館所蔵.

Chin Uirō keifu 陳外郎系譜. Held at Tōkyō Daigaku Shiryō Hensanjo 東京大学史料編纂所所蔵.

Chōhei ōsetsuki 朝聘応接記. By Arai Hakuseki 新井白石. In *Arai Hakuseki zenshū* 4 新井白石全集 4. Kokusho Kankōkai 国書刊行会, 1906.

Chōsei ryōyōhō 長生療養方. By Renki 蓮基. In *ZGR*, vol. 30.2, pp. 143–174.

Chosŏn wangjo sillok (*CWS*) 朝鮮王朝實録. Seoul: Kuksa P'yŏnch'an Wiwŏnhoe 國史編纂委員會, 1969–72.

Chungjong sillok 中宗實録. In *CWS*.

Chūyūki 中右記. By Fujiwara Munetada 藤原宗忠. In *ZHST*, vols. 8–14.

Daiganji monjo 大願寺文書. In *Hiroshima kenshi: Kodai chūsei shiryō hen*, 3 広島県史－古代中世史料編 3. Hiroshima 広島: Hiroshima-ken 広島県, 1978.

Daikaku Zenji goroku 大覚禅師語録. By Lanxi Daolong 蘭渓道隆. In *T.* 80, no. 2547; *DNBZ*, vol. 95.

Dai Nihon Bukkyō zensho (*DNBZ*) 大日本仏教全書. Ed. Bussho Kankōkai 仏書刊行会. 150 vols. Bussho Kankōkai 仏書刊行会, 1912–19 (various reprinted editions also).

Dai Nihon kokiroku (*DNKR*) 大日本古記録. Ed. Tōkyō Daigaku Shiryō Hensanjo 東京大学史料編纂所. Iwanami Shoten 岩波書店, 1952–.

Dazaifu, Dazaifu Tenmangû shiryô 大宰府太宰府天満宮史料. Ed. Takeuchi Rizô 竹内理三 and Kawazoe Shôji 川添昭二. 17 vols. to date. Dazaifu 大宰府: Dazaifu Tenmangû 太宰府天満宮, 1964–.

Denshi kashū 田氏家集, vol. 2 巻中. In *GR*, vol. 6, pp. 347–352.

Eisei hiyōshō 衛生秘要抄. By Tanba Yukinaga 丹波行長. In *ZGR*, vol. 31.1, pp. 205–218.

Entsū Daiō Kokushi goroku 円通大応国師語録. By Nanpo Jōmin 南蒲紹明. In *T.* 80, no. 2548, pp. 94-128.

Fukudenpō 福田方. By Yūrin 有林. Kagaku Shoin 科学書院, 1986.

Geihan tsûshi 藝藩通史. Comp. Rai Gyôhyô 頼香坪. Hiroshima 広島: Hiroshima Toshokan 広島図書館, 1908.

Genkō shakusho 元亨釈書. By Kokan Shiren 虎関師練. In *SZKT*, vol. 31; *DNBZ*, vol. 101.

Gikeiki 義経記. Ed. Okami Masao 岡見正雄. In *NKBT*, vol. 37. Trans. Helen Craig McCullough as *Yoshitsune: A Fifteenth Century Japanese Chronicle*. Stanford: Stanford University Press, 1966.

Gôdanshô chû 江談抄注. Ed. Kawaguchi Hisao 川口久雄 and Nara Shôichi 奈良正一. Benseisha 勉誠社, 1984.

Gozan bungaku shinshū 五山文学新集 (*GBSS*). Ed. Tamamura Takeji 玉村竹二. 6 vols. plus 2 vols. Tōkyō Daigaku Shuppankai 東京大学出版会, 1967–72.

Gozan bungaku shū 五山文学集. Ed. Iriya Yoshitaka 入矢義高. In *SNKBT*, vol. 48.

Gozan bungaku shū, Edo kanshi shū 五山文学集, 江戸漢詩集. Ed. Yamagishi Tokuhei 山岸徳平. In *NKBT*, vol. 89.

Gozan bungaku zenshū 五山文学全集 (*GBZS*). Ed. Uemura Kankō 上村観光. 4 vols. plus 1 vol. Kyoto 京都: Shibunkaku Shuppan 思文閣出版, 1973 reprint.

Gunsho ruijū (*GR*) 新校群書類従. Ed. Hanawa Hokinoichi 塙保己一. 24 vols. Naigai Shoseki Kabushiki Kaisha 内外書籍株式会社, 1931–37.

Gyokuyō 玉葉. By Kujō Kanezane 九条兼実. Ed. Kokusho Sōsho Kankōkai 国書叢書刊行会. 3 vols. Meicho Kankōkai 名著刊行会, 1993.

Hachiman gudōkin (kō otsu) 八幡愚童訓 (甲乙). In *Jisha engi* 寺社縁起, pp. 169–205, 207–273. Ed. Sakurai Tokutarō 桜井徳太郎 et al. In *NST*, vol. 20.

Hanazono tennō shinki 花園天皇宸記. By Hanazono tennō 花園天皇. 3 vols. In *ZHST*, vols. 1–3; *SS*, vols. 62, 66, 80.

Hanyang to 漢陽圖. In Hŏ Yŏnghwan 許英桓. *Chŏngdo 600 nyŏn Sŏul chido* 定道600년 서울地圖. Pŏmusa 汎友社, 1994.

Heiji monogatari 平治物語. Ed. Nagazumi Yasuaki 永積安明 and Shimada Isao 島田勇雄. In *NKBT*, vol. 31. Trans. E. O. Reischauer and Joseph Yamagiwa as "The *Heiji Monogatari*," in *Translations from Early Japanese Literature* (2nd edition, abridged), pp. 271–351. Cambridge: Harvard University Press, 1964.

Heike monogatari 平家物語. Trans. Hiroshi Kitagawa and Bruce Tsuchida as *The Tale of the Heike*. Tokyo: University of Tokyo Press, 1975; Helen Craig McCullough as *The Tale of the Heike*. Stanford: Stanford University Press, 1988.

Hejiju fang 和済局方. By Chen Shiwen 陳師文 et al. In *Kankoku zōkō Taihei Wazai Kyokuhō* 官刻増広太平和済局方. 2 vols. Ryōgen shoten 燎原書店, 1976; *Kunchū Wazai Kyokuhō* 訓注和済局方. Ed. Yoshitomi Hyōe 吉富兵衛. Yukari Shobō 縁書房, 1992.

Ho Ankei kazen shū 捕庵京華前集. By Ōsen Keisan 横川影三. In *GBSS*, vol. 1, pp. 201–310.

Hōgen monogatari 保元物語. Ed. Nagazumi Yasuaki 永積安明 and Shimada Isao 島田勇雄. In *NKBT*, vol. 31. Trans. William Wilson as *Hōgen Monogatari: Tale of the Disorder in Hōgen*. Tokyo: Monumenta Nipponica, 1966.

Honchō kōsō den 本朝高僧伝. In *DNBZ*, vol. 103.

Honzō wamyō 本草和名. (Alt. *Wamyō honzō*; *Sukebito honzō, Honin honzō* 輔仁本草). By Fukane Sukebito 深根輔仁. In *ZGR*, vol. 30.2, pp. 371–434.

Hyakurenshō 百錬抄. In *SZKT*, vol. 14.

Ikai gojō 遺戒五条. In *Kamakura shishi 2, shaji hen* 鎌倉市史 2 社寺編. Ed. Kamakura Shishi Hensan Iinkai 鎌倉市史編纂委員会. Yoshikawa Kōbunkan 吉川弘文館, 1959.

Ippanfū 一帆風. In *Shijiku shūsei* 詩軸集成, pp. 925–930; *GBSS, bekkan* 別巻 1, pp. 921–1120.

Ishinpō 医心方. By Tanba Yasuyori 丹波康頼. *Ishinpō: Nihon igaku sōsho katsujibon* 医心方日本医学叢書活字本. Osaka 大阪: Oriento Shuppansha オリエント出版社, 1991. Partial trans. Emil Hsia, Ilza Veith, and Robert Geertsma as *The Essentials of Medicine in Ancient China and Japan: Yasuyori Tanba's Ishinpō*. Leiden: E.J. Brill, 1986; Howard Levy and Ishihara Akira as *The Tao of Sex: An Annotated Translation of the Twenty-eighth Section of the Essence of Medical Prescriptions (Ishinpō)*. Yokohama: Shibundō, 1968.

Jisha engi 寺社縁起. Ed. Sakurai Tokutarō 桜井徳太郎 et al. In *NST*, vol. 20.

Kaksa sugyo 各司受敎. Ch'ŏngnyŏnsa 청년사, 2002.

Kamakura ibun komonjo hen (KI) 鎌倉遺文古文書編. Ed. and comp. Takeuchi Rizō 竹内理三. 42 vols. plus 4 vols. Tōkyōdō Shuppan 東京堂出版, 1971–96.

Kanke bunsō 菅家文草. In *Kanke bunsō, Kanke goshū* 菅家文草, 菅家後集. Ed. Yamaguchi Hisao 山口久雄. In *NKBT*, vol. 72.

Kenchōji kishiki 建長寺規式. In *Kamakura shishi 2, shaji hen* 鎌倉市史 2, 社寺編. Ed. Kamakura Shishi Hensan Iinkai 鎌倉市史編纂委員会. Yoshikawa Kōbunkan 吉川弘文館, 1959.

Kim Chongjik 金宗直. *Chŏmp'ilche chip* 佔畢齊集. In *Hanguk munjip ch'onggan* 12 韓國文集叢刊 12. Minjok Munhwa Ch'ujinhoe 民族文化推進會, 1988.

Kinsō ryōjishō 金創療治抄. Anonymous manuscript (originally compiled in the fourteenth century) held in the Sōda Collection. See *Sōda bunko mokuroku shoseki hen* 宗田文庫目録書籍篇. Ed. Kokusai Nihon Bunka Kenkyū Sentā

Sōda Bunko Mokuroku Henshū Iinkai 国際日本文化研究センター 宗田文庫目録編集委員会. Kyoto 京都: Kokusai Nihon Bunka Kenkyū Sentā 国際日本文化研究センター, 2001.

Kissa ōrai 喫茶往来. In *GR*, vol. 15, pp. 912–915.

Kissa yōjōki 喫茶養生記. By Myōan Eisai 明庵栄西. In *GR*, vol. 15, pp. 899–911. See also Furuta Shōkin 古田紹欽, ed. and trans. *Eisai Kissa yōjōki* 栄西喫茶養生記. Kōdansha 講談社, 2000.

Kiyomizudera engi 清水寺縁起. In *Zoku zoku Nihon emaki taisei, denki engi hen* 続々日本絵巻大成伝記縁起編, vol. 5. Chûô Kôronsha 中央公論社, 1994.

Kōjishō 香字抄. By Ken'i 兼意. In *ZGR*, vol. 30.2, pp. 467–540; Koizumi Enjun 古泉圓順 ed., *Kyōu* 杏雨, 10 (2007), pp. 2–95.

Kokon chomonjū 古今著聞集. By Tachibana Narisue 橘成季. Ed. Nagazumi Yasuaki 永積安明 and Shimada Isao 島田勇雄. In *NKBT*, vol. 84.

Kōra Tamataregū goengi 高良玉垂宮御縁起. In Kikutake Jun'ichi 菊竹淳一. "Kyūshū no engie 九州の縁起絵." *Bukkyō geijutsu* 仏教芸術 76 (1970.7): pp. 57–80.

Kōyakushō 香薬抄. By Ken'i 兼意. In *ZGR*, vol. 31.1, pp. 57–111.

Kōyōshō 香要抄. By Ken'i 兼意. In *ZGR*, vol. 31.1, pp. 1–56; Koizumi Enjun 古泉圓順 ed., *Kyōu* 杏雨, 11 (2008), pp. 109–246.

Kundaikan sōchōki 君台観左右帳記. Ed. Akai Tatsurō 赤井達郎 and Murai Yasuhiko 村井康彦. In *Kodai chūsei geijutsu ron* 古代中世芸術論, pp. 423–445. Ed. Hayashiya Tatsusaburō 林家辰三郎. In *NST*, vol. 23.

Kungnip Kyŏngju Pangmulgwan 국립경주박물관. T'ongch'ŏn Munhwasa 통천문화사, 1984.

Kyŏngguk taejŏn (KT) 經國大典. Asea Munhwasa 亞細亞文化社, 1983.

Lingnan weisheng fang 嶺南衛生方. By Jihong 継洪. Zhongyi Guji Chubanshe 中医古籍出版社, 1983.

Man'anpō 万安方. By Kajiwara Shōzen 梶原性全. Kagaku Shoin 科学書院, 1986.

Midō kanpakuki 御堂関白記. By Fujiwara Michinaga 藤原道長. 3 vols. In *DNKR*.

Mōko shūrai ekotoba 蒙古襲来絵詞. In *NET*, vol. 14; *Nihon emakimono zenshū* 日本絵巻物全集, vol. 9, *Heiji monogatari emaki, Mōko shūrai ekotoba* 平治物語絵巻, 蒙古襲来絵詞. Kadokawa Shoten 角川書店, 1964. Trans. Thomas Conlan as *In Little Need of Divine Intervention*. Ithaca: East Asia Program Cornell University, 2001.

Muchū mondō shū 夢中問答集. By Musō Soseki 夢窓疎石. Ed. and trans. Kawase Kazuma 川瀬一馬. Kōdansha 講談社, 2000.

Munjong sillok 文宗實錄. In *CWS*.

Muromachi dono gyōkō goshokuki 室町殿行幸御餝記. In *Higashiyama gyobutsu* 東山御物. Ed. Nezu Bijutsukan 根津美術館 and Tokugawa Bijutsukan 徳川美術館, 1976.

Myōkaiki 妙槐記. By Kazan'in Morotsugu 花山院師継. In *ZHST*, vol. 33.

Myŏngjong sillok 明宗實錄. In *CWS*.

Nanbokuchō ibun, Kyūshū hen (*NBI-Ky*) 南北朝遺文九州編. Ed. and comp. Seno Seiichirō 瀬野精一郎. 7 vols. Tōkyōdō Shuppan 東京堂出版, 1985–92.

Nihon emaki taisei (*NET*) 日本絵巻大成. Ed. Komatsu Shigemi 小松茂美. 27 vols. Chūō Kōronsha 中央公論社, 1977.

Nihon koten bungaku taikei (*NKBT*) 日本古典文学大系. 100 vols. Iwanami Shoten 岩波書店, 1958–68.

Nihon sandai jitsuroku 日本三代実録. In *SZKT*, vol. 4.

Nihon shisō taikei (*NST*) 日本思想大系. 67 vols. Iwanami Shoten 岩波書店, 1970–82.

Noritoki kyōki 教言卿記. By Yamashina Noritoki 山科教言. In *SS*, vols. 10, 20, 38.

Ŏ Sukkwŏn 魚叔權. *Kosa ch'waryo* 攷事撮要. Nammungak 南文閣, 1974.

Riben kao 日本考. By Li Yangong 李言恭. In *Shinshū yakuchū Nihon kō* 新修訳注日本考. Ed. and trans. Watanabe Mitsuo 渡辺三男. Shintensha 新典社, 1985.

Sakeiki 左経記. By Fujiwara Yoritsune 藤原頼経. In *ZHST*, vol. 6.

Sankaiki 山槐記. By Nakayama Tadachika 中山忠親. In *ZHST*, vols. 26–28.

San Tendai godaisanki 参天台五台山記. By Jōjin 成尋. Ed. Takakusu Junjirō 高楠順次郎. In *DNBZ*, vol. 115.

Sappan kyûki zatsuroku, kôhen 薩藩旧記雑録後編. Ed. Kagoshima-ken Ishin Shiryô Hensanjo 鹿児島県維新史料編纂所. 6 vols. Kagoshima 鹿児島: Kagoshima-ken 鹿児島県, 1981-1986.

Sejo sillok 世祖實錄. In *CWS*.

Sejong sillok 世宗實錄. In *CWS*.

Sekiso ōrai 尺素往来. By Ichijō Kaneyoshi 一条兼良. In *GR*, vol. 6, pp. 602–616.

Shaken nichiroku 蔗軒日録. By Shaken 蔗軒. In *DNKR*.

Shasekishū 沙石集. By Mujū Ichien 無住一円. Ed. Watanabe Tsunaya 渡邊綱也. In *NKBT*, vol. 85. Trans. Robert J. Morrell as *Tales of Sand and Pebbles*. Albany: State University of New York Press, 1985.

Shikaumi jinja engi 志賀海神社縁起. Owned by Shikaumi jinja 志賀海神社所蔵, held at Fukuoka Shiritsu Hakubutsukan 福岡市立博物館.

Shimada monjo 島田文書. Held at Kyōto Daigaku Bungakubu 京都大学文学部所蔵.

Shin Nihon koten bungaku taikei (*SNKBT*) 新日本古典文学大系. Ed. Satake Akihiro 佐竹昭広 *et al.* 100 vols. Iwanami Shoten 岩波書店, 1989–2005.

Shinsarugaku ki 新猿楽記. By Fujiwara Akihira 藤原明衡. In *Kodai seiji shakai shisō* 古代政治社会思想, pp. 134–152. Ed. Yamagishi Tokuhei 山岸徳平 et al., *NST*, vol. 8.

Shintei zōho kokushi taikei (*SZKT*) 新訂増補国史大系. Ed. Kuroita Katsumi 黒板勝美. 60 vols. Yoshikawa Kōbunkan 吉川弘文館, 1964–67.

Shiryō sanshū kokiroku hen (*SS*) 史料纂集古記録編. Zoku Gunsho Ruijū Kanseikai 続群書類従完成会, 1967–.

Shōichi Kokushi nenpu 聖一国師年譜. By Enni Ben'en 円爾辯円. In *DNBZ*, vol. 73.

Shōkenkō 蕉堅藁. By Zekkai Chūshin 絶海中津. *Gozan bungaku shū* 五山文学集 qv, pp. 1–194; *Shōkenkō zenchū* 蕉堅藁全注. Ed. Kageki Hideo 蔭木英雄. Osaka 大阪: Seibundō 清文堂, 1998.

Shotoshū 初渡集. By Sakugen Shuryō 策彦周良. In *DNBZ*, vol. 116.

Shōyūki 小右記. By Fujiwara Sanesuke 藤原実資. In *DNKR*.

Shujing 書経. In *The Chinese Classics*. Vol. 3, *The Shoo King or Book of Historical Documents*. Trans. James Legge. Taipei: SMC Publishing, 1991 reprint.

Shūkoroku 集古録. Manuscript held at Tōfukuji Reiun'in 東福寺霊雲院蔵.

Sin Sukchu, ed. 申叔舟撰. *Haedong chegukki* 海東諸國紀. Keijō 京城: Chōsen Sōtokufu 朝鮮総督府, 1933.

Sinjŭng Tongguk yŏji sŭngnam 新增東國與地勝覽. Myŏngmundang 明文堂, 1959.

Song Hŭigyŏng 宋希璟. *Nosongdang Ilbon haengnok* 老松堂日本行録. In *Rōshōdō Nihon kōroku: Chōsen shisetsu no mita chūsei Nihon* 老松堂日本行録朝鮮使節の見た中世日本. Ed. and trans. Murai Shōsuke 村井章介. Iwanami Shoten 岩波書店, 1987.

Songben lidai dili zhizhang tu 宋本歷代地理指掌図. Ed. Tan Qixiang 譚其驤 and Cao Wanru 曹婉如. Shanghai 上海: Shanghai Guji Chubanshe 上海古籍出版社, 1989.

Sŏngjong sillok 成宗實錄. In *CWS*.

Sŏnjo sillok 宣祖實錄. In *CWS*.

Sonpi bunmyaku 尊卑分脈. By Tōin Kinsada 洞院公貞. 4 vols. plus one vol. In *SZKT*, vols. 58–60, supplementary vol. 別巻 2.

Taejŏn songnok 大典續錄. In *Taejŏn songnok, Hu songnok* 大典續錄·後續錄. Asea Munhwasa 亞細亞文化社, 1983.

T'aejong sillok 太宗實錄. In *CWS*.

Taiheiki 太平記. In *NKBT*, vols. 34–36. Ed. Gotō Tanji 後藤丹治 and Kamata Kisaburō 釜田喜三郎. Partial trans. Helen Craig McCullough as *The Taiheiki: A Chronicle of Medieval Japan*. New York: Columbia University Press, 1959.

Taiki 台記. By Fujiwara Yorinaga 藤原頼長. In *ZHST*, vols. 23–25.

Taikō sama gunki no uchi 太閤さま軍記のうち. In *Taikō shiryōshū* 太閤史料集. (Vol. 1 of *Sengoku shiryō sōsho* 戦国史料叢書.) Ed. Kuwata Tadachika 桑田忠親. Jinbutsu Ōraisha 人物往来社, 1965.

Taiping shenghui fang 太平聖恵方. In Tōyō igaku zenpon sōsho 東洋医学善本叢書. Ōsaka 大阪: Oriento Shuppansha オリエント出版社, 1994.

Taishokan 大職冠. In *Mai no hon* 舞の本, pp. 15–42. Ed. Asahara Yoshiko 麻原美子 and Kitahara Yasuo 北原保雄. In *SNKBT*, vol. 59.

Taishō shinshū Daizōkyō (T) 大正新脩大藏經. Ed. Takakusu Junjirō 高楠順次郎 and Watanabe Kaigyoku 渡邊海旭. 85 vols. Taishō Shinshū Daizōkyō Kankōkai 大正新脩大蔵経刊行会, 1924–35.

Taketori monogatari 竹取物語. Ed. Sakakura Atsuyoshi 阪倉篤義. In *Taketori monogatari, Ise monogatari, Yamato monogatari* 竹取物語, 伊勢物語, 大和物語. In *NKBT*, vol. 9. Trans. Donald Keene as *The Tale of the Bamboo Cutter*. Tokyo: Kodansha International, 1998.

Tekkinshō 擲金抄. Ed. Abe Yasurō 阿部泰郎, Yamazaki Makoto 山崎誠 et al. Vol. 11 of *Shinpukuji zenpon sōkan* 真福寺善本叢刊. Kyōto 京都: Rinsen Shoten 臨川書店, 1998.

Tendai kahyō 天台霞標. In *DNBZ*, vol. 125.

Tenjin engi emaki, Hachiman engi, Amawakahiko zōshi, Nezumi zōshi, Bakemono zōshi, Utatane zōshi 天神縁起絵巻, 八幡縁起, 天稚彦草紙, 鼠草紙, 化物草紙, うたたね草紙. In *Kadokawa shinshū Nihon emakimono zenshū, bekkan 2* 角川新修日本絵巻物全集別巻 2. Kadokawa Shoten 角川書店, 1981.

T'ongmungwan chi 通文館志. Minch'ang Munhwasa 民昌文化社, 1989.

Tongnae-bu ŭpchi 東萊府邑志. In *Tongnae saryo*, vol. 3 東萊史料 3. Yŏgang Ch'ulp'ansa 麗江出版社, 1989.

Ton'ishô 頓医抄. By Kajiwara Shôzen 梶原性全. Kagaku Shoin 科学書院, 1986; Naikaku Bunko microfilm hard copy held at Kitasato Kenkyûjo Tôyô Igaku Sôgô Kenkyûjo Ishigakubu 北里研究所東洋医学総合研究所医史学部所蔵.

To sŏnsaeng an 道先生案. In *Kyŏngju sŏnsaeng an: Ojong* 慶州先生案 – 五種. Asea Munhwasa 亞細亞文化社, 1982.

Tsūken nyūdō zōsho mokuroku 通憲入道蔵書目録. In *GR*, vol. 21, pp. 545–554.

Tsurezuregusa 徒然草. By Yoshida Kenkō 吉田兼好. In *Hōjōki Tsurezuregusa* 方丈記, 徒然草. Ed. Nishio Minoru 西尾実. In *NKBT*, vol. 30. Trans. Donald Keene as *Essays in Idleness: The Tsurezuregusa of Kenkō*. New York: Columbia University Press, 1967.

Ukaikishō 宇槐記抄. By Sanjōnishi Kin'eda 三条西公条. In *ZHST*, vol. 25.

Unmon ikkyoku 雲門一曲. Manuscript held at Tokyo Daigaku Shiryō Hensanjo 東京大学史料編纂所所蔵写本.

Usa jingūshi shiryōhen 宇佐神宮史史料編. Ed. Nakano Hatayoshi 中野幡能. 14 vols. to date. Usa 宇佐: Usa Jinguchō 宇佐神宮庁, 1984–.

Weishi jiacang fang 魏氏家蔵方. By Wei Xian 魏峴. Microfilm copy held at Kitasato Kenkyûjo Tôyô Igaku Sôgô Kenkyûjo Ishigakubu 北里研究所東洋医学総合研究所医史学部所蔵; *Beijing Daxue Tushuguan Guancang Shanben Yishu, 7, Weishi jiacang fang* 北京大学図書館館蔵善本医書, 7, 魏氏家蔵方. Zhongguo Guji Chubanshe 中国古籍出版社, 1987.

Xin Tangshu 新唐書. 20 vols. Zhonghua Shuju 中華書局, 1975.

Yakushushō 薬種抄. By Ken'i 兼意. In *Tenri toshokan zenpon sōsho Washo no bu 31* 天理図書館善本叢書和書の部 31. Yagi Shoten 八木書店, 1977; *T.* (*zuzō* 図像) 11, pp. 177–230.

Yi Ŏnjŏk 李彦迪. *Hoejae sŏnsaeng pyŏlchip* 晦齋先生別集. In *Hoejae chŏnsŏ* 晦濟全書. Sŏnggyungwan Taehakkyo Taedong Munhwa Yŏnguso 成均館大學校大東文化研究所, 1973.

Yi Sŏm 李詹. "*Pak P'ansa Ilbon haengnok* pal" 朴判事日本行録跋. *Tongmunsŏn* 東文選 4. In *Hanguk hansi munsŏn chip* 韓國漢詩文選集 4. Kyŏngwŏn Munhwasa 慶苑文化社, 1992.

Yŏngga chi 永嘉誌. In *Chosŏn sidae sach'an ŭpchi 18, Kyŏngsang-do 3* 朝鮮時代 私撰邑誌 18: 慶尙道 3. Hanguk Inmun Kwahagwŏn 韓國人文科學院, 1989.

Yŏnsangun ilgi 燕山君日記. In *CWS*.

Youyou xinshu 幼幼新書. By Liu Fang 劉昉 et al. Renmin Weisheng Chubanshe 人民衛生出版社, 1987.

Yuriwaka daijin 百合若大臣. In *Mai no hon* 舞の本, pp. 43–69. Ed. Asahara Yoshiko 麻原美子 and Kitahara Yasuo 北原保雄. In *SNKBT*, vol. 59.

Yūzanroku ge 友山録,下. By Yūzan Shisai 友山士偲. In *GBSS*, vol. 2, pp. 99–162.

Zekkai oshō goroku 絶海和尙語録. By Zekkai Chūshin 絶海中津. In *T.* 80, no. 2561, pp. 731–760.

Zōho shiryō taisei (*ZHST*) 増補史料大成. Rev. and enlarged ed. 99 vols. Kyoto 京都: Rinsen Shoten 臨川書店, 1965.

Zoku gunsho ruijū (*ZGR*) 続群書類従. Ed. Hanawa Hokinoichi 塙保己一 and Ōta Tōshirō 大田藤四郎. 34 vols. Zoku Gunsho Ruijū Kanseikai 続群書類従完成会, 1929–33.

Zoku kojidan chūkai 続古事談注解. Ed. Kōbe Setsuwa Kenkyūkai 神戸説話研究会. Osaka 大阪: Izumi Shoin 泉書院, 1994.

Bibliography of Secondary Sources

Abe Ryūichi 阿部隆一. "Kanseki 漢籍." In Vol. 3 of *Abe Ryūichi ikōshū* 阿部隆一遺稿集, pp. 1–75. Kyūko Shoin 汲古書院, 1985.

Abe Yasurō 阿部泰郎. "Hachiman engi to chūsei *Nihongi* 八幡縁起と中世日本紀." *Gendai shisō* 現代思想 20.4 (1992.4), pp. 76–87.

Adolphson, Mikael, Edward Kamens, and Stacie Matsumoto, eds. *Heian Japan: Centers and Peripheries*. Honolulu: University of Hawai'i Press, 2006.

Ahn Hwi-joon. "Two Korean Landscape Paintings of the First Half of the Sixteenth Century." *Korea Journal* 15.2 (February 1975), pp. 31–41.

———. "Korean Landscape Painting of the Early and Middle Chosŏn Period." *Korea Journal*, 27.3 (March 1987), pp. 4–17.

Ames, Roger T. and Henry Rosemont, Jr. *The Analects of Confucius, A Philosophical Translation*. New York: Ballantine Books, 1998

An Hwijun 安輝濬. *Hanguk hoehwa ŭi chŏnt'ong* 韓國繪畫의 傳統. Munye Ch'ulp'ansa 文藝出版社, 1988.

Aoyama Sadao 青山定雄. "Ritsukyokuan shozō no *Yochizu* ni tsuite 栗棘庵所蔵の輿地圖 について." *Tōyō gakuhō* 東洋学報 37.4 (1955.3), pp. 49–77.

Asahina Yasuhiko 朝比奈康彦ed. *Shōsōin no yakubutsu* 正倉院の薬物. Osaka 大阪: Shokubutsu Bunken Hakkōkai 植物文献発行会, 1955.

Asami Ryūsuke 浅見龍介 et al. *Zen no genryū* 禅の源流. Exhibition catalogue, Tokyo Kokuritsu Hakubutsukan 東京国立博物館, 2003.

Batten, Bruce. *Gateway to Japan: Hakata in War and Peace, 500–1300*. Honolulu: University of Hawai'i Press, 2006.

Beal, Samuel. *Si-Yu-Ki: Buddhist Records of the Western Worlds, Translated from the Chinese of Hiuen Tsiang (AD 639)*. London: Kegan Paul, Trench, Trubner, 1884.

Berry, Mary Elizabeth. *The Culture of Civil War in Kyoto*. Berkeley: University of California Press, 1994.

Bielefeldt, Carl. "Kokan Shiren and the Sectarian Uses of History." In *The Origins of Japan's Medieval World: Courtiers, Clerics, Warriors, and Peasants in the Fourteenth Century*, pp. 295–317. Ed. Jeffrey P. Mass. Stanford: Stanford University Press, 1997.

Bol, Peter K. *"This Culture of Ours": Intellectual Transitions in T'ang and Sung China*. Stanford: Stanford University Press, 1992.

Borgen, Robert. "Jōjin's Travels from Center to Center (with Some Periphery in Between)." In *Heian Japan: Centers and Peripheries*, pp. 384–413. Ed. Mikael Adolphson, Edward Kamens, and Stacie Matsumoto. Honolulu: University of Hawai'i Press, 2006.

————. "Monkish Diplomacy: A Case Study in Eleventh-Century Sino-Japanese Relations." In *Contacts between Cultures: Selected Papers from the Thirty-third International Congress of Asian and North African Studies,* Vol. 4: *East Asian History and Social Sciences*, pp. 1–6. Edward Mellen Press, 1992.

————. *Sugawara no Michizane and the Early Heian Court*. Cambridge: Council on East Asian Studies, Harvard University, 1986.

————. "The Legend of Hanshan: A Neglected Source." *Journal of the American Oriental Society* 111.3 (July–September 1991); pp. 575–79.

Brinker, Helmut, and Hiroshi Kanazawa. *Zen: Masters of Meditation in Images and Writings*. Trans. Andreas Leisinger. Zurich: Artibus Asiae, 1996.

Chang Chiyŏng 장지영 and Chang Segyŏng 장세영, eds. *Idu sajŏn* 이두사전. Tosŏ Ch'ulp'an 도서출판, 1991.

Chen Jie 陳捷. "*Hakushi monjū no Sōhan shohon ni tsuite* 白氏文集の宋版諸本について" Trans. Wada Kōhei 和田浩平. In Hakushi monjū *no honbun* 白氏文集の本文, pp. 92–117. Vol. 6 of *Haku Kyoi kenkyū kōza* 白居易研究講座. Ed. Ōta Tsugio 太田次男 et al. Benseisha 勉誠社, 1995.

Chen Jie 陳捷 and Kosoto Hiroshi 小曽戸洋. "Hokusō kankoku isho no minkan e no ryūtsū 北宋官刻医書の民間への流通." *Nihon ishigaku zasshi* 日本医史学雑誌 43.3 (1997.9), pp. 54–55.

Cherniack, Susan. "Book Culture and Textual Transmission in Sung China." *Harvard Journal of Asiatic Studies* 54.1 (June 1994), pp. 5–125.

Chia, Lucille. "Mashaben: Commercial Publishing in Jianyang from the Song to the Ming." In *The Song-Yuan-Ming Transition in Chinese History*, pp. 284–328. Ed. Paul Jakov Smith and Richard von Glahn. Cambridge: Harvard University Asia Center, 2003.

————. *Printing for Profit: The Commercial Publishers of Jianyang, Fujian (11th–17th Centuries)*. Cambridge: Harvard University Asia Center for the Harvard-Yenching Institute, 2002.

Chibbett, David. *The History of Japanese Printing and Book Illustration*. Tokyo: Kodansha International, 1971.

Chikushi Yutaka 筑紫豊 and Nakano Hatayoshi 中野幡能, eds. *Shintō taikei jinja hen* 神道大系神社編, Vol. 44: *Chikuzen, Chikugo, Buzen, Bungo no Kuni* 筑前, 筑後, 豊前, 豊後国. Shintō Taikei Hensankai 神道体系編纂会, 1982.

Cho Pyŏngno 趙炳魯. "Chosŏn chŏngi yŏngno chŏngbi wa yŏngma kakpo 朝鮮前期 驛路整備와 驛馬 各保." In *Sohŏn Nam Toyŏng paksa kohŭi kinyŏm yŏksahak nonch'ong* 素軒南都泳博士古稀紀念歷史學論叢, pp. 223–280. Ed. Sohŏn Nam Toyŏng Paksa Kohŭi Kinyŏm Yŏksahak Nonch'ong Kanhaeng Wiwŏnhoe 素軒南都泳博士古稀紀念 歷史學論叢刊行委員會 編. Minjok Munhwasa 民族文化社, 1993.

Ch'oe Wangi 최완기. "Kyot'ong-Unsu-T'ongsin: Toro ǔi chǒngbi; Yǒk-wǒnje ǔi chǒngbi; Susang kyot'ong kwa choun 교통·운수·통신 – 도로의 정비; 역-원제의 정비; 수상 교통과 주운." In *Hanguksa 24: Chosǒn ch'ogi ǔi kyǒngje kujo* 한국사24 조선초기의 경제구조, pp. 495–538. Kuksa P'yǒnch'an Wiwǒnhoe 국사편찬위원회, 1994.

Ch'oe, Yongho. "Precious Metals." In *Sourcebook of Korean Civilization. Vol. 1: From Early Times to the Sixteenth Century*. Ed. Peter H. Lee. New York: Columbia University Press, 1993.

Clark, Hugh R. *Community, Trade, and Networks: Southern Fujian Province from the Third to the Thirteenth Century*. Cambridge: Cambridge University Press, 1991.

Coates, Bruce. "The Architecture of Zen-Sect Buddhist Monasteries in Japan, 1200–1500." Doctoral diss. Harvard University, 1985.

Collcutt, Martin. *Five Mountains: The Rinzai Zen Monastic Institution in Medieval Japan*. Cambridge: Council on East Asian Studies, Harvard University, 1981.

———. "Musō Soseki." In *The Origins of Japan's Medieval World: Courtiers, Clerics, Warriors, and Peasants in the Fourteenth Century*, pp. 261–294. Ed. Jeffrey P. Mass. Stanford: Stanford University Press, 1997.

———. "'Nun Shogun': Politics and Religion in the Life of Hōjō Masako (1157–1225)." In *Engendering Faith: Women and Buddhism in Premodern Japan*, pp. 165–187. Ed. Barbara Ruch. Ann Arbor: Center for Japanese Studies, University of Michigan, 2002.

Conlan, Thomas. *In Little Need of Divine Intervention: Scrolls of the Mongol Invasions of Japan*. Ithaca: East Asia Program Cornell University, 2003.

Cort, Louise Allison. "Shopping for Pots in Momoyama Japan." In *Japanese Tea Culture: Art, History, and Practice*, pp. 61–85. Ed. Morgan Pitelka. London: RoutledgeCurzon, 2003.

Daihonzan Kenchōji 大本山建長寺, ed. *Kyofukuzan Kenchōji* 巨福山建長寺. Kamakura 鎌倉: Daihonzan Kenchōji 大本山建長寺, 1977.

Drège, Jan-Pierre. "La lecture et l'écriture en Chine et la xylographie." *Études chinoises* 10.1–2 (1991), pp. 77–111.

Dumoulin, Heinrich. *Zen Buddhism: A History: Japan*. New York: Macmillan, 1990.

Dunn, Ross E. *The Adventures of Ibn Battuta, a Muslim Traveller of the Fourteenth Century*. Berkeley: University of California Press, 1986.

Ebine Toshio 海老根聰郎. "Kaizō-in zō Kokan Shiren zō 海蔵院蔵虎関師練像." *Kokka* 國華 1218 (1997), pp. 24–29.

———. 海老根聰郎. "Neiha [Ningbo] no bunjin to Nihonjin: jūgo seiki ni okeru 寧波の文人と日本人－十五世紀における." *Tōkyō Kokuritsu Hakubutsukan kiyō* 東京国立博物館紀要 11 (1975), pp. 219–260.

Feng Xianming 馮先銘. "Shin'an kaitei chinbotsusen hikiage tōjiki ni kanren shita mondai ni taisuru kentō 新安海底沈没船引き上げ陶磁器に関連した問題に対する検討." In *Kokusai shinpojiumu Shin'an kaitei hikiage bunbutsu hōkokusho* 国際シンポジウム新安海底引き上げ文物報告書, pp. 27–32. Nagoya 名古屋: Chūnichi Shinbunsha 中日新聞社, 1984.

Fontein, Jan, ed. *Zen Painting and Calligraphy.* Exhibition catalogue, Boston Museum of Fine Arts, 1970.

Fujita Motoharu 藤田元春. *Nisshi kōtsūshi no kenkyū: Chū-kinsei hen* 日支交通史の研究:中近世篇. Fuzanbō 富山房, 1938.

Fujiwara Shigeo 藤原重雄. "Chin Uirō kankei shiryōshū (kō), kaidai: Kyōto Chin Uirō o chūshin ni 陳外郎関係史料集稿, 解題—京都陳外郎を中心に." *Tokyo Daigaku Nihon Shigaku Kenkyūshitsu Kiyō* 東京大学日本史学研究室紀要 2 (March 1998), pp. 29–82.

Fujiyoshi Masumi 藤善眞澄. *San Tendai godaisanki no Kenkyū* 参天台五臺山記の研究. Suita 吹田: Kansai Daigaku Shuppanbu 関西大学出版部, 2006.

———. 藤善眞澄, trans. *San Tendai godaisanki, Jō* 参天台五臺山記,上. Suita 吹田: Kansai Daigaku Shuppanbu 関西大学出版部, 2007.

Fukushima Kaneharu 福島金治. *Kanazawa Hōjōshi to Shōmyōji* 金沢北条氏と称名寺. Yoshikawa Kōbunkan 吉川弘文館, 1997.

Fukushima Tsunenori 福島恒徳. "*Shikaumi jinja engi*-kō 志賀海神社縁起考." *Dearute* デアルテ 5 (1989), pp. 103–125.

Furth, Charlotte. *A Flourishing Yin: Gender in China's Medical History, 960–1665.* Berkeley: University of California Press, 1999.

Geddes, Ward. *Kara Monogatari: Tales of China.* Tempe: Center for Asian Studies, Arizona State University, 1984.

Gibb, H. A. R., trans. *The Travels of Ibn Battūta* 5 vols. Cambridge: Hakluyt Society, 1958–99.

Giles, Herbert A. *The Travels of Fa-hsien (399–414 AD).* London: Routledge and Kegan Paul, 1959.

Goble, Andrew Edmund. "Medicine and New Knowledge in Medieval Japan: Kajiwara Shōzen (1266–1337) and the *Man'anpō*." *Nihon ishigaku zasshi* 47.1 (2001.3), pp. 226–192 (part 1); 47.2 (2001.6), pp. 452–432 (part 2).

———. "Medieval Japan." In *A Companion to Japanese History*, pp. 47–66. Ed. William M. Tsutsui. Oxford: Blackwell, 2007.

———. "Social Change, Knowledge, and History: Hanazono's *Admonitions to the Crown Prince*." *Harvard Journal of Asiatic Studies* 55.1 (June 1995), pp. 61–128.

———. "War and Injury: The Development of Wound Medicine in Medieval Japan." *Monumenta Nipponica* 60.3 (Autumn 2005), pp. 297–338.

Goldschmidt, Asaf Moshe. "The Transformation of Chinese Medicine During the Northern Song Dynasty (A.D. 960–1127): The Integration of Three Past Medical Approaches into a Comprehensive Medical System Following a Wave of Epidemics." Doctoral diss., University of Pennsylvania, 1999.

Gomi Fumihiko 五味文彦. "Inseiki no sei to seiji, buryoku 院政期の性と政治,武力." *Bungaku* 文学 6.1 (Winter 1995), pp. 32–39.

Graham, Patricia J. "*Karamono* for *sencha*." In *Japanese Tea Culture: Art, History, and Practice*, pp. 110–136. Ed. Morgan Pitelka. London: RoutledgeCurzon, 2003.

Gu Wenbi 顧文璧 and Lin Shimin 林士民. "Neiha [Ningbo] ni genzon suru Nihon koku Dazaifu Hakata tsū no kakyō kokuseki no kenkyū 寧波に現存する日本国大宰府博多津の華僑刻石の研究." *Kaijishi kenkyū* 海事史研究 43 (1986.6), pp. 101–112.

Guo Xiumei 郭秀梅, Kosoto Hiroshi 小曽戸洋, and Okada Kenkichi 岡田研吉. "*Wan'anfang* yin zhongguo yishu guankai 万安方引中国医書管窺." *Journal of Chinese Medicine* 9.3 (1998), pp. 127–135.

Guy, John. "Tamil Merchant Guilds and the Quanzhou Trade." In *The Emporium of the World: Maritime Quanzhou, 1000–1400*, pp. 283–308. Ed. Angela Schottenhammer. Leiden: Brill, 2001.

Hall, John Whitney. *Government and Local Power in Japan, 500–1700: A Study Based on Bizen Province*. Princeton: Princeton University Press, 1966.

Hanabusa Hideki 花房英樹. "Sōbon *Hakushi monjū* ni tsuite 宋本白氏文集につ いて." In *Kanda hakase kanreki kinen: Shoshigaku ronshū* 神田博士還暦記 念: 書誌学論集, pp. 481–490. Ed. Kanda Hakase Kanreki Kinenkai 神田博 士還暦記念会. Heibonsha 平凡社, 1957.

Hanguk Munhwajae Kwalliguk 韓國文化財管理局編, ed. *Sinan haejo yumul chonghapp'yŏn* 新安海底遺物綜合編. Hanguk Munhwa Kongbobu Munhwajae Kwalliguk 韓國文化公報部文化財管理局, 1988.

Hasebe Gakuji 長谷部楽爾 and Imai Atsushi 今井敦. *Nihon shutsudo no Chūgoku tōji* 日本出土の中国陶磁. Heibonsha 平凡社, 1995.

Hashimoto Yoshihiko 橋本義彦. *Fujiwara no Yorinaga* 藤原頼長. Yoshikawa Kōbunkan 吉川弘文館, 1964.

Hattori Toshirō 服部敏郎. *Muromachi jidai igakushi no kenkyū* 室町時代医学史 の研究. Yoshikawa Kōbunkan 吉川弘文館, 1971.

Hayakawa Mitsusaburō 早川光三郎. "*Mōgyū* kaisetsu 蒙求解説." In vol. 1 of *Mōgyū* 蒙求. Meiji Shoin 明治書院, 1973.

Hayakawa Shōhachi 早川庄八. *Shoku Nihongi* 続日本紀. Iwanami Shoten 岩波 書店, 1993.

He, Li. *Chinese Ceramics: A New Comprehensive Survey*. New York: Rizzoli, 1996.

Hiroyama Hidenori 広山秀則. "Shōchūban *Kanzan shishū* ni tsuite 正中版寒山詩集について." *Ōtani gakuhō* 大谷学報 41.2 (1961), pp. 39–58.

Holyoak, Keith, and Paul Thagard. *Mental Leaps: Analogy in Creative Thought.* Cambridge: MIT Press, 1995.

Horton, H. Mack. *The Journal of Sōchō.* Stanford: Stanford University Press, 2002.

Hirth, Frederick, and W. W. Rockhill, trans. *Chau Ju-Kua: His Work on the Chinese and Arab Trade in the Twelfth and Thirteenth Centuries Entitled Chu-fan-chï.* Saint Petersburg, 1911; New York: Paragon Books reprint, 1966.

Hsia, Emil, Ilza Veith and Robert Geertsma. *Tanba Yasuyori: The Essentials of Medicine in Early Japan.* Leiden: E. J. Brill, 1986.

Hymes, Robert P. "Not Quite Gentlemen? Doctors in Sung and Yuan." *Chinese Science* 8 (1987), pp. 9–76.

Ibuki Atsushi 伊吹敦. *Zen no rekishi* 禅の歴史. Kyoto 京都: Hōzōkan 法蔵館, 2001.

Ichinose Yūichi 一ノ瀬雄一. "Nansō Rin'an no shoho ni kansuru ichi kōsatsu 南床臨安の書鋪に関する一考察." *Shisen* 史泉 63 (1986), pp. 1–22.

Ide Seinosuke 井出誠之輔. *Nihon no Sōgen butsuga* 日本の宋元仏画. *Nihon no bijutsu* 日本の美術 418 (March 2001), pp. 1-98.

————. "Sakuhin no kosei to aidentitii: Neiha butsuga to chiiki shakai 作品の個別性とアイデンティティー—寧波仏画と地域社会 ." *Ajia yūgaku* アジア遊学, 70 (2004.12), pp. 86–101.

Ii Haruki 伊井春樹. *Jōjin no nissō to sono shōgai* 成尋の入宋とその生涯. Yoshikawa Kōbunkan 吉川弘文館, 1996.

Imaizumi Yoshio 今泉淑夫. "Baigai san no Totō Tenjin zō 梅匡賛の渡唐天神像." In *Zen to Tenjin*, pp. 255–281. Ed. Imaizumi Yoshio 今泉淑夫 and Shimao Arata 島尾新. Yoshikawa Kobunkan 吉川弘文館, 2000.

Imatani Akira 今谷明. *Genchō Chūgoku tokōki: ryūgakusō Sesson Yūbai no suki na unmei* 元朝中国渡航記: 留学僧雪村友梅の数奇な運命. Takarajimasha 宝島社, 1994.

Inoue Mitsusada 井上光貞. "*Tōiki dentō mokuroku* yori mitaru Nara jidai sōryo no gakumon 東域伝灯目録より見たる奈良時代僧侶の学門." *Shigaku zasshi* 史学雑誌 57.3 (1948.3), pp. 27–48; and 57.4 (1948.4), pp. 23–45.

Iriya Sensuke 入谷仙介 and Matsumura Takashi 松村昂. "Kaisetsu 解説." In *Kanzan shi* 寒山詩, Vol. 13 of *Zen no goroku* 禅の語録. Chikuma Shobō 筑摩書房, 1970.

Ishihara Akira 石原明. "*Eisei hiyōshō* 衛生秘要抄." In *Gunsho kaidai* 群書解題, vol. 5, p. 288. Ed. Zoku Gunsho Ruijū Kanseikai 続群書類従完成会. Zoku Gunsho Ruijū Kanseikai 続群書類従完成会, 1960.

————. "*Honzō iroha shō* kaidai 本草色葉鈔解題." In *Honzō iroha shō* 本草色葉鈔. Ed. Ishihara Akira 石原明. Naikaku Bunko 内閣文庫, 1968.

Ishii Susumu 石井進. *Kamakurabito no koe o kiku* 鎌倉びとの声を聞く. Nihon Hōsō Shuppan Kyōkai 日本放送出版協会, 2000.

Ishimoda Shō 石母田正. "Shi to bankaku 詩と蕃客." In Ishimoda Shō, *Nihon kodai kokkaron* 日本古代国家論. Iwanami Shoten 岩波書店, 1973.

Itakura Masaaki 板倉聖哲. "Kankoku ni okeru Shōshō hakkei zu no juyō, tenkai 韓国における瀟湘八景図の受容, 展開." *Seikyū gakujutsu ronbunshū* 青丘学術論文集, 14 (1999.3), pp. 5–47.

Kamakura Shishi Hensan Iinkai 鎌倉市史編纂委員会, ed. *Kamakura shishi 2, shajihen* 鎌倉市史 2 社寺編. Yoshikawa Kōbunkan 吉川弘文館, 1959.

Kameda Tsutomu 亀田孜. "Tomofuchi Hachimansha no hakubyō engi 鞆淵八幡社の白描縁起." In *Bukkyō setsuwae no kenkyū* 仏教説話絵の研究, pp. 229–237. Ed. Kameda Tsutomu 亀田孜. Tōkyō Bijutsu 東京美術, 1979.

Kamei Meitoku 亀井明徳. *Nihon bōeki tōjishi no kenkyū* 日本貿易陶磁史の研究. Dōbōsha Shuppan 同朋舎出版, 1986.

Kanagawa Kenritsu Kanazawa Bunko 神奈川県立金沢文庫, ed. *Cha to Kanazawa Sadaaki* 茶と金沢貞顕. Yokohama 横浜: Kanagawa Kenritsu Kanazawa Bunko 神奈川県立金沢文庫, 2005.

Kawaguchi Hisao 川口久雄. *Heianchō Nihon kanbungakushi no kenkyū* 平安朝日本漢文学史の研究. 3 vols. Meiji Shoin 明治書院, [1959] 1988.

Kawase Kazuma 川瀬一馬. *Gozanban no kenkyū* 五山版の研究, vol. 1. Tokyo: Antiquarian Bookseller's Association of Japan, 1970.

———. *Zoku Nihon shoshigaku no kenkyū* 続日本書誌学の研究. Yūshōdō Shoten 雄松堂書店, 1980.

Kawazoe Shōji. "Japan and East Asia." In *The Cambridge History of Japan, vol. 3, Medieval Japan*, pp. 396–446. Ed. Kozo Yamamura. Cambridge: Cambridge University Press, 1990.

———. "Jōtenji no kaisō to Hakata gōshu Sha Kokumei [Xie Guoming]: Kamakura chūki no taigai kankei to Hakata 承天寺の開創と博多綱首謝国明─鎌倉中期の対外関係と博多." In *Hakata Jōtenji shi, hoi* 博多承天寺史補遺, pp. 1–41. Ed. Hirowata Masatoshi 広渡正利. Hakata 博多: Jōtenji 承天寺, 1990.

———. "Kamakura jidai no taigai kankei to bunbutsu no inyū 鎌倉時代の対外関係と文物の移入." In *Iwanami kōza Nihon rekishi* 岩波講座日本歴史 6 *chūsei* 中世 2, pp. 41–83. Iwanami Shoten 岩波書店, 1975.

———. "Kamakura makki no taigai kankei to Hakata: Shin'an chinbotsusen mokkan, Tōfukuji, Jōtenji 鎌倉末期の対外関係と博多─新安沈没船木簡, 東福寺, 承天寺." In *Kamakura jidai bunka denpa no kenkyū* 鎌倉時代文化伝播の研究, pp. 301–330. Ed. Ōsumi Kazuo 大隅和雄. Yoshikawa Kōbunkan 吉川弘文館, 1993.

————. "Mōko shūrai to chūsei bungaku 蒙古襲来と中世文学." *Nihon rekishi* 日本歴史 302 (1973.7), pp. 14–28.

Keene, Donald. *Essays in Idleness: The Tsurezuregusa of Kenkō*. New York: Columbia Univesity Press, 1967.

————. *Seeds in the Heart*. New York: Henry Holt, 1993.

————. *The Tale of the Bamboo Cutter*. Tokyo: Kodansha International, 1998.

Kelley, Liam C. *Beyond the Bronze Pillars: Envoy Poetry and the Sino-Vietnamese Relationship*. Honolulu: Association for Asian Studies and University of Hawai`i Press, 2005.

Kikutake Jun'ichi 菊竹淳一. "Kyūshū no *engie* 九州の縁起絵." *Bukkyō geijutsu* 仏教芸術 76 (1970.7), pp. 57–80.

Kitasato Kenkyūjo Fuzoku Tōyō Igaku Sōgō Kenkyūjo, ed. 北里研究所付属東洋医学総合研究所. *Shōhinhō, Kōtai daikei meidō* koshōhon zankan 小品方黄帝内経明堂古鈔本残巻. Kitasato Kenkyūjo 北里研究所, 1992.

Knechtges, David R. *Wen Xuan or Selections of Refined Literature*, vol. 1. Princeton: Princeton University Press, 1982.

Kobata Atsushi 小葉田淳. *Kingin bōekishi no kenkyū* 金銀貿易史の研究. Hōsei Daigaku Shuppankyoku 法政大学出版局, 1976.

————. *Nihon kōzanshi no kenkyū* 日本鉱山史の研究. Iwanami Shoten 岩波書店, 1969 reprint.

Komatsu Shigemi 小松茂美. *Heianchō denrai no* Hakushi monjū *to sanseki no kenkyū: Kenkyūhen* 平安朝伝来の白氏文集と三蹟の研究： 研究篇. Bokusui Shobō 墨水書房, 1965.

Kondō Seiseki 近藤清石. *Ōuchi shi jitsuroku* 大内氏実録. Ed. Misaka Keiji 三坂圭治. Tokuyama 徳山: Matsuno Shoten マツノ書店, 1974.

Kornicki, Peter. *The Book in Japan: A Cultural History from the Beginnings to the Nineteenth Century*. Leiden: Brill, 1998.

Kosoto Hiroshi 小曽戸洋. *Chūgoku igaku koten to Nihon* 中国医学古典と日本. Hanawa Shobō 塙書房, 1996.

————. "Gendai no iyakusho (1)–(6) 元代の医薬書." *Gendai tōyō igaku* 現代東洋医学 11.3 (1990.7), pp. 92–96; (2) 11.4 (1990.10), pp. 76–82; (3) 12.1 (1991.1), pp. 78–85; (4) 12.2 (1991.4), pp. 93–99; (5) 12.3 (1991.7), pp. 94–101; (6) 12.4 (1991.10), pp. 103–109.

————. "Hokusō jidai no iyakusho (sono 1) 北宋時代の医薬書その1. " *Gendai tōyō igaku* 現代東洋医学 8.3 (1987.7), pp. 83–91; (sono 2) 8.4 (1987.10), pp. 86–95.

————. "Kansu bon kara Sōgenban e: chūsei Nihon ni okeru Chūgoku isho juyō no yōsō 巻子本から宋元版へ—中世日本における中国医書受容の様相." *Nihon ishigaku zasshi* 日本医史学雑誌 44.4 (1998.12), pp. 451–480.

————. "Kindai no iyakusho (1)–(4) 金代の医薬書." *Gendai tōyō igaku* 現代東洋医学 (1) 10.3 (1989.7), pp. 101–107; (2) 10.4 (1989.10), pp. 105–112; (3) 11.1 (1990.1), pp. 108–113; (4) 11.2 (1990.4), pp. 99–105.

————. "Koisho dankan *Shinpukuji shozō reihon Kanzō-gan* tō hō kō 古医書断簡真福寺所蔵零本甘草丸等方考." In *Yakazu Dōmei sensei tainin kinen Tōyō igaku ronshū* 矢数道明先生退任記念東洋医学論集, pp. 179-189. Ed. Ōtsuka Yasuo 大塚恭男, Chŏng Chongchŏl 丁宗鉄, Kosoto Hiroshi 小曽戸洋, and Kunida Kinji 国田欣二. Kitasato Kenkyūjo Fuzoku Tōyō Igaku Sōgō Kenkyūjo 北里研究所付属東洋医学総合研究所, 1986.

————. "Nansō jidai no iyakusho (1)–(6) 南宋時代の医薬書." *Gendai tōyō igaku* 現代東洋医学 (1) 9.1 (1988.1), pp. 87–93; (2) 9.2 (1988.4), pp. 79–85; (3) 9.3 (1988.7), pp. 96–104; (4) 9.4 (1988.10), pp. 96–103; (5) 10.1 (1989.1), pp. 93–99; (6) 10.2 (1989.4), pp. 94–103.

————. "Sōban *Bikyū sōkōhō* (*Bizen sōkōhō*) no shoshi kenkyū 宋版備急総効方 (備全総効方)の書誌研究." *Kyōu* 杏雨 6 (2003), pp. 203–221.

————. "*Taihei keimin wazai kyoku hō* kaidai 2 太平恵民和剤局方解題2." In *Zōkō Taihei keimin wazai kyoku hō* 増広太平恵民和剤局方 (*Wakoku kanseki isho shūsei* 和刻漢籍医書集成, vol. 4). Ed. Kosoto Hiroshi 小曽戸洋 and Mayanagi Makoto 真柳誠. Osaka 大阪: Entapuraizu エンタプライズ, 1988.

Kuroda Hideo 黒田日出男. *Rekishi toshite no otogi zōshi* 歴史としての御伽草子. Perikansha ぺりかん社, 1996.

Kwon, Cheeyun Lilian. "The Ten Kings at the Seikadō Library." Doctoral diss., Princeton University 1999.

Kyōtofu Ishikai 京都府医史会編. *Kyōto no igakushi* 京都の医学史. Kyōto 京都: Shibunkaku Shuppan 思文閣出版, 1975.

Lambton, A. K. S. "The *Āthār wa ahyā'* of Rashīd al-Dīn Fadl Allāh Hamadānī and His Contribution as an Agronomist, Arboriculturalist, and Horticulturalist." In *The Mongol Empire and Its Legacy*, pp. 126–154. Ed. Reuven Amitai-Press and David O. Morgan. Leiden: Brill, 1999.

Latham, Ronald. *Marco Polo: The Travels*. London: Penguin, 1958.

Lau, D.C. *Confucius The Analects*. Harmondsworth, Middlesex: Penguin Books, 1979.

Lee Jang Moo. "The Divine Bell of King Sŏngdŏk." *Korea Journal* 39.4 (Winter 1999), pp. 270–283.

Lee Young-bae. "The Bell of Sangwonsa Temple." *Koreana* 14.4 (Winter 2000), pp. 81–82.

Legge, James. *A Record of Buddhistic Kingdoms*. New York: Dover, 1965.

————. *The Chinese Classics*, vol. 3, *The Shoo King or Book of Historical Documents*. Taipei: SMC Publishing Inc., 1991 (reprint).

————. *The Confucian Analects*. Taipei: SMC Publishing Inc., 1991 (reprint).

Leung, Angela Ki-che. "Medical Learning from the Song to the Ming." In *The Song-Yuan-Ming Transition in Chinese History*, pp. 374–398. Ed. Paul Jakov Smith and Richard von Glahn. Cambridge: Harvard University Asia Center, 2003.

Levey, Martin. *The* Medical Formulary *or* Aqrābādhīn *of Al-Kindi*. Madison: University of Wisconsin Press, 1966.

Li, Hui-Lin, trans. *Nan-fang ts'ao-mu chuang: A Fourth Century Flora of Southeast Asia*. Hong Kong: Chinese University Press, 1971.

Li, Rongxi, trans. *The Great Tang Record of the Western Regions*. Berkeley: Numata Center for Buddhist Translation and Research, 1996.

Liu Shukui 劉書奎. "*Youyou xinshu* yinyong yixue wenxian kao 幼幼新書引用医学文献考." *Zhonghua yishi zazhi* 中華医史雜誌 28.3 (1998), pp. 177–180.

Ludwig, Theodore M. "Before Rikyū: Religious and Aesthetic Influences in the Early History of the Tea Ceremony." *Monumenta Nipponica* 36.4 (Winter 1981), pp. 367–390.

Mair, Victor, ed. *The Columbia Anthology of Traditional Chinese Literature*. New York: Columbia University Press, 1994.

Mass, Jeffrey P. *The Development of Kamakura Rule, 1180–1250*. Stanford: Stanford University Press, 1979.

Matsuki Satoru 松木哲. "Chinsen wa kataru 沈船は語る." In *Ajia no naka no Nihonshi, III, kaijō no michi* アジアのなかの日本史, III, 海上の道, pp. 211–223. Ed. Arano Yasunori 荒野泰典, Ishii Masatoshi 石井正敏, and Murai Shōsuke 村井章介. Tōkyō Daigaku Shuppankai 東京大学出版会, 1992.

Matsuo Kenji 松尾剛次. *Nihon chūsei no Zen to Ritsu* 日本中世の禅と律. Yoshikawa Kōbunkan 吉川弘文館, 2003.

————. *Ninshō* 忍性. Minerubua shobō ミネルヴァ書房, 2004.

Mayanagi Makoto 真柳誠. "*Honzō iroha shō* shoin no igaku bunken 本草色葉鈔書引の医学文献." *Nihon ishigaku zasshi* 日本医史学雑誌 36.1 (1990.3), pp. 34–36.

McCullough, Helen Craig. *Yoshitsune: A Fifteenth Century Japanese Chronicle*. Stanford: Stanford University Press, 1966.

Minobe Shigekatsu 美野部重克. "Bunkaken to shite no sōbō 文化圏としての僧房." In *Henkakuki no bungaku* 1 変革期の文学 1. Vol. 4 of *Iwanami kōza Nihon bungakushi* 岩波講座日本文学史, pp. 259–270. Ed. Kubota Jun 久保田淳 et al. Iwanami Shoten 岩波書店, 1996.

Miya Tsugio 宮次男. "Hachiman Daibosatsu goengi to Hachiman engi (1)–(3) 八幡大菩薩御縁起と八幡縁起." *Bijutsu kenkyū* 美術研究 (1) 333 (1985.9), pp. 149–158; (2) 335 (1986.3), pp. 15–23; (3) 336 (1986.8), pp. 57–67.

Miyachi Naokazu 宮地直一. *Hachimangū no kenkyū* 八幡宮の研究. Ōfūsha 桜楓社, 1984.

Miyachi Naokazu 宮地直一 and Fukuyama Toshio 福山敏男, eds. *Jinja kozushū* 神社古図集. Kyoto 京都: Rinsen Shoten 臨川書店, 1942.

Miyawaki Takahira 宮脇隆平. *Eisai monogatari* 栄西ものがたり. Bungeisha 文芸社, 2003.

Miyazaki Noriko 宮崎法子. "Seikadō Bunko Bijutsukan zō 'Jūō-zu, ni shisha-zu' ni tsuite 静嘉堂文庫美術館蔵「十王図・二使者図」について." In *Bukkyō no bijutsu (mihotoke no osugata)* 仏教の美術（御仏の御姿, pp. 22–30. Ed. Seikadō Bunko Bijutsukan 静嘉堂文庫美術館. Seikadō Bunko Bijutsukan 静嘉堂文庫美術館, 1999.

Momo Hiroyuki 桃裕行. *Jōdai gakusei no kenkyū* 上代学制の研究. Meguro Shoten 目黒書店, 1947.

Moon, Hyungsub. "Matsura-tō: Pirate Warriors in Northwestern Kyushu, Japan, 1150–1350." Doctoral diss., Stanford University, 2005.

Mori Katsumi 森克己. *Nissō bōeki no kenkyū* 日宋貿易の研究. Kokuritsu Shoin 国立書院, 1948.

———. *Nissō bunka kōryū no shomondai* 日宋文化交流の諸問題. Tōkō Shoin 刀江書院, 1950.

———. "*San Tendai godaisanki* ni tsuite 参天台五台山記について." In Mori Katsumi, *Zoku Nissō bōeki no kenkyū* 続日宋貿易の研究, pp. 278–282. Kokusho Kankōkai 国書刊行会, 1975.

———. *Shintei Nissō bōeki no kenkyū* 新訂日宋貿易の研究 (*Mori Katsumi chosakushū* 森克己著作集, vol. 1). Kokusho Kankōkai 国書刊行会, 1975.

———. "Sōdai zanbon no kin'yu to Nihon e no ryūden 宋代槧本の禁輸と日本への流伝." In *Iwai hakase koki kinen: Tenseki ronshū* 岩井博士古希記念：典籍論集, pp. 697–711. Ed. Iwai Hakase Koki Kinen Jigyōkai Hensan Iinkai 岩井博士古希記念事業会編纂委員会. Iwai Hakase Koki Kinen Jigyōkai 岩井博士古希記念事業会, 1963.

———. *Zoku Nissō bōeki no kenkyū* 続日宋 貿易の研究 (*Mori Katsumi chosakushū* 森克己著作集, vol. 2). Kokusho Kankōkai 国書刊行会, 1975.

Mori Shikazō 森鹿三. *Honzōgaku kenkyū* 本草学研究. Osaka 大阪: Kyōu Shooku 杏雨書屋, 1999.

Murai Shōsuke 村井章介. *Ajia no naka no chūsei Nihon* アジアのなかの中世日本. Azekura Shobō 校倉書房, 1988.

———. "Chūsei ni okeru Higashi Ajia sho chiiki to no kōtsū 中世に於ける東アジア諸地域との交通." In *Nihon no shakai shi, 1, rettō naigai no kōtsū to kokka* 日本の社会史, 1, 列島内外の交通と国家, pp. 97–138. Ed. Amino Yoshihiko 網野善彦 et al. Iwanami Shoten 岩波書店, 1987.

———. *Chūsei Wajinden* 中世倭人伝. Iwanami Shoten 岩波書店, 1993.

———. *Higashi Ajia ōkan* 東アジア往還. Asahi Shinbunsha 朝日新聞社, 1995.

———. ed. and trans. *Rōshōdō Nihon kōroku: Chōsen shisetsu no mita chūsei Nihon* 老松堂日本行録朝鮮使節の見た中世日本. Iwanami Shoten 岩波書店, 1987.

———. "Torai sō no seiki 渡来僧の世紀." In *Miyako to hina no chūsei* 都と鄙の中世, pp. 170–198. Ed. Ishii Susumu 石井進. Yoshikawa Kōbunkan 吉川弘文館, 1992.

———. *Umi kara mita sengoku Nihon: Rettōshi kara sekaishi e* 海から見た戦国日本―列島史から世界史へ. Chikuma Shobō 筑摩書房, 1997.

Murai Yasuhiko 村井康彦. *Buke bunka to dōbōshū.* 武家文化と同朋衆. San'ichi Shobō 三一書房, 1995.

———. *Heian kizoku no sekai* 平安貴族の世界. Tokuma Shoten 徳間書店, 1968.

Murck, Alfreda. *Poetry and Painting in Song China: The Subtle Art of Dissent.* Cambridge: Harvard University Asia Center, 2000.

Nagasawa Kikuya 長沢規矩也. *Shina gikyoku shōsetsu no kenkyū* シナ戯曲小説の研究. Vol. 5 of *Nagasawa Kikuya chosakushū* 長沢規矩也著作集. Kyūko Shoin 汲古書院, 1985.

Nakamura Hidetaka 中村栄孝. *Nissen kankeishi no kenkyū*, vol. 1 日鮮関係史の研究上. Yoshikawa Kōbunkan 吉川弘文館, 1965.

Nakamura Teruko 中村輝子, Kawaguchi Naomi 川口直美, and Endō Jirō 遠藤次郎. "*Wazaikyoku hō* shōkanhen no kentō 和剤局方傷寒篇の検討." *Yakushigaku zasshi* 薬史学雑誌 35.2 (2000), pp. 218–223.

Nakamura Teruko 中村輝子, Matsuzaki Aiko 松崎亜衣子, and Endō Jirō 遠藤次郎. "*Wazaikyoku hō* ni okeru hōkōsei ken'i yaku no kentō: Seiiki no igaku no eikyō ni tsuite 和剤局方における芳香性健胃薬の検討―西域の医学の影響について." *Yakushigaku zasshi* 薬史学雑誌 35.2 (2000), pp. 153–158.

———. "*Wazaikyoku hō* issaikihen no kentō 和剤局方一切気篇の検討." *Kanpō no rinshō* 漢方の臨床 47.11 (2000.11), pp. 119–126.

Nakamura Teruko 中村輝子, Miyamoto Hirokazu 宮本浩和, and Endō Jirō 遠藤次郎. "*Wazaikyoku hō* ni mirareru seizai no tokuchō 和剤局方に見られる製剤の特徴." *Yakushigaku zasshi* 薬史学雑誌 38.2 (2003), pp. 185–192.

Nakano Hatayoshi 中野幡能. *Hachiman shinkō* 八幡信仰. Hanawa Shobō 塙書房, 1985.

———. *Usa Jingū shi, shiryō hen*, vol. 1 宇佐神宮史, 史料編 1. Usa 宇佐: Usa Jingū chō 宇佐神宮庁, 1984.

———. ed. *Hachiman shinkō* 八幡信仰. Yūzankaku 雄山閣, 1983.

Nakano Teruo 中野照男. *Enma, Jūō zō* 閻魔・十王像. *Nihon no bijutsu* 日本の美術 313 (June 1992). pp. 1–83.

Nakayama, Shigeru. *A History of Japanese Astronomy*. Cambridge: Harvard University Press, 1969.

Nanba Matsutarō 難波松太郎, Muroga Nobuo 室賀信夫, and Unno Kazutaka 海野一隆. *Nihon no kochizu* 日本の古地図. Sōgensha 創元社, 1969.

Nara Kokuritsu Hakubutsukan 奈良国立博物館, ed. *Shaji engi-e* 社寺縁起絵. Nara 奈良: Nara Kokuritsu Hakubutsukan 奈良国立博物館, 1975.

Narasaki Shōichi 楢崎彰一. "Nihon shutsudo no Sōgen tōji to Nihon tōji 日本出土の宋元陶磁と日本陶磁." In *Kokusai shinpojiumu Shin'an kaitei hikiage bunbutsu hōkokusho* 国際シンポジウム新安海底引き上げ文物報告書, pp. 37–58. Nagoya 名古屋: Chūnichi Shinbunsha 中日新聞社, 1984.

Needham, Joseph. *Science and Civilization in China*. Vol. 4, Pt. 1: *Physics*. Cambridge: Cambridge University Press, 1962.

———. *Science and Civilization in China*. Vol. 4, Pt. 3: *Civil Engineering and Nautics*. Cambridge: Cambridge University Press, 1971.

———. *Science and Civilization in China*, Vol. 5, Pt. 7: *Military Technology: The Gunpowder Epic*. Cambridge: Cambridge University Press, 1986.

Nezu Bijutsukan 根津美術館, and Tokugawa Bijutsukan 徳川美術館 eds. *Higashiyama gyobutsu* 東山御物. Nezu Bijutsukan and Tokugawa Bijutsukan 根津美術館, 徳川美術館, 1976.

NHK and NHK Promotion, ed. *Hōjō Tokimune to sono jidai ten* 北条時宗とその時代展. Exhibition catalogue, 2001.

Nienhauser, William N., ed. *The Indiana Companion to Traditional Chinese Literature*. Bloomington: Indiana University Press, 1986.

Nihon chimei daijiten 34: *Hiroshima ken* 日本地名大辞典 34: 広島県. Kadokawa Shoten 角川書店, 1987.

Nihon chimei daijiten 42: *Nagasaki ken* 日本地名大辞典 42: 長崎県. Kadokawa Shoten 角川書店, 1987.

Nishio Kenryū 西尾賢隆. *Chūsei Nitchū kōryū to Zenshū* 中世日中交流と禅宗. Yoshikawa Kōbunkan 吉川弘文館, 1999.

———. "Kamakura jidai ni okeru torai sō o megutte 鎌倉時代に於ける渡来僧をめぐって." *Nihon rekishi* 日本歴史 491 (1989.4), pp. 38–58.

Nishioka Reizō 西岡禮三 and Yanagita Yoshitaka 柳田純孝. *Genkō to Hakata: shashin de yomu Mōko shūrai* 元寇と博多—写真で読む蒙古襲来. Fukuoka 福岡: Nishi Nihon Shinbunsha 西日本新聞社, 2001.

Nojiri Tadashi 野尻忠. "Kinryō kisai kara mita Shōsōin tan uramonjo no kenkyū 斤量記載からみた正倉院丹裏文書の研究." *Komonjo kenkyū* 古文書研究 57 (2003.5), pp. 1–29.

Ōba Osamu 大庭脩. *Kanseki yunyū no bunkashi: Shōtoku taishi kara Yoshimune e* 漢籍輸入の文化史 — 聖徳太子から吉宗へ. Kenbun Shuppan 研文出版, 1997.

Ōita Kenritsu Fudoki no Oka Rekishi Minzoku Shiryōkan 大分県立宇佐風土記の丘歴史民俗資料館, ed. *Jishae no sekai: Chūseijin no kokoro o yomu* 寺社絵の世界—中世人の心を読む. Exhibition catalogue. Usa 宇佐: Ōita Kenritsu Fudoki no Oka Rekishi Minzoku Shiryōkan 大分県立宇佐風土記の丘歴史民俗資料館, October 1995.

Ōji Toshiaki 応地利明. "Echizu ni arawareta sekaizō 絵地図に現れた世界像." In *Nihon no shakai shi, 7, Shakai kan to sekaizō* 日本の社会史, 7, 社会観と世界像, pp. 299-318. Ed. Amino Yoshihiko 網野善彦 et al. Iwanami Shoten 岩波書店, 1987.

Okada Masayuki 岡田正之. *Nihon kanbungakushi* 日本漢文学史. Kyōritsusha Shoten 共立社書店, 1929.

Okanishi Tamendo 岡西爲人. "Chūgoku honzō no torai to sono eikyō 中国本草の渡来と其影響." In *Meijizen Nihon yakubutsugakushi* 明治前日本薬物学史, vol. 2, pp. 1–265. Ed. Nihon Gakushiin 日本学士院. Zaidan Hōjin Nihon Koigaku Shiryō Sentā 財団法人日本古医学資料センター, 1978.

———. *Song yiqian yiji kao* 宋以前医籍考. 4 vols. Taipei 台北: Ku T'ing Book House 公亭書屋, 1969.

Okazaki Kanzō 岡崎寛蔵. *Kusuri no rekishi* くすりの歴史. Kōdansha 講談社, 1976.

Ortiz, Valérie Malenfer. *Dreaming the Southern Song Landscape: The Power of Illusion in Chinese Painting*. Leiden: Brill, 1999.

Ōsaka Shiritsu Hakubutsukan 大阪市立博物館 ed. *Shaji sankei mandara* 社寺参詣曼荼羅. Heibonsha 平凡社, 1987.

Ōta Aya 太田彩. Emaki – Mōko shūrai ekotoba 絵巻=蒙古襲来絵詞. *Nihon no bijutsu* 414 日本の美術 414. Shibundō 至文堂, 2000.11.

Ōta Hirotarō 太田博太郎. *Chūsei no kenchiku* 中世の建築. Shōkokusha 彰国社, 1957.

Ōta Kōki 大田弘毅. *Mōko shūrai: sono gunjishiteki kenkyū* 蒙古襲来— その軍事史的研究. Kinseisha 錦正社, 1997.

Ōta Shōjirō 太田晶二郎. *Ōta Shōjirō chosakushū* 1 太田晶二朗著作集 1. Yoshikawa Kōbunkan 吉川弘文館, 1991.

Ōyama Kyōhei 大山喬平. *Chōkōdōryō mokuroku to Shimada ke monjo* 長講堂領目録と島田家文書. Kyoto 京都: Shibunkaku Shuppan 思文閣出版, 1987.

Pelliot, Paul. "Le Ts'ien tseu wen ou Livre des Mille Mots." *T'oung Pao* 24 (1926), pp. 179–214, 293.

Pollack, David. *The Fracture of Meaning: Japan's Synthesis of China from the Eighth through the Eighteenth Centuries*. Princeton: Princeton University Press, 1986.

———. *Zen Poems of the Five Mountains*. New York: Crossroads; Decatur: Scholars Press, 1985.

Quinter, David Ralph. "The Shingon Ritsu School and the Mañjuśrī Cult in the Kamakura Period: From Eison to Monkan." Doctoral diss., Stanford University, 2006.

Rai Kyōhei 頼杏坪, ed. *Geihan tsūshi* 藝藩通志. Hiroshima 広島: Hiroshima Toshokan 広島図書館, 1908.

Reischauer, Edwin O., trans. *Ennin's Diary: The Record of a Pilgrimage to China in Search of the Law*. New York: Ronald Press, 1955.

Robinson, Kenneth R. "An Island's Place in History: Tsushima in Japan and in Chosŏn, 1392–1592." *Korean Studies* 30 (2006), pp. 40–66.

———. "The Tsushima Governor and the Regulation of Japanese Access to Chosŏn in the Fifteenth and Sixteenth Centuries." *Korean Studies* 20 (1996), pp. 23–50.

———. "Treated as Treasures: The Circulation of Sutras in Maritime Northeast Asia from 1388 to the Mid–Sixteenth Century." *East Asian History* 21 (June 2001), pp. 33–54.

Rokutanda Yutaka 六反田豊. "Chōsen ōchō jidai no kōtsū seido to shukuhaku shisetsu 朝鮮王朝時代の交通制度と宿泊施設." *Kankoku bunka* 韓国文化 225 (1998.8), pp. 6–9.

———. "Richō shoki Kan-kō no suitan seido ni tsuite 李朝初期漢江の水站制度について." *Shien* 史淵 128 (1990), pp. 77–120.

———. "Richō shoki no denzei yusō taisei: kakudō tan'i ni mita sono seibi, hensen katei 李朝初期の田税輸送体制－各道単位にみたその整備·変遷過程." *Chōsen gakuhō* 朝鮮学報 123 (1987.4), pp. 35–152.

Rosenfield, John M. "The Unity of the Three Creeds." In *Japan in the Muromachi Age*, pp. 205–25. Ed. John W. Hall and Toyoda Takeshi. Berkeley: University of California Press, 1977.

Saeki Kōji 佐伯弘次. "Hakata 博多." In *Iwanami kōza Nihon tsūshi* 岩波講座日本通史 10, *chūsei* 中世 4, pp. 283–300. Iwanami Shoten 岩波書店, 1994.

———. "Kyōgen *Chikugo no oku* kara mita chūsei no Kyūshū 狂言筑後の奥からみた中世の九州." *Museum Kyūshū* 21 (1986), pp. 29–33.

———. *Mongoru shūrai no shōgeki* モンゴル襲来の衝撃. Chūō Kōron Shinsha 中央公論新社, 2003.

———. "Tairiku bōeki to gaikokujin no kyoryū 大陸貿易と外国人の居留." In *Higashi Ajia no kokusai toshi Hakata* 東アジアの国際都市博多, pp. 102–128. Ed. Kawazoe Shōji 川添昭二. Heibonsha 平凡社, 1988.

Sasaki Tatsuo 佐々木達夫. "Hakusai ibutsu no kōkogaku 舶載遺物の考古学." In *Ajia no naka no Nihonshi, III, kaijō no michi* アジアのなかの日本史, III, 海上の道, pp. 173–220. Ed. Arano Yasunori 荒野泰典, Ishii Masatoshi 石井正敏, and Murai Shōsuke 村井章介. Tōkyō Daigaku Shuppankai 東京大学出版会, 1992.

Sasaki Toshikazu 佐々木利和. "Hakubutsukan shomoku shikō Teishitsu bon no bu Igakukan hon hen, *Yūrin Fukudenpō* ni tsuite 博物館書目誌稿帝室本之部医学館本編有林福田方について." *Museum* 518 (1994.5), pp. 4-13 (part 1); 538 (1995.8), pp. 30–34 (part 2).

Satō Michio 佐藤道生. "Shitai to shisō: Heian kōki no tenkai 詩体と思想 ― 平安後期の展開." In *Iwanami kōza Nihon bungakushi* 岩波講座日本文学史 3, *Jūichi, jūni seiki no bungaku* 11, 12 世紀の文学, pp. 221–252. Ed. Kubota Jun 久保田淳 et al. Iwanami Shoten 岩波書店, 1996.

Satō Tetsutarō 佐藤鉄太郎. *Mōko shūrai ekotoba to Takezaki Suenaga no kenkyū* 蒙古襲来絵詞と竹崎季長の研究. Kinseisha 錦正社, 2005.

Schafer, Edward H. "Fusang and Beyond: The Haunted Seas to Japan." *Journal of the American Oriental Society* 109.3 (July–September 1989), pp. 379–99.

———. *Mirages on the Sea of Time.* Berkeley: University of California Press, 1985.

———. *The Golden Peaches of Samarkand.* Berkeley: University of California Press, 1963.

Schottenhammer, Angela, ed. *The Emporium of the World: Maritime Quanzhou, 1000–1400.* Leiden: Brill, 2001.

Seki Shūichi 関周一. "Kōryō no michi to Nihon, Chōsen 香料の道と日本朝鮮." In *Ajia no naka no Nihonshi, III, kaijō no michi* アジアのなかの日本史, III, 海上の道, pp. 265–280. Ed. Arano Yasunori 荒野泰典, Ishii Masatoshi 石井正敏, Murai Shōsuke 村井章介. Tōkyō Daigaku Shuppankai 東京大学出版会, 1992.

Seki Yasushi 関靖. *Kanazawa bunko no kenkyū* 金沢文庫の研究. Ōzorasha 大空社, 1992 reprint.

Sekiguchi Kin'ya 関口欣也. "Gozan to Zen'in 五山と禅院." Vol. 15 of *Shinpen meihō Nihon no bijutsu* 新編名宝日本の美術 15. Shōgakkan 小学館, 1991.

Sekino Tadashi 関野正. *Chōsen bijutsushi* 朝鮮美術史. Keijō 京城: Chōsen Shigakkai 朝鮮史学会, 1932.

Shibata Shōji 柴田承二, ed. *Hōryūji shozō iyaku chōzai koshō* 法隆寺所蔵医薬調剤古抄. Hirokawa Shoten 広川書店, 1997.

Shibuya-ku Shōtō Bijutsukan, ed. 渋谷区松涛美術館. *Chūsei shomin shinkō no kaiga: sankei mandara, jogoku-e, otogi zōshi* 中世庶民信仰の絵画―参詣曼荼羅・地獄絵・御伽草子. Tokyo: Shibuya-ku Shōtō Bijutsukan 渋谷区松涛美術館, Exhibition catalogue, 1993.

Shimao Arata 島尾新. "Sesshū to Totō Tenjin 雪舟と渡唐天神." In *Zen to Tenjin*, pp. 206–221. Ed. Imaizumi Yoshio 今泉淑夫 and Shimao Arata 島尾新. Yoshikawa Kobunkan 吉川弘文館, 2000.

Shimizu Hisao 清水久夫. "*Mōko shūrai ekotoba* no rekishi shiryō to shite no kachi: yumi no keitai o megutte 蒙古襲来絵詞の歴史資料としての価値—弓の形態をめぐって." *Hōsei shigaku* 法政史学 43 (1991), pp. 13–30.

Shinjō Toshio 新城敏男. "Chūsei Hachiman shinkō no ichi kōsatsu 中世八幡信仰の一考察." In *Hachiman shinkō* 八幡信仰, pp. 61-82. Ed. Nakano Hatayoshi 中野幡能. Yūzankaku Shuppan 雄山閣出版, 1983.

Shinmura Taku 新村拓. *Nihon iryō shakaishi no kenkyū* 日本医療社会史の研究. Hōsei Daigaku Shuppankyoku 法政大学出版局, 1985.

Shinno, Reiko. "Medical Schools and the Temples of the Three Progenitors in Yuan China: A Case of Cross-Cultural Interactions." *Harvard Journal of Asiatic Studies* 67.1 (June 2007), pp. 89–133.

Shiraishi Kogetsu 白石虎月, ed. *Tōfukujishi* 東福寺誌. Kyōto 京都: Shibunkaku Shuppan 思文閣出版, 1979.

Shōji Sensui 庄司浅水. *Insatsu bunkashi: insatsu, zōhon, shuppan no rekishi* 印刷文化史 – 印刷, 造本, 出版の歴史. Insatsu Gakkai Shuppanbu 印刷学会出版部, 1957.

Smith, David Eugene, and Yoshio Mikami. *A History of Japanese Mathematics*. Chicago: Open Court, 1914.

Smith, Richard J. *Chinese Maps: Images of 'All Under Heaven.'* Oxford: Oxford University Press, 1996.

Smits, Ivo. *The Pursuit of Loneliness: Chinese and Japanese Nature Poetry in Medieval Japan, ca. 1050-1150*. Stuttgart: Franz Steiner Verlag, 1995.

———. "Song as Cultural History: Reading *Wakan rōeishū*." *Monumenta Nipponica* 55.2 (Summer 2000), pp. 225-256 (part one), and 55.3 (Autumn 2000, pp. 399–427 (part two).

———. "The Way of the Literati: Chinese Learning and Literary Practice in Mid-Heian Japan." In *Heian Japan, Centers and Peripheries*, pp. 105-128. Ed. Mikael S. Adolphson, Edward Kamens and Stacie Matsumoto. Honolulu: University of Hawai'i Press, 2007.

So, Billy K. L. *Prosperity, Region, and Institutions in Maritime China: The South Fukien Pattern, 946-1368*. Cambridge: Harvard University Asia Center, 2000.

Sŏ Sŏngho. "Chosŏn-ch'o Han-gang ŭi uisang kwa yŏnan chiyŏk ŭi hyŏnhwang 朝鮮初 漢江의 位相과 沿岸地域의 現況." *Sŏurhak yŏngu* 서울학연구 23 (2004), pp. 1-28.

Song, Ki-Joong. "The Study of Foreign Languages in the Yi Dynasty (1392–1910)." *Journal of Social Sciences and Humanities* 54 (December 1981), pp. 1–46.

Stanley-Baker, P. Richard. "Mid-Muromachi Paintings of the Eight Views of the Hsiao and Hsiang." Doctoral diss., Princeton University, 1979.

Sugimoto, Masayoshi, and David L. Swain. *Science and Culture in Traditional Japan, A.D. 600–1854*. Cambridge: MIT Press, 1978.

Sugitatsu Yoshikazu 杉立義一, ed. *Ishinpō no denrai* 医心方の伝来. Kyoto 京都: Shibunkaku Shuppan 思文閣出版, 1991.

Sugiyama Shigeru 杉山茂. "Chūsei Nissen kōeki ni okeru Uirō (Sōju, Jōyū) no katsuyaku 中世日鮮交易における外郎(床寿, 常祐) の活躍." *Yakushigaku zasshi* 薬史学雑誌 35:2 (2000), pp. 195–201.

———. *Kusuri no shakai shi: Uirō Tōchinkō* 薬の社会史—外郎透頂香. Kindai Bungeisha 近代文芸社, 1999.

Suzuki Hiroyuki 鈴木廣之. "Ōkan suru kaiga: jūgo seiki kanji bunkaken no naka no kara-e no igi 往還する絵画—十五世紀漢字文化圏のなかの唐絵の意義." *Bijutsu kenkyū* 美術研究 361 (1995.3), pp. 1–20.

Suzuki Kei 鈴木敬. "Riku Shinchū hitsu Jūō-zu 陸信忠筆 十王図." *Kanazawa Bunko kenkyū* 金沢文庫研究 13.6 (1967.6), pp. 1–5.

Tada Keiko 多田圭子. "Chūsei ni okeru Jingū kōgōzō no tenkai 中世における神功皇后像の展開." *Kokubun Mejiro* 国文目白 31 (1991), pp. 191–203.

Takagi Sōkan 高木宗監. *Kenchōjishi: Kaizan Daikaku Zenji den* 建長寺史 — 開山大覚禅師伝. Kamakura 鎌倉: Kenchōji 建長寺, 1989.

Takahashi Kimiaki 高橋公明. "Gaikō girei yori mita Muromachi jidai no Nitchō kankei 外交儀礼より見た室町時代の日朝関係." *Shigaku zasshi* 史学雑誌 91.8 (1982.8), pp. 67–85.

———. "Jūroku seiki Chōsen, Tsushima, Higashi Ajia no kaiiki 十六世紀の朝鮮,対馬,東アジア海域." In *Bakuhansei kokka to iiki ikoku* 幕藩制国家と異域異国, pp. 143–177. Ed. Katō Eiichi 加藤栄一 et al. Azekura Shobō 校倉書房, 1989.

Takahashi Noriko 高橋範子. "Banri shūkyū no san no aru nifuku no 'Totō Tenjin zō' 萬里集九の賛のある二幅の「渡唐天神像」." In *Zen to Tenjin*, pp. 222–254. Ed. Imaizumi Yoshio 今泉淑夫 and Shimao Arata 島尾新. Yoshikawa Kobunkan 吉川弘文館, 2000.

Takahashi Shintarō 高橋真太郎. "Chūgoku no yakubutsu ryōhō to sono eikyō 中国の薬物療法と其影響." In *Meijizen Nihon yakubutsugakushi* 明治前日本薬物学史 vol. 2, pp. 267–513. Ed. Nihon Gakushiin 日本学士院. Zaidan Hōjin Nihon Koigaku Shiryō Sentā 財団法人日本古医学資料センター, 1978.

Takahashi Zenshichi 高橋善七. *Tsūshin* 通信. Kondō Shuppansha 近藤出版社, 1986.

Takashima Motomu 高島要. "Nihon koten ni okeru *Ri Kō Hyakuei* o megutte 日本古典における「李嶠百詠」をめぐって." In *Koten no henyō to shinsei* 古典の変容と新生, pp. 703–714. Ed. Kawaguchi Hisao 川口久雄. Meiji Shoin 明治書院, 1984.

Takeda Tsuneo 武田恒夫. "Daiganji zō Sonkai tokai nikki byōbu 大願寺蔵尊海渡海日記屏風." *Bukkyō geijutsu* 仏教芸術 52 (1963.11), pp. 127–130.

Tanaka Takeo 田中健夫. *Taigai kankei to bunka kōryū* 対外関係と文化交流. Kyoto 京都: Shibunkaku Shuppan 思文閣出版, 1987.

———. *Wakō to kangō bōeki* 倭寇と勘合貿易. Shibundō 至文堂, 1961.

Tashiro Kazui 田代和生. *Edo jidai Chōsen yakuzai chōsa no kenkyū* 江戸時代朝鮮薬剤調査の研究. Keiō Gijuku Daigaku Shuppankai 慶応義塾大学出版会, 1999.

———. "Kinsei zenki Chōsen iyaku no juyō to Tsushima han - igakusho, yakuju, ishi ni tsuite 近世前期朝鮮医薬の受容と対馬藩—医学書, 薬種, 医師について." In *Rekishi no naka no yamai to igaku* 歴史の中の病と医学, pp. 265–299. Ed. Yamada Keiji 山田慶児 and Kuriyama Shigehisa 栗山茂久. Kyoto 京都: Shibunkaku Shuppan 思文閣出版, 1997.

Teiser, Stephen F. *The Scripture on the Ten Kings and the Making of Purgatory in Medieval Chinese Buddhism*. Honolulu: University of Hawai`i Press, 1994.

Tochio Takeshi 栃尾武. "Nihon ni denrai shita ruisho to sono kōyō 日本に伝来した類書とその効用." In *Wakan hikaku bungaku to sono shūhen* 和漢比較文学とその周辺, pp. 57-79. Vol. 18 of *Wakan hikaku bungaku sōsho* 和漢比較文学叢書. Ed. Wakan Hikaku Bungakukai 和漢比較文学会. Kyūko Shoin 汲古書院, 1994.

Togawa Tomoru 戸川点. "Inseiki no daigakuryō to gakumon jōkyō: Fujiwara no Yorinaga no jiseki o chūshin ni 院政期の大学寮と学問状況—藤原頼長の事績を中心に." In *Ōchō no kenryoku to hyōshō: gakugei no bunkashi* 王朝の権力と表象—学芸の文化史, pp. 53–86. Ed. Fukutō Sanae 服藤早苗. Shinwasha 森話社, 1998.

Tōno Haruyuki 東野治之. *Kentōshi to Shōsōin* 遣唐使と正倉院. Iwanami Shoten 岩波書店, 1992.

———. "Nikki ni miru Fujiwara Yorinaga no nanshoku kankei: ōchō kizoku no buita sekusuarisu 日記に見る藤原頼長の男色関係: 王朝貴族のブイタセクスアリス." *Hisutoria* ヒストリア 84 (1979), pp. 15–29.

Ts'ao, Yung-ho. "Pepper Trade in East Asia." *T'oung Pao* 68. 4–5 (1982), pp. 221–247.

Tsuji Zennosuke 辻善之助. *Nihon Bukkyōshi* 日本仏教史. Vol. 2. Iwanami Shoten 岩波書店, 1949.

Tuge, Hideomi. *Historical Development of Science and Technology in Japan*. Tokyo: Kokusai Bunka Shinkokai, 1961.

Turner, Victor. *Dramas, Fields, and Metaphors: Symbolic Action in Human Society*. Ithaca: Cornell University Press, 1974.

Ury, Marian. "Chinese Learning and Intellectual Life." In *The Cambridge History of Japan* Vol. 2: *Heian Japan*, pp. 341–89. Ed. Donald H. Shiveley and William H. McCullough. Cambridge: Cambridge University Press, 1999.

————. *Poems of the Five Mountains*. 2d. ed. Ann Arbor: Center for Japanese Studies, University of Michigan, 1992.

Varley, H. Paul, and George Elison. "The Culture of Tea: From Its Origins to Sen no Rikyū." In *Warlords, Artists, and Commoners: Japan in the Sixteenth Century*, pp. 187–222. Ed. George Elison and Bardwell Smith. Honolulu: University Press of Hawai`i Press, 1981.

Verschuer, Charlotte von. "Japan's Foreign Relations, 600–1200 A.D.: A Translation from *Zenrin Kokuhōki*." *Monumenta Nipponica* 54.1 (Spring 1999), pp. 1–39.

————. "Japan's Foreign Relations, 1200 to 1392 A.D.: A Translation from *Zenrin Kokuhōki*." *Monumenta Nipponica* 57.4 (Winter 2002), 413–445.

————. *Across the Perilous Sea: Japanese Trade with China and Korea from the Seventh to the Sixteenth Centuries*. Translated by Kristen Lee Hunter. Ithaca: East Asia Program Cornell University, 2006.

————. "Looking from Within and Without: Ancient and Medieval External Relations." *Monumenta Nipponica* 55.4 (Winter 2000), pp. 537–566.

Wakabayashi, Haruko. "Hell Illustrated: A Visual Image of *Ikai* that Came from *Ikoku*." In *Practicing the Afterlife: Perspectives from Japan*, pp. 285–318. Ed. Susanne Formanek and William R. LaFleur. Vienna: Verlag Der Österreichischen Akademie Der Wissenschaften, 2004.

————. "Sangoku shisō and Japan's Identity in the Buddhist Cosmology as Depicted in the *Konjaku monogatarishū*." In *Image and Identity: Rethinking Japanese Cultural History*, pp. 15–28. Ed. Jeffrey E. Hanes and Hidetoshi Yamaji. Kobe: Research Institute for Economics and Business Administration, Kobe University, 2004.

Wang, Gungwu. "The Rhetoric of a Lesser Empire: Early Sung Relations with Its Neighbors." In *China among Equals: The Middle Kingdom and Its Neighbors, 10th-14th Centuries*, pp. 47–65. Ed. Morris Rossabi. Berkeley: University of California Press, 1983.

Wang, Yi-t'ung. *Official Relations between China and Japan, 1368–1549*. Cambridge: Harvard University Press, 1953.

Wang, Zhenping. "Manuscript Copies of Chinese Books in Ancient Japan." *Gest Library Journal* 5.2 (1991), pp. 35–67.

Watanabe Fumio 渡辺文雄. "Den Tosa Mitushige hitsu *Ōita Yusuhara Hachimangū engi emaki* ni tsuite 伝土佐光茂筆大分由原八幡宮縁起絵巻について." *Ōita ken Usa Fudoki no Oka Rekishi Minzoku Shiryōkan kenkyū kiyō* 大分県宇佐風土記の丘歴史民俗資料館研究紀要 2 (1985.3), pp. 39–59.

Watanabe Yūji 渡辺雄二. "Kyūshū no Hachiman engi-e: kakefukusō keishiki o chūshin to shite 九州の八幡縁起絵―掛幅装形式を中心として." *Bukkyō geijutsu* 仏教芸術 181 (1988.11), pp. 96–116.

Watson, Burton, trans. *Meng ch'iu: Famous Episodes from Chinese History and Legend*. Tokyo: Kodansha International, 1979.

Wheelwright, Carolyn. "A Visualization of Eitoku's Lost Paintings at Azuchi Castle." In *Warlords, Artists, and Commoners: Japan in the Sixteenth Century*, pp. 87–111. Ed. George Elison and Bardwell Smith. Honolulu: The University of Hawai`i Press, 1981.

Wilson, William, trans. *Hōgen Monogatari, Tale of the Disorder in Hōgen*. Tokyo: Monumenta Nipponica, 1966.

Yabe Yoshiaki 矢部良明. "Nihon shutsudo no Tōsō jidai no tōji 日本出土の唐宋時代の陶磁." In *Nihon shutsudo no bōeki tōji* 日本出土の貿易陶磁, pp. 105–127. Ed. Tōkyō Kokuritsu Hakubutsukan 東京国立博物館. Tōkyō Bijutsu 東京美術, 1978.

———. *Nihon tōji no ichiman nisen nen* 日本陶磁の一万二千年. Heibonsha 平凡社, 1994.

Yanagihara Toshiaki 柳原俊昭. "Chūsei zenki minami Kyūshū no minato to Sōjin kyoryūchi ni kansuru ichi shiron 中世前紀南九州の港と宋人居留地に関する一試論." *Nihonshi kenkyū* 日本史研究 448 (1999.12), pp. 102–134.

Yokoi Kiyoshi 横井清. *Chūsei o ikita hitobito* 中世を生きた人びと. Fukutake Shobō 福武書房, 1991.

Yŏm Yŏngha 廉永夏. *Hanguk chong yŏngu, chŭngbop'an* 韓國鐘 研究 增補版. Koryŏwŏn 高麗苑, 1988.

Yoshida Mitsukuni 吉田光邦. "Mōko shūrai ekotoba ni okeru buki ni tsuite 蒙古襲来絵詞における武器について." In *Mōko shūrai ekotoba* 蒙古襲来絵詞, pp. 75–80. Ed. Matsushita Takaaki 松下隆章. In Vol. 9 of *Nihon emakimono zenshū* 日本絵巻物全集. Ed. Tanaka Ichimatsu 田中一松. Kadokawa Shoten 角川書店, 1964.

Yoshikawa, Kōjirō. *An Introduction to Sung Poetry*. Trans. Burton Watson. Cambridge: Harvard University Press, 1967.

Yoshimura Shigeki 吉村茂樹. "Tsūken nyūdō zōsho mokuroku ni tsuite no gimon 通憲入道蔵書目録についての疑問." *Shigaku zasshi* 史学雑誌 39.10 (1928.10), pp. 96–107.

Yukkun Ponbu 陸軍本部, ed. *Hanguk kunjesa: Kŭnse Chosŏn chŏngi p'yŏn* 韓國軍制史 – 近世朝鮮前期篇. Yukkun Ponbu 陸軍本部, 1968.

Yule, Henry, and Henri Cordier. *The Travels of Marco Polo: the complete Yule-Cordier Edition*. New York: Dover, 1993 reprint.

Zainie, Carla M. "*The Muromachi Dono Gyōkō Okazari ki*: A Research Note." *Monumenta Nipponica* 33.1 (Spring 1978), pp. 113–118.

Zengaku daijiten 禅学大辞典. 3 vols. Taishūkan Shoten 大修館書店, 1979.

Index and Glossary

GPSR Authorized Representative: Easy Access System Europe, Mustamäe tee
50, 10621 Tallinn, Estonia, gpsr.requests@easproject.com